MW00991523

TERRY BRADSHAW

Sports Icons and Issues in Popular Culture

Series Editors
Bob Batchelor and Norma Jones

In an age when sports icons cross over into everyday lives and popular culture, the time is ripe for assessing, reassessing, and refocusing our gaze on the significance of athletes in the contemporary world. The Sports Icons and Issues in Popular Culture series engages with star athletes and significant sports issues to examine how they have influenced not just the sporting world, but also popular culture and society. By looking beyond the on-field stats and figures, this series helps readers further understand sports icons both as individuals and as cultural phenomena.

Titles in the Series

TERRY BRADSHAW

From Super Bowl Champion to Television Personality

Brett L. Abrams

ROWMAN & LITTLEFIELD
Lanham • Boulder • New York • London

Published by Rowman & Littlefield
A wholly owned subsidiary of The Rowman & Littlefield Publishing Group, Inc.
4501 Forbes Boulevard, Suite 200, Lanham, Maryland 20706
www.rowman.com

Unit A, Whitacre Mews, 26-34 Stannary Street, London SE11 4AB

British Library Cataloguing in Publication Information Available

Library of Congress Cataloging-in-Publication Data

Names: Abrams, Brett L., 1960– author.
Title: Terry Bradshaw : From Super Bowl Champion to Television Personality / Brett L. Abrams.
Description: Lanham, Maryland : Rowman & Littlefield, 2017. | Series: Sports Icons and Issues in Popular Culture | Includes bibliographical references and index. | Description based on print version record and CIP data provided by publisher; resource not viewed.
Identifiers: LCCN 2017006185 (print) | LCCN 2017017333 (ebook) | ISBN 9781442277649 (electronic) | ISBN 9781442277632 (hardcover : alk. paper)
Subjects: LCSH: Bradshaw, Terry. | Pittsburgh Steelers (Football team)—Biography. | Football players—Pennsylvania—Pittsburgh—Biography | Quarterbacks (Football)—Pennsylvania—Pittsburgh—Biography. | Television personalities—United States—Biography.
Classification: LCC GV939.B68 (ebook) | LCC GV939.B68 A37 2017 (print) | DDC 796.332092 [B] —dc23
LC record available at https://lccn.loc.gov/2017006185

∞™ The paper used in this publication meets the minimum requirements of American National Standard for Information Sciences Permanence of Paper for Printed Library Materials, ANSI/NISO Z39.48-1992.

Printed in the United States of America

CONTENTS

PREFACE

When series editors Bob Batchelor and Norma Jones offered me the opportunity to submit a book proposal for Rowman & Littlefield's Sports Icons and Issues in Popular Culture series, I wondered how many athletes fit this category. I spoke with several friends, and we played an equivalent of a bar game, naming different athletes, determining if they had iconic status, then figuring out whether they had a significant impact on popular culture.

Among the people we mentioned were Jim Brown, Martina Navratilova, Billie Jean King, Muhammad Ali, and Terry Bradshaw. These icons had fantastic careers and played a role in popular culture. Growing up in the 1970s, I had seen most of these athletes playing their sport near the top level and had an awareness of their roles in the larger popular culture.

Bradshaw stood out because he hails from the South. I lived my formative years in New Jersey and knew little of the Southern United States until I moved to Washington, D.C., two decades ago. After many encounters with transplanted Southerners, my interest peaked. This book on Terry Bradshaw provided the chance to learn more about the South and shake off existing antiquated perceptions I may have held.

The former Pittsburgh Steelers quarterback and current cohost of *Fox NFL Sunday* has written five books, so a lot is already known about his activities. What has received less attention are the images Bradshaw formed as he pursued those activities and the reactions of fans and less enthusiastic observers.

Unfortunately, Mr. Bradshaw declined to participate in this project. Fortunately, many people who have been involved in his life graciously volunteered their time and effort to help me with this endeavor. The people of the great state of Louisiana proved extremely helpful. Shawn Ryder pointed me to the Louisiana Sports Hall of Fame and its chairman, Doug Ireland. I had wonderful and informative conversations with Bradshaw's high school football and track coach, A. L. Williams, and journalists Nico Van Thyn, Bob Griffith, Louis Brewer, and Jerry Byrd and his wife Barbara. I received able help from Kristi Baronette of the Calvary Baptist Church in Shreveport, Louisiana.

Many people provided helpful insights into the various businesses that Bradshaw has pursued. I am grateful to Gerry Mullins and Bert Jones for the time and effort they provided regarding professional football. Bobby and Scarlett Walden were very kind and helpful. Terry O'Neil and Vern Lundquist offered keen insights into the television arena and fun personal stories. Author Richard Hyatt gave me a fan and expert view of the world of Southern gospel.

Fans served as a cornerstone of this book because their reactions provided an understanding about specific images Bradshaw has portrayed and Bradshaw's longevity as an entertainer. Some of these fans included Ernest Bryant, Thomas Cotter, Jeffrey Landou, Sam McClure, Mark Osele, and Dexter Germany.

Many libraries and research institutions helped me pinpoint Bradshaw-related items in their enormous collections. I'm particularly grateful to Kristine Krueger from the Academy of Motion Picture Arts and Sciences' Margaret Herrick Library; Marilyn Holt from the Pennsylvania Department in the Carnegie Library of Pittsburgh; Amy Kastigar from the Ohio County Public Library in Wheeling, West Virginia; and Suzanne Wise at the Appalachian State University Library in Boone, North Carolina.

I appreciate the willingness of my family and friends to listen and exchange ideas as I worked on this project. Of course, my parents and my longtime husband have been highly supportive. Deon Hankins and John Powell have provided inestimable insight and encouragement. Brian Rohal proved invaluable with great insight into the many draft chapters he read.

INTRODUCTION

Terry Bradshaw in the Entertainment Industry

The Super Bowl. It's the great American event, with football, pregame shows, halftime extravaganzas, and commercials for products vying for the attention of millions of television viewers. Terry Bradshaw has done it all. On the field, he won four Super Bowls with the Pittsburgh Steelers and twice earned the Most Valuable Player Award. Reporting in the studio, he has been a commentator and studio analyst in the pregame shows for CBS and Fox television. During the 2001 Super Bowl halftime show, even though he made country and gospel albums for more than three decades, he shocked many by singing the Beatles' "A Hard Day's Night" with Sir Paul McCartney. Bradshaw has appeared in regional and national advertisements for everything from websites to movies. In the featured television program or movie airing in the prime slot after the big game, Bradshaw has played characters in television comedies and dramas, costarred with Burt Reynolds in his popular road movies, and bared his buttocks in a romantic comedy.

Terry Bradshaw's 50-years-and-counting career has introduced him to many different entertainment industries. The sheer number and diversity of his projects are astounding for any entertainer. It is more remarkable for an athlete, as no other former player has had such a long and varied career. Not Jim Brown, who made many movies. Not O. J. Simpson, who was a football commentator and actor. Not Shaquille O'Neal, who is a studio analyst for professional basketball and has recorded a few albums. Bradshaw has created public images that make him appear as a fun-loving, risk-taking performer who wants to make people laugh. Many times the jokes fall on him, but he always appears to be in on the laughs. As a Southerner in a time when Southern culture and economic and political power increased rapidly, his images make interesting comments on what was going on in the United States during that time frame.

As today's culture of ubiquitous entertainment mediums developed, Bradshaw promoted and capitalized on the opportunities to appear on television and in movies, and record music. He made connections in these industries that led to additional appearances. Most importantly, he discovered the art of being a celebrity, selling an interesting personality that contained some semblance of his own. Bradshaw's play on the football field helped him become an iconic sports figure whose personality enabled him to forge an iconic status in broader popular culture for a generation of fans from the late 1960s through the early 1980s.

In recent years, as cohost of *Fox NFL Sunday* and in commercials and guest spots on numerous television programs, Bradshaw created the persona Terry Bradshaw. This zany figure of mania, humor, volume, and good old boy friendliness introduced Bradshaw to a new generation of fans. The persona has become so notable in popular culture that comedians have imitated him, a theatrical farce named a character after him, and a satirical news source has featured articles about him.

STAR, HERO, ICON, PERSONA

With its uncertain outcome—there are winners and losers—and dramatic moments, sport has gifted us some of the best entertainment events. Bradshaw entertained us with his play on the football field. As spectators, we admired his performance, as we do the actions of other athletes on the courts and in the arenas. We marveled at his strong arm and love for throwing the "bomb," just as we admire the abilities of other players to propel their bodies through time and space to jump and leap or elude and tackle opponents. We appreciated his strength and toughness, as we do sporting stars' agility, beauty, and fleetness.

While professional athletes have elite skills, some combine physical, mental, and emotional attributes to perform their best on an unwavering basis. They complete plays, especially the difficult ones, more often than their brethren. These players stand out and are called sports stars. Bradshaw was labeled a star when he became the number-one choice in the NFL Draft by the Pittsburgh Steelers, and a high salary provided fans with the expectation that he would indeed be star material.

Stars consistently give fans pleasure with their success. Thus, fans depend on stars to be successful in the most crucial moments of the game. When stars come through, fans expect that their teams will win games. Fans believe winning will get the team into the playoffs, ultimately achieving the foremost goal of winning a championship. In 1972, Bradshaw helped the Steelers win the division title and make it to the first round of the playoffs; however, he couldn't help the team make it to the Super Bowl that year or the next. Fans grew impatient, but he helped the team win its first championship in 1974. When stars help their teams win championships, they become short-term heroes.

If stars and their teams win more than one championship title, the hero status lasts much longer. Terry Bradshaw and the Pittsburgh Steelers achieved championship success on the field four times. Afterward, Bradshaw and other team members became lasting heroes throughout the Pittsburgh metropolitan region. The millions of viewers watching the worldwide television coverage and replays of the Super Bowls they won enabled Bradshaw to establish a broader fan base. He became heroic to people throughout the country and the world.

There are many heroes in team sports, but sometimes one of these heroes sets himself or herself apart from the rest. For example, he or she might perform a never-before-seen feat at an opportune moment, perhaps during a championship game or series. During the broadcast or soon thereafter, the media will link the hero's achievement to a larger idea, for instance, being a "big-game player" or being associated with the month in which the sport's championship is played—say "Mr. October." The hero becomes widely known among an entire generation of sports fans.

When the Steelers reached their fourth Super Bowl, the team earned the iconic status of "Team of the 1970s." Bradshaw had a lot to do with the team's success and thus in the team's status. In the fourth Super Bowl, he played a significant role in the team's victory and became the first quarterback to win four Super Bowls. Bradshaw's perfect record of four wins and zero losses led broadcasters to call him the greatest Super Bowl quarterback of all time. He became the epitome of the "big-game player" and attained that iconic position in the minds of a generation of football fans.

As he achieved this position of prominence, Bradshaw revealed his curious, restless nature and took advantage of opportunities in music, movies, and other entertainment fields. His fun-loving personality came through in these ventures, enabling him to elevate himself from the status of sports icon to a figure known by a larger segment of the public. As Bradshaw built his career after retiring as a professional football player, he realized that a successful entertainer needed to be much different from the iconic sports hero. He realized that entertainers need a style, personality, or gimmick that they become associated with; therefore, he forged a persona somewhat based on an exaggeration of his personality and Southern stereotypes and background.

As Bradshaw's sports career was drawing to a close, he and the Steelers organization had to deal with both the quarterback icon and an aging team. The most difficult aspect of the final years of Bradshaw's playing career involved the tumultuous relationship with another Steelers icon, coach and personal director Chuck Noll. But these difficulties could not diminish his accomplishments, his iconic status, or the new career opportunities he was forging.

SHORT CAREER/LONG LIFE

Players realize that age and injury will, at some point, interfere with their ability to perform their best and that their playing careers will only last for a limited number of years. The career of the average NFL player only lasts a little more than three years. The career of a star player lasts slightly less than 12 years. Athletes have a long life ahead of them after their retirement, with a need to remain active and vital, and earn a salary. Since the advent of free agency in sports, athletes make more money—sometimes millions—to help keep them from thinking about work outside their football job during the offseason.

However, athletes like Terry Bradshaw played before the era of free agency. They were never awarded the multi-million-dollar salaries we see players walking away with today. Bradshaw and others from his era needed jobs during the offseason for the additional income. Bradshaw served as a fishing guide, used car salesman, and pipeline welder during the offseason in his first few years in the NFL. After the Steelers won their second Super Bowl, he decided to take advantage of his name recognition, venturing into another area of the entertainment industry for his offseason work.

Recording, movie, and broadcasting industry executives often hired athletes to perform in their line of entertainment to see if they could make money off the big name or as a gimmick. Occasionally, athletes appeared on novelty songs, for example, Joe DiMaggio's spoken words in the song "Joltin' Joe DiMaggio." Such athletes as boxer Joe Frazier and basketball player Kobe Bryant believed they had musical abilities. They put out singles or an album on a small record label, which generally sold best where their team played in their hometown. While their musical careers proved short-lived, Terry Bradshaw recorded three albums in country and gospel styles on larger labels.

Beginning in the 1930s, movie studios started hiring athletes on a regular basis, first targeting individual Olympic stars. Decades later, the industry began hiring former NFL players for action and comedy films. For every Jim Brown and Alex Karras who succeeded in receiving regular roles in the movies and on television programs, there were Joe Namaths, Wilt Chamberlains, and Dennis Rodmans. Terry Bradshaw played roles in several Burt Reynolds movies in the 1970s and 1980s. Key people recognized and admired him in those films, creating an opportunity for Bradshaw to costar alongside Mel Tillis in a television program, an opportunity that nearly led to the quarterback retiring from the Steelers several years early.

Upon retiring from the game, many former players take work in sundry professions. Some leave the sports entertainment industries and head into sales, whether it be in real estate or the restaurant business, as in the case of former Cowboys quarterback Roger Staubach and former Lakers guard Magic Johnson. Many try to maintain involvement in the football entertainment world. They take jobs as assistants and coaches at the high school, college, and professional levels. On some occasions, they become successful head coaches. Former players once again become notable among fans of the sport, forging a new image outside of being a player.

Fewer retired athletes look for a new career in the related field of broadcasting collegiate and professional football games. Since the expansion of cable television in the early 1980s, the number of color commentator positions has increased, along with the number of games being broadcast. The number, however, remains limited, and competition for the positions increases with each new group of retirees. They quickly come to understand as they enter a new arena that they need to develop an ability to discuss football in an intelligent but entertaining way. Ex-stars and even icons who in their previous lives as athletes could let their play define them join the commercial world, where they must sell their personalities in the booth. From former Los Angeles Rams defensive lineman Merlin Olsen to former Oakland Raiders coach John Madden, some have forged the image of top-flight broadcaster. In the 1980s, Terry Bradshaw found success. Starting at CBS, he worked his way up to become one of the top commentators at the network.

Few commentators leave the broadcast booth, because the skills required to comment on the game do not necessarily translate into hosting a studio-based pregame or postgame program. Former Philadelphia Eagles defensive back Irv Cross transitioned from the booth to become the analyst for CBS's pregame show; however, Brent Musburger hosted the program. Former wide receiver Ahmad Rashad worked for several years on NBC's pregame show, but he spent only a year as a color commentator.

Bradshaw had appeared as an extra commentator on the pregame show in the past. When he left the color commentator position to become a football pregame host, some television critics expressed their doubts. He joined the long-running *NFL on CBS* program when it was revamped in 1990. After four successful seasons as a cohost, he and many members of the CBS staff moved over to the Fox network when it purchased the rights to the National Football Conference (NFC) football games. The network designed its pregame show, *NFL on FOX*, around Bradshaw and expanded the program to one hour. As the show won the annual pregame show ratings battle and Bradshaw won awards, a new generation of fans grew up appreciating Bradshaw's football impressions and opinions, as well as his antics, and the fun poked at him. He kept his old fans while finding more followers and expanding his audience.

The image he created on television as an analyst made him popular as a television show host and granted him the name recognition that helped him be featured in commercials in the 1990s and early 2000s. He returned to the recording studio and released a few more songs and albums in the gospel and country styles. His fame and personality also sparked guest appearances on television sitcoms and in movies, as well as on late-night talk shows. These forays into many areas of entertainment helped him establish a lasting image among more than just football fans. He became "Zany Uncle Terry," the ever-charming, ever-amusing, unpredictable, but always trustworthy, always welcome, loving member of the family.

Bradshaw illustrates what it takes for an entertainer to master many of the entertainment industries in the late twentieth century. He used his celebrity as an iconic athlete to join other entertainment fields. With talent and personality, Bradshaw engaged in the music and movie worlds, creating images as a singer and actor. More than a decade later, the iconic Bradshaw forged an indelible persona, allowing him to forge a career as an entertainer on a NFL pregame show. The fame he gained with a new generation of fans opened up new opportunities in the entertainment world for other athletes. Sometimes those appearances solidified the Terry Bradshaw persona we know today. More intriguingly, Bradshaw occasionally received opportunities to broaden his public image and comment on U.S. society.

I

BORN IN FOOTBALL COUNTRY

Making Heroes

"In Southern Hills football was a way of life. It made our hearts beat."—Jerry Byrd, sportswriter[1]

The high school football coach had often looked out at his big quarterback with the blond flattop as the young athlete reared back and fired a beautiful spiral to his friend from middle school, Tommy Spinks. Later, as the pair entered their senior year at Louisiana Technical University, that same quarterback, Terry Bradshaw, had gained national attention. NFL teams read reports from scouts regarding his strengths and weaknesses as a player. One reporter went back to Woodlawn High School to get background for his story on the quarterback. He asked Coach Lee Hedges, "How many times had Bradshaw and Spinks thrown the football back and forth?" "Start with a million," suggested Hedges.[2]

Despite a reputation for being a practical jokester, Bradshaw would have agreed with his high school coach. When the Bradshaw family returned home to the working-class Cedar Grove neighborhood of Shreveport, Louisiana, after living in Iowa for a few years, Terry made friends with Spinks. The boys played endless football games together, imagining greatness in their backyards and empty lots in the area. During the 1950s through the early 1970s, for many children in the United States, playing games of tag, football, and "army" served as a major amusement after school and on weekends through junior and sometimes senior high school. The video games that keep children indoors and the year-round traveling teams that structure a gifted athlete into a single-minded pursuit of a sport remained at least a decade away. Bradshaw and Spinks would throw the ball until they ran out of daylight. Terry got a new football each year and found throwing them endlessly fascinating.

Focusing on football came naturally to many citizens of northern Louisiana. Longtime sports columnist Jerry Byrd calls football a way of life and observes, "It made our hearts beat."[3] As a child, Terry would toss a football against the ceiling in his bedroom, despite the protestations of his parents. "I always had a dream, a burning ambition to play quarterback in the National Football League," he explained. But first he had to quarterback the city's junior high school football team, and his first coach, Ellace Bruce, only noticed the boy's enthusiasm. Terry showed his good character and work ethic, playing hard that year as a linebacker before he broke his collarbone.[4]

The 1958 NFL Championship Game between the New York Giants and Baltimore Colts drew a large crowd and produced high television

Figure I.I.   Bradshaw throwing to Spinks. *LSU-Shreveport Archives and Special Collections.*

ratings. The game established professional football as a bona fide sport and a television program. Colts quarterback Johnny Unitas became a hero to many would-be players. Bradshaw liked the style of the upstart American Football League (AFL) because in it, the quarterbacks wound up and threw the ball deep. They played wide-open, high-scoring games. The games showcased the quarterback, and the offensive players had a blast. Bradshaw enjoyed watching such quarterbacks as George Blanda, John Hadl, and Jack Kemp. As Bradshaw said, "That [style of play] always made sense to me."[5]

Bradshaw put his strong arm to use during physical education classes and what he called his auditions, throwing the ball to a friend on the sidelines at the team's practices. The junior high school football coaches made him their starting quarterback for the eighth grade. Bradshaw called this passionate interest in and talent for playing the game of football God-given gifts. He toiled at perfecting the skills of his position, worked on retaining his confidence, and remained enthusiastic and positive toward his teammates and the game. He accomplished all that while experiencing the highs and lows of the game and flatlining and sitting on the bench during his high school, college, and professional careers. The work ethic, confidence, and character of Terry Bradshaw emerged in a Shreveport that valued old-time religion, the masculine physicality of football, countryfolk toiling away at their work, and old-time country and gospel music. This enabled Bradshaw to begin developing the honest, homespun personality and natural charisma that would appear in his many public images in various entertainment forums throughout the next 50 years. He retained his roots from his Southern hometown—a city that evolved from its rough-hewn founding days.

Established in the 1830s, along the Red River, Shreveport became the seat of the new parish of Caddo. Cotton and forestry dominated the city's economy until the discovery of oil in the early twentieth century and the establishment of Barksdale Army Air Corp Base in the 1930s. Rural people came to the city for work and enjoyed the old-time country music broadcast weekly by the *Louisiana Hayride* program during the late 1940s and early 1950s. The townspeople also loved their football, but, like everything else in the city, white students did not play the game with or against African Americans.[6]

HIGH SCHOOL YEARS

The biggest rivalry in Shreveport football during the 1940s and 1950s was centered on Byrd and Fair Park high schools. Byrd High sat in the city's affluent area and, as a preparatory school, catered to the city's businessmen, large farmers, and public officials. But the school drew students from the southern and eastern portions of the city. Similarly, blue collar Fair Park drew its student body from areas outside the school district. Shreveport's population expanded from less than 100,000 to more than 127,000 between 1940 and 1950, and had climbed to more than 164,000 by 1960.

For many white Louisianans, Shreveport was an ideal place to live. Shreveport residents living in Fair Park held steady, decent-paying jobs with the railroad and as tradespeople. Terry's father, William "Bill" Bradshaw, worked at Riley Beaird in manufacturing and shared his love of sports and football with his three sons from an early age. According to Stan Powell, principal of Oak Terrace Junior High, "The Bradshaws were a close family. They brought dedication, discipline, and devotion to their children and family." Terry Bradshaw commented that his parents used to say their family was rich in love, which meant less rich in money. As a teen, Terry worked at a door manufacturer and performed other jobs during the holidays. Other new residents, including country people who were nice and easygoing, moved into the city to take jobs in the oil fields and related businesses. The vast majority were highly religious, choosing the local Methodist or one of the Baptist congregations. The Bradshaws attended Calvary Baptist Church.[7]

Bradshaw recalled years later that as a youngster the church proved one of the few places where he could sit still. The pastor, Brother Henry Grady Buchannan, better known as H. G., held the young Bradshaw spellbound with his mesmerizing sermons. The pastor made certain the parishioners knew about heaven and hell, and the right way to live in the world, to guarantee a presence in the positive world in the hereafter. The reverend instilled in Bradshaw that there were choices in life and that good folks made the proper ones to stay on the right side of the Lord. The church had several thousand members during the early 1960s but remained a small and home-folksy meeting place with informal sociability and entertainment—a place where sin could be shed and souls saved.[8]

This significant population growth in the metropolitan area led the school board to build another high school in the Southern Hills neighborhood in the late 1950s. The neighborhoods of Cedar Grove on the east, Summer Grove to the far south, and Sunset Acres also sent their teenagers to attend this school. The Bradshaws went to Oak Terrace Middle School in the Sunset Acres area, on the west side of Brush Bayou and Route 171. Small ranch houses with two bedrooms and a single bath within reach of blue-collar workers and lower-middle-income families dotted the neighborhood. Air conditioning repairmen and railroad engineers lived in the neighborhood and helped their neighbors build dens and extra bedrooms and bathrooms onto their houses. Southern Hills contained larger houses and had a suburban-enclave look and feel to it. Many of the household heads worked in the same decidedly blue-collar occupations as in Sunset Acres.

The construction of an additional high school shrank the school boundaries for both traditional sports powerhouses. The administrators immediately sought to start a football program at the new Woodlawn High School in 1960. The new school quickly demonstrated how much the sport meant to it, arranging to hire chemistry teacher and football coach Lee Hedges, who had previously coached the Byrd Yellow Jackets. Hedges convinced A. L. Williams to come to the new school and serve as his assistant coach, as well as the track and field coach.

Woodlawn started in 1960, and played in the state's highest classification. "We didn't win a game that first year . . . and we didn't score until the sixth ballgame," Williams recalled. The locals embraced the Knights, as they had long wanted a high school in their neighborhood. The people in the area loved their football, Williams noted.[9] Since this era predated busing children to schools located in different districts, the residents in the neighborhood experienced a stronger connection to the local school because the student body included the local children. As newsman and sportscaster Robert Griffin explained, "Back in the '60s it was neighborhood schools playing against one another, so it was neighborhood versus neighborhood."[10] This same phenomenon sparked many men and women to root for Auburn against Alabama or vice versa and refer to themselves as Auburn or Alabama men despite never having attended either college.[11]

In its second season, Woodlawn's football team also proved smaller and featured less football experience than most of its opponents. The coaches decided to abandon the "wing-T" offense they had used the previous season and started putting the ball in the hands of quarterback Billy Laird. Hedges and Williams started throwing the ball more than the five to seven times per game that most high school teams averaged. They designed play-action passes and passes on spread formations, attempting to provide ample time for the plays to develop and enable receivers to get free. Because the young school lacked depth on its team, many of these offensive players also had to play on the defensive side of the ball.

The changes brought immediate success. Woodlawn won the first game in school history on a last-minute touchdown. The Knights jumped out to a 6–0 record before facing the Byrd powerhouse. The two teams played the first of what would be a string of games in front of a crowd of more than 20,000, with Byrd winning, 26–0. The Woodlawn bounced back and won two before taking another loss. The district championship was on the line in the final game of the season. Woodlawn defeated Bossier, 12–7, to go from last to first in one season and win their first district championship.

The rags-to-riches story of Woodlawn's 1961 football team inspired the entire neighborhood. "I wanted to be another Billy Laird. He was our model," Bradshaw recalled later. He and the other players from Southern Hills focused on more than simply the offense or the most prominent figures on the team. Bradshaw said, "We were going to school with a bunch of family kids. Everyone felt equal. There was a great sense of unity."[12]

Bradshaw soon had the chance to experience that camaraderie. The Knights won 9, 8, and 10 games, respectively. during the first three years that Bradshaw attended high school. This strong team featured Trey Prather, an All-State quarterback and gifted athlete in several sports. Hedges admitted years after Bradshaw's Super Bowl successes that in Bradshaw's junior year, even though the team stayed with Prather as their quarterback, "[W]hen we could get Terry in, he played." These entrances may not have occurred as frequently as Bradshaw would have liked, but with a 10-win season, the Knights did provide some chances for the starters to rest. Bradshaw lettered that year. Williams worked with the backfield players and described Bradshaw as "young but very competitive, confident but not cocky. He just felt he could throw the ball anywhere." Woodlawn did not make it far in the state playoffs. [13]

The next season, Prather left to become a freshmen quarterback with Louisiana State University. Bradshaw inherited the reins of a team that had two starters returning from their squad from the previous season. The team did not get off to a rousing start. Woodlawn suffered a loss and a tie in the early part of the season, mostly because the team's defense had trouble stopping other teams. The offense contributed as well. At times Bradshaw struggled to run the play the coaches sent in during the games. "I was a little slow, but A. L. was patient with me," he remembered. [14] The team won a few games. As Coach Hedges remembered, "I was a ball-control coach back then . . . we were trying to get more into passing . . . but finally we decided to let Terry just drop back there and throw the ball. Terry could throw the football as far as one would want anyone to throw it." [15]

The victories led to the annual showdown with archrival Byrd High School. Byrd had won every time the teams played during the previous five years. After each victory, the Byrd students and parents would celebrate by serenading Woodlawn supporters as they left with the taunt, "Good Night Knights." This grew tiring for the large number of

Figure 1.2. The team encircled around the marching band. *LSU-Shreveport Archives and Special Collections.*

faculty who came to the games and especially for the pep squad, which stood at nearly 200 strong. The size of the squad caused one opposing player to comment, "Before the game starts you are already intimidated." Bradshaw completed two passes that evening, and combined with his running and the team's defensive stands, Woodlawn won their first game against Byrd. The Woodlawn supporters acted like they had won the championship.[16]

If the Woodlawn neighbors and fans thought the defeat of Byrd proved to be the greatest victory, some sports reporters had other opinions. One argued that every great player experiences crossroads in their career. In these moments, success or failure on the field can build the athlete's confidence and prepare them to reach the next rung on the ladder of success or destroy their confidence and leave them plagued with doubt.

Bradshaw's first big game was the 1965 Woodlawn–Airline matchup, held at State Fair Stadium. "It was billed as the 'Game of the Year,'" sportswriter Jerry Byrd noted. The two defenses dominated the vast majority of the play, with neither team scoring for more than 45 minutes of the game. Airline led by two touchdowns early in the second quarter when Bradshaw hit Tom Hagin on a 65-yard middle screen for Woodlawn's first touchdown. The Airline Vikings immediately got the touchdown back with a 40-yard run around right end. Bradshaw then hit Tommy Spinks in stride on a 66-yard touchdown bomb to cut the lead to six. An eight-yard run by Hagin in the second half won the game for Woodlawn, 21–20.[17]

The season continued to be successful. Bradshaw set a record with 21 touchdown passes during the year. The Woodlawn Knights completed the season with an 11–2–1 record to capture the district title. Woodlawn had qualified in previous years for the state championship but never won a game. The teams played in a wind storm brought on by a hurricane raging in the southern portion of the state, and Woodlawn won the game, 13–2. Next, the Knights faced off against the number-one ranked Lafayette High School Lions. The Lions completed the first undefeated season in Louisiana high school football history and were ranked as the best defensive team in the state. Bradshaw and the offense led the team to victory, with the quarterback throwing two touchdown passes. The school made their first-ever appearance in the state championship finals. Woodlawn played against Sulphur High School from Calcasieu Parish in a rain storm. Bradshaw ran for 14 yards and led the Knights to a 7–6 halftime lead. In the second half, Sulphur outscored Woodlawn and won the game, 12–9. Coach Williams observed, "They were worn down by the size of the opponent."[18]

Despite the disappointment, Woodlawn's 1965 football season ranked as one of the school's best ever. The school reached the state playoffs 29 times in 56 seasons between 1960 and 2015. The Knights only reached the championship round on two occasions. While the 1965 team lost, it won in 1968. The 1965 playoffs had a significant impact on the next development in Bradshaw's football career. He believed that his performance in the semifinals prompted several of the area colleges and universities to want him to sign to play on their football squads.[19]

Many high school athletes played multiple sports during each school year. At Woodlawn High, former quarterback Billy Laird played baseball, while Trey Prather lettered in four sports: football, basketball, baseball, and track. Bradshaw's top receivers, Ken Liberto and Tommy Spinks, were no different. Liberto played football, basketball, baseball, and track, while Spinks lettered in football, baseball, and track. Terry Bradshaw decided early on that he did not like baseball, so he lettered in track. The most athletically gifted players often had teams from two professional sports draft them. Among NFL quarterbacks, Otto Graham played professional basketball during the late 1940s, Dallas Cowboys star quarterback Troy Aikman was drafted by the New York Mets out of high school, and Russell Wilson of the Seattle Seahawks went to spring training with the Texas Rangers of Major League Baseball.

Before Bradshaw could devote much time to considering colleges, he needed to prepare for the upcoming track and field season. Terry threw the javelin, and his strong arm made him a natural at the event. He broke local and state records, gathering increasing media attention. Confronted with the overflow traffic of bystanders and media covering the event, officials decided to move the javelin toss from its usual fringes into the middle of the football practice field. Then Bradshaw hurt his elbow, prompting great concern from track coach A. L. Williams and others. Williams restricted Bradshaw to a single javelin throw per week.

Williams recalled having to weigh his concern about the young athlete's well-being with the desire to set a national record. The coach bought Bradshaw a javelin that was heavier and traveled better. The

Figure 1.3. Senior Superlatives, Most Athletic: "Ever heard of Terry Bradshaw? Anyway, you remember him don't you? He was the great Knight quarterback. He also broke the national javelin throw record (several times). That's 'Most Athletic' male." *LSU-Shreveport Archives and Special Collections.*

salesman asked Williams if he was sure he wanted to buy it because the javelin proved harder to throw. Williams told him he understood but that his athlete could handle the greater weight. He made the purchase and gave Terry the new javelin. Williams told the seventeen-year-old Bradshaw, "You've got the opportunity to set the national record." Bradshaw responded, "Coach, you don't believe that?" Said Williams, "I wouldn't tell you if I didn't believe it."[20]

The team attended the Alexandria meet after a hard week of working out. The Bolton Relays represented one of the last chances for Bradshaw to set a new national mark. To be scored officially, a javelin throw had to be measured by a licensed engineer, and there had to be a limit to the incline of the field. With everything ready, Bradshaw was set for his throw. He threw his javelin 240 feet and two inches, nearly eight feet longer than the previous national record of 232 feet and nine inches, set the year before. Lee Reece worked the Bossier City Invitational. Many decades later, he recalled the amazing throw, which remained the high school record for years.[21]

If the football season drew local and some state newspaper coverage, the track season generated blurbs in media sources throughout the country. Local newspapers discussed the many impressive performances, including Bradshaw's throw. Newspapers on both the East Coast and West Coast mentioned the feat. National magazine *Sports Illustrated* mentioned Terry's achievements in its "Faces in the Crowd" section. Most amazingly, actor and fellow high school javelin thrower Michael Landon—then starring as the popular Little Joe of *Bonanza*—visited Woodlawn to see Bradshaw. While fewer fans knew about his track exploits than his football efforts, Bradshaw generated more than 200 inquiries from schools interested in having him on their track teams.

STARTING COLLEGE

Terry Bradshaw faced the same question as most scholarship athletes and other students during their senior year of high school: deciding which school best suits them. Despite the numerous inquiries, including a few from European universities, Bradshaw focused on the schools that were offering him the opportunity to go out for their football teams. After the Louisiana state high school all-star game, he received offers from numerous colleges, including Louisiana State University (LSU), Louisiana Tech, and Baylor, as well as Notre Dame, the service academies, Florida State, Alabama, and several other schools in the South. Some of these schools wanted him badly. A few employed boosters and alumni to take inappropriate actions, for example, promising payments to Terry's father if Bradshaw signed with them.

Illegal and scandalous recruiting practices overlap with the origins of big-time college football. It is widely known that the Marx Brothers mock the practices in their 1933 movie *Horse Feathers*. The Southeastern Conference (SEC) allowed its members to pay for tuition, room, and board for athletes. During the immediate post–World War II era, the conferences dominated and made their own rules regarding recruitment procedures. The NCAA codified this ability of colleges to pay for school-related items with its Sanity Code. By the 1950s, the Pacific Coast Conference established rules limiting the types of jobs being offered, but slush funds paid players directly. Yet, through the mid-1960s, the rules in the SEC and Southwestern Conference enabled schools to give athletic scholarships and provide jobs for players, funded by the boosters. Indeed, throughout the era boosters could participate in recruiting and funded players' scholarships.[22]

The recruitment of Terry Bradshaw shows how difficult it was for the NCAA as they wrestled with how to differentiate between "honest" boosters and "crooked" ones, between the boosters who offered Bill Bradshaw money and the ones who drove Terry to events on campus and gave him the hard sell for their various schools. Bradshaw liked the current quarterback and coach at Baylor and went to visit the campus. He saw players partying and hanging out with women at the Baptist College and felt shocked and unable to comprehend the behavior. Upon his return, many people who knew Terry resumed their push for him to attend a college in the state. Woodlawn coaches and some other locals wanted him to go to Louisiana Tech, like many of his teammates. Others, including a local businessman and friend named Ken Hanna, really wanted Terry to attend LSU. LSU boosters and representatives turned up the heat. A local man loaned Terry his Mustang to drive around Shreveport for a few days. A group of alumni drove him down to Baton Rouge, pressuring him to sign. On the return trip, Terry agreed to sign.

This decision displeased Bradshaw's girlfriend, Penny Clarke, who planned on attending Louisiana Tech. At Woodlawn, A. L. Williams reacted by no longer talking to Terry. Bradshaw began to reconsider whether he wanted to play in the big-time competitive environment of LSU. He also realized that with Prather only in his second year there, there was a good chance he would be sitting behind the quarterback, as he had at Woodlawn. To escape this predicament and get out of his commitment to LSU, Bradshaw said he intentionally failed the College Board ACT exam. LSU officials wanted him to take the test again, and the second time he created a Christmas tree design with his multiple-choice answers. Unfortunately, the correct responses were not in that layout. From there, Bradshaw was free to pursue his interest in attending Louisiana Tech, and he successfully passed the ACT exam. [23]

Louisiana Tech sits in the midst of Piney Woods forest in Ruston, about 90 miles from Shreveport. Historically, it has drawn many of its students from Woodlawn and neighboring high schools. The school and one other college, along with the timber industry, fuel the town's economic engines. The residents have lived there for multiple generations, and everyone knows one another. It is a conservative area and was "dry" (alcohol was not legally sold) through the early 1970s. Alcohol was sold by bootleggers, like the Bandit figure in the *Smokey and the Bandit* movies. During that time, the city and the surrounding area generally had better employment rates and more money than other parts of the state, but the residents tended to be modest and kept their good tidings to themselves. Louisiana Tech conducted itself in a similar conservative manner. Women could not enter the college's engineering building, and men were required to remove their caps and hats when they entered a building.

A legendary figure in northern Louisiana, Louisiana Tech's head football coach, Joe Aillet, played high school and college sports before launching a successful career as a high school coach in Haynesville. He won more than 60 percent of his games during the next 26 years and won or shared the conference title in 13 of them. Bradshaw enjoyed the thought of playing in Aillet's pass-oriented offense, but sophomore Phil Robertson played the majority of the time. While some reporters considered Tech's two quarterbacks promising, they often noted that they rarely sustained an offensive drive. Louisiana Tech's team, the Bulldogs, won only one game in 1966. Despite the poor performances on the field, Bradshaw remained a gracious, open person. [24]

The next season, Aillet resigned, and Maxie Lambright took the reins. Bradshaw knew Lambright's reputation from Southern Mississippi University was run, run, and run some more. Bradshaw was concerned with the new hire, as the coach installed a new system. But Lambright was low key and said things to instill confidence in his players. When Robertson announced that he was quitting to pursue hunting and fishing, Lambright asked boosters and others to help convince him to return.

As a younger, slightly less mature man and a highly competitive individual, Bradshaw took issue with Robertson making a surprise return right before a game. When he found out that Phil had received the starting nod, Terry threw the ball at Lambright. Bradshaw entered the game after Robertson suffered an injury, leading the team to victory but playing poorly in the next game, during which Robertson relieved him. During Lambright's first season, Louisiana Tech's football team finished with a 3–7 record and failed to win a conference game; however, players like offensive lineman Glenn Murphy recalled how long and hard Bradshaw and the group of receivers worked after practice to improve and get in sync with one another. [25]

COLLEGE CHAMPIONSHIP YEARS

Entering Bradshaw's junior year, Louisiana Tech had a strong football team, featuring Tommy Spinks, Ken Liberto, and many other talented players. These guys practiced on their own during the offseason in Ruston with other college and would-be NFL players, including Bert Jones and his brothers, Jones's cousin Andy Hamilton, and James Harris. As an African American, Harris played at Grambling State, a historically black college located in Grambling, Louisiana. Grambling belonged to the Southwestern Athletic Conference and played against other schools with predominantly African American student bodies.

Those teams did not play the teams in the Gulf States Conference because racial segregation continued to exist. The mixing of these players stands out even if only on a practice field. Bradshaw mentioned that he rarely came into contact with African Americans while in Louisiana. As a child in Shreveport, he had seen the "White Only" and "Colored Here" signs. He remembered the separate toilet facilities. He occasionally ventured over to Grambling to play tag-team football or watch a basketball game because of the school's close proximity to Ruston.

The segregation of public facilities received legal sanction by the U.S. Supreme Court in 1896, with the *Plessy v. Ferguson* decision. Unequal funding and services to schools prompted a 50-year desegregation battle in the courts that ended with the Supreme Court overturning the earlier decision in *Brown v. the Board of Education of Topeka* . Colleges and universities, particularly those in the Northern states, began providing African Americans with more scholarships, improving their football teams. As Michael Oriard noted, " Because football in the South was a hugely important symbol of Southern manhood and Southern culture, integration meant a major readjustment." But Southern universities began losing more football games and slowly decided that winning games meant more than continuing racial separation. Louisiana Tech integrated their football team in 1971.[26]

The Louisiana Tech football team opened the 1968 season in the university's new stadium. While not quite complete—an open-to-the-group gap remained near the press box—the stadium seated 25,000, and those who missed the first game expressed frustration with the minimal coverage provided by the *Shreveport Times*. As starting quarterback, Bradshaw struggled, and the team was sporting a 2–2 record. In late October, Tech played the Northwestern Demons in the annual Louisiana State Fair Classic at State Fair Stadium in Shreveport. The schools each had about 10,000 students, generally from northern Louisiana and east Texas, and the game served as a neighborhood rivalry, with bragging rights and an extra day off of school at stake. There were rides, exhibits, IMCA races at the racetrack, fair food, and livestock. The coed courts from both schools acted in regal fashion as the students filed into the stands dressed in sports jackets, with their dates donning wool plaid skirts, boiled wool jackets, and elegant mum corsages. About 28,000 onlookers packed the stands—the most for a Louisiana Tech game all season.

Northwestern had the edge in the rivalry and had won the last two games at the fairgrounds. It looked as if things would continue along that path, with Northwestern leading, 19–7, at the half. The second half began with a Louisiana Tech explosion with two touchdowns on offense. The Demons responded with one of their own TDs to reclaim the lead. The teams proceed to swap touchdowns until Northwestern led, 39–35, and had the ball with one minute to play. They failed to get a first down and punted the ball to the Bulldogs. With 25 seconds left, Bradshaw stood behind center on his own 18-yard line. The Demons opted to play in a semiprevent defensive formation. Bradshaw reared back and unloaded a bomb to Ken Liberto, who streaked down the west sideline. Cornerback Ken Hrapmann went for the interception, and the ball zipped through his hands. Liberto pinned the ball to his chest at the Northwestern 40-yard line and ran as fast as he could toward the end zone. Demons linebacker Dick Concilio clipped Liberto's cleat with his hand, causing Liberto's shoe to fall off, but this did not stop Liberto from scoring a touchdown. Northwestern's defensive coordinator, Gene Knecht, dropped to his knees, pitched forward face-first, and pounded the ground. "It still haunts me," Knecht said a decade later.[27]

Decades later, the game—and the pass—remains memorable for those who were in attendance. Shirley Cobb, a resident of Ruston, wrote that her family still remembers the "State Fair" game "where [Bradshaw] won the game with that long 'Hail Mary' pass." Cobb added, "That's been a while back, but only seems like yesterday . . . folks around here still talk about it."[28]

The Louisiana Tech Bulldogs football team benefited greatly from the comeback victory at the State Fair. They reeled off five more wins to complete the season with an 8–2 record, earning the chance to play in one of the four regional quarterfinal bowl games used to help decide the champion of the NCAA College Division.

The College Division, for smaller colleges and universities, is now known as Division II. In 1964, the division started the bowl-game format. After the Camellia Bowl in the West, the Pecan Bowl in the Midwest, the Grantland Rice Bowl in the Mideast, and the Tangerine Bowl in the East, a wire service poll enabled coaches to vote for the team they thought to be the best.

The Rice Bowl, named after early twentieth-century sportswriter Grantland Rice, was played in Murfreesboro, Tennessee, near Vanderbilt University. Rice himself attended the games. Louisiana Tech won the conference championship in 1964, but the team did not receive an invitation to the inaugural quarterfinal bowl games, with Middle Tennessee State University going up against Muskingum University from the Ohio Athletic Conference. But Louisiana Tech's first appearance in a bowl game—the Rice Bowl in 1968—proved memorable.

"[It was] the most miserable day I have ever spent in my life," Mickey Slaughter, the Tech backfield coach recalled. The temperature reached a high of 20 degrees. Sleet and snow were falling from the sky, and a hard wind was blowing across the field. The ABC-TV network carried the game on a national broadcast. The Tech Bulldogs jumped out to a 21–0 lead. Offensive lineman Jesse Carrigan remembered, "It was so cold. The band couldn't march at halftime because their wind instruments were frozen." The daughter of one player said her father and other players couldn't feel their fingers or toes, but their adrenaline and excitement gave them the ability to play through it. [29]

In the third quarter, the University of Akron Bulldogs made it a game, scoring to cut the lead to 21–13. By the fourth quarter, only the heartiest of the 1,000 people in the stands remained. Bradshaw and the offense buried their opponent. On the way to a 33–13 final, Bradshaw threw an amazing touchdown pass that Mike Richey, a reporter for the Monroe, Louisiana, morning paper, called the "statute play." Bradshaw rolled out, fought off would-be tacklers, and, with three men hanging on him, tossed a six-yard touchdown pass to tight end Larry Brewer. "That play, that game is what sold NFL scouts on him," Slaughter said. Bradshaw recalled that interest in him picked up from that game onward. He was named to the All-America Team as one of the nation's top collegiate football players. [30]

Sadly, tragedy hit the Woodlawn football community in 1968. They lost quarterback Trey Prather, who left LSU after his sophomore year and enlisted with the U.S. Marines to serve in Vietnam. He helped secure the infamous Liberty Bridge in Quang Nam Province during the North Vietnam Tet Offensive but died days later from wounds sustained in the battle. Two other Woodlawn High football players are named on a memorial plaque at the school.

Bradshaw and others in Shreveport felt great sorrow about the loss of Prather. Like most men his age, Terry faced the possibility of being drafted to serve in the country's armed forces as the Vietnam War raged on. But as a student, Bradshaw had a deferment from being drafted. Like 90 percent of the males of his generation, the quarterback was not among the 648,000 drafted men who served in Vietnam. [31]

The Bulldogs lost a significant amount of talent during Bradshaw's senior year. The team's two cocaptains finished their college careers in 1968. The NFL's Pittsburgh Steelers drafted Ken Liberto. Three of the five players to win All-Conference honors graduated. For the new season, the remaining two to win All-Conference honors, Bradshaw and his friend Tommy Spinks, took over as cocaptains, along with John Harper.

The team continued to build chemistry, including through playing pranks. Bradshaw, for one, would call teammates in the middle of the night with a "chicken call." The player who answered the phone would hear the "cluck" of a chicken and then a squawk before getting hung up on. [32]

As college football began its centennial year, much of the conversation was focused on the "year of the quarterback." Bradshaw had topped the College Division quarterbacks in total offense the previous season, so his name was on many lips. Other top signal callers seeking 1969 All-America quarterback honors included Dennis Shaw (San Diego State), Rex Kern (Ohio State), Bill Montgomery (University of Arkansas), Bob Anderson (University of Colorado), Jim Plunkett (Stanford), and Bill Cappleman (Florida State University). These men played in Division I, against larger schools and more difficult competition than Bradshaw. Despite having his college described as "little known," Bradshaw received mention in the media throughout the country and made the list of possible professional quarterbacks. The *New York Times* dubbed him a "big man" at a "tiny college." Touting his strong arm and quick release, scouts like Gil Brandt of the Dallas Cowboys said, "Right now Bradshaw is an almost certainly first-round choice. It's conceivable he could go number one." [33]

Winning the Rice Bowl spurred greater attendance at Louisiana Tech games throughout the 1969 season. A quick start to the campaign helped fill the stands even more. Almost 20,000 spectators came to see the team win its third game, followed by more than 30,000 to see another victory at the State Fair Classic. Tech suffered its first loss after five wins during the homecoming game against the University of Southern Mississippi. Known as the "rivalry in Dixie," the Bulldogs lost, 24–23.

As the season wound down, the Bulldogs had a 9–2 record and won the Gulf States Conference championship. They were preparing to play in another Rice Bowl, this time against East Tennessee State University. Stanley Galloway, commissioner of the Gulf States Conference, argued that the game needed to be moved from Murfreesboro. "If the Sugar Bowl got Mississippi because Archie Manning is such a drawing card, then Terry Bradshaw ought to have a bigger stadium because he is the most exciting college quarterback today," Galloway stated. He succeeded in moving the game to Baton Rouge, Louisiana. They sold 20,000 tickets, and others watched the game regionally on ABC-TV. As one northern Louisiana sportswriter observed, Bradshaw received press from throughout the country. The sportswriter said friends sent him clippings about Bradshaw from everywhere, adding, "[H]e deserves every click of the typewriter that has been transformed into print."[34]

Bradshaw made the Associated Press Little All-America Team, but the game did not go as well as the year before, as the Bulldogs lost, 33–14. Bradshaw completed 20 passes for 299 yards and threw three interceptions. He spent too much time on his back side, as he was sacked 12 times for 143 yards; however, as one reporter noted, "Bradshaw showed why the pros are interested in him with bullet-like passes."[35]

With his final game for Louisiana Tech complete, Bradshaw had little time to think about his past and what he had done for the school. But others did take a moment to reflect on his collegiate career. One alumnus observed that the college would not have "come out of the 70s as they did" without Bradshaw having attended the school. Bradshaw worked constantly to be at his best, and fellow student Mike Guzman noted that being around him, "he could definitely get you to take that extra step" toward accomplishing your goals. The effect Bradshaw had on Louisiana Tech as a football player has been well documented. The positive influence he had on players and nonathlete students on campus may not have been as well known, but his impact illuminates the human dimensions to Bradshaw as a person.[36]

NFL DRAFT

The quarterback concentrated on making the transition from collegiate to professional ball. While conjecture flew about when Bradshaw would be taken in the upcoming NFL Draft, Bradshaw was readying himself for the all-star games. The top quarterbacks in the country—Bill Cappleman, Dennis Shaw, and Mike Phipps—played alongside Bradshaw in these games. During the 37–37 tie in the Senior Bowl, Bradshaw engineered two scoring drives of more than 70 yards to impress the many pros who were on hand for the contest.

After watching these games, the professional talent scout companies and scouts for some team organizations reported on what they witnessed to executives for the 26 NFL teams. The Pittsburgh Steelers and Chicago Bears were tied with the worst record in the league. Since the team with the worst record received the first pick in the draft, the two teams met with commissioner Pete Rozelle for the coin toss to determine the draft order. The Steelers won and got the first pick. The media began to speculate about what their selection might be. Steelers owner Art Rooney had visited Ruston earlier in the year to watch Bradshaw practice. "Raw ability, that's what this nation was built of," he mumbled. One could imagine that he figured the natural talent and charisma of Terry Bradshaw likely made him a good candidate for being a successful quarterback in the pros.[37]

Although the era lacked a 24-hour-a-day/seven-day-a-week media cycle, newspapers and sports news on television and radio carried stories about the upcoming draft. Early on, some media sources speculated that the Steelers would select Heisman Trophy winner Steve Owens, the running back from Oklahoma University. Others mentioned that Bradshaw would surely be chosen in the first round.

With the increasing possibility that Bradshaw would be the top pick in the draft, reporters focused on whether this guy from the College Division could succeed in the NFL. They asked experts, including his college coaches. Mickey Slaughter said, "Terry can throw the football as well as anyone alive. Anyone. Sure he has a lot to learn. He's got the arm, the quickness, the mind, everything. He's the finest pro prospect I've ever seen." They even asked the quarterback himself. Bradshaw told the media, "I chose Louisiana Tech to play at a college that uses a pro-type offense and pro formations. And I've had just great coaching. I've worked real hard, and the coaches have been very patient with me and taught me a lot."[38]

Media coverage also featured the opinions of the men who made a living evaluating football talent. A few of these evaluators provided comparisons to explain their view of Bradshaw and his football ability. "He's a bigger Sammy Baugh," said Jim Lee Howell, chief talent surveyor for the New York Giants. "He's the best passer since Joe Namath. But he had two things Namath doesn't have, good knees and good habits," offered another scout.[39]

The comparison with New York Jets quarterback Joe Namath emerged as a way for the media to understand the Bradshaw situation. Namath had a similar physical stature, standing at 6-foot-2, 200 pounds, to Bradshaw's 6-foot-3, 215 pounds. Like Bradshaw, Namath had a strong arm and the ability to throw the ball long distances. Most importantly, Namath was a major celebrity, having led the Jets to a Super Bowl championship just one year earlier. He lived in the media capital of the nation and drew attention with his good looks and active social life. But the pair had notable differences, aside from the ones mentioned by the scout. Namath played college ball in Division I at the University of Alabama, and the Jets picked him as the 12th selection of the first round in the 1965 NFL Draft. Bradshaw responded to reporters' questions about how the publicity and comparisons to Joe Namath were affecting him, saying they were not a factor because pressure is self-made.

The sports reporters missed some interesting comparisons that reporters and bloggers today would no doubt readily make. In the two decades from 1950 to 1969, teams selected 41 quarterbacks with their first-round selections. Almost 75 percent of the picks fell short of expectations. Beginning with the Los Angeles Rams selecting Billy Wade with the first pick in 1952, six other quarterbacks went as the top selection overall. While Wade had a decent career and one great year where he won a ring with the Chicago Bears, the others proved less successful. Another 23 first-round selections failed to become effective long-term quarterbacks. Only 10 played well enough to enjoy long and effective careers. Table 1.1 lists the most successful of these helmsmen. Among the rest, four picks have had good careers (from Babe Parelli to Craig Morton). John Brodie, Roman Gabriel, and John Hadl developed into top-flight quarterbacks. Namath, Len Dawson, and Bob Griese built Hall of Fame careers.

Perhaps the odds of finding a top-notch hall of famer six times out of 41 selections made drafting a quarterback seem a risky proposition. Quarterback ranked as the fourth most popular position to fill with a first-round selection. In this same era, teams drafted running backs in the first round 76 times, offensive linemen 52 times, and defensive

Table 1.1.   Notable Quarterbacks Selected in the First Round of the NFL Draft, 1950–1969.

Name	Draft Year	Main Team(s)	Status
Babe Parelli	1952 (4th overall pick)	Green Bay Packers,	solid career
Earl Morrall	1956 (2nd overall pick)	Baltimore Colts, Miami Dolphins	solid career
John Brodie	1957 (3rd overall pick)	San Francisco 49ers	top-flight career
Len Dawson	1957 (5th overall pick)	Kansas City Chiefs	HOF career
Billy Kilmer	1961 (11th overall pick)	New Orleans Saints, Washington Redskins	solid career
Roman Gabriel	1962 (2nd overall pick)	L.A. Rams, Philadelphia Eagles	top-flight career
John Hadl	1962 (10th overall pick)	San Diego Chargers	top-flight career
Craig Morton	1965 (5th overall pick)	Dallas Cowboys, Denver Broncos	solid career
Joe Namath	1965 (12th overall pick)	New York Jets	HOF career
Bob Griese	1967 (4th overall pick)	Miami Dolphins	HOF career

"Draft   Finder,"   *Pro-Football-Reference.com*,   http://www.pro-football-reference.com/play-index/draft-finder.cgi.

linemen 48 times. Ten running backs from the era played Hall of Fame–worthy ball, while another six had very good careers. Similarly, 10 defensive linemen from the era reached Hall of Fame worthiness, with another four being major contributors. Six offensive linemen reached the Hall of Fame level, with another six playing very well.

Perhaps the motivation came from a greater possibility of selecting a very good to excellent player when choosing from one of these other positions in the first round. The Steelers already had three quarterbacks on their roster. But sometimes teams follow the simple logic of selecting the best player available regardless of their position on the field. Steelers coach Chuck Noll announced his logic to the media, saying, "We made a decision on him as the best player in the draft. This is not a reflection on our people, just an analysis of the draft as it stands."[40]

Several other NFL teams expressed interest in Bradshaw. A reported 17 teams offered the Steelers some type of deal to obtain the first overall selection in the draft. The Baltimore Colts supposedly offered up Bubba Smith, John Mackey, and Willie Richardson. Chicago Bears defensive coordinator Abe Gibron expressed his amazement at the proposal. "Baltimore offered half a team for the kid—and he's still at least two years away," Gibron said. [41]

The Steelers picked Terry Bradshaw as their first selection in the 1970 NFL Draft. Reporters observed that he was the first player from a small college to be the number-one choice. One columnist noted that Bradshaw would be able to tell his grandchildren about that achievement but that people would soon forget unless the choice was surrounded with an aura of either tragedy or romance. The latter bloomed in Pittsburgh. Bradshaw beamed confidence, and the fans in the heavily Catholic area thought that he would be their savior. Even one of the veteran players offered similar comments. Ray Mansfield, the team's center, said that Bradshaw was going to be their "Moses," adding, "He's going to lead us out of the desert." [42]

After speculation concerning the draft choices ended, a few reporters and columnists began guessing how high Bradshaw's salary would be. They wondered if he would outpace the top pick from the 1969 draft, O. J. Simpson, who received a record contract of more than $300,000 for four years. Bradshaw stayed in Ruston and greeted the media circus willingly. He told them he "wanted to go with a loser," continuing, "I wanted to go someplace like Pittsburgh or Chicago, where if I made it they would make it with me." When he flew to Pittsburgh, some in the media said it was disappointing to Pittsburgh fans because he proved to be the opposite of Superman. Although Bradshaw came across as modest, he expressed his confidence. "I think I can make Pittsburgh a winner. If I didn't, I would have stayed home," he said. [43]

The quarterback had been very active. He and a few other Louisiana Tech players and coaches visited President Richard Nixon at the White House and presented him with a football signed by Bradshaw, Tommy Spinks, Larry Brewer, and coach Maxie Lambright. Nixon took the opportunity to show how small his hand was compared to the quarterback's mitt. Bradshaw spent time traveling and giving talks about his faith in Jesus Christ at various church functions and banquets. He also began his long career in the commercial world. He modeled slacks at a retail convention, telling reporters after the event, "Gosh, they give you a $100 a day to wear a pair of slacks. I'd wear a dress for $100."[44]

While he earned little money, the venture in modeling represented one of Bradshaw's first forays into endorsements. "The athlete provides recognition. More than that, he also supplies the image. For most people the athlete is still the all-American boy," said Steve Arnold, co-founder of Pro Sports, Inc., a company that represents athletes in their sundry negotiations. For decades, athletes from all professional sports have pitched products ranging from cereals to cigarettes and services for companies ranging from banks to insurance agencies. Only one year earlier, top draft pick O. J. Simpson received $250,000 to promote Chevrolet, one of the largest-ever endorsement gigs for an athlete.[45]

By mid-spring, Terry Bradshaw had signed his contract with the Steelers. Along with his chain-smoking father and Shreveport lawyer-agent, Bradshaw inked the document at a mock signing held with the construction of Three Rivers Stadium going on around them. He received a $110,000 bonus to sign a five-year contract worth $25,000 the first year, with a $5,000 increase each year. The "Blond Bomber" soon discovered that nearly half of the players in the NFL hailed from the South. The Midwest region ranked second, with about 20 percent. Louisiana has three of the most prolific areas for birthing NFL players in the country, with New Orleans, Lafayette, and Monroe producing three to four players per 100,000 births. Only Pine Bluff, Arkansas; Billings, Montana; Midland, Texas; Victoria, Texas; Hinesville, Georgia; Greenville, North Carolina; and Blacksburg, Virginia, have come close.[46]

The combination of selecting the top pick in the NFL Draft and the construction of a new stadium fueled a narrative of a "new" Steelers. Part of the multipurpose phase for stadiums during the late 1960s and early 1970s, Three Rivers shared attributes with the Astrodome, Busch Memorial Stadium, and Riverfront Stadium. These facilities looked like "concrete doughnuts," held more than 50,000 spectators, and had suites for the corporate and wealthy classes of patrons. The expansive parking areas served the large number of suburban clientele. Cost overruns, stolen materials, and lack of lighting slowed construction, which continued on into the beginning of the exhibition season.

The team's top draft pick also endured a few bumps from the get-go. A sports columnist for the *New York Times* used Bradshaw to illustrate the large number of college athletes who failed to graduate. Overall, 53 percent of athletes graduated between 1960 and 1969, but the numbers were lower in football and basketball. The columnist did not indicate that Bradshaw needed only nine more credits, or three courses, to complete his degree.[47]

A day later, word emerged that Bradshaw had undergone surgery to remove a calcium deposit on his right thigh. The injury kept him from playing in the annual American Football Coaches Association all-star game in Lubbock, Texas. A pulled muscle on the same thigh cost him the chance to play in the College All-Star Game later in the summer. But these little blips between Bradshaw's college and professional careers failed to temper the high expectations fans held for their new quarterback and the Pittsburgh Steelers. Inevitably, high expectations can result in disappointment.

2

THE BRADSHAW IMAGE

Moses vs. Li'l Abner

"Oft expectation fails, and most oft there / Where most it promises."—William Shakespeare[1]

The large crowd filling brand new Three Rivers Stadium roared as their team burst onto the artificial turf for the first football game ever held there, on September 20, 1970. Pittsburgh's tall, golden-haired rookie quarterback generated enthusiasm with his great play and excitement on the field. While playing host, the Steelers routed the New York Giants, and one visiting sports columnist observed, "[The rookie] immediately looked like a bigger bargain than the nearly completed $36 million stadium rising just across the river from downtown."[2] The allure of the shiny and new helped fans and reporters forget about the assessments of the more sober-minded.

Old hands in the game had voiced their high expectations of Bradshaw. Steelers owner Art Rooney asserted, "This team has a chance to make it big. This quarterback . . . he's as good as any rookie quarterback I've ever seen." As a team owner with a new stadium, Rooney certainly wanted everyone to have positive thoughts about his team. Players like veteran linebacker Andy Russell offered highly complementary views as well. "The veteran players on this team really almost wanted someone to come in and take over. We needed a leader, just someone to move the ball, not even score touchdowns," he admitted.[3]

PITTSBURGH AND ITS SPORTS

The city's steel, iron, and coal production enabled it to play a major role in U.S. history, serving as the "Arsenal of Democracy" during World War II. The large factories on the north and south sides of the Allegheny and Monongahela rivers generated the product. The Pittsburgh Terminal Properties on the city's South Side helped store and ship the resources, and served as the largest warehouse between New York and Chicago. But thick smog and dirty rivers made the city unhealthy and unattractive. Areas with housing stock and businesses appearing rundown and often lacking indoor plumbing became ripe locations for urban renewal in Pittsburgh, as was the case in many American cities. The city contained nearly one hundred neighborhoods, most enclaves made primarily of one or two ethnic groups.

In the immediate postwar years, Pittsburgh's mayor, David L. Lawrence, and other civic leaders developed an urban renewal plan called Renaissance I. The plan contained several components, nearly all focused on downtown revitalization. The skyscrapers of Gateway Center replaced factories, and Point State Park and Civic Arena appeared along the Allegheny and Monongahela rivers. But anticipated neighborhood revitalization stalled. People moved to the suburbs and out of the metropolitan area after 1960. Corporate leaders continued to prefer that their offices be located downtown, which helped keep the area somewhat vital throughout the 1960s and 1970s.

While corporate and civic leaders talked for years about building a new stadium for their sports teams, little happened. For many years, the Steelers played at Forbes Field, a baseball stadium and home of the Pittsburgh Pirates. The Steelers made the playoffs once during those three decades, and the team's poor play limited its fan base. The Steelers regularly gave away tickets and drew 18,000 to 23,000 diehard fans who enjoyed rooting for the defensive players to hurt someone on the other team. Many of the players lived near the South Park Fairgrounds in low-rise red-brick apartment complexes. Players' hometowns were frequently near the city, and they enjoyed having a few drinks with fans at such places as Dante's Restaurant and Lounge and Chiodo's Tavern. After years of delays, the ownership broke ground for the construction of Three Rivers Stadium in 1968. It took 29 months, but the facility finally held its first baseball game. Now the Steelers were ready to play their first regular-season game in their new digs.[4]

For the first time in his football career, Terry Bradshaw had won the starting quarterback job in his first year on the team. He took the reins from Dick Shiner and Terry Hanratty, who had led the team to its 1–13 record in the previous season. Reporters and columnists said the Steelers had at last found a competent quarterback in Bradshaw, but more often than not, he was described as a quarterback "sensation." They also liked his personality, especially in contrast to some of the other quarterbacks in the NFL. One observed that Bradshaw had a positive attitude, unlike such quarterbacks as Joe Kapp, who demanded a higher salary to keep playing. He expressed enthusiasm, unlike Joe Namath, who did not know if he wanted to continue playing pro football.

Bradshaw's looks and personality made him appear to be "All-American," distinguishing him from those who held the countercultural values of the Woodstock generation. In 1970, in the midst of regular demonstrations against the Vietnam War and occasional "be-ins," "love-ins," and rock concerts, Bradshaw was perceived as being conservative.

Figure 2.1.   Aerial view of Three Rivers Stadium in Pittsburgh, Pennsylvania.

The media described his short hair; deep blue eyes; small, white teeth; and large dimples. The publicity he received, especially in the Northern states, painted him a study in virtue, a young man of impeccable personal habits. Bradshaw appeared enthusiastic about his profession, the good old American game of football. He was aware of his role and willing to shoulder the responsibility that came with it. "From the moment I walked in here, I could tell that this was a football team in search of a leader," he proclaimed, "the people who operate the Pittsburgh Steelers . . . and they're paying this kid from the bayou—that's me—lots and lots of money to do just that . . . to be a leader." Bradshaw praised his teammates on the Steelers' offense and said that he would help in the effort to shake the team from the idea of losing.[5]

The quarterback most associated with the playboy life and countercultural ethos, Joe Namath of the New York Jets, wore the tag "controversial." While being noted for his natural playing abilities, Namath received heavy media coverage and some criticism for dating numerous women and enjoying the nightlife in the city, including places frequented by gamblers. They admired and bemoaned his ability to be his own man. The media asked him, "Has Hollywood spoiled Joe Namath?" "Maybe," the long-haired football hero acknowledged, adding, "Hollywood offers a great opportunity. The money is fantastic." In his first movie, Namath played a role that both represented the counterculture and opposed rebel members of that culture. He played a more average Joe in his next movie, *Norwood*.[6]

The attention—and, consequently, the expectations—loomed larger and remained more intense for quarterbacks than any other position on the field. Even running back O. J. Simpson, who began his professional football career in the fall of 1969, was not proclaimed as the answer for the woeful Buffalo Bills franchise. In their articles, reporters mentioned that Simpson was "less than a sensation as a pro." But one of the deans of the sports columnists, Arthur Daley, stated that progress had been slow but steady. "Some day [*sic*] O. J. will even live up to fan expectations," he declared.[7]

SHAPING AN IMAGE

Before Terry Bradshaw played his first games during his first season in 1970, many sports reporters and, consequently, a large number of fans held a conflicted image in their minds of the man from Shreveport. Being drafted number one and having been a highly successful player in college led many to conclude that Bradshaw would be the Steelers' Moses, leading the team out of the desert of no playoffs and championship titles.

But at times reporters interpreted Bradshaw's looks and personality in a stereotypical manner. His striking looks and enthusiastic, ebullient, loquacious nature made for great copy. One reporter referred to the rookie as "Li'l Abner in shoulder pads." Shreveport and northern Louisiana became Dogpatch. A shorthand reference to the new quarterback arose.[8]

Created by cartoonist Al Capp, Li'l Abner featured a fictional family of hillbillies from a poor mountain village in Appalachia. Abner was the oldest boy of Mammy and Pappy Yokum. He was a strapping, 6-foot-3 teenager who acted naïve and gullible but sweet and none too smart. What started in eight newspapers syndicated through United Feature grew within three years to appear in more than 250 newspapers, reaching 15 million readers. At its apex, coverage included 70 million readers in almost 900 newspapers in both Europe and North America. Other media formats also portrayed Li'l Abner and Dogpatch, including a movie, a musical comedy on Broadway, and a television series.

The comic ran its last strip in November 1977, after helping shape the cultural perceptions of Southerners, Pittsburghers as much as anyone. Residents who had been living in their communities for generations described Pittsburgh as a big small town with roots, "the classic shot and a beer town, and its people held classic grievances and got into fights." And the angle on Bradshaw was that he was a dummy—in fact, anyone from outside the Pittsburgh area had their judgments, and many Pittsburghers had the image of a Southerner in mind.[9]

As one sportswriter put it years later, the sporting press latched onto an angle for their stories about every player. For Bradshaw, beat reporters played on the stereotype as they emphasized the Bradshaw quotes that illuminated his fun personality. Bradshaw brought his infectious enthusiasm to the team. "I'm a jolly kind of fellow," he said, "I don't take things too seriously. To me football is a bunch of fun, a blast. I just love what's happening. I can't wait to play." Sports reporters again tied these traits to the Li'l Abner vision when they observed that Bradshaw came to play with the city slickers, sporting his man–child combination of honesty and naiveté.[10]

In most situations, the tie between Bradshaw and Li'l Abner hardly proved complementary to the quarterback and was not based on factual similarities with him. Instead, the perception emerged from a stereotypical view that saw all rural Southerners as being the same. The Kentucky Mountains surrounding fictional Dogpatch sat nowhere near Shreveport, Louisiana. The hillbilly culture emerging in the small Appalachian enclaves was significantly different from that within an urban area with a population of almost 165,000 (76th in the nation in 1960). The city's department stores alone showed that its culture had au courant tendencies by featuring pillbox hats a la Jackie Kennedy for sale when Bradshaw was a boy in the early 1960s. At the same time, the high schools and institutions of higher learning in the United States expanded immensely beginning in the middle of the Great Depression. Bradshaw took advantage of that experience, wildly surpassing the formal training that would have been available to Li'l Abner. But because Bradshaw had a "Southern" accent, used some country phrases, and stood at 6-foot-3, he received the nickname.

The image made fun of people from Appalachia and Southerners in general. A series of television programs during the era, including *Gomer Pyle U.S.M.C.*, *The Beverly Hillbillies*, and *Green Acres*, depicted "Southerners" who seemed well meaning yet often goofed things up. Scholar Nancy Isenberg described these figures as crude objects of audience laughter for mockery and not admiration.[11]

One truth about much of the South and Bradshaw's hometown was the segregation between the races. Jim Crow laws resulted in Bradshaw living a generally separated existence from the city's blacks. Yet, Bradshaw smartly realized that he knew little about black culture. While Northern cities did not have laws mandating racial segregation, blacks and whites lived in different neighborhoods in such Northern cities as Pittsburgh. The destitution and limited economic opportunities in some of the ghettos made several of these urban areas combustible until even a few years ago. In April 1968, violence, looting, and arson ran rampant in many Northern cities after the assassination of Dr. Martin Luther

King. For many, particularly young blacks, the Black Power and separatist groups and organizations advocated fighting for political and cultural power. They questioned the white power structure and whether blacks should be separate from that society and culture. By choice, many Steelers players, black and white, ate and did off-field activities in same-race groupings.

Two Steelers rookies from totally different backgrounds met when Bradshaw and receiver John Staggers joined the team. Bradshaw asserted that he took the role of leader of the team and saw the squad as a mixture of several cultures, particularly African American and Caucasian. An open person, he admitted to Staggers that he did not know much about "coloreds." Staggers offered a quick first lesson by suggesting that the quarterback stop using the word *colored* and substitute the word *black*.

A young man, Bradshaw came to the Northern city of Pittsburgh, Pennsylvania, with much to learn both on and off the field. One teammate who asked to remain anonymous observed the quarterback's major personality attributes of confidence and naiveté, and was worried. He spoke of the reality that every player has a bad day once in a while. The teammate observed, "There are going to be times when he has three or four passes intercepted. Every quarterback goes through it. But I don't believe he realizes this."[12]

What made the player raise this issue? Did he believe Bradshaw was unaware that he would have to suffer through tough games? That seems hard to believe, because Bradshaw had experienced bad days in his high school and college games. Did he wonder if Bradshaw could accept having a bad game on the big stage? Was his biggest concern how the media and Steelers fans would react?[13]

FIRST YEAR

Four consecutive victories to close out the exhibition season excited Steelers players and fans, but they experienced a rude awakening as the regular season began. The crowd of more than 45,000 at Three Rivers Stadium for the first game against their Central Division rival, the Houston Oilers, left unhappy. Bradshaw could not get the offense moving, and Houston's pass rush jarred him throughout the day as the

Steelers lost, 19–7. The next week against Denver, Bradshaw completed half his passes and had his team in front, 13–7, after the half. But Bradshaw got caught for a safety, and Denver scored a touchdown that provided the victory margin. Clearly, the rookie's inexperience with the speed and style of the professional game limited his effectiveness, but so far observers appeared patient.

On the road against Central Division powerhouse Cleveland, the Browns again caught Bradshaw for a safety. They intercepted three of his passes, including one they returned for the touchdown that gave them a 15–7 victory. Against the Buffalo Bills, neither Bradshaw nor Hanratty threw often or particularly accurately, but their lack of mistakes and the defense's three interceptions of rookie Dennis Shaw enabled the Steelers to defeat the Bills for their first victory. Against Houston the following week, solid defense and Bradshaw's first touchdown pass of his career enabled the Steelers to exact revenge on the Oilers. With a 2–3 record, the team looked forward to getting back into the division race.[14]

Since Houston sat so close to Bradshaw's hometown, he stopped in Shreveport to visit his parents. Days later, East Coast metropolitan newspapers featured a story stating that Bradshaw received a "substantial" fine for missing practice on Tuesday. They added that he had already received a $25 fine when he was five minutes late for a team meal. Was Bradshaw a bad boy? Then one newspaper explained that fog at the Shreveport Airport caused him to miss his planned flight out, so he arrived in Pittsburgh late. He also had stopped to talk with a scout, which caused him to be late for the team meal.

The story in this newspaper and one of the local weeklies reestablished the view of Bradshaw as a flip, fun-loving, sometimes facetious rookie. "This guy has more charisma than all the Kennedy's put together," said Ed Kiely of the Steelers. Sportswriter Pat Livingston confirmed this, noting that Bradshaw went to a local mall to promote a crippled children's fund drive, adding that they needed four policemen to keep the fans away from him.[15]

Local reporters mentioned another side of Bradshaw's personality, describing a man who kneeled down in his room each night and prayed. "I say God, I want to be the greatest quarterback who ever played this game, and then I'll use all the honors I'll ever receive to glorify Your name," Bradshaw said. They viewed him as completely refreshing, aware of his talent for throwing a football without being abrasive and bone honest. They noted that he had room for improvement on the field and a perception that fans felt down on him. This represented the first time Bradshaw faced any kind of adversarial relationship with football fans. He had not heard boos while playing in high school and college. "They were saying what a bum I was and where is this Savior of ours and when was he gonna do it?" Bradshaw provided a response, declaring, "I didn't say I'd do it this year, but I know I'm gonna do it. I know it."[16]

The team's next game came against the formidable Oakland Raiders in California. The Steelers offense didn't know what hit them. The Raiders defense hit Pittsburgh with their intense pass rush, sacked Bradshaw a few times, and forced the rookie into four interceptions in clobbering the men from Steel City, 31–14. The next week the Steelers returned home to take on division rival Cincinnati. Bradshaw started the first half and completed only four of 12 passes. A halfback option, thrown by running back Dick Hoak, enabled Pittsburgh to score the touchdown that left the game tied at seven each at halftime. Terry Hanratty replaced Bradshaw and led the team to a victory.

Bradshaw was left with the impression that many fans were happy with the switch at quarterback, thinking the fans seemed to prefer Terry H. to Terry B. When Bradshaw won the starting job, he felt the burden of having beaten out a local hero. Hanratty hailed from nearby Butler, Pennsylvania, and achieved success in high school and in college at Notre Dame. Hanratty's background was more similar to that of the locals as well, as he was half Italian and Catholic.

The national newspapers featured the rookie's tribulations. After he played poorly against Cincinnati, they deridingly described the ineffective performance of the "Steelers' glamour boy." Unlike Pittsburgh, where the reporters tagged Bradshaw as Moses, many of the national sports reporters highlighted the quarterback's status as the top draft pick and hefty contract, and viewed him as this glamour boy. Hanratty became the starting quarterback for the next week. Reporters concentrated on Bradshaw's frustration with playing second fiddle to Hanratty. The rookie admitted that he felt unhappy with his play and that Hanratty deserved to start because he led the team to victory. Still, Bradshaw said if he was going to be on the bench, he wanted to do it behind a veteran so he could learn. Reporters asked him if he had heard the crowd of 39,000 during the game. "Yeah, I heard the boos," he commented, "'You deserve it,' I told myself." A large group of fans, particularly boys in their preteen years, loved the Steelers regardless and saw Bradshaw as their hero. One wrote years later, "He is no dummy! . . . Even though he and Chuck Noll didn't get along we own him a big THANK YOU."[17]

In his first seven games as a professional, Bradshaw completed 41 percent of his passes for 898 yards and only two touchdown passes. "I think my main trouble is the ups and downs as a rookie, not necessarily just a quarterback is going to face during his learning period in pro football," Bradshaw explained. A sportswriter for the *New York Times* appeared to agree, noting that even the most notable collegiate performers who received the recognition of winning the Heisman Trophy had failed in the pro game. Being drafted first offered no assurances of success.[18]

Hanratty took control in front of the first sellout crowd in seven years. He led the Steelers to a victory over the Jets in his first start, 21–17. But Hanratty struggled against the Kansas City Chiefs, and Bradshaw entered the game and also struggled in the team's loss. The following week, each played worse in a division loss to the Bengals; however, no team seemed to want to seize control of the division's top spot. The Browns came into Three Rivers Stadium one game ahead. They forced Hanratty out of the game with a concussion, and Bradshaw entered the contest to throw two touchdown passes. The Steelers won and grabbed a share of the top spot in the Central Division, but they only stayed at the top for one week. Bradshaw threw four interceptions in a loss to the Green Bay Packers. He and Hanratty combined for five more interceptions in a loss to the lowly Atlanta Falcons.

Announcements of the awards for the league's top players came with the end of the year. Buffalo Bills quarterback Dennis Shaw received the award for Offensive Rookie of the Year by Associated Press reporters, as well as the award for American Conference Rookie of the Year from United Press International reporters. Reporters underlined that at the beginning of the season, most of the publicity featured fellow rookie quarterbacks Terry Bradshaw and Mike Phipps, shunning Shaw. In a discussion about the 1970 All-Rookie Team, another reporter discussed the tough going several young quarterbacks had that season. He argued that despite this, Bradshaw was an excellent, heady player. Bradshaw had amazing qualities, including an exceptional arm, the ability to run well, and the capacity to take punishment from opposing linemen. He predicted Bradshaw would lead the team to a division title.[19]

With the 1971 draft approaching, stories discussed the methods talent scouts use to evaluate players. One of the Dallas Cowboys' four national scouts, Red Hickey, ranked players on a scale of one to nine (poor to exceptional) in several areas: character, quickness, ability, balancing competitiveness and aggressiveness, mental alertness, and strength/explosion. Hickey had ranked Bradshaw as a nine the previous season and would not alter his opinion. The insights from the scouts were put through one of the first computing programs in the NFL. Chief scout Gil Brandt noted, "We look for a number of things in a quarterback. In our system he must have an IQ of around 120." Brandt viewed Bradshaw as a winner, relating, "He had flashes. His release is so quick it's unreal. Sometimes he tries to force a pass, but he'll learn. He'll be great."[20]

The new draft cast Stanford's Jim Plunkett into Bradshaw's position of a young quarterback being drafted number one overall by a weak team. Quarterbacks manned the draft's top three choices, as Mississippi's Archie Manning went to New Orleans and Houston took Santa Clara's Dan Pastorini. Comparisons between the two most recent number-one draft selections continued throughout the summer. Many fans and members of the media contested that the Steelers had put too high a value on Bradshaw, like others were doing with Plunkett. The scouts who placed that value on Bradshaw insisted they remained correct in their evaluations. They argued his play would improve greatly with experience. After the exhibition season began and Pittsburgh won a few games, reporters quickly noted, "The can't-miss label on Bradshaw is smudged and has a damaged-in-transit sticker on it. He is now back in the ranks with the rest of the boys."[21]

Bradshaw took heat for taking ill-advised risks. He ran for yardage when he thought it was best, and sometimes it ended up successful. In an exhibition game against division rival Cincinnati, linebacker Bill Bergey hit Bradshaw with a forearm that sent the young quarterback to the local hospital for observation. Reporters and columnists critiqued Bradshaw's play, saying he liked to run too much for his own welfare. The professionals working for the team would agree on this point. Predictions on where the Steelers would finish boiled down to how well Bradshaw played, and they emphasized that the big quarterback had the physical tools to succeed.[22]

Despite the continuous mention of Bradshaw as a flop in sports columns, the quarterback felt that he was in a better place. He made friends with guard Gerry Mullins and another rookie, safety Mike Wagner. They found a place to live near Squirrel Hill, in a 12-story building with only two finished units at the time they moved in. While it was noisy because of the ongoing construction, the price and ability to sign a half-year lease made it a good choice. The players returned home in the offseason and could not afford to pay for living spaces in two places. But many players found Pittsburgh natives to be very friendly. "People in Pittsburgh were super nice. In Minnesota, you didn't know your neighbors," said Bobby Walden's wife Scarlett.[23]

YEAR TWO

The first game of the 1971 season was against the Chicago Bears. Despite Bradshaw's four interceptions, the Steelers led and were running out the final minutes of the matchup. Bradshaw handed the ball off to Warren Bankston, and he failed to get the first down. Chicago scored a touchdown to win by two. As the local and national media questioned Noll on the play choice, the coach absolved both players and blamed the media for putting too much pressure on Bradshaw. One local reporter linked the play choice to Bradshaw's level of intelligence, playing on the Li'l Abner image. He observed a comment from a wily and successful football figure, who said, "If he's such a brain, why didn't he play for Louisiana State instead of Louisiana Tech? Think about it."[24]

The Steelers opened at home against the Bengals and won. Bradshaw threw two touchdown passes. He continued playing well, and the Steelers earned a .500 record. They went before the Monday night television audience in a tough road game against Kansas City. The team was taken to task by the strong veteran squad. Back at home for the next game, Bradshaw and Hanratty threw interceptions, and the team suffered three fumbles and multiple penalties. Yet, behind one rushing touchdown by Bradshaw and another by John Fuqua, the Steelers won. Punter Bobby Walden, who played with the team during the lean years of the late 1960s, took his nieces and nephews into the locker room to introduce them to the players. One niece, Franki McCartney, wrote several years later about how badly she felt about Mr. Terry having to get his skin toughened up. She understood why Bradshaw felt that way. She wanted people to know "she was honored to have been around him as a child." Mrs. Scarlett Walden, Bobby's wife, grew to love Bradshaw and said, "Terry was very naïve [during his first years in Pittsburgh] and said too much, and reporters ran with what he said."[25]

The alternating wins and losses continued. The division lead went up for grabs as the Browns come to Three Rivers just past the midpoint of the season. Behind their quarterback, the Steelers took a 16–0 halftime lead. Despite losing Bradshaw to a badly sprained ankle, they won the game and tied for the division lead. Playing hurt, Bradshaw threw three touchdowns, but the Steelers lost to Miami. They defeated the New York Giants the next week. With a record of 5–5, they remained in the running for the division title, which would be the first in the team's 39-year history.

As the season progressed, the media continued to come up with new ways of expressing images of Bradshaw's promise and how he was playing. While not using the comparisons of Moses and Li'l Abner, one major reporter referred to Bradshaw's image at the draft as Sir Lancelot and contrasted it with him playing more like Don Quixote. The statement had originated from Bradshaw being tackled for safeties three times and was being used to illustrate his "muddledom." Despite the loss of some of the shine from the Bradshaw star, Terry remained the figure who advertisers identified with the Steelers. One advertisement featuring a single player from each of the 26 teams, an ad promoting the Personna 74 razor, singled out Bradshaw to represent the Steelers.

As the season was coming to a close, the team's title hopes disappeared. The Steelers suffered their first home loss of the season. Hanratty replaced Bradshaw after the latter hurt his shoulder, but Bradshaw returned from the injury and promptly threw three interceptions in a loss at Houston, knocking the team two games behind the Cleveland Browns, who won their final two games to earn the division title. Despite struggling down the stretch, the Steelers ended the season with their best record since 1963. While Noll and the players realized this, many fans remained critical of their star quarterback. Some of the younger Steelers fans recalled how Bradshaw used to get booed all the time.[26]

Even as the quarterback was failing to live up to expectations on the field, the image of national glamour boy continued off it. As a practicing Christian, Bradshaw limited the type of women he dated, as well as his sexual engagements with them. For a few months during the season, Bradshaw dated Melissa Babish, and the announcement of their engagement sounded like a fairy tale—the big, brawny hero quarterback marrying the beautiful winner of a Miss Teenage America pageant. The media got cute with her acceptance of his proposal, noting that Bradshaw's passes clicked.

The pair hardly waited, getting married six weeks after the engagement. The media heralded the match as the all-American boy and the all-American girl tying the knot. She was 19 and in the middle of undergraduate studies at the University of Pittsburgh. Bradshaw revealed that he immediately felt as if he had been bound in an emotional knot, as he quickly realized he did not love her. The stories he read in the media about his marriage only made him feel worse about his choice.[27]

While Bradshaw processed his feelings, the team drafted several important new contributors to the team. Franco Harris became the team's top running back, John McMakin came on as a tight end, and three contributors helped the defense. They also drafted Tennessee State University's Joe Gilliam, who became the third quarterback. Gilliam told the press that he intended to compete with the Terrys for the top quarterback spot.

YEAR THREE: MAKING THE PLAYOFFS

Bradshaw took the lion's share of snaps during the exhibition season. Although he suffered some injuries, he played well. The team had come close the previous season, and Chuck Noll was expecting more from his players. He stated, "If our top 40 players operate at top efficiency, we can win the Central Division title." Bradshaw was his starting quarterback.[28]

Bradshaw seemed inspired from the start, leading his team to a victory over a tough Oakland Raiders squad. The division rival Bengals won the following week, although Bradshaw played well and the Steelers lost primarily because of three missed field goals and five fumbles. Despite the team's 2–2 record, a final drive on the road against St.

Louis spurred some belief in both the offense and the team. One long-time coach certainly believed in Bradshaw. Jets coach Webb Ewbank observed that there were several quarterbacks who he expected to be great. "Dan Pastorini of Houston, for instance. Jim Plunkett, Dennis Shaw, and Terry Bradshaw are going to make it big," he said.[29]

The Steelers began winning and seized control of the division. After defeating Houston, the team routed several clubs before getting revenge against the Bengals, with Bradshaw completing three touchdown passes. Fans filled the stadium. The number of season ticket holders climbed from 29,000 to 40,000, and the games regularly drew more than 50,000 spectators, setting records for the team. Bradshaw pronounced that the team was good enough to defeat anyone and that they would win the Central Division title.

Perhaps he jumped the gun. The very next week, the Steelers played against Cleveland. Although they scored first, the team trailed, 20–3, before Bradshaw found his buddy Gerry Mullins for a touchdown pass before halftime. After taking a 24–23 lead in the fourth quarter, the Steelers watched as the Browns moved into field goal range to win the game, 26–24, grabbing a share of the division lead. Pittsburgh defeated the Minnesota Vikings and the Browns won again to set up a battle for the division.

The Steelers used a balanced attack, scored in each quarter, and rolled to a 30–0 win in front of a delirious crowd at Three Rivers Stadium. Fans identified with several of the players. Rookie sensation Franco Harris had parents of Italian and African American descent, so a large number of fans formed "Franco's Italian Army." Several other banners proclaimed things like, "Run Pisano Run." Frank Sinatra asked to join. Placekicker Roy Gerela had a fan club known as "Gerela's Gorillas," and Jack Ham had a club called "Dobre Shunka," which is Slovak for "Great Ham."[30]

After the defeat of the Browns, the Steelers rolled through their last two games to seal the deal on their first-ever title. Fans turned out in droves to see their team upon its return from San Diego at 1 a.m. While mostly young people, the crowd included members of Gerela's Gorillas and Franco's Italian Army. Army members donned helmets and arm bands, and their Great Dane mascot had a hammer strapped to his head. In the bitter cold, facing powerful winds, two elderly men realized the dream of their football-watching lives. "It's been a long time coming, but how sweet it is," one said. Several groups of fans began lining up in front of the ticket window at 3 a.m. to get tickets for the game, which were set to go on sale seven hours later.

While playing a leading role as quarterback, leading the franchise to its first title, Bradshaw did not receive acclaim as the team's Moses from the media, but he did not care, because he was more worried about the team than individual accolades. Nonetheless, the lack of recognition in the media cemented a perception of Bradshaw being a subpar quarterback in the minds of fans.[31]

PLAYOFF GAME 1: THE IMMACULATE RECEPTION

The prognosticators projected that the Steelers–Raiders playoff game would be close. Some wondered if Bradshaw, with his 47 percent completion rate, could actually guide the team to victory. In Louisiana, the media discussed Bradshaw's success. He was compared to Namath as a winner. While Harris and the defense received the majority of the publicity, a small number of fans constituted the "Bradshaw Brigade." Those supporters expressed concern when the media said Bradshaw's middle finger on his throwing hand was badly swollen at its base.

Whether or not his injury handicapped him during the game, both the Steelers and the Raiders failed to score in the first half. Good defense hampered both teams' running and passing games. In the third quarter, Bradshaw led the Steelers on a long drive that ended in Gerela making a chip shot field goal. The Steelers began the fourth quarter with another long drive that amounted to a 6–0 advantage. Kenny Stabler, in the game as a replacement for Daryle Lamonica, scored on a 30-yard run that put the Raiders in the lead, 7–6.

The Steelers took control of the football with a little more than a minute remaining. They ran several plays, but the ball sat on their 40-yard line with 22 ticks left in the game. Bradshaw dropped back to pass and stepped back further and to his left to avoid the pass rush. He slipped around the attempted sack from Raiders defensive end Horace Jones and winged the ball 37 yards to an open John "Frenchy" Fuqua, before getting knocked onto his behind. Raiders safety Jack Tatum moved toward the Steelers' running back and determined that he couldn't intercept the pass. He unloaded a forearm to Fuqua's upper body, sending him backward, while denying him the ability to catch the pass. The ball hit someone in the Tatum–Fuqua pile and caromed 10 yards backward, end over end. Franco Harris followed the play, cupping his hands under the ball before it hit the artificial turf and took off toward the corner of the end zone. Raiders defensive back Jimmy Warren angled to catch Harris, but the big back gave him a stiff arm that forced Warren to the turf as Harris completed the touchdown play.

NBC television announcer Curt Gowdy quickly gathered his wits and summarized the play as it was replayed for the television audience. "You talk about Christmas miracles, here's a miracle of all miracles. . . . Bradshaw's lucky to even get rid of the ball. He shoots it out, Jack Tatum deflects it right into the hands of Harris." As scouts and fans knew from his play at the Grantland Rice Bowl, which Louisiana Tech had won in 1969, Bradshaw had great strength and resiliency in the pocket and a strong arm to be able to wing the ball hard and for a significant distance. One of his bullets could rebound off a player's shoulder pads and stay in the air for more than 10 yards. This remained one of the underdiscussed aspects of the play.

Steelers players ran from the bench to mob their teammate. Hundreds of fans poured onto the field to celebrate. Two of the back judges on the field interpreted the play as a legitimate touchdown, and after a brief discussion with the head of officials in the press box, the ruling on the field was a touchdown. According to news outlets, observers watched a replay to make the determination, but like the play, the official decision had several versions. Despite protests, Pittsburgh won, 13–7.

That night, Steelers announcer Myron Cope received a phone call in the newsroom at the television station from Sharon Levosky. Her friend, Steelers fan Michael Ord, dubbed the Harris reception the "Immaculate Reception." During the 11 o'clock news, Cope conferred the name on the play, and it stuck. For the next 40 years, the play became known as the greatest play of all time, as well as the most controversial.[32]

The play became the talk of the city. Fans and other residents thought that their team was destined for victory. Composer Henry Mancini asked where he could enlist in Franco's Italian Army, while Frank Sinatra received induction into the fan club. A year or so before, Bradshaw had stopped going out around town because the fans had grown impatient while waiting for him to produce. Now when he visited a mall, his friend Gerry Mullins said Terry was like the Pied Piper, with everyone following him in hopes of catching a glimpse and getting an autograph.

THE FIRST OF MANY

The Steelers were busy preparing for the American Football Conference (AFC) Championship Game. Their opponent was the undefeated Miami Dolphins. Both sides exhibited respect for one another. The Dolphins' Manny Fernandez stated, "Terry Bradshaw can create quite a problem all by himself. He's big and fast for a quarterback and just as dangerous as any runner." Bradshaw responded, "Miami is a fine football team. They aren't 15–0 for nothing."[33]

Unfortunately, Melissa Bradshaw called Pittsburgh trainer Ralph Berlin in the early morning hours. Her husband had been feeling dizzy all week, and the flu finally slammed him. From his hospital bed, Bradshaw declared, "I'll play, you can bet on it." When he rejoined his teammates at practice, he looked wan.[34]

Fans from throughout the area were ready for the game. Since the NFL had a 75-mile blackout rule, those living in small towns and cities could watch the game in their homes, so Steelers fans drove to Oil City, Meadville, and Erie to see the matchup at local businesses. Youngstown and East Liverpool received cable television feeds from Cleveland for Steelers fans desperate to see their team. Even fans of other teams jumped onboard the Steelers' Cinderella bandwagon.

Fans witnessed a titanic battle. Miami held a 7–3 lead when Bradshaw tried to carry the ball into the end zone. Safety Jake Scott met Bradshaw at the goal line with a thunderous hit that caused a fumble. Mullins fell on the ball for a 10–7 lead, but Bradshaw was forced to retire to the bench for half of the game. Hanratty mustered one drive for a field goal but little else. Bradshaw returned and threw four completions to narrow the Dolphins lead to 21–17. The Italian Army, the Gorillas, Russell's Raiders, and Frenchy's Foreign Legion began whooping it up, expecting another miracle finish. But the woozy Bradshaw threw two interceptions, sealing the Miami victory. The Steelers offense suffered without Bradshaw at the helm. As Miami safety Jake

Scott observed, "The Steelers lost a lot when Bradshaw was out. Hanratty is smart, but Bradshaw had the arm." Scott intended to be respectful of both quarterbacks. Unfortunately, his comment associated Bradshaw with physical ability and Hanratty with mental toughness, which could be interpreted as diminishing Bradshaw's mental capabilities.[35]

Bradshaw enjoyed a busy offseason. He and his buddy Gerry Mullins went fishing off of Key West, Florida, along with host Curt Gowdy from the television program *The American Sportsman*. The quarterback made the rounds on the annual winter banquet circuit as well. Other football players included Larry Brown of the Washington Redskins and Mercury Morris of the Miami Dolphins. Pete Rose of the Cincinnati Reds and Gaylord Perry of the Cleveland Indians came from the baseball world.

Amid the banquet circuit, Bradshaw found time to write a book about his life, with Charles Paul Conn. Called *No Easy Game*, the book describes various games, including high school and college football, as well as his current coaches and teammates. Of course, there is a section about the "miracle" plays and the anguished moments on the bench. He wrote about the role of his personal faith in seeing him through life's ups and downs. The quarterback dedicated the book to his wife Melissa.

Bradshaw returned to the field just before the start of training camp. His abilities as a quarterback had earned him a spot as a teacher. The Steelers' leader joined teammate Franco Harris and fellow quarterback Jim Plunkett as professionals at the Instructional Football Camp. More than 100 boys did drills and received tips for playing the game at the week-long program, held in Sparta, New Jersey.[36]

As soon as Bradshaw returned, the frequent criticisms returned as well in the area metropolitan news media and local weekly newspapers. "Not enough upstairs," became the most frequent condemnation. The comment tired the quarterback. "I may not be the smartest football player around, but I think I have good football savvy," Bradshaw said. Others brought up his statistics. "I've had my belly full of people telling me my stats are not good enough. . . . But what good is it if you lost and completed 60 percent of your passes," he countered. But Bradshaw reacted furiously to comments made by Super Bowl–winning quarterback Bob Griese, who stated that Bradshaw needed to study more game film to learn to read defenses better and work harder to be a star. Bradshaw bristled: "Griese has no right to evaluate another quarterback. He's never shook hands with me. He's only seen me in two games, and in one of them I was knocked half groggy. He doesn't know what I do in Pittsburgh."[37]

YEAR FOUR: AN UGLY SEASON

The 1973 exhibition season started poorly for Bradshaw and the team. He threw two interceptions in a loss to the Vikings and three against the Giants toward the end of camp. Chuck Noll screamed at his helmsman and even pulled him back to yell some more. "I lost my poise," Noll admitted after the game. "That stuff's hard to take, but he's the head man." Bradshaw must have recalled how his high school and college coaches remained laid back and relaxed.[38]

They won the next game, as Bradshaw played well. "The coach—it was beautiful tonight. He let me alone. Let me get it straight. You got to be involved in the game, do what you can do," said Bradshaw. Noll offered his vote of confidence, stating, "Terry's had a good camp. He's a lot more confident this year." The beat reporters talked about the Steelers giving the Dolphins a battle for the AFC title.[39]

Another journalist, who was profiling the team for a book, noted that the fans seemed ready to explode into a frenzy again like they picked up right where they left off the previous season. It was thought that the cost of tickets would lead to the loss of the average Steelers fan—the mineworkers and millworkers, who drank hard and fought hard, and accepted losing out on life with violent resignation. In its early years, Three Rivers Stadium could accommodate more than 50,350 fans, 6,000 less than Pitt Stadium, where the team played during the 1960s. At the new stadium, about 115 enclosed lounge boxes were sold to businesses and individuals for $55,000 a year. This seating occupied 4 percent of the stadium's total seating capacity, the ninth-highest total of premium seating as a percentage of total seating in the league. Alcoa, Heinz, USX, and other area corporations purchased these locations most frequently.

During the first few years at the new stadium, average fans did not lose their seats, as predicted. Even the 1973 Arab Oil Crisis, which led to the rationing of gasoline, did not stop fans from driving their cars and trucks to the game. The Steelers ranked second lowest in the NFL's no-show rate. But deindustrialization began leading to the loss of jobs, with middle-class salaries disappearing throughout Pittsburgh in the steel and related industries, and many Steelers fans could no longer afford to attend games.[40]

After winning their last two exhibition games, the Steelers opened the season against the Detroit Lions. After throwing an interception to begin the game, Bradshaw righted himself with a two-touchdown scoring spurt in the beginning of the second half to seize the game from Detroit. In the press box, Roy McHugh of the *Pittsburgh Press* said, "Bradshaw's I.Q. is way up this half." Perhaps he was having fun with the inanity of linking Bradshaw's play on the field with his intelligence. Later on, as Bradshaw kept the ball and ran through a bunch of tacklers to score from the two-yard line, McHugh said, "I guess he was too dumb to realize they had him stopped."[41]

Convincing wins against division rivals, the Browns and Oilers, came from the mixture the team used to win its title the previous season. According to their star quarterback, that mix included "solid defense, timely passing, better ball control, and fewer mistakes." The Steelers reached 4–0 before the Bengals held the offense in check to hand the team its first loss.[42]

Pittsburgh rebounded the next week, defeating the Jets. But Hanratty replaced Bradshaw at quarterback. One game behind in the standings, the Cincinnati Bengals entered Three Rivers Stadium supposedly angry about comments that appeared in Bradshaw's book. He wrote, "There are some teams you just like to beat more than others, and I believe I'd rather beat Cincinnati than anybody. I don't know why, but lots of guys on our team feel the same way. They are obvious rivals." In addition, Bradshaw called out Bengals linebacker Bill Bergey for giving him a cheap shot and complained about lineman Mike Reid. Both shrugged off the comments.[43]

In the second quarter, defensive tackle Steve Chomyszak smashed Bradshaw's right shoulder into the turf. As the quarterback got up holding his right shoulder, many Steelers fans cheered. While some reporters commented about the cheering being a discredit to the crowd, longtime football man and Bengals coach Paul Brown blasted spectators. "Here's a crowd cheering its own injured guy because he is forced to leave the game. It's sickening," Brown said. Defensive end Joe Greene agreed. "You could hear it loud and clear. He hadn't taken two steps, and he was holding his shoulder, obviously in pain, when that shit started," Green said. [44]

Fans called the local sports talk show, and one admitted to being among those cheering. In explaining his position the caller asserted, "The Steelers have always played the wrong guy." "Would you cheer if they shot him?" Myron Cope asked. The caller responded, "Well, I wouldn't cheer if they shot him." "You're saying its fine to cheer when he's hurt, just to get him out of there?" said Cope. "How else you gonna get him out of there? How about his gray matter? If he's so smart, why didn't he go to LSU?" the caller asked. Another supposed personality trait influenced the viewpoint of another Steelers fan. While sitting in a bar, the fan complained that Bradshaw would never be the quarterback Bobby Layne had been because Bradshaw was never seen out on the town drinking. [45]

A few regional and national newspaper reporters attempted to understand the fans' attitudes. The *Washington Post* asserted that Bradshaw performed like a conservative, ball control-type quarterback, which got him on the fans' bad side. Those fans clamored for Hanratty most of the season. Another claimed that Hanratty had an easy disposition that made fans happy and kept the team loose. As one player stated, inside the huddle, "Bradshaw is liable to say, '19 Power Right, uh, Left, uh timeout.' Hanratty came in and said, 'Okay boys we're going downtown with this one.' And you know you are." Another chimed in saying, "You want your quarterback to be tricky, wily, like Bugs Bunny, or Daffy Duck. Bradshaw's too much like Elmer Fudd." [46]

These comments surely only added to the lingering "intelligence" questions and the image problems surrounding the quarterback. Bradshaw was not a ball-control quarterback by choice, but as a result of the offense that Chuck Noll wanted to run. Being decisive in the huddle does not necessarily result in success on the field. Hanratty completed 39 percent of his passes in 1970, completed 24 percent in 1971, barely played in 1972, and completed almost 45 percent in 1973—definitely not setting the NFL on fire. Being wily seemed like it would help, but it wasn't one of those skills acquired though playing experience.

Several local reporters sought Bradshaw's reaction to the fans booing him. "It makes you hard," he admitted. "If you don't block them out of your mind, you'll go batty. . . . I've decided that I just have to take a downright rough, tough kind of approach and say the heck with them."

He viewed the sport as fickle and observed that there are some people who can never be pleased. He insisted that their reaction would change the next time he went out and threw three touchdown passes. Bradshaw's wife noted that she did not mind when fans made booing noises at a botched play. "But the cheering hurt," she said. "It was bad enough knowing Terry had been injured, but the cheering made it worse."[47]

Bradshaw's past experiences left him ill prepared to deal with Steelers fans. In high school and college, players and fans supported one another. As the quarterback recalled, "In college you got a whole group of people united for one cause." The small size of the town and the possibility of seeing the players in person forged that sense of connection at Louisiana Tech and in Ruston. Steelers and other football fans did not seem to share that sentiment. They wanted to win every game, and if a player could not produce, they wanted some who could. This concept was so alien to Bradshaw that he assumed many of the fans hated him. Certainly, receiving letters with the following message might help you reach that conclusion: "Dear Mr. Bradshaw: My husband and I watch you on TV, and we think you are degenerate." But he also received 300 encouraging letters in one week alone during his recuperation period.[48]

Observers commented that many fans cared how the game was won, but most fans cared more about the players as characters. The NFL produced dramas, and spectators sought heroes and villains. The mentality was if "we" cannot win with you, then you cannot be our hero and we need someone else who can. The opposing teams, specifically rival teams, became the obvious villains. Players on favorite teams who fans feel have deserted them or who never lived up to their potential become villains or, worse, objects of derision. While Bradshaw certainly helped the Steelers win, somehow it proved not enough for a good number of fans.

The Steelers took on the Washington Redskins at home. Hanratty and Gilliam each threw two interceptions, but their combined three touchdown passes gave the team enough for a 21–16 victory. Hanratty played the entire game against the tough Oakland Raiders and contributed a touchdown and an interception. The defense yielded only nine points, more than enough for the Steelers to reach an 8–1 record. A loss to Denver at home did little to faze Noll, as he commented, "Two of our best players, Terry Bradshaw and Joe Greene, have been hurt." In

Cleveland, Hanratty suffered a thumb injury. Gilliam took over the position and could not get the team in the end zone the final three quarters. In Miami, Gilliam started disastrously, tossing three passes that were caught by the Dolphins without throwing a completion to his own team. Bradshaw also threw three interceptions, but his touchdown passes nearly led his team to a miraculous victory.[49]

Fortunately, the Steelers had two weak teams remaining on their schedule. Bradshaw's two touchdown passes in the chilly drizzle helped defeat the Houston Oilers and kept Pittsburgh tied with Cincinnati in the AFC Central Division. His teammates felt heartened by the quarterback's return, and Bradshaw threw one touchdown in the romp over the San Francisco 49ers at Candlestick Park. A Cincinnati defeat of Houston gave the Bengals the same 10–4 record, but their better conference record of 8–3, compared to the Steelers' 7–4, gave them the title. The Steelers made the playoffs as the wild card entry.

The Oakland Raiders hosted the Steelers for the divisional round playoff game. Things were rough from the start for Bradshaw, as he stayed on the West Coast and called Melissa to let her know he wanted a divorce.

Some columnists provided advice to those interested in gambling on the game. *Washington Post* sports columnist Bob Maisel related that despite the Steelers winning the last three games between the two teams, the real question was how healthy Harris and Bradshaw were. He predicted an Oakland victory. The Steelers walked into the Coliseum, where fans were dressed in black to create the "black hole." Signs featured simple statements like "Murder Franco" or had two sides, with "Hurt Bradshaw" on the front and "Blood" on the back, for example.[50]

The Raiders dominated the opening half but led only 10–7 at halftime. With the game still within reach at 16–7, Bradshaw made an ill-advised pass that Willie Brown picked off and took 54 yards for the touchdown, That put Oakland ahead by three scores.

After the 33–14 loss, Noll responded to media questions bluntly. "They beat the hell out of us, it's as simple as that," he said. But Noll focused on the Brown interception, stating, "It was a play-action pass. Bradshaw was supposed to preread the coverage, and he didn't. It was the turning point of the game as far as we are concerned." The play may have represented the "last straw on the camel's back"; however, other reporters noted that Bradshaw faced an onslaught of Oakland defenders on every play. Moreover, the Steelers had little success running the ball. Harris carried the ball 10 times and only gained 29 yards in the game, and the two other backs finished with 27 yards on seven carries. There were no heroes; certainly, expectations went unmet. The image of the less intelligent quarterback would remain for some time, despite the team's forthcoming run of enormous success.[51]

3

TWO GOLDEN RINGS
Becoming the Leading Man

When Terry Bradshaw started playing in the NFL, most professional football players did not earn large salaries, with many averaging a little more than $25,000 per year in 1969. This rose to $30,000 by late 1973. NFL teams earned a fair profit in the late 1960s—the average net was $635,000, before adding accounting and tax strategies into the mix. The advent of richer television contracts boosted the profits immensely.

Meanwhile, the nation fell into a recession beginning in November 1973. The combination of the rise in oil prices, the greater competition from foreign businesses, and inflationary pressures created an economic downturn called "stagflation." People were laid off from their jobs and the unemployment rate soared. While the prices for most goods and services climbed during the next 18 months, the value of the football players'—and everyone else's—salaries dropped. Despite these harsh conditions, some businessmen saw the growing profits among NFL teams and thought another football league could be successful in the United States.

The NFL and its 26 teams faced competition as a group of owners announced the founding of the World Football League (WFL) in October 1973. Started by California lawyer Gary Davidson, the WFL promised 12 teams that would play 20 games beginning in July 1974. The new league had franchises in Boston, New York, Toronto, Anaheim, and Vancouver, and was considering expanding to Chicago, Seattle,

Tampa Bay, Memphis, Birmingham, and Honolulu. Davidson was the driving force behind the development of the American Basketball Association and the World Hockey Association in the late 1960s and early 1970s, respectively. Both of these leagues continued but remained on tenuous financial terms. These experiences made Davidson assert that the new WFL owners would have to accept big losses in the initial years. The teams would need to average 25,000 in paid attendance to succeed.

The WFL offered football players new opportunities. Team officials identified personnel that they wanted to bring into the new league. While word leaked of "secret" lists of players whom they were seeking to join their ranks, news came from NFL teams about players who were unhappy with their contracts and saw the chance to increase their earnings. Joe Namath, Joe Theismann, Ken Stabler, Mercury Morris, Jim Kiick, and Calvin Hill were among the names in either or both of these groups.[1]

Terry Bradshaw also appeared on the WFL lists as a player they wanted to bring into the new league. Bradshaw had reached the last years of his contract and was interested in engaging in negotiations for a new one. Terry Hanratty turned down an offer from the New York Stars and signed a new two-year deal with the Steelers. Then Bradshaw turned down his first contract offer from the New York Stars. "I flew to New York with my lawyer, Les Zittrain, to meet Parilli and club officials," said Bradshaw. "After two hours, we said no and flew back here. We set a higher price and expect it to be forthcoming."[2]

The WFL began taking talent from the NFL. Numerous veterans jumped to the new league, including Richmond Flowers, George Sauer Jr., Duane Thomas, Jim Kiick, Larry Csonka, Craig Morton, and Paul Warfield. The Steelers watched as John "Frenchy" Fuqua signed for the 1976 season. L. C. Greenwood signed to play in the future with the Birmingham Americans. More than 40 percent of football fans thought the new league would be good because competition in sports was healthy. Only 20 percent saw the WFL having bad consequences.

Bradshaw's negotiations with the Stars of the WFL and the Steelers of the NFL ended when he signed a multiyear contract with the Steelers. The quarterback stated, "I didn't want to give up this team for one which I just didn't know would be there in two years. Very simply,

Pittsburgh is a fine town with great football and a great organization . . . and when you travel first class you want to continue first class."[3]

The quarterback adroitly used the leverage of the additional team seeking his services to improve his contract. He accurately noted that organizations needed a few million dollars to operate a football team and wondered how the owners of the WFL franchises would manage that. A little swagger came through. "I don't like the idea of playing in small stadiums that might not be filled," Bradshaw declared.[4]

The quarterback also kept busy during the offseason, participating in television sports events. In the 1970s, the television broadcasting industry remained dominated by three major networks, with a few independent stations in the largest cities. The American Broadcasting Corporation (ABC) hired Roone Arledge, who headed an inventive sports division and devised a new show. Called *The Superstars*, the program featured active athletes competing in a series of different sports events, similar to a decathlon competition, to determine the best overall athlete. The show began in 1973, becoming an immediate hit.

The Columbia Broadcasting System (CBS) television network quickly devised a similar program. Called the *All Pro Football Olympia*, it featured 33 NFL players in 10 events, with prize money for finishing first, second, or third. About 4,000 spectators watched the men battle in distance passing, accuracy passing, and running tests. Bradshaw finished second in distance and third in accuracy. Oakland Raiders punter Ray Guy won the competition, accumulating $8,000 in prize monies. While one observer called it a "wacky day," the guys enjoyed the contests and being around one another.[5]

STRIKE ONE

While some players considered the new league as a possible earning bonanza, others turned to their union representation. Although the average player salary was two to three times more than the average median income in the era, the salaries were often not guaranteed, so an injury could limit or end this earnings potential. And for most players, their career had a limited life span.

The greatest disadvantage to the players was the lack of control of their worth on the market. Unlike most workers who could theoretically ply their trades with any business in their career area, NFL players could not. Professional football players signed contracts that contained option clauses, enabling the team to resign a player for an additional year beyond the end of the contract for 90 percent of the expired contract. After this year, the player became a free agent. But the freedom had limitations, as the player experienced the effects of the "Rozelle Rule," written into the NFL Constitution and the league's by-laws. Named after NFL commissioner, Pete Rozelle, the rule provided the commissioner with broad powers during certain free-agency situations. When a team lost a free agent, they expected to negotiate with the player's new team for "appropriate compensation." The move effectively limited movement of players, as teams did not want to risk losing players if they signed a free agent.[6]

The National Football League Players Association (NFLPA) was formed in late 1956, but the owners often ignored the union representatives. During the 1960s, despite a rise in salaries due to competition between the NFL and AFL, gains in pension funds and other benefits proved slow and sometimes less than satisfactory to the players. In 1970, the NFLPA and the NFL emerged with a four-year contract agreement that the union believed fell short on many important issues.

Four years later, with a larger staff and an ample strike fund, the union entered the new collective bargaining negotiations with a slogan: "No freedom, No football." As Dan Rooney of the Steelers interpreted things, the NFLPA sought to eliminate the "Rozelle Rule" but also sought arbitration for disputes, to eliminate the draft and the waiver system, and to guarantee salaries.[7]

Negotiations for the bargaining agreement went nowhere. The owners believed that they could win their position through the courts, and the NFLPA stood fast on its advocacy for players' "freedom." On July 1, 1974, the players went out on strike. As with any strike, the majority, if not the entirety, of the workforce must remain out of work. Among football fans, almost 40 percent sided with the players and 20 percent with the owners. Like the Major League Baseball players who decided to go on strike during the beginning of the season two years earlier, the football players needed to keep the stars from returning. Bradshaw joined the NFLPA and went out on strike. Of the three quarterbacks on the team's roster, Joe Gilliam returned to camp first. After the first month of the stoppage, of the more than 1,000 players league-wide, about 300 returned, including nearly 100 starters. Terry Hanratty returned to the Steelers camp.

The NFL drew more than 230,000 fewer fans and lost $2 million during the first exhibition games. On the eve of a continuation of negotiations, things became bleaker for the union when Roger Staubach and a few others returned. The Cowboys quarterback had several other quarterbacks follow within days, as John Hadl, Bob Griese, and Terry Bradshaw returned to their teams' respective training camps. Bradshaw expressed his support of the NFLPA's cause, but after many sleepless nights, he decided to enter training camp. He had watched Gilliam help win the team's opening exhibition game and realized that Gilliam might win the starting quarterback job.

The return of the NFL offered an opportunity to determine how well the WFL performed. The crowds in cities from New York to Birmingham had reached into the upper 40,000s, but the paying crowd neared one-third to half of the total. The New York Stars needed to move to Charlotte, North Carolina, to survive; Houston's franchise moved to Bradshaw's hometown of Shreveport. Detroit and Jacksonville folded by midseason. The TVS television contract, which provided $1 million in revenue, only kicked in if all the advertising slots were sold. After beginning the season in July with ratings of 7.4 and 6.1, two of the last three games garnered ratings of 5.0 or less. In direct competition with the NFL's final exhibition game, the Philadelphia–Jacksonville WFL game garnered a rating of 2.3, while the Steelers–Cowboys matchup reached a 9.6 rating.

The WFL increasingly struggled. Commissioner Davidson resigned, and members of the executive committee talked about "turning their league around and being very bullish on it now."[8]

THE THREE-HEADED QUARTERBACK

During the exhibition season, the quarterback competition was reignited. Gilliam, Hanratty, and Bradshaw were locked in an audition for the starting role. Gilliam threw the ball more often when compared to Bradshaw or Hanratty and played well. He directed three touchdowns in the next two Steeler victories. Bradshaw also played well when he entered but left the third game with a sore arm. Chuck Noll expressed

Figure 3.1. Bradshaw in a pensive moment. LSU-Shreveport Archives and Special Collections.

satisfaction with Gilliam's performances. The media fluttered around Bradshaw, who tried to towel dry his hair as he spoke to them. "I can do the job," he gestured with his large hands and bulging forearms. He threw in a shrug. "Hell, I've proved that in the past. There's no question in my mind about that. I just need to be in there."[9]

The competition boiled down to Bradshaw and Gilliam. Media stories tracked how many scores each man had led the team to and added pointed adjectives. After a game in early September, a national story noted that Gilliam threw a couple of touchdown passes and Bradshaw totaled a touchdown and two field goals. The reporter described Gilliam as unflappable. The competition came to a close when Noll opted for the seemingly unflappable player as his starter.[10]

This decision prompted Bradshaw to express his frustration. He acknowledged his fellow quarterback's performances, saying, "Gilliam earned the job," but that did not mean he felt he was a backup quarterback. Bradshaw added, "I feel that I'm good enough to be starting for some team in the NFL, so if I'm not going to be starting here, I wish they would trade me to a team that needs me." The next day, Steelers vice president Dan Rooney said that he didn't think Bradshaw meant what he said. "He has not asked to be traded. I don't think we really are concerned about it," Rooney commented; however, local columnists like Bill Christine crowed, "Terry Bradshaw is the wrong guy to be living in a town with so many bridges." His article continued the theme, adding other ways in which he could kill himself if the Steelers lost due to Bradshaw.[11]

In 1974, no other black player except James Harris of the Los Angeles Rams had received a decent chance to make one of the supposed "intelligent" positions, until Joe Gilliam took over the Steelers huddle. Sports columnists for African American newspapers in large Northern cities had long been advocating integration in professional sports and other significant causes. Now they proudly discussed Gilliam's success. But some people wondered whether Bradshaw's reaction of asking for a trade resulted from losing his position to a black man. His similar reaction to losing out to Hanratty in 1970 indicated that it had nothing to do with race.

Race played a role for an unfortunate number of Steelers and football fans. Gilliam received death threats, and hate mail filled his mailbox daily. The Steelers themselves got bomb threats. Gilliam later said he always walked around strapped. His ascendancy propelled some fans to attack Bradshaw. Racists wrote to Bradshaw and made fun of him, saying he must be "really dumb" because he'd been beaten out by a black quarterback. For these fans, with their narrow racial views, he became someone they could look down on; however, few athletes had been placed in a similar situation. By remaining a solid citizen on the team, he handled the circumstances bravely.[12]

In the first game of the season, Gilliam received boos after completing two of nine passes. He improved markedly and led the Steelers to an easy victory. The following week, the Steelers got into a shootout with Denver and walked away with a 35–35 tie. Oddly enough, Gilliam threw only one touchdown pass despite the high score. Their major rivals, the Oakland Raiders, came into Three Rivers Stadium and shut out the Steelers, 17–0. The crowd chanted "We want Bradshaw" on a few occasions. The media asked Bradshaw for his reaction. "I didn't like it," he stated. "It's bad enough when you're getting beat without all that. I think it's uncalled for, but that's football. It's part of the game."[13]

Still, Gilliam led the league in attempts, completions, and yards. He transformed the Steelers from being primarily a running team into one of the most exciting teams in pro football. But the team scored only one touchdown in their win over Houston. In Kansas City, Gilliam threw a touchdown and an interception in another game where the Steelers scored more than 30 points. Back home against the lowly Cleveland Browns, Franco Harris returned from injury and helped reestablish the team's running game. Gilliam connected on five of 18 passes for 78 yards and heard the boo birds throughout the game. "I wonder if it would be better for us to play on the road," Noll commented. According to Bradshaw, Chuck Noll had let Gilliam get away with obvious problematic behavior like sleeping through film sessions.[14]

With Gilliam's performance in question, Noll had to make a decision. The team had a 4–1–1 record with Gilliam. The quarterback's critics argued that when he passed, he passed too much, and when he called a run, he called too many runs in succession. A fan or other observer could then ask, Why not have coaches call the plays instead of the quarterbacks?

During his playing days with the Cleveland Browns of the 1950s, Noll served as a guard who rotated in to carry the plays from the coach, Paul Brown, to his quarterback. Perhaps Noll did not enjoy that. Noll provided his own telling response, insisting that quarterbacks should call their own plays. "It emasculates your quarterback. It's for coaches who want to be quarterbacks," he insisted. Bradshaw called his own plays in college and certainly wanted to continue doing so in his professional career. Complicating Noll's decision was the fact that Bradshaw apparently also had the support of the majority of the players, who liked Bradshaw and found Gilliam aloof.[15]

Bradshaw took over for Gilliam and played okay, but Noll inserted his third option, Terry Hanratty. His poor performance led to Bradshaw's return. After two good performances, Cincinnati's Ken Anderson outplayed Bradshaw, and the Steelers stood only a half-game ahead of the Bengals for the top spot in the title chase.

Hanratty took the reins against the Cleveland Browns and struggled. He developed leg cramps and exited the game. Gilliam went in and threw four passes, completing one. Four field goals and a fumble recovery for a touchdown enabled the Steelers to win, 26–16. Media outlets came out with pithy statements, one of which posited that the Steelers were winning without a quarterback.

Wide receiver Ron Shanklin spoke for most of the team's offense. The five-year veteran who had gone to the Pro Bowl the previous season told reporters, "We've got to clean up this act and get more precision on offense." Bradshaw offered his opinion on the situation, saying, "This is no way to operate a team. You have to have a number-one quarterback. Hanratty hasn't played in six years. They put him in a game, and he gets leg cramps."[16]

Bradshaw returned to the starting position for the next game, against the New Orleans Saints. He led the team in a romp. The quarterback threw two touchdowns and ran for 99 yards. His humor returned. He knew he had experienced a great day running with the ball himself. Bradshaw joked that if he were O. J. Simpson, he'd have scored a few more touchdowns. Being the top quarterback and having a good day while the team won returned Bradshaw to his jester's nature.

Noll remained uncertain, saying he was waiting for a leader to emerge from among his quarterbacks and take the bull by the horns. The city's major newspaper asked fans their opinions on the quarterback controversy. This public referendum on job performance and personality had to hurt each of the three men. Bradshaw received a 41 percent approval rating, Hanratty 32 percent, and Gilliam 20 percent. The next week, the Oilers defeated the Steelers after knocking Bradshaw out of the game with a sore rib cage. Hanratty replaced him and struggled.

The loss to Houston didn't help anyone's case with Noll. Bradshaw threw a touchdown and an interception, but he had to leave the game

with bruised ribs. Hanratty entered and proceeded to throw two interceptions. Bradshaw led the team to a victory over New England the
following week. The win was the only victory against an opponent with
at least a .500 record. Gilliam struggled in the series he ran for the
Steelers. In the season finale, Bradshaw played well but had to leave the
game in the third quarter with soreness coming from a hard tackle.
Gilliam came in and also performed fine in the 27–3 romp.[17]

THE 1974 PLAYOFFS

For the third consecutive year, the Steelers made the playoffs. As winner of the Central Division, they drew the Buffalo Bills, this season's
wild-card entrant. The week before the game, the media focused on the
Steelers' quarterbacks and agreed that having three quarterbacks
proved detrimental to all of them. "It's been tough, particularly mentally, particularly on the three of us," Bradshaw noted. Meanwhile, stories
again circulated about Bradshaw's mental abilities, many of them retold
from previous years, like an end-run call on a third down and 35 yards
to go. The frequency of the accusations coming from Pittsburgh television stations led one national columnist to suggest that Bradshaw receive equal air time to make his case for being intelligent.[18]

The playoff game represented a rare occasion. The starting quarterbacks from each team shared the same hometown, as Bradshaw and
Bills quarterback Joe Ferguson had both played for Woodlawn High in
Shreveport. Both men performed well in the game. Ferguson had two
touchdown passes and threw for 160 yards, while Bradshaw threw a
single touchdown pass but passed for more than 200 yards. Bradshaw
ran effectively as well. Reporters for the large metropolitan newspapers
expressed surprise that Bradshaw did not rank very high among the
worshipped in football-frenzied Pittsburgh.

Prior to the next playoff game, the media coverage of Bradshaw
differed from the previous game. A few outlets focused on Bradshaw's
faith. The quarterback explained the tribulations of divorce and losing
his starting position on the field. He turned to reading the Bible as a
source of solace and comfort. The quarterback noted, "I'm not saying
that I'm playing better because of getting back my faith. It's just something I believe in. It helps me accept the good and the bad." As Terry

explained that everyone needs something to lean on, he also felt the need to clarify his faith, saying, "I'm not a religious fanatic but put himself in God's hands. And when I did that, I kind of relaxed. I'm very relaxed now—I know He's taking care of me."[19]

The team was headed to Oakland for the second year in a row. Playing against a team that featured the Player of the Year, Ken Stabler, many gave the Raiders the advantage at the quarterback position, as well as in the game. Pittsburgh lost a touchdown in the first half on a blown call, and the teams went into halftime tied at three. After three quarters, the Raiders had the lead, but the Steelers drove the ball down the field for a tying touchdown. Running back Rocky Bleier said, "[Bradshaw] got rattled a couple of times in the huddle, but now we're not getting uptight about it. We settle him down and he comes through." The next time they had the ball, Bradshaw connected on a short touchdown pass to put the Steelers ahead for good. One sports reporter summarized the first meaningful win in the team's 42-year history. He predicted that the snickers and jeers about Bradshaw being a dumb quarterback would be put to rest, perhaps forever.[20]

The city exploded after the game. The Steelers had reached Super Bowl IX. Thousands of fans gathered at the city's airport and waited for their team to return. A chilly rain did little to stop the crowd, which broke into sustained screaming and cheering as the players exited the airplane. Another large crowd met the team downtown. A band struck up "When Irish Eyes Are Smiling," for Art Rooney Sr., and the owner responded with his thanks. Coach Noll offered his thanks to the fans who had sent telegrams of encouragement to the team. When the fans gathered at the airport noticed that Bradshaw had not accompanied the team on the trip home, they broke into chants of "We want Bradshaw" and "Where's Bradshaw?"[21]

SUPER BOWL MANIA: IX

The quarterback joined the rest of his team in western Pennsylvania for practices during the first of the two weeks separating the conference final from the Super Bowl. One of the earliest predictions for the game had the Minnesota Vikings over the Steelers. The prognosticator mentioned that Bradshaw was not too clever in reading defenses and could be rattled into making costly misplays. He believed that the friendly player would get distracted by friends and media coverage of the big game. Another noted that he would prefer to have Tarkenton on his side over Bradshaw, thus the Vikings would win.[22]

The Steelers arrived in New Orleans, site of the Super Bowl, on Monday of week two. The photographers took pictures of the teams. Afterward, Bradshaw declared, "It looks like its [sic] going to be a wild and wooly week. I love it. I could see where you might get kind of sick of it after a while. But I still love it." The questions from the assembled media of about 600 people would help change his mind to some extent. Among the almost 1,000 reporters gathered for media day, Bradshaw faced questions about his intelligence. Those present asked if the coaches called the plays. "No, only at the goal line sometimes; that ought to answer the 'dumbness' question," he answered. Another reporter asked if he resented being likened to Li'l Abner. In full jester mode, Bradshaw responded, "I do if he's thought of as a dumb country hick, blond and with big muscles." He then flexed his arms.[23]

The questions continued, with some national reporters adding that Bradshaw resembled the character Ozark Ike. Rufus A. Gotto developed Ozark Ike McBatt while serving in the U.S. Navy during World War II. The comic strip emerged in late 1945, and the likeable, strong but dumb Ike lived in a family of hillbillies in a small backwoods community called Wildweed Run. While the comic's hillbilly roots prompted people to draw parallels to Li'l Abner, the sports star reminded others of the strip Joe Palooka. At its peak, the strip appeared in 250 newspapers, far fewer than the other two. Regardless of which character reporters referenced, by week's end Bradshaw admitted, "I'm so sick and tired of it [the dumb issue] that I've given up. I'll just have to live with it. I've played well for six weeks, and people still question me." Chuck Noll received a grilling on the question as well. He responded, "That is a vast bad rap. It is unfair and unfounded . . . down the line, I don't know where that came from, it did not come from anyone in our organization."[24]

While most people were resigned to watching the game on television, several Steelers fan clubs sent members to New Orleans in droves. Steelers jerseys were visible in bars throughout the city. "This is our first Super Bowl, that's why," said Tom Peterson of Washington, Pennsylvania. A small group from Turtle Creek, Pennsylvania, said they would do their celebrating after the game. Everyone anticipated the Steelers would emerge victorious. [25]

The teams were set to play at Tulane University Stadium because the Louisiana Superdome remained unfinished. It poured throughout the week, making for soggy conditions. A wind with gusts as high as 25 miles per hour and a temperature of 46 degrees made for a rough day. The largest audience for a Super Bowl, 29 million, settled in to watch the broadcast.

The teams engaged in a defensive struggle during the first half. The only score came when Tarkenton and running back Chuck Foreman botched a handoff. The ensuing fumble bounced off L. C. Greenwood's shoes and spun backward. As the Pittsburgh defense chased the ball, a sliding Tarkenton fell onto the ball and rolled into the end zone. He gave up the safety. Pittsburgh's 2–0 lead held through halftime. Bradshaw walked into the locker room and called for more, yelling, "We're whipping their asses off and still ain't got but two points!" [26]

Franco Harris and Terry Bradshaw played well enough to lead the Steelers to a touchdown in the second half; however, the Vikings blocked a Steeler punt and recovered it for a touchdown. With the score 9–6, the fans, the media, and the players knew that Pittsburgh's offense needed to show their ability. Harris gained eight yards. On third down and two yards to go for a first down, Bradshaw felt a sense of control and confidence. He stepped up to the line of scrimmage, dropped back, and hit Larry Brown with a 30-yard pass completion. Rocky Bleier carried the ball on first down. He got it on an audible that Bradshaw called and gained 17 yards. Four more plays ended with a four-yard touchdown pass to Brown.

The team felt great with a 16–6 lead. With a little more than three minutes remaining, Mike Wagner intercepted Fran Tarkenton's pass. The Steelers offense came onto the field. Harris, Bleier, and Bradshaw combined to set a new team rushing record in the Super Bowl. Lynn Swann had not caught a pass in the game. With a second down and four deep on Minnesota's side of the field, Bradshaw called for a reverse to Swann. Harris told the receiver, "Don't lose any yards." When the team broke up the huddle and lined up, an official held up play momentarily to change the ball. Swann heard Carl Eller of the Vikings yell, "Look out for the reverse." Harris and Bradshaw looked at Swann and laughed. Bradshaw called the play anyway. The play lost yardage, but

Bradshaw and teammates enjoyed a laugh. After the victory, the quarterback summed up his feelings, commenting, "I've looked at all sides—being a hero and being a jerk. I think I can handle this very well."[27]

At game's end, some national reporters chose to emphasize the fact that "Bradshaw did not have to do much" in the game, but others focused on the reality that Bradshaw was for real. They described his key third-down completions that kept the drives going. At the press conference after the game, a few reporters gave Bradshaw the chance to gloat about being referred to as a dumb country hick, but he declined, stating that he "did not want to get into that." The quarterback mentioned that he had engineered the drives to keep the Viking defense off balance with the help of his line and the running, but reporters returned to their main focus. The questions about being "Ozark Ike" and a "dummy" resurfaced. Nonetheless, Bradshaw showed poise, answering, "That's all over and done with. I have to go on living with that; I've been living with it. They can say what they want, but I got the Super Bowl ring."[28]

After the game, the fans in Pittsburgh poured out of their homes and the bars, screaming, honking horns, and reveling in the moment. Some broke windows in downtown buildings, leading to nearly 250 arrests and many injuries. A large crowd again met the team at the airport much later that night. On Monday, one estimate claimed 500,000 fans had lined the streets in 20-degree weather to cheer their team. The players rode in a parade of 60 cars and 15 floats through Fort Pitt Tunnel. Fans rushed through police barricades and slammed on the hoods of the cars to make contact with the players.

QUARTERBACK CONTROVERSY

One month later, the controversy concerning the NFL and African American quarterbacks flared up again. A columnist for an African American newspaper raised the question of why Gilliam lost his position when he "led the team to 11 wins in a row." The columnist was incorrect about that claim, and the six wins that occurred during the exhibition season were meaningless to the team's season. He snidely referred to Bradshaw as the "man of the hour." The *Washington Post* noted that Redskins All-Pro running back Larry Brown had expressed dismay about there being only two black quarterbacks in the league. Ironically, the supposed lacking-in-intelligence issue that had limited the drafting of black quarterbacks hung like an albatross around the neck of Caucasian quarterback Terry Bradshaw.

Steelers middle linebacker Jack Lambert weighed in on the topic, saying that neither the city nor its media appeared ready for a black quarterback. "I think the pressure of the press had a lot to do with the change in quarterbacks," he related. He advised Gilliam to go to a place where he could play. Lambert acknowledged, "Bradshaw certainly deserves to be our starter next season." When training camp started, Chuck Noll stated, "Terry Bradshaw is my quarterback." Gilliam and Hanratty continued their efforts to win the top position. [29]

Winning the Super Bowl sparked offers for players to appear in advertisements and at various events. Ten Steelers went to Honolulu, Hawaii, for another faceoff with the Minnesota Vikings in the "Super Teams" competition on *The Superstars*. In addition to such big names as Terry Bradshaw and Franco Harris, other Steelers involved were Mel Blount, Jim Clack, L. C. Greenwood, Ernie Holmes, captains Ray Mansfield and Andy Russell, Lynn Swann, and Mike Wagner. Pittsburgh won the tandem bike relay and the volleyball game, while losing the running relay and the war canoe race. The final event centered on the massive tug of war. The Steelers took the edge at first, but Alan Page saved the Vikings, giving his squad some much-needed momentum. After 16 minutes, the Vikings exacted a small measure of revenge.

Most intriguingly, Bradshaw received a recording contract. Jerry Kennedy, a producer with Mercury Records, noted, "Bradshaw has a smooth, easy voice. So, we're going to sign him up." Plans called for Bradshaw to travel to Nashville later in the summer to record, with the record slated for release by the end of the football season. [30]

The team began practicing at training camp for the upcoming exhibition season. Despite Noll's assertions regarding Bradshaw being the number-one man, the press foresaw another quarterback controversy. As has been stated, quarterbacks often receive too much of the credit for a win and too much of the blame for a loss. They are in a high-profile position, touching the ball on most plays, which usually makes them a star. Members of the media benefit from quarterback controversies because the fans care about the position, and the featured stars at the position sell newspapers and airtime.

Quarterback controversies occurred with the Los Angeles Rams in the 1950s and the Dallas Cowboys and Washington Redskins during the 1970s. Fans took sides, using bumper stickers, among other things, to show their support. The Gilliam–Bradshaw debate ranks among the top quarterback controversies in NFL history. Many fans in Pittsburgh perceived Bradshaw as a hero after the Super Bowl victory, but a minority denigrated his role as merely making handoffs (akin to the term *game manager* in the 2000s). Other fans and observers, many in the African American press, believed Bradshaw to be no hero, nor villain, but a pretender to the throne. One of these sports reporters, columnist Chico Renfroe, wrote that it paid to be white in sports and implied that Gilliam played better than Bradshaw and only sat because of his skin color. Columnist A. S. Doc Young reminded readers of his support for Gilliam, writing, "I've already said that I believe he will displace Terry Bradshaw as Pittsburgh number-one quarterback."[31]

The pot was stirred after Bradshaw played poorly during the annual All-Star Game between the winner of the Super Bowl and the College All-Stars. Gilliam entered the game in the fourth quarter and led the Steelers to victory. Noll told the media, "You don't lose your job playing poorly in one game." During the exhibition season, all three quarterbacks played. Hanratty struggled, Gilliam had ups and downs, and Bradshaw played some good games and some poor ones. One national sports columnist observed the play during the preseason and concluded that Bradshaw had been erratic and Gilliam uneven as well. Hanratty had slipped. He predicted that the quarterbacks would keep the team from establishing a dynasty.[32]

DEFENDING THE TITLE

When the regular season began, Bradshaw and the Steelers appeared ready to play. In the season opener, Bradshaw threw two touchdowns, and the team scored the first four times they had the ball for an easy win against the San Diego Chargers. Then the Bills came to Pittsburgh, and Bradshaw threw one interception and fumbled twice. Gilliam replaced him and threw one touchdown and an interception in the loss.

At Cleveland, Bradshaw started well but sustained a deep cut on his passing hand. Gilliam came on and led the team to victory with two touchdown passes but unfortunately hurt his index finger. Against Denver and then Chicago at home, Bradshaw and Harris led the offense, while the defense played rock solid as the Steelers won for the third straight time.

Historically speaking, the Steelers have played well at home. Thus, playing the next two games on the road was a test for the team to discover just how strong they were. Harris's running complemented Bradshaw's passing in a win against Green Bay. But now the Steelers had to take on the undefeated Bengals in Cincinnati's Riverfront Stadium. The home team jumped out to an early 3–0 lead. The Steelers owned the second quarter and took a 10–3 lead at halftime. They picked up where they left off in the third quarter, scoring one running and one passing touchdown to grab a 23–3 lead going into the final quarter. The Bengals scored 14 unanswered points, narrowing the deficit to six points. But Bradshaw took his team on a drive that he completed with a touchdown run that cemented the game. One media correspondent said the Steelers won despite Bradshaw being an unpredictable quarterback.

Another division rival, the Houston Oilers, came into Pittsburgh with a 6–1 record and tied for first in the division with the Steelers. The Steelers took a 10–0 lead after the first of Bradshaw's three touchdown passes. Houston narrowed the deficit before the Steelers reinstated their 10-point lead before halftime. After scoring the only points of the third quarter, Houston marched down the field and tied the game in the middle of the last quarter. The Steelers offense responded. John Stallworth caught a 21-yard touchdown from Bradshaw to win the game. "Just lucky," was how the game's hero described his performance as he spat chewing tobacco into the souvenir Super Bowl mug on the floor near his locker stool. Houston's coach, Bum Phillips, drawled, "Pittsburgh is a much better team this year because of Bradshaw's poise."[33]

Pittsburgh kept winning. After defeating the Jets, they needed a comeback behind Bradshaw's two touchdown passes to overtake the Cleveland Browns. Despite winning 10 games in a row, the Steelers held only a one-game lead over their rival Cincinnati. The Bengals arrived in Pittsburgh with the chance to even things up and play for the title the following week. A crowd of 49,000 screamed during the introductions. They kept yelling as their team undertook a flawless 12-play drive, ending with a three-yard touchdown to Lynn Swann. Pittsburgh took a 14–0 lead after recovering the only Bengals fumble of the day and taking it in for the score. Cincinnati cut the lead in half, but Pittsburgh put 21 more points on the board and set a club record with their 12th victory.

As in the previous season, the Steelers faced the team that had won the Eastern Division of the AFC in the first round of the playoffs. This time it was the Baltimore Colts. Whereas Bradshaw had faced off against a fellow Shreveport native just one season earlier, this time he faced a guy he knew from his days in Ruston. Bert Jones, his friend from his offseason practice days, played quarterback for the Colts. They had maintained their friendship for more than 11 years, and this game represented their first meaningful contest against one another. The game stood tied at seven apiece when Bradshaw got flipped into the air by Colts defensive back Lloyd Mumphord, landing so violently he sprained his knee and his foot went numb. The quarterback limped to the locker room, and the half ended with the two teams tied.

At the beginning of the third quarter, the Three Rivers crowd cheered wildly as Bradshaw came out onto the field. The Pittsburgh crowd responded to their man's toughness and heart. "The way the crowd responded when I came back on the field was just fabulous," Bradshaw said. He completed three of his four attempted passes and twice ran the ball on his stiff leg. The running game and a defensive touchdown enabled the Steelers to walk away with the win, 28–10. Afterward, Bradshaw went to see Jones and sat next to him in the visitors' locker room, chewing tobacco. "I'm sad for you but glad for me," Pittsburgh's quarterback said softly.[34]

Several fans commented on this part of Bradshaw's game, with one saying, "Bradshaw had guts. He never whined or complained, he just got the job done. . . . No doubt, Terry Bradshaw ranks among the best quarterbacks that ever played the game." The quarterback fit with the image of the team, which the Steel Curtain defense embodied. According to another fan, "Bradshaw was what the Pittsburgh Steelers image was all about, tough as nails and a hard-to-bring-down kind of guy." For some fans, writing years later, Bradshaw embodied a tough, working-man style that symbolized football—if not the era—and contrasted favorably with the football and players of the early twenty-first century. One fan appreciated Bradshaw's ability to enjoy the game while playing it and his simple dignity and honest class. These attributes are what made the football hero, not the heroes of today with their "off-field fiascos involving law enforcement, ridiculous celebratory end-zone dances, and endless fines."[35]

Through the early 1980s, NFL players exerted little control of their physical well-being and were treated simply as workers. Bradshaw and other players were tough and went back into games quickly, but the awareness of health and welfare among the players and teams rose significantly with each decade beginning in the 1970s and early 1980s. In today's game, neither the players nor their teams want the player to return to play in certain circumstances and risk making the injury or condition worse.

Other factors, notably, free agency, significantly higher salaries, and the 24-hour sports media cycle, have changed the game and its culture even more dramatically. Players have greater freedom to eventually choose their workplace and more money to pursue hobbies, whether legal or illegal, during the offseason. The omnipresent media cover these events, fueling the perception of fans that the game is focused on individuals rather than teams. The wall-to-wall coverage and number of players who seek it out have also spurred the perception that today's players behave like, and perhaps are, narcissists.

As always seemed to be the case, the Steelers were set to meet the Raiders in the playoffs. This time the game was scheduled to take place at Three Rivers. The temperature at game time felt like two degrees, with wind gusts approaching 20 miles an hour. According to one play-by-play announcer, the weather was "favorable to no one." The sidelines, which were slick as ice, drove most of the play into the middle of the field, where Noll said he witnessed the hardest hitting he'd seen the entire season. The teams combined for 13 turnovers.[36]

Oakland dominated play for much of the first half; however, Pittsburgh put together one drive that enabled them to make a short field goal. Those three points constituted the scoring for the entire first half, as both quarterbacks threw interceptions. In the second half, players had difficulty holding on to the ball. Swann, Harris, and Bleier fumbled, along with each of Oakland's three running backs. Neither team scored in the third quarter. The Raiders blocked the attempt by Pittsburgh to double their lead with another field goal. A strong drive by each team ended in a touchdown, with Pittsburgh clinging to a 10–7 lead.

The Steelers defense recovered another fumble. With the short field, Pittsburgh wanted to score at least three more points. Two running plays left them with a third down and long. Bradshaw dropped back to pass, eluding one defensive end who reached out to grab him. He stepped up and threw toward receiver John Stallworth, who had double coverage in the end zone. The Raider moving in front of Stallworth slid to the ground, leaving Stallworth free. He jumped into the air and pulled the ball down for the touchdown.

Conditions on the field grew worse as the temperature dropped. The Steelers had the chance to run out the clock. Bradshaw carried the ball for a 16-yard gain before the two-minute warning. He took a head hit, felt groggy, and needed to be helped off the field. The rest of the offense stayed on the field for the first-down play and an attempt to seal the victory.

Franco Harris fumbled, and Oakland recovered. The Raiders took over and drove down the field for a field goal, cutting the lead to six points. With 17 seconds left, Oakland lined up for an onside kick. The Steelers sent out their "hands people" to make sure that the team held on to the ball. The kick bounced off a Pittsburgh player's foot, and Oakland recovered. Ken Stabler dropped back with seven seconds remaining and threw a pass from his own side of the field, caught by his receiver, Cliff Branch, on the Steelers 15-yard line. The clock ran out; Pittsburgh would return to the Super Bowl.[37]

SUPER BOWL MANIA: X

The Steelers were slated to face the Dallas Cowboys in Super Bowl X, at the Orange Bowl in Miami, Florida. The Cowboys were returning to play in their third Super Bowl, having lost in 1971 and won in 1972. The hoopla and media circus featured two unusual elements: production companies filming a documentary and a feature film. A group called Top Value Television (TVTV) filmed the players relaxing and practicing for a behind-the-scenes look at the game. Among the commentators for the program were Bill Murray and Christopher Guest. The Steelers' wives talked while lounging at the hotel pool. They discussed the players' small salaries and the deleterious physical effects of playing the game. Filmmakers traveled throughout the city, getting the fans' perspectives as well. Steelers fans flocked to a man dressed in a gorilla outfit behind a large sign that read, "Gerela's Gorillas." Members of the Jack Ham Dobre Shunkas proclaimed that the Dobre Shunkas and the Gorillas were the first two fan clubs in the new stadium. Franco's Army came a year later. At game time, fans were waiting outside the stadium, trying to see the players or buy tickets. One paid $75 apiece for tickets on the 40-yard line. Others crowded around the cab that Franco Harris and Terry Bradshaw stepped out of.

Paramount Pictures gained permission to film during the Super Bowl. They needed the realistic footage for the drama *Black Sunday*, which features live shots. As the blimp came closer to the stadium, various plays from the game appeared. These included the opening kickoff, a few plays from scrimmage, and the touchdowns scored by each team. Terry Bradshaw made his first motion-picture appearance in *Black Sunday*, playing himself in an uncredited role. The terrorism plot proved timely, as the 1970s were the "golden age of terrorism." Unfortunately, nationalist ethnic groups, religious zealots, and antiwar organizations created nearly 1,500 incidents of terrorism in the United States between 1970 and 1979.[38]

Among the early topics of interest for the 1,800 assembled members of the media was the health of various players. Swann and Bradshaw had suffered concussions, but the Steelers expected both men to play. One small-town Ohio sports columnist admitted that he was not a Terry Bradshaw admirer but that he enjoyed Bradshaw's sheer joy of playing and disregard for his personal safety. This love of contact and the hit Bradshaw had taken that forced him out of the game were reportedly two other reasons why some media figures questioned the quarterback's intelligence.

The media focused their attention on the Steelers' quarterback, as well as Dallas' Roger Staubach, during the hour-long period each day. The reporters and journalists waved their microphones and notebooks in Bradshaw and Staubach's faces, backing them up against the wall. As had been the scenario in the previous Super Bowl, Bradshaw was deemed the lesser of the two quarterbacks by media types and such players as Washington receiver Charlie Taylor.

While some reporters acknowledged that the intelligence issue was a "bad rap," others chose not to let last year's story lay dormant. A television interviewer pushed to the front of the pack and said, "Some people say the Cowboys are going to win the Super Bowl because Roger Staubach is a smarter quarterback than you." "Aah," Bradshaw began, before stopping short. Another reporter began, "Last year your intelligence . . ." Bradshaw's face reddened. He interjected, "I don't want to talk about that. I just walked away from a guy who tried that." "Are you sensitive about it?" asked the newsman. "Wouldn't you be if somebody made you out to be a dummy?" Bradshaw replied. His coach offered a sage take on the issue, saying, "High-level educators are in a snit about what criteria to use in measuring intelligence. . . . All I can tell you is that Bradshaw is a good football player who calls most of his own plays and does an excellent job of it."[39]

CBS was set to air the Super Bowl on Sunday afternoon. On Saturday night, they aired a program called *Saturday Night at the Super Bowl*. Among the stars appearing on the show was Burt Reynolds, who told jokes, including a few about Bradshaw's intelligence. On the upside, the program aired on the night of the week when the fewest people watched television. The annoyances and the public humiliation were aspects that sports heroes were not supposed to have to go through; however, a silver lining would eventually emerge.[40]

Fans for both teams exerted confidence that bordered on arrogance. Supporters of the Cowboys pointed to their Flex defense and miracle worker of a quarterback. Steelers fans claimed Franco Harris was an irresistible force, that the Steel Curtain was immovable, and that Terry Bradshaw was Superman. The well-dressed fans, frequently sporting Cowboy hats, started cheering beginning with the first play. The Cowboys pulled a reverse on the kickoff and brought the ball to midfield. Kicker Roy Gerela saved a touchdown but also hurt himself on his tackle. Minutes later, Pittsburgh punter Bobby Walden fumbled the ball. Dallas took over on downs at the Steelers 29-yard line and immediately scored the game's first touchdown.

Steelers fans came out of their seats as Bradshaw connected with Swann for 32 yards on Pittsburgh's first pass play. They waved their golden pennants frantically in the air, while a few people whipped their terrible towels in celebration. The second play resulted in the tying touchdown. Dallas went ahead early in the second quarter with a field goal. Bradshaw led Pittsburgh on a drive the length of the field, but Gerela missed the tying field goal at the end of the half. He missed another one in the third quarter, when neither team put any points on the scoreboard.

In the middle of the final quarter, the Steelers blocked a Dallas punt. The ball rolled out of the end zone for a safety. Trailing 10–9, Bradshaw and the Pittsburgh offense took over after the Dallas free kick in Dallas territory. They kept the ball on the ground. Harris and Bleier made one first down, but after Bradshaw gained eight yards on his one carry, Harris was stopped short on the attempt for the second first down. This time Gerela kicked a field goal, and the Steelers took their first lead of the game, 12–10. Fans waved their towels and banners in celebration. As Dallas came out on offense, Steelers fans chanted, "Defense, defense." Staubach threw an interception. The score was now 15–10, as the Steelers converted the turnover into another field goal.

The Cowboys again failed to move the ball against a tough Steelers defense. They punted, and Pittsburgh had the ball on their own 30-yard line with almost five minutes left to play. Two running plays left the Steelers needing four yards for a first down that could clinch the game. If Dallas got the ball back, everyone expected Staubach to work one of his miracle endings to win the game. Instead of calling a short pass, Bradshaw called "69 Maximum Flanker Post" in the huddle, sending Stallworth and Swann on long routes down the field. This did not surprise Dallas, who blitzed the Steelers. D. D. Lewis poured through the Pittsburgh line, but Bradshaw took a step to his right, evading Lewis's grab. Bradshaw reared back and fired the ball 70 yards in the air before being smashed by blitzing safety Charlie Waters. Swann observed, "All I did was run under the ball." "One of the most beautiful passes and receptions we've seen all season," said one of the announcers. A group of Steelers fans seated in the end zone celebrated by torching the Dallas pennant they had purchased just minutes before.[41]

Bradshaw was so groggy he knew nothing about what happened. Mike Wagner ran out and helped him up, but the quarterback was unable to stand on his own. Wagner draped his arm around Bradshaw's shoulder while a trainer did so on the other side, with Rocky Bleier standing by to help if necessary. Bradshaw dragged his feet as they moved toward the sideline. "I was in the locker room, and the game was just about over when I understood it," Bradshaw said later. He couldn't play, so Hanratty took over on the team's final set of offensive plays of the game.[42]

The adjectives being used to describe Bradshaw changed. One major sportswriter called him indomitable and joked that Bradshaw seemed to collect concussions and championship rings with equal facility. Dallas coach Tom Landry credited Swann with being the difference in the game but also admired Bradshaw. "We had Bradshaw dead to rights with the blitz, but he was still able to get the ball to Swann," said Landry. Common opinion was that this was the best of the first 10 Super Bowls. Pittsburgh was now among the ranks of the best teams in football history.[43]

Throngs of screaming fans were again waiting for the team at the airport. Some lines stretched from the airport 15 miles into the heart of the city. Signs read, "Twice is not enough" and "1, 2, 3!" Drivers pulled their vehicles off the highway, honking their horns as the team rode by. Escorted by a high school marching band and police officers on motorcycles and horseback, the team traveled down Grant Street in buses. Despite freezing temperatures, a crowd of 100,000 screamed their appreciation while behaving calmly. Only 190 celebrants faced charges of drunken and disorderly behavior. Still, many were disappointed that the players stayed inside the buses. "We didn't see any players," lamented Gary Zurawski, who came from the city's South Side to celebrate with friends. Many of the team's stars had to miss the parade to play in the upcoming Pro Bowl. The team's Pro Bowlers and others worked with agents to set up postseason appearances to augment their salaries and playoff earnings.[44]

4

TWO MORE GOLDEN RINGS

Taking Center Stage

A WILD OFFSEASON

The Super Bowl–winning quarterback enjoyed some unique experiences during the offseason. Weeks after the game, Bradshaw and his fiancé, champion ice skater JoJo Starbuck, attended a state dinner for the prime minister of Israel. Also there were Super Bowl–losing coach Tom Landry and his wife, tennis star Chris Evert. Seen as a folk hero, lifestyle journalists continued to stick Bradshaw with the Li'l Abner designation. JoJo Starbuck became a miniature Daisy Mae. A week later, Bradshaw received an award as Pittsburgh's sports figure of the year. He enjoyed the moment by recollecting jokes from the *Saturday Night at the Super Bowl* program. "I have only one regret That Joe Namath and Burt Reynolds aren't here to help me receive this award," Bradshaw said.[1]

During the summer, Bradshaw married Starbuck. The ceremony took place at a Los Angeles hotel in front of 250 guests. Ice skater Janet Lynn served as bridesmaid. They left to honeymoon in Hawaii and would have their permanent home in Louisiana, with a summer place in Pennsylvania. Their marriage projected an image of two clean-cut, religious All-American athletes forming a wonderful bond. Bradshaw gave off an aura of traditional masculinity. Yet, as JoJo said, he was not afraid to be gentle and was very sweet. Their images appeared in an era when most young people liked scruffy types. Many popular television shows and movies featured antiestablishment types as heroes or antiheroes. But members of the older generation, football fans, evangelical Protestants, and many residents of the South appreciated the Bradshaws.

Young boys played imaginary repeats of the Super Bowl in their backyards, outside their schools, and in parks. One Steelers fan in Ohio found two other boys who liked the team. While his friends pretended they were Jack Lambert and Franco Harris, respectively, the younger boy was Terry Bradshaw. Another boy started copying Bradshaw's style in his backyard and emulated him throughout high school and college years, wearing the number 12 jersey. He can still recall being six years old and getting his first Steelers helmet and number 12 jersey for Christmas. One little girl, a diehard Steelers fan, lived in the house with the biggest yard in the neighborhood, and the boys had to include her in the game to play there. She played some serious ball and imagined herself in a place where Bradshaw and the Steel Curtain ruled.[2]

A TRYING YEAR

Professional athletes, members of the Steelers organization, and sports announcers knew how difficult it was for a team to repeat as champion of its sport. The reality is, as Bradshaw noted, players have busy offseasons when they win. For the Steelers, it proved tough to get mentally prepared for the grind of training and playing the next season. The team started the 1976 campaign with one win and four losses.

The Steelers found imaginative ways to lose. They dropped their opener to Oakland, scoring 28 points but giving up 24 points on defense in the final period. They fumbled seven times in the game against New England. On their only appearance on *Monday Night Football*, Bradshaw tossed four interceptions against Minnesota. Finally, the Browns avenged their earlier loss to Pittsburgh, scoring on six field goals. Defensive end Joe "Turkey" Jones lifted Bradshaw off the ground and dropped him on his neck and spine. The quarterback was carried off the field on a stretcher. A visibly upset Jones came over and apologized to Bradshaw. "It's okay. I understand," Bradshaw responded. Steelers defensive tackle Ernie Holmes hoisted the stretcher onto his shoulders and carried his quarterback to the chartered airplane. They laid the stretcher across three seats to limit movement during the flight.[3]

The team significantly changed its backup quarterback position. Terry Hanratty left the squad, becoming one of three quarterbacks with the expansion Tampa Bay Buccaneers. He left the NFL after that season. The Steelers released Joe Gilliam, who began an odyssey of battling heroin, cocaine, and alcohol addiction. He failed to make the New Orleans Saints roster in the mid-1970s and spent years in and out of various semiprofessional leagues. New backup quarterback Mike Kruczek took over, and the team began winning behind its defense and running game.

Longtime fans like those who were part of the Chiodo Football Club hung in for the turbulent ride. "When you're a fanatic, you're a fanatic," said founder Joe Chiodo. Many went along for the road trip to Cleveland and saw the injury to Bradshaw. At one time as large as 72 members, the number of season ticket holders on the club dropped to half that number during the 1976 season. "The prices are getting out of reach. You know, the boys are from Homestead, Munhall, Duquesne, Hazelwood. These are steelworkers. Nine dollars and 15 cents a ticket is kind of high for them. They just can't go," said Chiodo.[4]

Bradshaw suffered undisclosed neck and back injuries. Both the quarterback and the team were thrilled he had not broken his neck. After the doctor performed a physical examination, Bradshaw continued to feel pain in his neck. In the culture of football, particularly in the 1960s and 1970s, players played through pain. Bradshaw returned to the field two weeks later. He threw three touchdowns in leading the Steelers to a win over the Bengals. But the injury bug stayed with the team. Two weeks later, Bradshaw suffered a wrist injury that forced him out of a game against the Dolphins. Fortunately, the defense continued its amazing streak of five games giving up six points or less. The defense continued its stinginess in the final three games of the season, enabling the Steelers to win nine consecutive contests and finish with a 10–4 record. The Bengals had the same record, but the Steelers, with two wins over Cincinnati, won the division title.

For the second year in a row, the Steelers and Colts were matched up in the divisional playoffs. This time, they were set to do battle at Memorial Stadium in Baltimore. Almost 1,000 $12 and $15 tickets remained unsold at the risk of the game not being broadcast on television.

Amoco Oil Company came to the rescue and purchased them. None-theless, at 11–3, the Colts had an exciting team with an offense that became the center of the talk throughout the week. Despite the close proximity of Pittsburgh and Baltimore, the number of fans coming from Pittsburgh to see the game seemed small. Presumably, the financial strain experienced by members of the Chiodo Football Club explained some of the limited fan turnout.

Despite the talk, the Colts offense generated 14 points. Bradshaw generated 21 points with three touchdown passes. Reporters called the quarterback the key to Pittsburgh's victory. Bradshaw downplayed his role in the 40–14 win. He had been angered when Colts players began laughing after Steelers returner Ernie Pough was hurt on the opening kickoff. The quarterback told the media after the game that he turned to the players on the sideline and said, "All right if that's the way they want it let's do a number on them."[5]

As had been the case in consecutive years, the Steelers and Raiders were set to meet again in the playoffs, with the Steelers journeying to Oakland. Pittsburgh would have to play with half of their offense miss-ing, as two key running backs, Rocky Bleier and Franco Harris, were out of the equation with injuries. Guard Gerry Mullins observed, "[We] only had one running back, so the coaches changed the whole offense around at the last minute, and it is hard to break the way you did things all year." It was a tough game for the visitors and Bradshaw in particu-lar. A reporter noted, "[He] often seemed uncertain, threw poorly, picked the wrong receivers, but the aggressive Oakland defense had something to do with that." Oakland claimed an easy 24–7 victory. Two hundred faithful fans weathered a temperature of 20 degrees and snow to meet the team's airplane when it landed in Pittsburgh. The largest ovations went to retiring players Ray Mansfield and Andy Russell.[6]

A MORE DIFFICULT YEAR

Aside from two veterans leaving, the team underwent a few other major changes. Ernie Holmes and Jimmy Allen left on disputes. Jack Lambert and Mel Blount were holding out in contract disputes. The latter re-turned to the team for the season, but the group experienced sizable disruption during the exhibition season. At the annual NFL meetings, the owners often make rule changes and other adjustments. Earlier that year, they voted to institute the "in-the-grasp" rule, requiring officials to blow their whistles to stop play when a defensive player has a solid hold on the quarterback. The intention was to protect quarterbacks, and a major illustration of the potential danger for quarterbacks happened to be the Terry Bradshaw–Joe Jones tackle from the previous season. Bradshaw asserted, "It [that rule change] was, 'Oh my god we can't lose our star quarterbacks.' It wasn't 'He may never walk again.' It was, 'It hurt the league! It's bad for ratings!'"[7]

For the first time in six years, the Steelers had a .500 record a little more than halfway through the season. Their division rivals were performing slightly above average. The Steelers won one and lost one against Cincinnati and Houston, respectively. The strongest teams in the AFC, including the Colts, Raiders, and Broncos, defeated the team from Steel City. Everyone had anticipated that the Steelers–Raiders game would turn into a bloodbath. Commissioner Pete Rozelle issued explicit warnings to limit the violence, and players complied. Neither Ken Stabler nor Terry Bradshaw played well, but Stabler did slightly better.

Two weeks later, in the loss to Houston, Bradshaw broke his wrist; his replacement, Mike Kruczek, suffered a shoulder separation. The team had to use cornerback Tony Dungy as an emergency quarterback. But the next week, Bradshaw proved his toughness and cemented an image of masculine strength when he played. According to Steelers physician Paul Steele, who put the quarterback's left forearm in a cast, "Terry's an amazingly rapid healer." He added, "I'm going back to medical school and take a class on Bradshaw." Perhaps, but just as likely, the physicians did everything they could to get him ready to play because he wanted to play, and the sport's culture of playing while hurt motivated the quarterback to get back into the game. He played well enough to secure a victory over the Bengals and led a revenge victory over Houston, during which he made a one-arm tackle.[8]

Because of the injury, Bradshaw tended to throw the ball much less than usual; however, against the Colts, the Steelers fell behind, so Bradshaw had to throw to get his team back into the game. Of his 26 passes, he had five interceptions. His decorum in the locker room after the game made some reporters emphasize his quality of spirit and manli-

ness, which few possess. He answered questions from the media directly and without issue.[9]

The Steelers won five of their final six games. Their 9–5 record left
them waiting for the result in the season finale between Cincinnati and
Houston. If the former won, they would win the division title. Steelers
fans crowded into such bars as Don's Restaurant, waiting for the ver-
dict. The mood grew euphoric when Houston sealed the victory.

The team returned to Denver, where they lost in early November.
Denver opened the scoring, but Pittsburgh tied the game at 14 before
halftime. The Broncos grabbed the lead in the third quarter, and Pittsburgh tied the score on a Bradshaw touchdown pass. The remainder of
the fourth quarter belonged to Denver, with the Broncos scoring 13
unanswered points to win the contest. The Steelers uncharacteristically
threw the ball 37 times, and Bradshaw threw three interceptions.
"That's not our game," the helmsman noted. But as he discovered later,
the Steelers' game had changed, and the offense had to become more
explosive.[10]

There remained a few media members who recycled the "limited
intelligence" issue on occasion. One major Washington, DC, sports columnist, Dave Brady of the *Washington Post*, called Bradshaw a basic
thinker and an uncomplicated fellow in the first two sentences of his
November 1977 article. He combined these comments with the claim
that the quarterback spoke words stained with chew tobacco. While
descriptive, the reference also carried some negativity about country,
rural, and Southern habits of chewing tobacco. From one sportswriter's
perspective, Bradshaw's Bible Belt philosophy made him appear more
foolish than sincere among the supposedly sophisticated. These differences emerged concerning opinions on evolution, school prayer, and
alcohol during the late 19th and 20th centuries. By the mid-1970s, the
economic growth and population expansion in the old states of the
Confederacy had greatly enhanced their political and cultural influence
on the United States. While people poked fun at Bradshaw's Southern
ways, Georgian Jimmy Carter became the country's president and pro-
fessed that Jesus Christ was the driving force in his life. A political
movement arose with the essence of promoting a new personal morality
tied to religious fundamentalism.[11]

A month before the start of training camp for the 1978 season,
Bradshaw surprised his wife with a visit to New York City. JoJo per-

formed as one of nine company members in 1976 gold medal winner John Curry's ice dance and skating show at 33rd Street and 10th Avenue. Dancer Mikhail Baryshnikov, actress Lauren Bacall, choreographer Twyla Tharp, author Gay Talese, and *Rolling Stone* magazine owner Jann Wenner also numbered among the 650 luminaries. The media asked Bradshaw about his appearance. "I love New York," he said huskily.[12]

NEW YEAR, NEW OFFENSE

The exhibition season proved to be a mixed bag for Bradshaw and the team. In one game, Colts linebacker Stan White tackled Bradshaw after the quarterback ran downfield, breaking Bradshaw's nose. A few games later, Bradshaw was forced to sit out because of an injury. The team needed to cut down on the number of penalties and turnovers from the previous season. They had fewer practice games than in earlier seasons. The NFL expanded its regular-season schedule from 14 to 16 games and cut back on exhibition games from six or seven to four. The addition of Tampa Bay and Seattle into the league in 1976 created an off-balanced schedule that could effectively be remedied by expanding the number of regular-season matchups. The season started earlier in September.

The rule changes on the playing field proved just as significant. During the last several years, the league had sought to expand the passing part of the offensive game. In 1974, new rules were put in place in an attempt to reduce incentives for kicking field goals, with a few changes. The goal was to invigorate the passing game by reducing offensive holding penalties from 15 to 10 yards and limiting the "chucking" a defender could do to a receiver within three yards of the line of scrimmage. In 1978, additional rule changes were made to help loosen the interpretation of offensive holding, enabling linemen to extend their arms. Offensive receivers would be "freed up" more, with the illegal contact rule restricting defensive players from hitting a receiver beyond five yards downfield.

The Steelers greeted the change with Bradshaw throwing two touchdown passes in the victory in Buffalo. In the home opener against Seattle, Bradshaw's throwing hand met the top of a Seahawks helmet and grew large and bruised. Despite that, he completed half his passes and threw for two more touchdowns. The Steelers offense overran the Bengals in Cincinnati, but then Bradshaw jammed his knee against the Jets in New York. Tough as nails, he returned and threw three touchdowns in the team's fifth straight victory. The offense scored more than 30 points against lowly Atlanta and Cleveland to take the Steelers to 7–0, before a tough Houston Oilers squad came to Three Rivers and defeated them, 24–17. The 24 points scored by the Oilers and the 24 scored by the Kansas City Chiefs in the following game, in a 27–24 Steelers victory, proved to be the most the men from Pittsburgh gave up all season.

The win against the Chiefs and one against the Saints the following week put the Steelers at 9–1. They went to Los Angeles to take on the 8–2 Rams. Regardless of the success of the team and the offense, the media set their story lines to follow the contrast between the two quarterbacks. As he had during his two Super Bowl appearances, Bradshaw received plaudits about his knowledge and skills, and coverage of the quarterback included tales of his physical strength and supposed limited intellect. Rams quarterback Pat Haden was a Rhodes Scholar, thus one media story depicted Haden translating Homer, while Bradshaw supposedly scratched his head while reading the comic page.[13]

The Steelers went to Cincinnati and played a nail-biter. The offense generated a touchdown in the second quarter, and the defense held the Bengals to two field goals. They went on to San Francisco. The NFL rejected the request to postpone the game for 24 hours because the city had experienced the grief just one day earlier of the assassination of mayor George Muscone and supervisor Harvey Milk by a man named Dan White. Bradshaw completed three touchdowns in the win.

The team flew to Houston and scored one touchdown and two field goals to defeat the Oilers. Back home against the Colts, snow and biting cold made for tough conditions. After throwing for three touchdowns, Bradshaw's hand was so shaky and numb he could barely hold a cup of coffee in the locker room. The Steelers and Broncos won their respective division titles before facing off in the final game of the season. The Steelers went to Denver and jumped out to a 21–0 lead. Bradshaw sat out the second half, and the team held on for a 21–17 victory.

The NFL made a change to the playoff format. The two wild-card teams were set to face one another, with the winner playing the team with the best record, the Steelers. But the Oilers defeated the Miami Dolphins. Since they played in the same division as Pittsburgh, the new playoff rules sought to avoid having teams in the same division play one another in the divisional round. Hence, Houston played in New England, against the team with the second best record in the league. The Steelers played the Broncos again, this time at Three Rivers Stadium.

As he waited for the playoffs to begin, Bradshaw received the Maxwell Football Club award as the nation's outstanding professional player for 1978. They would bestow the honor on him at a banquet on January 31, in Philadelphia. The Steelers' quarterback felt "certainly honored and humbled by the award." The top college player, Penn State University quarterback Chuck Fusina, also came from Pennsylvania. The western Pennsylvania native admitted to being a big fan of Bradshaw, saying, "I've been a fan of his through the good times and the bad times. The press in Pittsburgh put him down a lot. But I admire the way he took the pressure. It was really something to watch the way he came through. I hope I can take pressure like that."[14]

Fans waited anxiously for the opening playoff game. Tom Leonard, an art student in Donora, showed his Steelers pride by painting Terry Bradshaw riding herd on the Denver Broncos on a window at the McCue-McCans Agency. The image perfectly summed up the game. Bradshaw threw and Harris ran over the Broncos defense. While Franco gained more than 100 yards, Terry threw for nearly 300. Lyle Alzado, Broncos defense end, said, "Terry Bradshaw was incredible. . . . That was the best offensive performance against us in the last two years."[15]

After the victory, the Steelers celebrated the win. The media observed that celebrating was unusual for the Steelers. "I think there is a genuine affection for everyone on this team. We don't want to shortchange each other," said center Mike Webster. Bradshaw made sure he enjoyed himself, and many of his teammates did as well. The quarterback had mismatched receiver Lynn Swann's cleats and tied them together before neatly restacking them so that Swann wouldn't notice. "There are a lot of practical jokes played on this team, and Terry starts a lot of it," Swann agreed. Not really an act of teasing, Bradshaw had to run into the locker room during practice for the upcoming Oilers game while suffering from an intestinal flu.[16]

In the 1978 AFC Championship Game at Three Rivers Stadium, a deluge of cold rain battered the players, froze parts of the turf, and made the footballs slick. Puddles collected on the field and grew larger as the game progressed. Houston running back Earl Campbell, as well as Swann and Bradshaw, said afterward that the cold took the feeling out of their hands. Steelers fans roared before the start of the telecast and created an enormous din as Curt Gowdy talked with commentators Merlin Olsen and John Brodie before the game. Brodie summed up what Bradshaw sensed during the loss to Denver in the last playoffs: "Their team was different. They've thrown it [the ball] more than they've run it."[17]

After Houston punted on their first series of the game, the Steelers marched down the field. They scored on a Franco Harris run. Minutes later, the Oilers committed the first of six fumbles. Rocky Bleier did the honors this time. The Oilers kicked a short field goal to get on the board. The Steelers responded with a touchdown pass—Bradshaw to Swann. Bradshaw proceeded to throw another scoring pass, this time to wide receiver John Stallworth. Roy Gerela kicked a field goal to close out the first half, with Pittsburgh ahead, 31–3. The rain poured down, and both teams struggled to hold on to the football in the second half. The teams combined for 12 fumbles, six a piece, and seven interceptions, five by Houston. The Steelers held on to reach their third Super Bowl with a 34–5 victory.[18]

SUPER BOWL MANIA: XIII

Super Bowl XIII shared many of the same characteristics as Super Bowl X. Both featured the Steelers and Cowboys, and both took place at the Orange Bowl in Miami. Aside from Bradshaw, nine other offensive players took part in both contests. These included running backs Rocky Bleier and Franco Harris; receivers Lynn Swann, John Stallworth, and Randy Grossman; the versatile Larry Brown; linemen John Kolb and Gerry Mullins; and kicker Roy Gerela. The seven men on the defensive side of the ball who served in both tours were Joe Greene; L. C. Greenwood; Dwight White from the defensive line; Jack Lambert and Jack Ham from the linebackers; and Mel Blount and Mike Wagner at corner and safety, respectively. Five players from the Cowboys offense played in both, while three defensive linemen, two linebackers, and the two safeties also played in the two games.

Miami turned football crazy as the teams battled to become the first team to win three Super Bowls. The $30 tickets netted $200. The local media in Pittsburgh gave Bradshaw the nod for winning the league passing title and having better playoff games than Roger Staubach. Lynn Swann had his best year, and he quickly credited the man who had been voted the AFC's Most Valuable Player. "Terry's ability to read defenses this season, to pick out the open receiver, has made my job a lot easier. His consistency has reflected on all of us," Swann observed; however, a large group of fans leaving snowy western Pennsylvania for Miami expressed doubt because of how close some of the games were that the Steelers had won.[19]

As the media descended on the city, one Cowboys linebacker helped capture the attention and reopened seemingly healing wounds. Thomas Henderson had played as a kick returner in the 1975 battle between the two teams. Now the loquacious Thomas Hollywood Henderson was making daring comments, saying Dallas' defense would shut out the men from Steel City. He grabbed some additional spotlight with a pithy insult harking back to Bradshaw's "dumb" image. "Bradshaw couldn't spell cat if you spotted him the c and a," Henderson said. He made himself the star of the press conference. A latecomer to the presser asked Henderson to repeat his appraisals of Bradshaw and tight end Randy Grossman. Henderson obliged, restating, "He only plays when everyone else is dead." The comments landed him on the front page of the *New York Times*, in *Time* magazine, and on the cover with Bradshaw for *Newsweek*. To Bradshaw, this represented the culmination of the insults.[20]

As in the past, Bradshaw had to answer questions about the image. Initially, he used humor in his response to the Henderson remark. "Yeah, I've heard about it. But it's 'o,' isn't it? There I got him didn't I?" said the smiling quarterback. He elaborated. "I've always said you never live down an image once it's created. It'll haunt you the rest of your playing career and possibly when your playing days are over. . . . I don't like talking about it. It's a touchy subject. I've lived with it 10 years. I don't like it." Reporters sought out other Steelers players for their input. Guard Jon Kolb offered another image. He and Bradshaw had attended a country music jamboree in Wheeling, West Virginia. They walked into an alley and found a man who told them he was going to kill himself. Bradshaw talked to the guy for 30 minutes until he felt better.

"Terry's always being maligned," said Kolb. Longtime coach Dick Hoak said the reputation was both underserved and unfair. Hoak thought Bradshaw picked up the reputation because he was a Southern boy from Louisiana, a good ol' boy. [21]

With game day approaching, the final views on the teams emerged. Las Vegas oddsmakers posted the Cowboys as a four-point favorite to win. President Carter bet his mother Lillian Carter $5 that the Cowboys would win. Reggie Jackson of the New York Yankees and tennis professional Arthur Ashe both supported the Steelers. Fans standing in front of the stadium chanted, "Super Bowl, Super Bowl." Inside, Steelers fans in the stands wore a range of Steelers jerseys, ranging from Harris to Ham and Lambert.

Lynn Swann observed, "Terry was as loose as I've ever seen him." Presumably, he felt happy to be on the field and away from the media. The Steelers scored on a touchdown pass on their first drive. An announcer credited Bradshaw with catching Dallas by surprise, throwing rather than establishing the run. Swann related, "Terry called a play that I had suggested for our game plan. In the huddle, Terry smiled when he called my play, with John [Stallworth] as the receiver." [22]

Shortly thereafter, Bradshaw fumbled, and Dallas evened the score with one of their own before the end of the quarter. Bradshaw fumbled after colliding with Harris on the next possession, and the Cowboys recovered and ran it into the end zone for a 14–7 lead. If Steelers fans felt any concern, it dissipated quickly. On third down, Bradshaw passed, and Stallworth took it to the end zone to even the score. Trainers administered smelling salts to Bradshaw, but he returned to the field after the Cowboys punted. As NFL Films commented, "The Steelers are a mature, physically powerful squad with a special confidence that allows them to reach for heroism instead of merely trying to avoid mistakes." Bradshaw, "like a skilled conductor, directed his teammates on a classic two-minute drive," intoned the NFL Films announcer. On a third down, he called a pass-run option and tossed a high pass that Bleier pulled down as he landed on his back in the end zone for the touchdown that ended the first-half scoring. [23]

The second half started much more calmly, with only one field goal denting the scoreboard in the third quarter. Leading 21–17, Bradshaw engineered a long drive that culminated in a Harris running touchdown after the quarterback read a giant hole in the defense. Dallas fumbled the ensuing kickoff. Swann noted that in this situation, Bradshaw again called his play for another touchdown. Bradshaw threw touchdown passes to Stallworth, Bleier, and Swann, and gave Franco Harris the chance to score a rushing touchdown, demonstrating the leadership involved in sharing the ball so that everyone could contribute.

But everyone knew better than to count out Roger Staubach and the Cowboys. They scored a touchdown in four minutes, recovered an on-side kick, and scored a second touchdown, using two of the remaining two minutes and 23 seconds. The onside kick failed this time. The offense, led by Terry Bradshaw, ran onto the field. The quarterback kneeled twice, and time expired. Even today, the NFL lists the game as one of its greatest. The matchup thrilled everyone watching. The highest-scoring, most suspenseful Super Bowl in the history of the game ended with the Steelers winning, 35–31. The ratings for this and the previous Super Bowl jumped to 47 percent, with 35 million households tuning in, much higher than the previous high of 44 percent.

Bradshaw was named Most Valuable Player. He had set new records for touchdowns thrown and passing yardage. In the locker room, without malice, a jubilant Bradshaw told the assembled reporters, "Go ask Thomas Henderson if I was dumb." He continued spitting tobacco juice into a plastic cup.[24] Reporters from Canada chimed in as well:

> Finally a Super Sunday assigned to the satisfaction of one of man's most ancient desires—to ram his fist down the throat of some poor soul and walk away laughing. The Steelers made as many mistakes on the soggy grass in Miami as the Denver Broncos did last year, but the difference in the two games was Bradshaw and his third-down mastery.[25]

After the victory, about 5,000 revelers partied in downtown Pittsburgh. Police officers wearing helmets and armed with billy clubs sealed off the streets, preventing vehicles from entering the inner city. Other police officers lined Liberty and Fifth avenues, arresting about 100 people, mostly for public intoxication. The city did not have a parade for the team, as several Steelers players went to the Pro Bowl within days of returning from the Super Bowl. "I'm very sore . . . I'm very glad to be here and have the chance to meet a lot of the other players," Bradshaw said. He had made the Pro Bowl once before, but a concussion he suffered during the Super Bowl three years earlier kept him from attending.[26]

A HERO IN STEEL CITY

Bradshaw's success in the Super Bowl cemented his status as a hero among Pittsburgh Steelers fans. He was now thought of as a winning player in the minds of the tens of millions who had watched the big game. Winning a third Super Bowl and setting passing records firmly lodged his name in the annuals of professional football, the most popular sport in the United States. His name was now one of those mentioned by fans in rankings of the all-time great quarterbacks. As fans watching this generation of the NFL became advocates for the greatness of the style of football in the era, they argued for the greatness of Bradshaw and others from the time period, just as an earlier generation had supported Johnny Unitas and the championships of the 1950s, and just as the next generation supported Joe Montana and the 49ers teams of the 1980s and Troy Aikman and the Cowboys teams of the 1990s.

The younger cadre of fans also felt a powerful attraction to Bradshaw, seeing him as one of the best and a heroic figure. Such college football quarterbacks as Dan Marino and Jim Kelly had their favorite players—both were Bradshaw fans. Younger children saw the Steelers winning on television and made them their favorite team and Bradshaw one of their favorite players regardless of whether they lived in New York, Arkansas, or California. As one boy from South Dakota said years later, "I really enjoyed watching the Steelers play week after week." Fans of other teams, even those the Steelers defeated, sometimes accepted Bradshaw's greatness. A fan of the Raiders and Rams said, "Terry whipped them both. . . . He always got the job done with much the same inspiration and won four big ones." A Dallas Cowboys fan agreed that Bradshaw whipped up on his team too. Bradshaw's name recognition led to opportunities for endorsements and other appearances on radio and television.[27]

The beginning of the next season found most experts picking the Steelers as the top team in the AFC. One referred to them as being in a "class by themselves." The players thought the team had improved over last year's Super Bowl champion. The perception in the Pittsburgh media was that the rushing game had lost a step and the defense had weakened. The team jumped out to a 3–0 record but had a close call with the Patriots. In their third game, Bradshaw left the contest on a stretcher with a badly bruised left ankle. He returned at the start of the third quarter and led the team to 17 points in the final quarter to defeat the St. Louis Cardinals, 24–21. The quarterback went out injured during part of the game against the tough Colts as well but led the Steelers to victory. Chuck Noll commented that Bradshaw played better hurt. Bradshaw responded, "Heck, I'd much rather play when I'm healthy. But I'll tell you, if I play better when I'm hurt, Chuck coaches better when he's hurt."[28]

They suffered a tough loss to their cross-state rivals, the Philadelphia Eagles. Then coaches and players alike felt embarrassed after suffering their worst loss in nearly a decade during a blowout against the Bengals, 34–10. The Steelers vented their annoyances on Denver, defeating them, 42–7. Next, Bradshaw and the defense shut down Dallas, before taking Washington's challenge to throw against its fine secondary, carving it up for four touchdowns.

The Houston Oilers stayed right behind the Steelers in the division. With two games left in the season, the Oilers hosted the Steelers in the Astrodome on the *Monday Night Football* stage. Houston grabbed a 13–3 lead in the final quarter. The two teams traded rushing touchdowns, and Bradshaw's only touchdown pass of the day left Pittsburgh three points short with no time left. The Steelers and Oilers sat tied for the Central Division title. Next up, the Steelers entertained the Buffalo Bills, shutting them out, 28–0, while Houston failed to defeat the Eagles.

Pittsburgh enjoyed the bye week, as Houston took on the wild card Denver Broncos. Houston won and flew to San Diego to battle the West Division–winning Chargers. The Steelers welcomed the East Division champion Miami Dolphins. The two teams had not met in a playoff game since the 1972 AFC Championship Game. Pittsburgh fired on all cylinders, taking a 20–0 lead into halftime. Bradshaw tossed touchdowns to both of his wide receivers, and the defense gave the Dolphins little room to operate. After the 34–14 victory, the media lauded Bradshaw. One reporter called him the premiere quarterback in the AFC. Another said he exemplified the Steelers, being physically and mentally tough and playing through injuries. He and Noll were known for their displays of temper and combativeness, shouting at one another on the sidelines. As one of the team's front-office officials observed, the embrace between a large contingent of fans and the star quarterback came slowly. "This is a glass-of-beer-and-a-shot town. It took time for them to accept Terry," he said.[29]

For the third time in a year, the Oilers and Steelers were preparing to do battle. The teams were set for a rematch of the 1978 AFC Championship Game in Pittsburgh. While the Oilers complained about playing in the cold, the Steelers exhibited little sympathy. The media talked about Pittsburgh perhaps being the team of the decade. Bradshaw said, "I got tired watching it when Green Bay was winning all the time in the 60s, but when you're a part of it . . ." The Oilers also faced tens of thousands of crazed Steelers fans whipping their Terrible Towels into a frenzy throughout the game.[30]

Bradshaw threw an interception on the opening drive, which was returned for a touchdown. The game announcers and media observed that Bradshaw, too mature and confident to let one setback rattle him, drove the team down the field. On third down and 14, he showed a little of the old running quarterback when he ran for 25 yards, setting up the team's first points, a field goal. During the half, he passed 19 more times, with 14 completions, and his two touchdown passes left his team ahead, 17–10, at halftime. The defense stopped Oilers star running back Earl Campbell in his tracks, holding him to 17 yards for the game. Dan Pastorini drove his team to an apparent tying touchdown, but the referees ruled that the receiver was out of bounds and Houston had to settle for a field goal, cutting the deficit to four early in the fourth quarter.

The bad call presumably hurt the Oilers, but some players thought it did not represent the turning point of the game. Bradshaw told the media that he agreed the play ought to have been a touchdown but responded, "I thought: 'So they score; we'll just score again.' They had to stop us, and they didn't." The Steelers marched down the field for their own three points to restore the seven-point advantage. Pittsburgh doubled the advantage and put the game out of reach.[31]

SUPER BOWL MANIA: HOLLYWOOD STYLE

Pittsburgh traveled to Pasadena, California, for their fourth trip to the
Super Bowl. Steelers fans came out in large numbers, as they had for
the game at the Orange Bowl the previous year. They wore their number 58 Jack Lambert sweatshirts and Terry Bradshaw hardhats, and the
yellow Terrible Towel appeared everywhere. Dancin' Danny and His
Derelicts wore the team colors in imaginative ways. Chuckie Lazar
painted his bare body yellow and black with Harris's number 32 on his
chest. Danny Conners donned a black tuxedo and yellow cape. Dave
Byer wore a yellow and black hardhat, but his wife limited their baby to
a Terry Bradshaw t-shirt. One well-known fan came on assignment as a
photographer. Willie Stargell of the world champion "We Are Family"
Pittsburgh Pirates claimed the Steelers were family too, saying, "Sure
I'm a big Steelers fan, I saw every game I could on television and the
playoffs from the stands."[32]

Many who stayed home picked up the spirit of the times and donned
outfits befitting their favorite team. Sid Snyder, an assistant fire chief in
suburban North Irwin, joined his six buddies in painting Steelers helmets on their heads. Snyder added Terry Bradshaw's number 12 smack
dab in the middle of his forehead. They watched the game amid the
Steelers signs and slogans in the Trafford Triangle Club.

Las Vegas oddsmakers and the media seemed to expect a big win for
Pittsburgh. Bradshaw had reached the pinnacle of his career, going up
against a relative rookie, Vince Ferragamo. The Steelers had won 12
games to the Rams' nine, and Pittsburgh had dispatched their playoff
opponents much more efficiently than Los Angeles. The betting line
put the Steelers as 11-point favorites. But the Rams now had former
Steelers defensive coordinator Bud Carson as their defensive coordinator. He made plans to stop the Steelers' running and short passing
game, revealing, "In obvious passing situations we can get a fifth defensive back in there who will give us double coverage on both wide receivers. And against Bradshaw, you need that. I think Bradshaw is the best
quarterback there is."[33]

The Rams punted after their first possession. The Steelers took over
and mixed runs and one long pass to move down the field for a Matt
Bahr field goal. Los Angeles got a break on a short kickoff. Beginning at
their own 41-yard line, Ferragamo threw a short pass for a decent gain

and then ran the ball against the tough Steelers defense. As one announcer commented, "The Rams were winning the battle of the line of scrimmage against the Steelers' defense." It worked, and they went in for a short touchdown. Not to be outdone, the Steelers received an excellent kickoff return that put them near midfield. Five running plays and four passing plays later, they had a 10–7 lead. The Rams drove down the field again and settled for a short field goal that tied the game. "They made it look easy," said a Rams assistant coach seated in the booth overlooking the field.[34]

Both defenses stiffened, and then the Rams' Dave Elmendorf intercepted a Bradshaw pass deep in Pittsburgh territory. The Steelers defense yielded two first downs but then tightened up, and the Rams settled for a long field goal that gave them a 13–10 halftime lead. "Nothing seemed right for the Pittsburgh Steelers. Players that are usually lighthearted were guarded and somber," said one announcer.[35]

The Steelers took the second-half kickoff. The offense made many wonder, as they took a curiously conservative approach. The daring and explosive attack came when Bradshaw slipped a long bomb into Lynn Swann's arms between two Rams defenders. But the Rams showed resilience. After completing a 50-yard bomb of their own, they threw in trickery. A halfback option pass led to a score, and the Rams regained the lead, 19–17. For two consecutive drives, the Steelers found their inside running game clogged up. Then the Rams knocked Swann out of the game when he landed hard after making a catch. The defense continued to pressure Bradshaw, who threw one off-the-mark pass that ended up being intercepted and another that got batted around before being intercepted.

The Rams opened the fourth quarter still ahead but were unable to mount a drive. They punted, putting the Steelers back near their own 20-yard line. The first running play went for two yards. The next short pass fell incomplete. On third down, Bradshaw stepped back in the pocket and saw that the Rams had employed five defensive backs; however, the safety ignored John Stallworth as he ran through the middle of the field. Bradshaw tossed a ball that sailed more than 45 yards, over the head of the Rams' jumping corner back and into the arms of Stallworth, who galloped untouched into the end zone for the go-ahead score. The Rams refused to quit, but a Ferragamo interception stopped the team's best bid to retake the lead. Bradshaw and the offense faced another third down and long. He went long again and connected with Stallworth for the first of two plays that put the Steelers one yard shy of the clinching touchdown.

After the game, the media discussed Pittsburgh's toughness and ability to find a way to win. Noll noted that the closeness of the game didn't surprise him. "When you have two fine defensive teams, it's a question of how often you can hit the big play." Rams middle linebacker Jack "Hacksaw" Reynolds stated, "We gave them three big plays." "Pittsburgh's ability to hit the long ball made the difference," said Tom Bass, defensive coordinator for the Buccaneers. "There was going to be a guessing game going on between the Steeler offense and the Ram defense on passing downs," noted Oilers defensive coordinator Ed Biles.[36]

Both men thought Bradshaw made the difference in the game. The quarterback again received MVP honors. Inside the locker room after the victory, one California reporter heard Bradshaw say, "You spell cat with a 't,' good for tail and then we kicked your ass." He was obviously still angered by the comments regarding his intelligence, even a year later. For the larger media consumption, he observed, "I'm tired of football. It was one of the toughest Super Bowls I ever played in." But he said that talk of retirement disappeared when Joe Greene and Jack Lambert cornered him during the postgame celebration and gave him a message. "They told me they were going to kick my bleep if I didn't come back," Bradshaw said. He had reached the status of untouchable hero in Steeler Nation. Within the week, Bradshaw flew to Nashville to resume the recording career he started a few years earlier, singing about the important people in his life.[37]

5

A LITTLE BIT COUNTRY AND
A LITTLE BIT GOSPEL

An Old -School Southern Singer

"I just couldn't believe what happened."—Terry Bradshaw, reacting
to people from Shreveport booing him as he tried to sing during the
summer of 1979[1]

Terry Bradshaw had discovered the joy of music while sitting around
with his grandparents at their farm in Hall Summit, listening to the
Grand Ole Opry on the radio. Back home they had the *Louisiana Hayride* programming by KWKH Radio in Shreveport. Bradshaw sang with
the choir at Calvary Baptist Church in Shreveport for a few years. The
quarterback also sang at various times in the locker room and other
places where his teammates had heard him. Most times they ignored
his singing because few of them liked the country western or southern
gospel songs he sang; however, Bradshaw believed in himself and his
ability to sing, and tried to make things happen for himself. But the
limited audience would be a reality he would have to face.

Bradshaw sought to come out of the shadows as a singer. "I've always
been interested in country music and singing. But I was scared to approach anybody about it," he told the media as he prepared to go on
tour to support a forthcoming album. During the offseason in 1975,
while in an airport, Bradshaw spotted a recording industry agent and
joked with him about wanting to sing. That agent-representative, Till-

man Franks, invited Pittsburgh's quarterback back to his house to hear
him perform. Reportedly, the men wagered $100 on whether Franks
could get Bradshaw a recording contract. Bradshaw auditioned on the
telephone, singing "Your Cheatin' Heart" to an executive in Nashville,
and got a contract with Mercury Records. Franks and Bradshaw signed
a contract for the former to manage the latter in his music career.[2]

Franks linked his new client with Jerry Kennedy, a producer at the
label, in the summer of 1975. Kennedy said Bradshaw had a "smooth,
easy voice," adding, "So, we're going to sign him up." News of Bradshaw's recording contract circulated throughout Pittsburgh, Baltimore,
and a few locations in the South, where executives thought Bradshaw
had the largest fan base. Initially, record executives planned to record
later in the summer and release the album after the end of the football
season.[3]

Things did not happen as planned. The recording session happened
later in the year. Steelers lineman Gerry Mullins accompanied his
friend to Nashville, and when they walked into the recording studio
they saw a band already there, ready to record. Bradshaw did not know
what he wanted to sing, and they gave him a landing, a book of songs.
Bradshaw thumbed through it and asked Mullins what he should sing.
Mullins's folks were country music fans, and he picked "I'm So Lonesome I Could Cry" because he liked the song when his parents played
it. They recorded four songs in four hours in early December 1975. "I
was scared I'd lose my voice," Bradshaw said, but he hung in there, just
as he would have waited for his receivers to get open. "The funny thing
is, when we did it, I didn't like 'Making Plans.' And I wasn't too pleased
with 'I'm so Lonesome I Could Cry' either. But those were the two they
picked out, and they're the pros."[4]

During the two-week media fest before Super Bowl X, readers and
fans in Lakeland, Florida, and a few other locales heard about Bradshaw's singing. In an article about his football ability and Li'l Abner
personality, Dave Anderson of the *New York Times* mentioned that
Bradshaw recorded "Making Plans" and "I'm So Lonesome I Could
Cry." But fans and readers located in more populated areas of the
country learned little about Bradshaw's country western activities. The
company released the first single in Shreveport during the first week of
the Super Bowl hoopla, and it came out in Florida during the second
week. Mercury planned for Bradshaw to record the remainder of the

Figure 5.1. Country western singer. LSU-Shreveport Archives and Special Collections.

album the second week in February. With the selling of the music single, Bradshaw officially used his platform as a Super Bowl–winning athlete to begin a possible career in the world of country western music. He was not alone in the pursuit of success in more than one entertainment field.[5]

SINGING ACTORS AND ATHLETES

The advent of multiple entertainment mediums provided the potential for a person who had gained success in one medium to try and establish a name for themselves in a second medium. Many actors and athletes had made the trek to the recording studio before Terry Bradshaw. As disc jockey and music writer Gerry House said, "There's always some producer or record exec who sees dollar signs attached and is ready to lead the way into a recording studio." One of the earliest to partake in these possibilities was a corporation, Walt Disney. The company provided *Mickey Mouse Club* member Annette Funicello with the songs and structure to record and release 14 albums from 1958 to 1967, in a range of musical styles. Most of the singles that made the charts came early in her career.[6]

By the mid-1960s, several actors had engaged in recording careers while starring in hit television programs. One of the earliest to do so, actress Shelley Fabares, released five albums between 1962 and 1965, with her third, *Teenage Triangle*, doing the best. It reached number 48 on the music charts, probably because it also included heartthrobs James Darren and Paul Petersen. Richard Chamberlain, star of the program *Dr. Kildare*, released an album in 1962, with the obvious title *Richard Chamberlain Sings*. The album spawned a few hit singles, with his version of "Love Me Tender" reaching number 21 on the charts. By the late 1960s, everyone from Clint Eastwood and Loren Greene to Leonard Nimoy and William Shatner had albums where they "talk-sang."[7]

More infrequently, athletes have gone into recording studios to create singles and albums. A few of the earliest tracks came from a baseball player. Outfielder Tony Conigliaro broke in with the Boston Red Sox as a 19-year-old in 1964. He acted wildly on the road, jumping on stages at nightspots to sing with the band. Ed Penny, a public relations executive and Boston radio personality, got the slugger into a New York City recording studio. "Playing the Field" quickly sold out its 15,000-copy pressing, as did "Play Our Song." RCA signed him for $25,000 and reissued the first single. His new label released two singles, but neither "Little Red Scooter" nor "When You Take More Than You Give" did significantly well despite Conigliaro making a few promotional appearances. Another RCA single followed in 1966, with "When You

Take More Than You Give," on the A side. It failed to move units like his previous singles and the label cut him. Other players making music included Detroit and Washington pitcher Dennis McLain, whose records featured him playing lounge music on an organ.[8]

Sometimes athletes from individual sports tried recording. Heavyweight champion Joe Frazier's first single, "Knock Out Drop," originally came out in 1969, but the song received a reissue after Frazier's victory over Muhammad Ali. His voice sounds flat on both sides, but he supported the song's release in Europe with a tour of the continent. As one reporter noted, the tour did not generate tremendous interest. "Joe Frazier, world heavyweight boxing champion, opened a two-day engagement on June 1, at the Cine Monumental of Madrid. Attendances at both performances were poor."[9]

Terry Bradshaw had more musical background than most of the athletes and actors who released singles and albums, and did not require a voice double (like Danny Bonaduce did for his 1973 album). As disc jockey, House described Bradshaw's singing, relating, "It's a voice you'd hear in church on Sunday when somebody stepped out of the choir to sing a verse by his lonesome." Bradshaw labored under no great illusions. "They signed me because I'm a jock. Let's face it, it helps. They figure if he can sing and play football, we have something," he admitted. The quarterback might have hoped to reach the same level of success as actor David Soul, who had several Top 20 singles between 1976 and 1978, and engaged on regular musical tours worldwide until 1982.[10]

After the win in Super Bowl X in January 1975, Bradshaw recovered from his concussion and began practicing for his tour. "I can tell my stage presence is improving," he told members of the press as he practiced performing and grew more at ease about his career as a country western singer. He rehearsed extensively during the month of February, aiming to get ready for his debut later in the month. "Sure I'm nervous," he declared, "but that will go away once I'm accustomed to standing on stage and singing to people. Singing in public is a lot different than singing in the shower or the Steeler locker room."[11]

PLAYING GIGS

The first tour started in Los Angeles and lasted five days. Bradshaw played a one-night stand at the Palomino Club in North Hollywood. With a façade of an Old West corral and a neon bucking bronco sign outside the door, "The Pal" ranked as one of the top country western music spots in the United States. Old cowboy actors and stuntmen from 1930s and 1940s Hollywood westerns cohabitated with long-haired cosmic cowboys. Since the mid-1950s, they had been listening to hardscrabble singers, rockabilly, and many of the top acts in country western.

Bradshaw froze when he reached the stage. The musicians restarted the piece, and it took him a bit to rise above the fear that had paralyzed him. The gig received notice in newspapers throughout the country. While the *New York Times* included a quote displaying Bradshaw's confidence—"I know a lot of guys have tried this. But I think I may be the first guy from sports to go into entertainment who might make it on merit"—the Washington, DC, media referred to the music as "hillbilly songs" and snidely called Bradshaw a "little old Southern country boy" and the "Steelers' brainy quarterback."[12]

Due to its location and the presence of his fiancée, Olympic skater JoJo Starbuck, the show contained more of a Hollywood aura than would usually be present at Bradshaw's shows. In his dressing room, Bradshaw received a horseshoe-shaped ring of carnations. A note from Burt Reynolds sought forgiveness for the jokes he had told on the Super Bowl variety show. Gerry Mullins said that he and Bradshaw went to see Reynolds later that night at Dinah Shore's home. The pair of Southerners also had football and horses in common. Reynolds asked Bradshaw to come by the set where the star happened to be filming the movie *Hooper*.

Completing his circuit in Albuquerque, New Mexico, Bradshaw sang "Jambalaya," "I Can't Stop Loving You," "By the Time I Get to Phoenix," "Pass Me by If You're Only Passing Through," and his hit record, "I'm So Lonesome I Could Cry." One critic observed that while no threat to his singing heroes, Hank Williams and Johnny Rodriguez, Bradshaw had a strong, lively voice. Among the crowd, as one woman talked about caressing his dimple, another grumbled, "I've heard better, but when you have a name like that, you can play anywhere."

Bradshaw noted another factor he had not accounted for when he started: "The concerts are really tough because you can't sleep afterwards. With these shows, you're keyed up after singing. You just can't go to bed. I didn't get to sleep last night until 4:30." Mullins added that the bar owners often held meet-and-greet parties after the show ended in the wee hours of the morning. Good friend Mullins lost 20 pounds from touring the country western bars. "It wasn't conducive to eating and sleeping well," he admitted. [13]

With Mullins as road manager, Bradshaw played a few gigs with other country western performers. He appeared at the Capitol Music Hall in Wheeling, West Virginia; at the Old South Jamboree, a two-and-half-hour show with five other performers; in a matinee; and in an evening program. *Jamboree U.S.A.* represented one of the most influential radio programs and country western concert series. By the early 1970s, there were new performers associated with the show, as well as such stars as Buck Owens, Tammy Wynette, and Charlie Pride.

Bradshaw felt frustrated with Franks's management and personal behavior, severing their contract in July 1976. Bradshaw said Franks repeatedly exaggerated album sales and the number of bookings. He noted that during the first set of shows, nothing was set up right and people at the bars and other locals complained to him about the problems with the shows. Bradshaw said he spent so much time making bar owners happy and smoothing things out after Franks had created problems that he wanted out of the singing or simply out from his association with Franks. Bradshaw paid Tillman and his wife Virginia $2,100 to settle Franks's civil case regarding his dismissal as Bradshaw's singing manager.

West Virginia was Steeler Country, and Bradshaw received positive reviews about his new career. "This work kills me. I'm more tired now than when I'm practicing football," he said. He appeared in two big shows in the early and late evening, appearing second to last on a bill that included Leon Douglas, Bob Wood, Holley Garrett, the Morris Brothers, Johnny Rocker, Lynn Steward, and the Country Roads with MC Buddy Ray. Only two of his teammates enjoyed country music, and Bradshaw said punter Bobby Walden did not like the way Bradshaw sang. Scarlett Walden disagreed, saying both she and Bobby liked Terry's singing and attended a few of his concerts. She remembered talking with country star Johnny Rodriguez at a show, and he expressed amazement at the quarterback's singing. "He's impressive, think about what it would be like if I played football," Scarlett recalled the slightly built Rodriguez saying.[14]

Bradshaw did make several other appearances in person. But instead of performing inside the Los Angeles Coliseum, he found himself in the parking lot, where he sang between a knife thrower and a high-wire act. A more threatening crowd appeared in Dallas, where Bradshaw feared the Cowboys faithful would boo him off the stage because of Super Bowl X. He bought a cowboy hat and came out on stage, and tipped the hat and waved a white flag, arousing laughter from the crowd.

The touring experiences introduced the quarterback to the life of a musician. The routine of a performer proved quite different from that of a football player. The musician toured regularly, moving from one location to another, staying in a town for only one or two days and performing two shows almost every evening. Bradshaw discovered that the schedule put stress on his voice, which had never been trained in the way his body was groomed to play football. During his performances, Bradshaw engaged with the songs and found himself highly emotional and "keyed up" afterward. While a typical reaction for many performers, the experience was somewhat different to Bradshaw. He did not understand how to "decompress" after the show. As an accessible man, many bar and club owners found it easy to convince Bradshaw and Mullins to stay and partake in private parties to meet the owners' friends and relatives.

These performances drew more mixed reviews. After the Wheeling event, where Bradshaw sang his hit, one critic wrote, "It was so loathsome, I could've cried." But a Steelers chronicler wrote in a *Sports Illustrated* article that Bradshaw delivered real feeling at Dwight White's birthday party at Bruiser's Pub and received some well-earned applause. Bradshaw brought his usual levity to the views of his performances. "I've done only one encore," he stated. "In fact, I've asked the people to give me a standing ovation because I doubted if I'd ever get one and I wanted to see what it'd be like." A reporter reviewing the album observed that the quarterback had an untrained voice and problems staying on key but believed the issues could be worked out and that Bradshaw had his own unique style. Final assessment: "The promise is there."[15]

Pittsburgh's helmsman soon realized how demanding the business side of the industry could be. People with the label, including managers and others, needed to figure out the logistics for concert tours. Others needed to market the bands that were performing to generate interest among local audiences and get people in the seats. Even with these elements properly addressed, Bradshaw claimed a show might cost $20,000 to put on, and he might only earn $15,000 from the performance. The earnings from his appearances on television programs and concerts between October 1975 and March 1976 amounted to a little more than $15,000, or about $64,000 in 2016.

OTHER AUDIENCES

Daytime television programs offered Bradshaw another platform to appear as a singer. During their domination of television from the 1960s to the mid-1980s, CBS, NBC and ABC aired the most popular of the variety talk shows of the era, including *The Mike Douglas Show* and *Dinah!* and *Dinah's Place*. Mike Douglas and Dinah Shore were popular singers in the 1940s, and as hosts, they offered a charming and jovial environment for music and conversation. The programs combined old performers, from Milton Berle to George Jessel, who talked about the old days or a new book, to such present-day actors as Jack Nicholson, touting clips from their latest product.

Terry Bradshaw made his first appearance on both of these programs as a singer. Shore had him on in March, and he appeared on *The Mike Douglas Show* in early April. He sang "I'm So Lonesome I Could Cry" both times. These shows provided Bradshaw the chance to show different aspects of his personality, including his "good ol' boy" comedy and Southern raconteur skills. Both his singing and humor were rarely on display during football games. For the first time, football fans and other viewers had the opportunity to see this side of the star player, in as many as 230 cities nationwide. The audiences being reached by the shows opened up a new fan base for Bradshaw. The single "I'm So Lonesome I Could Cry " moved into the Top 10. Terry sang the song on the notable country program *Hee Haw*, on an episode that aired in November.

The live shows reached listeners who spent time in country western bars and attended jamborees. The television shows also reached a large number of women who frequently watched daytime television and could easily forget one performance, interview, or song. The most proven method for the marketing of music during the era involved the repetition of the song over the airwaves so the melody and lyrics grabbed listeners' attention and became repeatable.[16]

RECORDING AND RECEPTION

The radio represented the most important method for marketing music. This industry expanded significantly in the United States in the 20 years from 1950 to 1970. The number of stations on the FM and AM dials more than doubled in the two decades. The vast majority of stations played styles of music based on what the people in their individual markets preferred, and local disc jockeys made selections of songs with a significant amount of choice. During the mid-1970s, more than one-third of the radio stations in the United States played contemporary music as their format. Middle of the road (MOR), the broadly popular music crossing multiple styles, proved the second most popular, followed closely by country, which played on about 17 percent of the nation's stations. The stations playing country music—predominantly existing in the South—drew about 1.3 million listeners, slightly more than the 1.25 million who listened to news and talk radio stations. Most radio listeners kept their dial on only a few radio stations during the day and spent most of that time committed to one type of music format. The opportunities for Bradshaw and country western artists blossomed with this growth in the radio industry. But how did Bradshaw's single do on these country stations?

The "B" side of the 45 rpm single gained the most traction. It caught the attention of Bill Gavin, and *Variety* publicized the B-side song "I'm So Lonesome I Could Cry" by Bradshaw, along with "Love Fire" by Jigsaw and "I Do, I Do" by ABBA as probable climbers. The Gavin Report monitored radio airplay and served as a guide for programming content of radio shows. After releasing "I'm So Lonesome I Could Cry" with great success in Shreveport, country radio stations in Akron and Canton, Ohio, and Sacramento, California, added the song to their playlists. By the third week, stations in cities from Albuquerque and Jackson, Mississippi, to San Jose and Seattle were spinning the record on a regular basis. Fourth-week additions included such larger cities as Buffalo, Denver, Dallas, and Los Angeles. The song cracked *Broadcasting Magazine's* country music playlist on March 8, at number 16. After country locales of Charlotte, North Carolina, and Houston, Texas, added the disc to their playlists, "I'm So Lonesome I Could Cry" reached its high point of play in seven weeks. *Cash Box* magazine's "Top 100 Country" ranked it at number 32.

Bradshaw did many of the promotional appearances in radio booths throughout the nation. He visited with Marty Sullivan, known as the PD, MD, and chief beer taster at KRMD in Shreveport. He stopped by the KITS studios in Los Angeles for an interview session with the station's morning personality, Charlie Tuna. In early March 1976, a trade magazine announced that Bradshaw had received the honor of being named Country Artist of the Week. The quarterback explained that the first recording session was quite scary, stating, "I was sweating so bad I had to take my shirt off. It was tougher than any NFL afternoon." The industry wags observed that there had never been a professional athlete to successfully make the transition from playing field to recording studio. Terry Bradshaw was the first. [17]

Despite stations from Chicago and Oakland, and later Palm Beach, Florida, adding the song to their playlists, the track lost momentum. Phone calls and other requests slowed. More significantly, the song's lack of staying power on the charts was attributed to its limited traction in larger U.S. cities. From New York to Boston and Atlanta to Detroit, attracting a large number of listeners in these cities would have added substantially to sales, even if country appealed to a small share of the total market.

Most of the album's songs would have been considered classic country standards, even today. Two were favorites from the Hank Williams catalog, and then there was "Four Walls," made famous by Jim Reeves in the late 1950s, all telling sad stories of lost love. Webb Pierce's "Slowly," from the mid-1950s, tells a potentially happier love story. Nonetheless, the album also contained several songs from the pen of Roger Miller. The influential songwriter of the 1960s combined lyric inventiveness and the presentation of everyday human problems. Finally, the album featured one song from a female songwriter, Dottie West.

The hit from 1964, "Here Comes My Baby," carried another tough-luck-in-love message, which permeated Bradshaw's debut album. The country-pop style reigned at the time, and Bradshaw would have to move in that direction on future country albums to increase his popularity.

Recording industry executives continued to express surprise at Bradshaw's abilities and success. Mercury released the next single, a Roger Miller hit, "The Last Word in Lonesome Is Me." In describing the rendition, a *Billboard* reviewer used the terms "smooth" and "relaxed." Entering the Hot Country Singles chart at number 100 in early July, the song moved up to number 90 in four weeks. Meanwhile, another reviewer analyzed the album *I'm So Lonesome I Could Cry*, which Mercury released in early July. Bradshaw's voice received praise for being mellow, pleasant, and carefully controlled. Five of the songs reached designation as best cuts. The reviewer predicted that Bradshaw's immense name value would generate buyers in both the pop and country arenas.

During the 1976 football season, which ended with the Steelers falling to Oakland in the AFC Championship Game, Bradshaw received good news from the music world. He ranked number nine on the list of New Artists in Country Western Music, and two of his singles charted. But the last two tracks from the album did not perform as well. The song "The Last Word in Lonesome Is Me" peaked at number 90, and "Here Comes My Baby" went nowhere fast. Still, Bradshaw received mention with Dave and Sugar and Joni Lee as a new face on the landscape, brightening the quarterback's future in country music.[18]

More than three decades later, the Internet has enabled the sharing of videos and recordings of Bradshaw singing his various singles. A site called Rate Your Music allows listeners to rate the music in its collection and includes four ratings for the first single released by Bradshaw. Done between 2007 and 2015, one rating gave the single three and a half stars, and two settled for two and a half stars. The total rating shows that the single received high regard. The second single drew only one review. AlRog also gave the second single a rating of two and a half stars. Moreover, this site offers a platform for listeners to rate the album that spawned the singles. While one person thought highly of *I'm So Lonesome I Could Cry* and gave it five stars, two others gave it one and a half out of five stars. One of the commenters simply gave the album a "D+."

Writer and commentator Andy Thomas started a discussion about Bradshaw's country singing because, he said, "I'm learning that the singer's ability to express some deeper, personal meaning is a big differentiating point in country music. Pretty obvious, I know, but I sense I am not alone in being impressed by Bradshaw's abilities." Of the small group that offered comments, most thought that Bradshaw sounded "too technical" and needed to "roll out and evade a few blockers." The sole comment on a site selling the album embraced each of the two perspectives provided in the previous conversation. The commenter stated, "[T]he guy can sing pretty well, as heard in this country compilation of smooth arrangements in the style of the Nashville sound." The commenter also noted, "He sounds at times somewhat like Glen Campbell though he lacks the vocal range."[19]

Most commentators have expressed cynicism regarding athletes engaging in music careers. One disc jockey at a country station in Sioux Falls, South Dakota, posted the video of Bradshaw singing his hit single. At first, he admitted he thought of the song as a novelty when he had heard it the first time years earlier, but after listening to it he said that it "really is pretty good." Another article approached athletes as singers with a "snarky tone." The author disbelieved in their musical abilities. The attitude seemed justified. Since the 1990s, a number of sports figures, including football and particularly basketball players, have perceived that they have a gift for singing, rapping, and music in general. Several of them could not even stay in time with the music. Andy Thomas critiqued the abilities of Deion Sanders, LaDainian Tomlinson, Troy Aikman, and Doug Flutie; he then paused and admitted that Bradshaw was a good musician. He praised Bradshaw as having a silky smooth voice and eyes like two crystal pools of water.[20]

BEST-LAID PLANS

The record company and Bradshaw planned for the offseason of 1977 to be filled with musical performances. Bradshaw performed in Nashville, at Four Guys Harmony House, in late January, before moving on to the Florida State Fair outside of Tampa, where he appeared with artists ranging from Barbara Mandrell and Johnny Rodriguez to Brian Collins and Jim Ed Brown. Rodriguez included Bradshaw among the performers on his United Cerebral Palsy Telethon, which aired in Texas in early March 1977. That same month, he appeared on the bill with Tammy Wynette and the Statlers at Civic Arena in Pittsburgh.

Plans went astray when Terry came down with tonsillitis. He could not sing, but promoters had invested resources in the performance and wanted to know what the problem was. They discovered that there was no doubt that the quarterback could not perform; however, some of the promoters still sought to be recompensed. They brought lawsuits. The "political hassles" and lawsuits soured Bradshaw on the music business. "I'm just too easygoing and fun-loving for all that," he said. As accurate as that statement might have been, others in the music business perceived shows as an important part of how they made their livelihood. They sold an entertainment product, just as the NFL sold performances. If Bradshaw missed too many games, the Steelers would look for a new quarterback, one who would be more reliable and allow them to maximize the investment that they made in him.[21]

The issue of singing commitment flared up later in the middle of spring. It played a role in Bradshaw losing his contract with Mercury. According to the quarterback, the record company disliked that he "bad-mouthed them in a Dallas paper," so they cancelled his contract. Bradshaw complained about the methods the company used to promote his records. He smiled, saying, "If I can't speak my mind, I might as well go back and sell milk and beef cattle." Bradshaw also admitted that a second factor had played a part in the contract's dissolution: The concert promoters did not like that he could only work at his singing on a part-time basis, in the offseason.[22]

The label's executives denied that the newspaper comment had influenced their decision. The director of country music promotions, Frank Leffel, said, "That article had nothing to do with our decision. It was just a matter of Terry's being unable to work as much as he had to work to advance in the business." Leffel offered a positive view of Bradshaw's abilities as a singer, relating, "Our opinion was that he had a lot of talent. I haven't seen anyone come out of the sports field and do any better in the record business than he did." Despite the assessment, the label ultimately decided that Bradshaw could not accomplish what was required while playing football and singing. "Because of his football career, Terry was not able to devote the time necessary for his singing career," Leffel clarified. Bradshaw received an exclusive booking arrangement with the Lavender Blake Agency in the middle of the summer, just as Mercury released his album.[23]

Perhaps Mercury's executives did not take kindly to the media attack, but they certainly knew that a newer act needed to travel the country on tour to gain name recognition. Playing with other, more established acts introduced new music to fans previously disposed to liking country music. When the Bellamy Brothers released an album with Warner Brothers, they toured the United States and Canada for most of 1976. Established acts like George Jones toured more than 100 dates a year.

Bradshaw may have meant that he would settle into being a "gentleman farmer" in the moment. That changed. An advertisement in industry magazines promoted Fred Rose's record company, Hickory. For more than 25 years, the company had released numerous hits; its roster of current talent included Don Gibson, Don Everly, and Ray Price. They mentioned the 25 songs at the top of the 1977 charts, including "Take These Chains from My Heart," from Bradshaw's album.

Hickory promoted Bradshaw, and he appeared with several influential radio disc jockeys to talk and promote his music, visiting Gerry House's popular Nashville radio morning show three times during the late 1970s. The quarterback grabbed the attention of DC's king of country music, morning disc jockey Red Shipley. A poster of Bradshaw occupied a rear wall of the booth, along with one from the National Rifle Association, a calendar showing a fisherman in action, and photographs of four attractive women.

Bradshaw also sought the counsel of other figures in the industry on his own initiative. He took up the offer of the sports director of a small radio station, WIXZ (1360 AM, now WPTT) in East McKeesport, to submit for an interview in 1977. Bradshaw knew that Jack Maloy also served as a disc jockey for a small country music station. He discussed his singing career with Maloy. "He wanted to talk about airing some of the country songs he recorded, including the classic 'I'm So Lonesome I Could Cry,'" noted Maloy. Maloy suggested that Bradshaw create shorter songs that could be played near the top of the hour as a lead-in to the network newscast.[24]

The Steelers' quarterback retained friendships and connections in the music industry. After his successful performance against the Dallas Cowboys in Super Bowl XIII, he received a telegram. Mercury Records artists the Statler Brothers regularly sent congratulatory telegrams to friends and acquaintances in poetic verse. The telegram Bradshaw received read as follows:

> In the annals of 100-yard goal,
> There was a quarterback with perfect control.
> He was the first to win three in football history.
> And now it's called the Bradshaw Bowl.[25]

After the Super Bowl victory against Dallas, Bradshaw returned to Shreveport. He arranged with another of his industry friends, Larry Gatlin, to make a singing appearance at Gatlin's concert in Bradshaw's hometown. Gatlin had written a new song for Bradshaw to perform, and they hoped to premiere it at the show. Gatlin had recently become "Peck's Bad Boy" of the country music industry after getting into an argument with fans and coverage of the incident in the media. Some of Gatlin's fans were known for getting rowdy at his shows.

As mentioned earlier in the chapter, Bradshaw was set to sing in front of an enormous crowd of Cowboys fans in Dallas after Super Bowl X. He realized that they were unlikely to feel warm toward him after the Steelers had defeated the hometown team, so he made light of the situation. But three years later, he came unprepared to face a hostile crowd. The large number of northern Louisiana, East Texas, and Arkansas Cowboys fans disliked what Bradshaw had done during Super Bowl XIII and decided to act petulantly. The quarterback was shocked. Gatlin tried to let the crowd know that Bradshaw would sing, but many people booed voraciously. Gatlin asked them to stop, but they kept going, even as Bradshaw tried to sing.

The crowd showed a truth about fan behavior—that allegiance to football teams outweighed the support of a hometown hero. They felt comfortable and justified in booing one of "them" standing there in the flesh. Bradshaw, the man, represented the area with pride. He received attacks from the media because he spoke like a fellow bayou guy. But this did not matter to these Cowboys fans. The crowd weighed their identity as Cowboys fans more heavily that their identity as residents of the Shreveport metropolitan area. The realization that the fans were angry about the recent Super Bowl did not make Bradshaw feel better.

"I just couldn't believe what happened. . . . I was really humiliated," he said.[26]

The crowd could not or would not separate Bradshaw the singer from Bradshaw the football player. They may have been able to forgive him for defeating their favorite team once, but the second time proved too much. Other motivations and considerations may also have played a factor in the crowd's reactions. Some football and nonfootball fans might have preferred to place someone like Bradshaw in a box and see him as just a football player and nothing else. Many came to see Gatlin, the headliner, and had little interest in seeing Bradshaw or anyone else.

Area officials heartily supported the quarterback. The local newspaper's editorial board called Bradshaw a rugged character who is the epitome of what Americans like their sports heroes to be. Sheriff Harold M. Terry of Caddo Parish praised Bradshaw in a letter to the editor, writing, "I consider you a credit to our city, an outstanding athlete in your field, and, most importantly, a Christian gentleman."[27]

Bradshaw represented a Christian gentleman in the country at a time when evangelical Protestants had increased vitality and resources more so than at any time since the Second Great Awakening. A political movement of religious people called the "Moral Majority" allied with the Republican Party to defend a "Protestant-based moral order." The group advocated for the election of Ronald Reagan as president of the United States and conservatives to Congress. The organization expected that the election of these leaders would lead to legislation promoting their religious values. The limited action during Reagan and George H. W. Bush administrations helped prompt Pat Buchanan's challenge to Bush in the 1992 Republican primaries.

While enacting political change was of great importance to the Christian Right, the primary focus of most evangelical Protestants involved personal salvation for themselves and others. The public revivals in the evangelical tradition on radio and television, downplay of doctrinal differences, and promotion of personal conversion brought many Christians together. Like them, Bradshaw renewed his faith in Christ in 1975. He devoted himself to his personal relationship with God through such activities as regular observances and reading of the Bible. As Florida governor Reubin Askew asserted, "[Y]our faith has to be at the center of your life, and from it must emanate all your decisions."[28]

As a believer, Bradshaw visited Reverend Jerry Falwell of Liberty University and the "Moral Majority" for guidance during his divorce from JoJo Starbuck. Although Bradshaw felt emotionally spent, Falwell wanted him to speak on his Sunday morning program. Even though he admired Falwell and felt the reverend knew what God wanted him to do, Bradshaw felt he was being used and declined to make the appearance. He viewed spiritual growth as something that needed cultivation. Thus, it had to occur in small groups where people met on a regular basis and had a reverend concerned more about the flock than the offering plate.

Bradshaw's personal search for meaning, fulfillment, and use of a moral compass inspired many others as well. Evangelical church memberships surged. With the opportunities provided by cable television, more evangelists started programs and broadcasting networks to meet the needs of and create more congregants. The growth in church memberships only started leveling out in the late 1980s. The churches tended to attract more males than other denominations, and these men started family lives earlier than others of their generational cohort and resided in Southern states in rural and small towns in the United States. Would this be the fan base for Bradshaw's latest musical adventures?[29]

SOUTHERN GOSPEL

With the 1979 NFL season nearing, Bradshaw wrapped up his near-term plans for a singing career. MCA Music Nashville, under vice president Jerry Crutchfield, signed the quarterback. Crutchfield planned to assume production responsibilities for the forthcoming Bradshaw album. By the time of the 1979 playoffs, news stories were mentioning that a new album was soon to be released. Bradshaw needed to get to Nashville to record, or as one outlet said, "sing the praises of the Lord." Crutchfield explained, "We've already recorded the music, and all Terry has to do is add his voice to the tracks. It's a gospel album with just a little flavor of some pop-country mixed in. . . . Terry is a good Christian boy." Terry wanted to record a gospel album to mark the reinvigoration of his Christianity in 1975.[30]

An athlete putting out another album seemed challenging for some people to understand. Members of the media made an effort to understand what motivated Bradshaw. He told them he did not need the money. To others, he responded, "I'm not pursuing it as a hobby." Finally, he had confidence in his abilities. "Larry Gatlin . . . told me point-blank at the *Tonight Show* . . . I should give up singing. . . . He said I couldn't sing. I'm going to prove him wrong." A few months later, Bradshaw performed at a muscular dystrophy fundraiser sponsored by Larry Gatlin and the Gatlin Brothers.[31]

Others in the industry demonstrated their support for Bradshaw's singing career. The Benson Company held a reception for Terry inside the Opryland Hotel. Notables in the local music industry enjoyed the festivities. After the party, the singer got down to the promotional work. He appeared on the scene to discuss his new single, "Until You." He went to WKDA-AM in Nashville and talked with deejay Marijo Monette as well. He joined James Blackwood, Pat and Shirley Boone, and Shirley Caesar as a host for the annual gospel music industry awards television program early in the year.

The single broke onto the country singles chart at number 87. "Until You" moved up to number 80, before settling at number 73 for weeks four and five. The album came out a few months later and received a review in a local Wisconsin newspaper. The reviewer considered the compilation more gospel than country, emphasizing that Bradshaw was trying to make it in another area: "No Lanza or Como, Terry still puts a heap of heart and feeling into the 10 hymns he sings with the Jordaniars, the Shelley Kurland Strings, and other friends."[32]

The religious music market on the radio had real limits in the early 1980s. Less than 200 stations existed on both dials, grabbing less than 250,000 listeners, or 2 percent of AM and less than 1 percent of FM listeners. The largest market share amounted to 9 percent and was claimed by the stations located in Shreveport. Most of the metropolitan areas in the top 10 were in the South, except for Eugene, Oregon, Billings, Montana, and Lancaster, Pennsylvania. Women and people 50 years of age and older comprised the majority of the listeners.

Fortunately for Bradshaw, the song and the album used country styles as well. The market for country continued to climb. As Southerners and others who liked country music moved throughout the country, they took their tastes in music with them. While the number of country stations increased by only a small amount, they drew almost 20 percent more listeners. Three stations playing the country music format ranked among the top 50 in listeners, one in Chicago, one in New York, and one in Dallas. The stations attained great listener loyalty and appealed to a great number of listeners aged 50 and older who spent a fair amount of time listening after turning the station on. Executives for the Benson label arranged for Bradshaw to reach country audiences, putting him on tour with such artists as Tammy Wynette and Alabama, who played places like the Amarillo Coliseum, a 7,500-seat facility, for three nights.

This album drew mixed reactions from listeners. A disc jockey doing the late-night shift at the Louisiana Tech student-run radio station KLPI said that the radio station had all the Bradshaw albums. During the early 1990s, when he was on his shift, the deejay recalled that he and a friend, while spinning the records, used to threaten to play a Bradshaw gospel song if someone did not call in with a song request. People used to call in and say, "Keep playing what you've got on," or they would say, "Just play anything." The disc jockey, named Sam McClure, said, "Bradshaw's gospel was not what the demographic wanted to hear at that time of the night."[33]

Decades later, fans also had a range of opinions. One person who had rated the earlier album a "D+" thought the second album was worthy of a "D." A fan of Bradshaw found the album highly enjoyable. He played it and caused his wife to comment, "It's ok, who is it?" When he told her she said, "What the F**K?!?!" He recommended that people open their minds and give the songs a listen.[34]

Bradshaw and Crutchfield united again for a new album in late spring of the following year, working on the tracks for an album project called *Here in My Heart*, scheduled for a fall release. One review came out just after Christmas in 1981. Again, the writer started with the requisite identification of Bradshaw as a football player and surprise about how nice his voice sounded, writing, "The title tune is probably the best cut, but other gems include 'What a Way to Go' and 'In the Middle of the Night.' Country PDs should take a listen."[35]

A number of programming directors at the country-formatted stations took a liking to the sounds. The album garnered some regional country airplay, according to Don Klein, public relations director for Benson records. He observed that much of the airplay came on secondary country stations, whereas most radio stations continued to play the songs from Benson's artists in the gospel time slots. Stations like KSDY in Sidney, Montana, played 75 percent country and 25 percent gospel. General manager Becky Fisher preferred to opt for a total gospel format but determined early on that it probably would not work. The gospel side steered between old-time Southern quartet gospel and gospel rock. The popular artists ranged from the Rambos, the Imperials, and the Mercy River Boys to Jeannie C. Riley and Terry Bradshaw.

While the *Here in My Heart* album did not score the chart-making single of the previous album, *Until You*, it did draw some attention from fans. Several liked the approach of adding the country style. Years later, two listeners gave it an overall "good" rating. One person who rated all three of the early albums rated this one a "C." The other rater gave it one and a half stars.

Most significantly, musicians from throughout the music community recognized the albums' strengths. A choir director and organist at one North Carolina Methodist church recalled one of her special moments when Terry Bradshaw walked into a studio while she was there. Trish Williams Warren said, "He had a pretty good record." Notable songwriters and lyricists contributed songs to his album. These included two from Claire Cloninger, who has won significant recognition in the music world, and Ric Gorden, a country singer-songwriter with numerous credits to his name.[36]

Here in My Heart received a high honor, earning a Dove Award nomination as one of 1982's top gospel albums of the year by a secular artist. It appeared in the category with B. J. Thomas's *Amazing Grace*, Jeannie C. Riley's *From Harper Valley to the Mountain Top*, Chris Christian's *Just Sit Back*, and Bob Dylan's *Shot of Love*. To appear in a category with these notable performers represented an incredible achievement for Terry Bradshaw and recognition of his ability to sing. Thomas won the award, but Bradshaw had finally gained recognition as a country gospel singer.[37]

Another compliment came a few years later, when members of the group the Witnesses discussed one song that went over well with audiences. Singer Jim Barilow mentioned that pianist Becky Dundas had heard the song "Create in Me," performed on a Terry Bradshaw album. Fellow musicians who had listened to Bradshaw's work indicated many viewed his albums as good productions, containing strong musicianship. A group adopting for its own use a song Bradshaw had sung gave the piece new life, representing a legacy in music for the quarterback. By the mid-1980s, Bradshaw had slowed his activities in the recording industry as interest in making a new album waned. He waited for another opportunity to record to arise. Meanwhile, he hoped to pursue his interest in acting.[38]

6

FROM ADVERTISING TO ACTING

Being a Good Ol' Boy

"It was just a gig, but it limits the way people perceive you."—Bernie Casey, on being known as an ex-football player when trying to be an actor[1]

Like many successful athletes, Terry Bradshaw started appearing on radio and television in interviews before and after football games. Once he moved up to the professional ranks as a player in the notable position of quarterback, Bradshaw started receiving the attention of advertisers. Many companies believed that the athlete could give their product recognition. They also wanted to associate their product with the image of the athlete. The converse worked as well, with the athlete's image becoming linked to the product. Bradshaw started small with a local clothier during a convention immediately after signing his first Steelers contract.

The earliest opportunities to appear on radio and television came from Pittsburgh media outlets and commercials for regional products. He and Terry Hanratty, in the middle of their trading off as the team's top quarterback, both appeared on local radio in a program called *Terry's Back to Back*. Local sportscaster Bob Tatrn arranged for the program to get on the air. He hosted the 15-minute show, which ran for 20 weeks and was broadcast to radio stations in Pennsylvania, Ohio, and West Virginia in the early 1970s. The players learned that the first commodity that sold was themselves, and then they sold the product they endorsed. Second, they were selling the position as quarterback of the Steelers. Bradshaw expanded on the selling of his self and his position as successful NFL quarterback. Bradshaw, teammate Franco Harris, O. J. Simpson, and Billy Kilmer had their stories profiled as one of the entertainment programming options on Trans World Airlines (TWA) flights.

PRODUCT ENDORSEMENTS

Bradshaw admitted that he turned down few advertising opportunities, as he saw the value of making money while he could. The commercials he made for radio and television included regional products, ranging from Kuppenheimer's Men's Wear and Furr Bishop's Cafeterias to Dick's Clothing and Sporting Goods. The Kuppenheimer Company started in the Midwest, eventually being based in Chicago. They sold tailored clothing and men and women's sportswear to middle-class consumers. The Furr Cafeterias, another Midwestern company, sold down-home cooking like chicken-fried steak, baked fish, and carved meats, along with salads and breads, to working-class families. Cafeterias started in the urban North but spread quickly throughout the growing cities in the South after World War II. Their décor and variety of inexpensive dishes appealed to a family-oriented clientele, and cafeterias became places to go for the main meal after church on Sundays. When Bradshaw signed with them, Furr had recently issued public stock, and after a few years they had 57 restaurants in seven states throughout the United States.[2]

As Bradshaw achieved success in his first two Super Bowls, his advertising opportunities expanded to include national brands. Some of the first were Tony Lama's Cowboy Boots, Red Man chewing tobacco, and TBZ Cattle Dewormer. Some of these opportunities included ones in which he did not have to appear in commercials. He received a check for $2,500 to wear Puma shoes while playing in Super Bowl X. Interestingly, the quarterback chewed Red Man, wore cowboy boats, and raised cattle, so the products dovetailed neatly with his personality and persona as a good ol' boy.

Chewing tobacco reached the zenith of its popularity in the late nineteenth century. Its portability, low cost, and ease of use made it

Figure 6.1.   The man who created the TBZ Cattle Dewormer ad. *LSU-Shreveport Archives and Special Collections.*

highly popular with cowboys and miners in the American West, baseball players in the East and Midwest, and many males in the South. Despite the issuance of the U.S. Surgeon General's report on the hazards of smoking, younger men became the primary users of the product. Bradshaw's image and success on the field certainly made him an attractive figure to those users. While the prohibition of cigarette advertising on broadcast mediums occurred in 1970, smokeless tobacco products continued to be advertised on radio and television until their ban in 1986.

The Red Man brand started in a small number of states before spreading throughout the South in the 1950s and going national in 1963. The Bradshaw image after the Super Bowls offered a national name; however, his image as a Louisianan and a Southerner enabled the brand to gain traction in that area of the country. When Bradshaw joined their campaigns, the brand was aimed solidly at the athlete or sports audiences. Print advertisements appeared in sports magazines during that time, but this changed once a broader magazine approach came into use by the late 1990s.

Cowboy boots were a bit less controversial, with a fairly long history in the United States. Necessity being a strong motivator, the men on the western trail drives discovered that the boots they wore during the Civil War served them poorly out West. By the early 1870s, H. J. Justin had brought the western boot into being.

The commercial for TBZ Cattle Dewormer became Bradshaw's favorite because the company allowed him to ad lib during the filming of the ad. The film crew came to Bradshaw's ranch and shot footage of Terry, his dad, his uncle Bobby, and his dog Goldie. The highlight centered on Bill Bradshaw stepping on Goldie's tail, causing the dog to squeal. That noise scared the cattle, and one banged into Uncle Bobby's horse, causing it to spin around.[3]

Bradshaw's balding scalp became one notable physical attribute a few years into his professional career. Sportswriters commented on his blond hair in the early years, but they switched to his balding or receding hairline during the first Super Bowl. Cultural biases toward male baldness have existed since the time of the Egyptians and the Romans. By the 1970s, physical fitness, body shape, sexual dysfunction, and hair represented one aspect of American males devoting more time to their looks. A full head of hair purportedly indicated a man's youth and vitality. Men wanted others to know that they were young and vital. The U.S. hair replacement industry grew markedly in the twentieth century. Beginning in 1954, advertisements in major magazines and newspapers spurred the increase from an estimated 350,000 men wearing toupees to a business that was grossing $15 million a year by the close of the decade. As the technology for hairpieces improved, more than 2.5 million men out of a potential 20 million wore toupees in the early 1970s.

Instead of his hair loss becoming a hindrance to his opportunities, it enabled Bradshaw to become a spokesperson for hair replacement products. After winning his second Super Bowl, a newspaper advertisement contained a testimonial Bradshaw offered for a new hair product. Supposedly, Qaylar provided customers with hair replacement that looked good, as it covered your balding scalp. The market for this and other versions of a solution to combat male baldness seemed endless. As a result of Bradshaw's national fame, a toupee company offered him $15 million to endorse its product.

First, they made plaster copies of his head while he was wearing the toupee, putting them in salons throughout the country. The artists were so proud of their cast they sent one to his parents in the mail. Neither knew what it was, but at least his mother Novis thought it looked nice. Next, Bradshaw filmed some commercials. One had him swimming in a pool while the announcer exclaimed, "You too can have a full, robust life with our toupee. Look, Terry's in the pool swimming. Look how natural it looks." Bradshaw later wrote that he thought it looked like synthetic road kill stuck on his head. But the company liked that this he-man football player was not embarrassed to wear a toupee, thus no one else should be.[4]

However, unforeseen problems emerged. The quarterback had to wear the toupee in public. The synthetic material and dense silicone base trapped body heat. When he wore the piece, he would start sweating. He used to detach the clips from the toupee and put it on his dachshund when he got home. He felt so uncomfortable they ditched the clips and sewed it to his hair. After a day of fishing in Florida, the hairpiece looked like he had stuck his finger in an electric socket. It became so problematic he cut it off while playing in a pro-am golf tournament, getting himself fired and losing the endorsement deal.[5]

DINAH!, THE MIKE DOUGLAS SHOW, AND OTHER TELEVISION PROGRAMS

Television has always needed programming to capture the most viewers. As part of their popular Saturday afternoon program *Wide World of*

Sports, producers created a mock three-day trout-fishing competition between the United States and Argentina. It generated such fantastic ratings that the executives aired several one-hour outdoor segments on *Wide World of Sports*, called "The American Sportsman." The program eventually received its own time slot. Often shown on Sunday afternoons, the series *The American Sportsman* featured major sports celebrities and Hollywood stars of the era in some of the most spectacular destinations in the world, hunting and fishing. Host Curt Gowdy observed, "It was more than a hunting and fishing program. Every episode told a story." Gowdy recalled the highest-rated episode of the series, a show he dubbed, "Tarpon Catches Man."[6]

After the Steelers lost to the eventual Super Bowl champion Miami Dolphins in early 1973, the show's producers invited Bradshaw and his roommate and friend Gerry Mullins to Key West on a fishing trip. Bradshaw's appearance on the show fit nicely with the appreciation for the great outdoors held by most Southerners, as they were generally physically and psychologically bound to its mountains, woods, lakes, streams, and shores.

With Bradshaw, viewers embarked on a sport-fishing expedition aboard a charter boat. Popular during the Roaring Twenties, sport fishing declined during the Great Depression. World War II put the industry on a hiatus, but it returned stronger than ever beginning in the late 1940s. Bradshaw and the program arrived during the heady days of Key West and its tourism and fishing industries.

The opportunity provided Pittsburgh's quarterback with a platform to present a genuine aspect of his personality. He appeared as a funny, goofy, pleasant, exciting guy, appealing to the program's viewers, who one critic called "armchair adventurers." After hooking a fish, an enormous tarpon, Bradshaw fumbled his fly rod. He then instinctively dove into the water, only to save the rod and lose the fish. "Looks like old Terry got sacked again," the guide quipped. Mullins recalled that the entire crew laughed heartily and could not believe that he had destroyed the expensive recording equipment. "Curt Gowdy's favorite episode of the whole series," Mullins remembered. Reviewers placed the episode among the highlights of the week.[7]

A successful appearance on a program usually generated another. After winning the first Super Bowl, Bradshaw returned for a fishing expedition, this time in his home state. *The American Sportsman* went to the Chandeleur Islands in Louisiana. Living-room adventurers tagged along on the trip to these slowly shrinking, uninhabited barrier islands that are part of the Breton National Wildlife Refuge. Bradshaw and outdoor editor Grits Gresham caught their limit, while Gresham kidded the quarterback about his earlier fishing expedition.[8]

Later in the offseason of 1975, Bradshaw appeared on a different variety program. Bob Hope, comedian and actor from Hollywood's Golden Era, carved a highly successful niche for himself on television. The July 4 holiday Bob Hope special *The Stars and Stripes Show* contained singing, dancing, and requisite comedy bits. During a scene about annual fairs and games, they held an "annual tug-of-war game." First, the announcer for the fair announced legendary athletes Johnny Unitas and Mickey Mantle, and then out came Terry Bradshaw to grab onto the rope on the same side as the two legends. Mean Joe Green and Rocky Bleier joined on the same side, along with numerous other players. They supposedly lost the battle to two women on the other side of the rope. None of the athletes spoke, and the scene ended within a few minutes.

As part of his singing career, Bradshaw made appearances on two major daytime variety programs in early 1976. Dinah Shore enjoyed his personality and invited him to appear on her program for a second time one month later with longtime actor and representative of the old Hollywood studio system Douglas Fairbanks Jr. and comedian Dick Gautier. Bradshaw enjoyed being on the program. He found Shore remarkable, saying, "So classy, a Southern gal. She had a mom's attitude toward me." They connected in friendship as Southerners.[9]

During the offseason in 1977, the producer for *The Mike Douglas Show* met Bradshaw while he and the crew were filming Bradshaw's wife, JoJo Starbuck, for an upcoming program. Erni DiMassa enjoyed Bradshaw's story about JoJo being scared by rattling noises while staying at their ranch. He liked Bradshaw's story-telling style enough that he decided to include him in the program. Later, when Burt Reynolds served as Mike Douglas's cohost for a week, Bradshaw and Starbuck were invited as guests to appear with mogul Ted Turner and Daniel Bouchard.

As the Steelers won their next two Super Bowls, Bradshaw made a number of appearances on variety and national morning news programs. He and JoJo appeared with comedians Milton Berle and Dody

Goodman, as well as actors Mackenzie Phillips and Anson Williams on a show that aired in the spring of 1978. Almost a year later, the married couple accompanied actors Michael Douglas and Dom DeLuise. Bradshaw also joined fellow quarterbacks Roger Staubach and Don Meredith in singing "The Glory of Love." His last appearance with Mike Douglas came while Cher served as cohost. Her children, Chaz Bono and Elijah Allman, rounded out the invitees. The ABC morning news/entertainment show *Good Morning America* included Bradshaw as part of their program the day after the Super Bowl victories in 1979 and 1980.[10]

During the same period, the quarterback gave in-depth interviews for major articles in several magazines, including *Redbook*, *People*, and *Playboy*. While some readers were sports fans already familiar with him, many people were not. The articles provided this new audience with the chance to appreciate Bradshaw and develop a connection with him as fans. The piece in *Redbook* presented his story and offered a glimpse into his personality for women with little interest in sports.

Being married to another celebrity served as the primary focus for the pair of articles in *People*. The first article started with a mention of Bradshaw's Super Bowl victory before highlighting the absence of his wife. After a presentation of his history as a player, the piece featured Bradshaw and Starbuck's differing professional obligations, which kept them apart for half the year. "When you love someone it's hard to stay away from that person a great length of time," Bradshaw said.

Readers learned that their marriage was a Joe DiMaggio–Marilyn Monroe union and that Bradshaw was a passable country western singer. His album had flopped commercially. "No promotion," Bradshaw said. The piece may have generated sympathetic reactions from some readers. More than a year later, the second article featured the pair's divorce due to JoJo's urban lifestyle having little in common with the down-home tastes of Bradshaw. The writer reminded readers of Bradshaw's commercial album being a failure.[11]

The interview for *Playboy* magazine stunned most people involved with the Steelers organization and in Bradshaw's life. President Jimmy Carter had given an interview to the magazine before winning the presidency, so why shouldn't another good Christian? Bradshaw explained his choice, declaring, "Well, if Jesus were on earth today, he'd want to be interviewed by *Playboy*. . . . I don't think Jesus ever shied down.

And, as one of his children, neither should I." People thought Bradshaw might get "slickered" by the reporters from *Playboy*. "I was honest, but I was guarded. I liked the way it came out," he said. Indeed, he laughed a few times while reading an advance copy of the piece on an airplane. Steelers players laughed about Bradshaw "using" the magazine for his religious message instead of being exploited. Bradshaw spoke about his continued love of football, as well as his realization that faith played the most important role in his life. [12]

MAKING MOVIES

Before Bradshaw began appearing in magazines and on television programs, when he was nothing more than quarterback for the Steelers, the perception that he was dumb reemerged in a television special. The Saturday evening before Super Bowl X, CBS ran a variety program called *Super Night at the Super Bowl*. Andy Williams and Jackie Gleason shared hosting duties; the Pointer Sisters, KC & the Sunshine Band, and Dinah Shore sang; and O. J. Simpson and Joe Namath appeared, along with performers Mary Tyler Moore, Bob Newhart, and others. Actor Burt Reynolds also delivered a routine. He focused on winning few games as a quarterback at Florida State and went on to portray Bradshaw as a dumb country hick. One generous reviewer called the routine "half-funny," but at least one columnist thought the comments about the football player's intelligence were inaccurate. Bradshaw's mother became irate after seeing the portrayal. [13]

After the Steelers' victory in Super Bowl X, Reynolds heard that the jokes he had told on the variety program before the big game hurt Bradshaw's feelings. As an apology, he sent carnations arranged in the shape of a horseshoe with a note asking for forgiveness. In early March 1976, Reynolds also arranged for his manager to bring Bradshaw to the set where the star was filming a movie. Reynolds greeted the pair and pointed to the script, and asked director Hal Needham to get rid of the guy playing a specific part. Reynolds looked at Bradshaw and said, "Terry, read this line." Bradshaw read it, unsure of how he should perform the reading. "That's as good acting as I've ever seen," Reynolds said. Two weeks later, a Hollywood columnist announced that Bradshaw would make his acting debut in the new Reynolds movie, entitled *Hollywood Stuntman*.[14]

HOOPER

As the quarterback returned for training camp, he gave an interview to the local media about his activities in Hollywood. One reporter noted that Bradshaw rated as a celebrity just as the country appeared ravenous for football and its stars. Bradshaw explained his role in the film, stating, "I play a SWAT officer who is in Los Angeles for a convention." But his fans would have to wait until the summer to see for themselves.[15]

The movie reached the theaters with the title *Hooper*. A top Hollywood stuntman, Sonny Hooper (Reynolds), and a younger stuntman (Jan-Michael Vincent) perform increasingly complex stunts to earn the title of the "greatest stuntman alive." In a scene in the middle of the movie, Hooper, his girlfriend, her stuntman father, and their friends hoot and holler as they eat a meal in the Palomino Club. Playing a SWAT officer named Sherman, Bradshaw is also at the Palomino with fellow policemen. Dressed in jeans and a black-striped polo shirt, he and his friend put money in the jukebox and return to their seats. Despite being only a few tables away from the jukebox, they grumble like aggrieved customers that they cannot hear the music because of the noise at the stuntmen's table. Sherman says, "I tell ya I got 50 cents in that jukebox, and I can't hear any of it. Let's go over there and get our money's worth." Sherman and his friend get up and walk over to the stuntmen's table.

Sherman puts his hands on the table and speaks calmly but firmly. "Hey granddad, I got 50 cents in that jukebox over there, and all I can hear is your mouth flapping," he says to Jocko (Brian Keith). Jocko jokingly cups a hand around his ear and says, "What did you say son, I'm a might bit deef." The gang laughs, but Sherman repeats his request, this time more loudly.

When Sherman asks about his money again, Hooper calls for a motorcycle helmet and rams Sherman's head into the jukebox. He removes 50 cents and gives it to the men as the crowd cheers. Sherman and his friends line up across the restaurant. Sherman steps forward and tears

Hooper's shirt open. The stuntman throws a punch to Sherman's jaw, and the two begin fighting. The rest of the men soon follow suit.

The Palomino manager directs the bartender and bouncers to stop the fight. Men in white t-shirts grab Hooper and throw him through a window. Others do the same to Sherman, who lets out a cowboy yell while crashing through the glass. As he lands on the other side of a pile of trash, Sherman excitedly shouts to Hooper, "Damn is that fun. Come on, let's go, let's go back in there." Hooper replies, "Are you crazy? Let's just sit here and talk about it." Reynolds and Bradshaw's characters are good ol' boys. Their mano a mano battle is good, harmless fun, and they walk away feeling happy.[16]

Bringing in $78 million, *Hooper* performed well at the box office. It placed sixth among the top-grossing films of 1978, slightly ahead of *Jaws 2*. The movie also started the trend in Hollywood of advertising movies on country radio stations, playing throughout the South, from Palm Beach, Florida, to Austin, Texas, and as far North as Indianapolis, Indiana. Many of these working-class male listeners were already Reynolds fans who also enjoyed the cars his characters drove, and the radio station promotions accordingly included a *Hooper* Trans-Am Contest. Men appreciated that Reynolds's characters had the traditional appetites and were accessible because they did not take themselves too seriously. Playing a role in the movie enabled Bradshaw to become noticeable to these audiences and bask in the reflected glory of the star.

The majority of movie critics liked *Hooper*. They liked its action and thought it funny and an accurate portrait of moviemaking. One specifically mentioned Bradshaw's appearance in the movie as one of a "knuckle-dusting collection of conventioneering SWAT force members." Another reviewer praised the movie as having sentiment, warmth, comedy, and likeable performances. Later that year, sportswriter Al Goldstein described the character Bradshaw played as a tough guy who picked a fight with a celluloid hero. He concluded that in typical Hollywood fashion, they break up all the furniture, brutalize one another, and, in the end, embrace in brotherly love.[17]

By the end of filming, Reynolds and Bradshaw had become friends. The men shared Southern roots, football, and involvement with horses and registered cattle in common. Reynolds was among the top Hollywood stars of the late 1970s, making several top-grossing films. Bradshaw achieved parallel success in the NFL, quarterbacking for a four-time Super Bowl champion. These movies were set and filmed in the South. In the 1970s, the South grew as a filmmaking area because it cost less to make films there than in Hollywood. The larger number of people and businesses moving into the region in the 1950s and 1960s provided movie companies with financial incentives to create those characters and movies. Reynolds and Bradshaw built reputations playing redneck rebel characters in some of these movies.[18]

FAN REACTIONS

Middle-class commenters had complicated reactions to characters like Hooper. Many found his bravado and look appealing. As one noted in a more recent comment on the Internet, the movie pulsated with good ol' boy charm. When this fan discussed the movie with his friends, they said, "Oh, that's right! The rocket car! The Terry Sherman fight! Wow, I loved that when I was a kid!" Still, even after decades have passed, some of these same middle-class viewers cringe when it comes to aspects of the traditional appetites and attitudes. Placing Terry Bradshaw in the Sherman role offered advantages, especially with Bradshaw's physical presence, as he stood at six-foot-three and weighed 215 pounds. Since many in the audience recognized him as a football player, Hooper's opponent gained authenticity as a tough guy who could withstand the punishment Hooper doled out. This adds another level of rooting interest for the movie's audience, making *Hooper* more memorable and cementing Bradshaw as an actor.[19]

PORTRAIT OF A MARRIAGE

In the spring of 1979, Bradshaw and wife JoJo Starbuck received an intriguing offer. Writer Alan Milberg proposed that the pair star as themselves in a two-hour telefilm called *Star Marriage*. Milberg had recently completed a television movie documentary called *When the West Was Fun: A Western Reunion*, featuring cast members from some of television's most successful westerns of the 1950s and 1960s. Hollywood producer Brad Parks and Milberg convinced Bradshaw and Starbuck to sign on to the project. Parks and Milberg planned on using the movie as a pilot for a half-hour series starring the couple. The pair visited the networks to drum up interest. Unfortunately, they found no takers, and the project vanished. The program's interest in combining celebrity with the interworkings of a marriage proved innovative and far ahead of its time.

The Bradshaw–Starbuck program would have pioneered decades earlier the merging of reality show and infotainment into celebrity voyeurism known as "docusoaps starring celebrities." In the summer of 2002, *The Anna Nicole Show* became one of the first of these programs to be produced. Also debuting in 2002, *The Osbournes* featured father Ozzy, mother Sharon, daughter Kelly, and son Jack. One year later, pop music stars Nick Lachey and Jessica Simpson got their own show, giving viewers a glimpse into the life of another celebrity family. Their program, *Newlyweds: Nick & Jessica*, ran for 40 episodes in three seasons from 2003 to 2005. This genre exploded during the next decades, with nearly 100 such shows being made or nearing production.[20]

ATHLETES AND THE NOBLE PROFESSION

The movie and television industries have featured athletes in a variety of roles throughout the years, from walk-ons to novelty programs. Hollywood studios have rarely missed an opportunity to capitalize on a person's notoriety. A few athletes took their sports stardom and parlayed it into acting careers. Among the early successes was swimmer Johnny Weissmuller, winner of five Olympic gold medals. He starred in six Tarzan movies with MGM, before moving over to play the role at Radio Keith Orpheum (RKO). Figure skater Sonja Henie made movies during the 1940s, and swimming champion Esther Williams made "aqua musicals" into the 1950s. Years later, bodybuilder Lou Ferrigno costarred in a television series, and Arnold Schwarzenegger became a top movie star.

Beginning in the 1950s, some professional athletes from team sports retired from their sports careers and went on to act in Hollywood. Chuck Connors left baseball to become a television western star. Rosey Grier parlayed his location, playing with the Los Angeles Rams, into appearances on a variety of television shows during the mid-1960s, and in recurring character roles through the mid-1970s. One-time Ram and

49er Bernie Casey got his biggest break in the made-for-television dra-ma *Brian's Song*. The prolific Casey totaled 78 credits in television and movies.

After an amazingly successful NFL career, running back Jim Brown appeared in a western called *Rio Conchos* in 1964, and in one episode of a television series the next year. His big break came in the supporting role of Robert Jefferson in the World War II movie *The Dirty Dozen*. After that 1967 success, Brown started making several movies a year, starring in many of them. Other former athletes who found success in the movies have included Fred Williamson, who starred in some of the best-known movies in the "blaxploitation" catalog; Alex Karras, Merlin Olsen, and Fred Dryer, who starred in television programs; and Ka-reem Abdul-Jabbar, who played a notable character in *Airplane!* For-mer Buffalo Bills running back O. J. Simpson had success as a recurring character in the *Naked Gun* movies and on television in commercials and the HBO comedy series *1st and 10*.[21]

As befitting his personality, Terry Bradshaw made light of his own involvement in the movie business. He returned to his full-time job and joked during training camp about the broken nose he suffered in an earlier exhibition game. "I guess this is the end of my movie career," he said laughing. The director of *Hooper*, Hal Needham, got to "know Bradshaw and loved him." He happily invited Pittsburgh's quarterback to partake in his latest movie. Needham, Reynolds, and the other cast and crew enjoyed working hard, cutting off after they had put enough hours in, and then having a good time, and Bradshaw fit right in.[22]

But in early spring 1980, another opportunity arose when Reynolds returned to play his definitive rebel redneck character Bo "Bandit" Darville in *Smokey and the Bandit II*. A sequel to the highly successful movie from 1977, *Smokey and the Bandit II* included many returning characters and also featured Bradshaw and four other NFL players, with the football players playing themselves. The plot featured a mud-slinging campaign for the spot as governor of Texas between John Coen and Big Enos Burdett. The outgoing governor upbraids both men and gives them the responsibility of transporting a crate from Miami to the Republican National Convention in Dallas. Burdett enlists Bo "Bandit" Darville (Reynolds) and friend Cledus "Snowman" Snow (Jerry Reed) to pick up the crate and take it to Dallas. Sheriff Buford T. Justice tries to catch the friends as they transport the cargo.

Along the way, Darville stops his car in an area near a stadium outside of Miami and sees a football player. He asks the man if he plays for the Dolphins. After the guy responds that he plays for the Steelers, Darville pauses. He asks if Bradshaw is around. The player says, "Of course, coach doesn't let us go anywhere without him." Darville takes off toward the entrance to the facility. Playing himself this time, Bradshaw grins when he spots the Bandit's car driving on the track near the stands. The quarterback greets the Bandit and his passenger, and Darville asks for a favor, as well as whether Bradshaw still has his ranch in Shreveport. When Bradshaw responds, "You bet!" the Bandit points to the police car that has just entered the stadium. The Bandit asks if Bradshaw can delay the lawman for a while, so Bradshaw calls out for his teammate, "Mean Joe" Greene, to tackle the police car. As the Bandit starts driving off after thanking Bradshaw, the quarterback calls out, "You owe me, Bandit."[23]

While the first Bandit movie did well with critics, the sequel did poorly. Most thought the second film lacked the energy and originality of the first. Some complained that guest stars like Bradshaw entered only for a few moments and then never returned. A rare positive review observed that Reynolds embodied the fast-living, hard-driving, infamous minor-league legend and that Bradshaw, "Mean Joe" Greene, and others accelerated the action. The Southern "outlaw" characters of Bradshaw and Greene outwitted the authority figure. The scene showed that the outlaw and other rednecks, like the jock redneck, shared a common background and could overcome their differences. These rednecks opposed "The Man," represented by the sheriff in this instance, and enjoyed the chance to best the people in power. The players' supportive action illustrated a class solidarity that crossed racial lines and remained intact despite the football players having more money than they once did.[24]

As the reviewer for *Variety* predicted, *Smokey and the Bandit II* proved popular, earning $66 million. The movie ranked eighth among films released in 1980, $1 million behind *Coal Miner's Daughter*. It had wide appeal throughout the United States, showing in nearly 1,200 theaters. Only *Any Which Way You Can* and *Bronco Billy*, both starring Clint Eastwood, screened in more movie theaters. One female online commenter recalled watching the movie with her working-class dad, who loved it primarily because it contained great action. A New

Yorker who saw the movie as a young adult recalled years later that it was childishly fun and really fun for those who liked cowboys, big trucks, and car jumps. Some viewers in the early 1980s and even modern times saw more to the movie. One middle-class male movie aficionado stated, "Simply brilliant."[25]

TOURING WITH KENNY

Perhaps not brilliant but a television highlight late in the 1980 season featured musician Kenny Rogers offering viewers a seat on his tour bus. Calculated to broaden Rogers's appeal to other fan bases, guests included pop singer Kim Carnes, funk/soul band the Commodores, and three members of the Super Bowl champion Pittsburgh Steelers. Filmed during the midst of the musician's U.S. concert tour, the special featured scenes from his concerts and Rogers meeting average Americans.

After different musical interludes, Rogers played one-on-one basketball with a farmer's daughter. He threw baseballs at milk bottles at the Wisconsin State Fair. He mixed with Terry Bradshaw, Rocky Bleier, and Lynn Swann from the Steelers and joked around. Finally, Rogers drove a tractor 100 yards in New York City and backed it into a loading bay, linking Bradshaw with a good ol' boy bringing country fun to the big city.[26]

STOCK CAR RACER

Reynolds and his gang of friends and fellow workers began filming their next movie in late 1980. The plot for *The Cannonball Run* came from a cross-country outlaw road race that was held a few times in the 1970s. Events that had occurred with various members of the 46 teams who competed in the 1979 race became part of the movie. Hollywood stars from the past and present, from Dean Martin to Roger Moore, and such television figures as Bert Convy and Jamie Farr, and part of the Reynolds's gang, including Mel Tillis and Terry Bradshaw, each drove an entry in the race. But before the public was able to see the film,

Bradshaw's celebrity and involvement in the movie led him down a new possible career path: television.[27]

As *The Cannonball Run* awaited its planned summer release, the principals involved in making the movie realized that the pairing of Bradshaw and Tillis proved very funny. Director Hal Needham, among others, thought that they could create a television show based on the characters. The television pilot entitled *The Stockers* was the first show created by Johnny Carson's production company. Bradshaw played a stock car driver and Tillis his mechanic in the fast-paced life of a two-man racing team traveling the rugged, rural stock car racing circuit. Bradshaw's Terry dressed like his character would in the upcoming movie *The Cannonball Run*, wearing jeans and casual collared shirts. Network executives for NBC saw the rushes of the pair and decided to give the pilot a one-time shot in the schedule during early spring 1981.

As the pilot was being shot, Bradshaw's agent began talking about his client's potential television career and the possibility that he might have to retire from professional football. While Bradshaw stayed quiet, the Steelers front office expressed their understanding of their star's situation, saying every player needs to work on their future career. But the team's spokesman made sure to let the world know that Steelers fans had expressed their unhappiness with Bradshaw. Spokesman Joe Gordon stated, "The fans feel Terry is betraying the team. Their attitude is, 'We'll tell him when he can leave.'" This came across as a harsh and negative attitude toward Bradshaw. Despite these sentiments, *The Stockers* would receive serious consideration for a full-blown series based on the response to the pilot, which the station scheduled to air on a Friday night in late April.[28]

The pilot aired after a repeat of *Harper Valley PTA*, going up against a new *The Incredible Hulk* on CBS and a repeat of *I'm a Big Girl Now* on ABC. This did not offer the show the greatest scenario for success. It faced a first-run show on one network and did not receive the benefit of a full audience from its own lead-in show because that show was a repeat. One sample audience of a few dozen Pittsburgh Steelers fans watched inside the Poor House in downtown Pittsburgh. Only a few lasted through the entire program. Noted New York sports columnist Red Smith called the show dreadful. He claimed that Bradshaw overacted, squirmed, and shrugged in an effort to depict some kind of emotion. Two differing views came from professional reviewers. One thought the show and the actors came off poorly; the second thought the script poor but said Bradshaw had nothing to be ashamed of concerning his *Stockers* participation coming over likably.[29]

The critical reviews included unkind comments toward the show's intended audience. As one said, "[The Stockers] was the mediocre county-bumpkin type of show which evidently tries to seek the level of 'The Dukes of Hazzard.'" The punch line was that it failed to reach even that level. Unlike *The Stockers*, *The Dukes of Hazzard* came from Warner Brothers' television production company and received a beneficial mid-season placement in CBS's schedule. Unfortunately, *The Stockers* did not come close to those ratings. While a 30 share was considered the minimum threshold to be considered for a network schedule at the time, the program garnered only a 23 share. It did poorly in New York, Chicago, and Los Angeles. Not surprisingly, NBC's executives decided against taking a chance on the series.

Accepting the network's decision, Bradshaw announced he would report to the Steelers' quarterback school. During the press conference when he returned to the team for spring practices, Bradshaw said, "So it all happened, and I'm glad it did. It brought me to the realization of where I came today, which is, 'Thank God it failed.'" Needham thought the show was great. He believed the show did not make it because it was associated with the old regime at NBC. "And we took the film back to New York to show it to the exec back there. We got there on Thursday and were supposed to show it to him Friday. He got fired on Friday. So we went into the new regime on Monday . . . showed it to them, and it wasn't going to make the grade after that."[30]

Early in the summer blockbuster season, *The Cannonball Run* embarked on its theatrical release. Most of the prominent reviewers expressed confusion. For one, the no-holds-barred cross-continental highway race was a virtual unending series of highway gags. Another referred to the movie as an aggressive shambles. The latter found promising items, for example, the comic compatibility in the Tillis–Bradshaw and Chan–Hui teams, but the movie ended just as things started going positively.

Despite generally poor reviews, *The Cannonball Run* earned a respectable return for its producers, making $72 million in nearly 1,700 theaters throughout the United States. Only *Superman II* played in more theaters, one of only five other movies that grossed more than *The*

Cannonball Run. The movie finished in a solid sixth position, $13 million ahead of *Chariots of Fire* and roughly the same amount behind the fifth-place Bill Murray comedy *Stripes*.[31]

Several people, particularly males, recalled being children or young teenagers when they saw the movie for the first time. As one stated, "I find it as enjoyable now as I did as a kid 31 years ago." A few of these people mentioned the stellar cast, listing the individual performers, including Bradshaw, and saying that they "play good roles/parts throughout this movie." They loved it then, and a few continue to enjoy it today. They emphasized that the movie appealed to those who wanted to laugh and have a good time with their entertainment. One woman who led the brigade now finds the movie embarrassing. With the success of *The Cannonball Run* at the box office, *The Stockers* would have had a built-in audience and might have been a ratings success had it appeared after the film's release.[32]

With the beginning of football exhibition season, several reporters asked Bradshaw to summarize his experiences in Hollywood. Evaluating his own acting, Bradshaw said "[he was] better than Joe Namath but not as good as Don Meredith." The quarterback enjoyed a wild ride on the "great American celebrity machine," but as one interviewer concluded, he was pleased to return to football and get away from the Hollywood types. Perhaps he did feel mistreated, but he kept an agent and received an offer to play the part of Joe Hardy in a production of *Damn Yankees* at the Bucks County Playhouse in Pennsylvania. After he decided against signing the contract to perform in the show, the producer brought suit against him, charging that he failed to star, as advertised, in the playhouse's April 19, 1983 season opener, with the show expected to run through May 15. In the fall, a district judge dismissed the charges against him.[33]

The popularity of the "Southern road movie" declined as the filmmaking industry began to gravitate away from that genre. Nonetheless, playing roles in his friend Burt Reynolds's movies enabled Terry Bradshaw to participate in creating images of a new South. In this growing and increasingly prosperous region, harmless and fun-loving rednecks rebelled against corrupt authorities and elites, helping their friends and making new ones after having manly fights and disagreements with them. Exposure in these movies enhanced Bradshaw's celebrity and enabled him to increase his fan base among all types of moviegoers.

Bradshaw's personal appearances on television and in magazines, as well as in these movies, gave him the image of a happy good ol' boy. It meshed with a time in the country when the interest in Southern country had hit an apex, particularly in popular culture.

7

LEAVING IT ON THE FIELD

The Hero Digs Deep

"There are not many happy endings in the NFL."—Bert Jones, former NFL quarterback[1]

Terry Bradshaw spent a significant amount of time during the 1980 and 1981 offseasons in Hollywood, making movies and television programs. He strongly considered moving into that entertainment avenue on a full-time basis. Still, he had time for the more traditional rounds that big-name athletes engaged in. The quarterback held court in the halls of Congress when Senator John Heinz held a party in the Dirksen Senate Office Building for his Pittsburgh Steelers. He attended several banquet dinners for various clubs. In Hartford, Connecticut, during the winter of 1980, Bradshaw admitted to being drained after the Super Bowl. He had needed to pull from reserves—what athletes called "digging deep"—to have the energy to lead the offense on the comeback in the final quarter. Bradshaw then announced his future plans to the media, stating, "Two more years. I'm going to play two more years, then I'm finished."[2]

His plan to retire made sense, but athletes know how difficult it is to take off the uniform for good. Bradshaw had reached hero status throughout the Pittsburgh region, as well as throughout the United States and worldwide. He stood as an icon who embodied the "big-game quarterback." By leaving while he was on top, fans would have fresh memories of his Super Bowl triumphs.

A NEW DECADE

Pittsburgh wore the "City of Champions" badge proudly, with both the Pirates and Steelers taking championships in their respective sports for the 1979 season. The tough, clannish Pittsburgh people expressed pride in their neighborhoods even when they had a good high school football team. Steelers tributes appeared throughout the city, and Gimbel's downtown department store sold Steelers paraphernalia at the sports souvenir counter.

Thousands had attended the Super Bowl in January 1980, despite it being held far from Pittsburgh. Now fans were visiting Latrobe, Pennsylvania, at a clip of more than 5,000 daily to see the team at training camp practices. From retirees living in Ford City to local college students and even nonfootball fans, everyone enjoyed the Steelers.[3]

But winning a third consecutive championship would be difficult. Each opponent would play the Steelers as if the game was the Super Bowl. The team had aged and slowed, particularly on defense. Joe Greene claimed that Bradshaw was now the only indispensable player on the team, relating, "Terry took control of a tight situation. On the field. On the sidelines. In the locker room." Center Mike Webster noted that Bradshaw's greatest asset was his "application of the game plan." This involved frequent use of what are known in the trade as audibles—late signals at the line of scrimmage to give or change a play on the basis of the defenses set by the rival team. As they had done during the previous two Super Bowls, this team planned to win with a big offense as much as a stingy defense.[4]

The team hung up the championship banner and went on to score 31 points in an easy defeat of the Oilers in the home opener. The Baltimore Colts proved tougher, but the Steelers scored a late touchdown to grab the three-point victory. Fans expressed a little surprise at the outcome of the game but realized that they had grown so used to having the best of everything that they failed to accept the good. A bigger surprise came the following week at Riverfront Stadium, where old rivals the Bengals had forged an improving team. The Bengals scored 10 points to seize the lead, but Bradshaw, the old pro, brought his team down the field for the chance to win with a field goal. But Matt Bahr missed, and the team went down in defeat.

If the defeat unsettled the Steelers it did not appear immediately obvious. The Steelers offense rolled over two NFC Central Division teams, the Chicago Bears and Minnesota Vikings, with Bradshaw throwing five touchdowns and running for another in the two games. The Steelers looked geared up for the arrival of the Bengals at Three Rivers despite being short one of their best receivers, as John Stallworth had broken his leg and was finished for the season. Again, the Bengals held a narrow lead. Bradshaw directed the offense down the field and set up Bahr for a 39-yard field goal attempt, but he missed. The tight loss set off a run of two more defeats. The first, against the Raiders, featured explosive offense, with the Raiders scoring the last 10 points to win the game after Bradshaw got knocked out of the contest in the third quarter. Cliff Stoudt replaced Bradshaw in the Cleveland game and played well in the team's loss.

Some fans began blaming Bradshaw's dissolving marriage to JoJo Starbuck for impairing his concentration during the 1980 season. A jammed thumb on his throwing hand made playing more difficult. Bradshaw had developed an image as a tough player, as he had proven he could play with residual pain that would sideline many other athletes. This presumably kept most fans from knowing how hurt he truly was and how limiting a particular injury was to his effectiveness as a quarterback. As he aged, Bradshaw had to dig deep to be able to play when he was experiencing constant pain.[5]

A few weeks earlier, Bradshaw had taken a brief trip to visit a breeder of quarter horses in Kansas. Duane and Jo Walker ran TJ Ranch, and along with Francis Esely, president of Farmers State Bank, they arranged for the sale of some horses to Bradshaw. The quarterback pleased them with his personality, a good ol' boy with a real sense for farming and breeding. "I've been a Terry Bradshaw fan for a long time. . . . He's just like talkin' to the good ol' country boy next store," said Duane.[6]

The recent losses had been such a surprise and carried such an intensity that the next game, a victory, was followed by the national headline, "Steelers Finally Win." Working-class fans retained their excitement as the second-place Cleveland Browns came to Pittsburgh. The regulars in the Chodo Fan Club traded verbal digs, and heated debate raged as the 50-member gang from Cleveland came to watch the game at the bar in Homestead. The visitors had the best of the conversation, with their team leading the game and the Steelers drop-ping touchdown passes and committing penalties that wiped out other big plays. With only 11 seconds left, the hero tried one more time. He flipped a three-yard touchdown pass to Lynn Swann in the end zone, and the Steelers bested the Browns, 16–13. The Steelers moved into a tie with the Browns for second place in the Central Division, one game behind Houston.

Next, the team went to Buffalo to play a tough Bills squad. The defense gave up a touchdown per quarter, and the offense could not keep pace. The next week, a win against a weak Miami team kept the squad's playoff hopes alive. Both the Oilers and the Raiders held a one-game lead on the Steelers with only three games remaining in the season. The Steelers traveled to Houston and lost in a defensive show-down, 6–0. Bradshaw faced a fierce attack from Houston's front four and threw three interceptions. Combined with two fumbles, the turn-overs undid the last-gasp attempt to stay in the playoff hunt. "They had a great run, like they had been on Broadway" wrote one reporter. Old pro Joe Greene noted, "It's just another experience. There's always two sides to a coin. We've been fortunate to live on the good side for a long while." Webster was thinking about his upcoming visit to a children's hospital, saying, "It's still only a football game."[7]

The quarterback felt the same. But he loved the game and believed players needed to do their best. Bradshaw also knew that the game and the team meant a lot to the fans. During the game against the Kansas City Chiefs at Three Rivers, the capacity crowd saw the Steelers score a touchdown in the beginning of the fourth quarter to narrow the visitors' lead to 16–14. The Steelers engineered another drive and neared their opponents' end zone. Bradshaw called a trap play. Thirty-four-year-old Rocky Bleier took the handoff from his quarterback and ran 14 yards for the go-ahead touchdown. The crowd of 50,000 stood and ap-plauded, showering the veteran with appreciation during the last home game of his career.

Bradshaw headed to Hollywood and met up with director Hal Need-ham. He teamed with Mel Tillis and Needham to film a pilot for a television series that NBC's executives chose to not add to its fall sched-ule. "I was gone—definitely gone. It was time to put out the lights," Bradshaw admitted later. He clearly would have retired from professional football if the pilot had been a hit and added to the network schedule.[8]

Even after the official network announcement, Bradshaw allowed his theatrical agent to speak for him. "Terry hasn't decided. There are a number of options open, and certainly football is one of them," said David Gershenson. He reportedly would have roles in two more movies. Needham wanted him for a part in the movie *Megaforce*, and another movie entitled *The Texans* was to follow but did not happen. Before the summer, Bradshaw told the Steelers organization and fan base he felt happy to return. He claimed to be satisfied that the pilot had failed, announcing that he felt great, even as many of the team's megafans knew he had played through some pain the previous season. He then recognized his current position and informed the Steelers organization that he would continue to play football until Chuck Noll, the coach, "cuts me, trades me, or I wear out my welcome."[9]

Bradshaw admitted he did not want to leave football until he surpassed Fran Tarkenton's passing records and won a fifth Super Bowl. "An athlete doesn't like to think his career will ever end. I don't want people to tell me I'm old. I don't think I'm getting old. And I still love to play," he declared. Some Steelers players heard the claims that they were getting old from sportswriters and others. At training camp, one longtime writer noted, "The sign with the arrow on the campus road says 'St. Vincent Cemetery,' and it has its symbolism." Bradshaw denied these claims but admitted, "It seems odd, but you can't say the Steelers are the team to beat anymore."[10]

The team's injury list continued to grow during training camp. Outside linebacker Jack Ham, tight ends Randy Grossman and Bennie Cunningham, and offensive tackle Ted Petersen missed time. Still, several experts predicted the Steelers would win the Central Division, regardless of Bradshaw's lack of interest or health, due mostly to Cliff Stoudt's playing ability at quarterback. But the team struggled on all accounts in their opening game. They scored 33 points; however, they fumbled the ball eight times. They made mental mistakes, for example, having too many men on the field, and the defense yielded the Kansas City Chiefs more than 350 yards of offense and 37 points. The reporters covering the game observed Steelers players on the sidelines laughing, joking, and possibly dreaming of postgame beer on their way to a 37–33 loss.[11]

The situation only got worse. The Steelers lost again, falling to 0–2 for the first time since Bradshaw's rookie season. "I'm going to play better," Bradshaw said. But when opponents are averaging 35 points per game, the offense can only take a small share of the responsibility for the team's losses. A true sports hero, Bradshaw never called out teammates in the media and always focused responsibility for negative situations on himself. [12]

The Steelers won their first game of the season the next week. Reporters commented that the game represented the first time the Steelers had dominated a game with their running attack in several years. The offense kept rolling as the team won three more. They faced off against division rival Cincinnati, which also had a 4–2 record. The Steelers fell apart on both sides of the ball and got trounced, 34–7.

After defeating Houston to get back on the winning track, the Steelers suffered two heartbreaking losses. The 49ers intercepted three of Bradshaw's passes and scored in the final quarter to win the game. "It's just so frustrating. You'd like to go somewhere and hide, but there's no place to go," Bradshaw told the media in the locker room after the game. The following week, in Seattle, the Seahawks scored two touchdowns in the fourth quarter to seize the victory. [13]

The injury bug continued to plague the team. Backup quarterback Cliff Stoudt sidelined himself for the season by breaking his arm while hitting a punching bag. Bradshaw led the team to a victory over the Atlanta Falcons. The veteran broke the tied score with a touchdown pass while becoming the 17th player to throw for more than 25,000 yards in his career. Reaching that mark indicated Bradshaw's greatness as a player, toughness, and longevity in a brutal environment. [14] Table 7.1 lists the quarterbacks who threw for more than 25,000 yards prior to 1981.

This list compares only those men who achieved this mark before or during the era in which Bradshaw played in the NFL. Bradshaw ranked among the lowest in number of games played—only Joe Namath and Bob Griese appeared in fewer contests. Six, or one-third of the players, attempted more passes per game than Bradshaw, a surprising figure given how much the Steelers seemingly concentrated on rushing the ball between 1972 and 1977. He ranked in the middle in completions per game. Those completions went for a high yards per catch average. Bradshaw ranked sixth on the list, or in the top two-thirds, in this

Table 7.1. Quarterbacks Who Threw for More Than 25,000 Yards

Player	Games Played	Attempts	Att/ Game	Completions	Compl/ Game	Yards	Yards/ Completion
Fran Tarkenton	246	6,467	26.3	3,686	15.0	47,003	12.8
Johnny Unitas	211	5,186	24.6	2,830	13.4	40,239	14.2
Jim Hart	201	5,076	25.3	2,593	12.9	34,665	13.4
John Hadl	224	4,687	20.9	2,363	10.5	33,503	14.2
Y. A. Tittle	204	4,395	21.5	2,427	11.9	33,070	13.6
Sonny Jurgensen	218	4,262	19.5	2,433	11.1	32,224	13.2
John Brodie	201	4,491	22.3	2,469	12.3	31,548	12.8
Norm Snead	178	4,353	24.4	2,276	12.8	30,797	13.5
Roman Gabriel	183	4,498	24.6	2,366	12.9	29,444	12.4
Len Dawson	211	3,741	17.7	2,136	10.1	28,711	13.4
Terry Bradshaw	**168**	**3,901**	**23.2**	**2,025**	**12.1**	**27,989**	**13.8**
Ken Stabler	184	3,793	20.6	2,270	12.3	27,938	12.3
Craig Morton	207	3,786	18.3	2,053	9.9	27,908	13.6
Joe Namath	140	3,762	26.9	1,886	13.5	27,663	14.7
George Blanda	340	4,007	11.8	1,911	5.6	26,920	14.1
Bobby Layne	175	3,700	21.1	1,814	10.4	26,768	14.8
Bob Griese	161	3,429	21.3	1,926	12.0	25,092	13.0

Pro-Football-Reference, "NFL Career Passing Yards Leaders," *Pro-Football-Reference.com*, http://www.pro-football-reference.com/leaders/pass_yds_career.htm; individual players records from same site.

category. Most of the players with higher averages, including Bobby Layne, Johnny Unitas, George Blanda, and John Hadl, played the majority of their careers in the era before Bradshaw.

The season did not stop for monumental achievements. Pittsburgh defeated the Rams behind the combined efforts of Franco Harris and Bradshaw. The team had an 8–5 record, two games behind the Bengals for the top slot in the Central Division with three games left. Their playoff hopes rested on winning a wild-card spot. They were tied with the Bills, Broncos, and Chiefs for the second wild-card slot.

For a number of fans, this position was not nearly good enough. They booed the quarterback, the defense, and the coach. "They've come to expect not just excellence, but dominance," explained Bradshaw. The quarterback added, "And we've come to expect a lot out of ourselves, too." The team had barely been more than a 50–50 proposition thus far that year and was relying on its leading man more than ever. In the last game, Bradshaw hurt his knee and finished the game limping. Chuck Noll admitted, "We were only going to take him out if he couldn't walk." Fans with high expectations never came to realize the amount of emotional and psychological energy it took for the star to play at a high level while ailing physically.[15]

The Steelers flew to Oakland to take on their archrival in the nationally televised, *Monday Night Football* game. Both teams needed to win to keep their slim chances of making the playoffs alive. Pittsburgh took a 7–0 lead on a Bradshaw touchdown pass to tight end Bennie Cunningham. In the second quarter, the Raiders tied the score. Bradshaw rallied his offensive team when he called a play-action play. "They had a safety blitz on, and I was trying to lay it off in the corner for a touchdown," he said. On the follow throw, Bradshaw's hand hit Rod Martin's helmet. He tried to stay in the game but realized that he could no longer hold on to the ball. With backup quarterback Mark Malone playing, the Steelers held a 20–14 lead going into the third quarter, but Oakland outscored them, 16–7, in the fourth quarter to win the game.[16]

Bradshaw became the fifth quarterback to be knocked out of a game by the Raiders that season. Reporters summarized his loss as "devastating" to the Steelers, and although Bradshaw thought the team still had a chance to make the playoffs, most observers did not. Pittsburgh lost two close games to division rivals Cincinnati and Houston and finished the season at .500, at 8–8. While the playoffs did not include the Steelers, they did feature Bradshaw. He joined CBS Sports as a member of their football commentator crew. His accepting this job started him on a path to being a color commentator with the network.

With the season's conclusion came the end of the collective bargaining agreement between players and owners. The potential for a strike loomed large after they failed to reach a workable free-agent arrangement. The union had prioritized getting a fixed percentage of gross revenues, preferably 55 percent, and a wage scale based on years of service. The wage scale had the support of a majority of the players, but some did not like the idea of everyone making the same amount of money if they have been in the league the same number of years.

Franco Harris stood up at one meeting and asked, "How would you allow for a player like me who makes $350,000 a year?" One young pro stood up in the back and said, "Heck Franco, you deserved $500,000 a year." Franco smiled and sat back down. The players knew they needed to stay united. As Philadelphia Eagles safety John Sciarra noted, "As a group, [the owners] they're a very smart, shrewd group of individuals with a lot of business sense." He stated that the NFL players were underpaid relative to baseball and basketball players.[17]

At the start of 1981, Ronald Reagan took over the presidency after defeating incumbent Jimmy Carter. Reagan advocated for tax cuts as a way to stimulate the U.S. economy. The White House worked to lower the high inflation rate but, in the process, sparked a recession in 1982 and 1983. With unemployment rates at more than 10 percent and the effects of losing jobs overseas hurting the steel and other manufacturing industries, Bradshaw thought football players striking would look bad. "With the economy the way it is people aren't going to be sympathetic with a guy making $100,000 going on strike," he said to reporters just before the announcement of the players' strike.[18]

However, the unionized working person in the Pittsburgh region did not appreciate the declaration. Westinghouse Air Brake assembly work-er Larry Williams said, "A working man making $20,000 gross like me with a wife and family, who can barely live on his salary, isn't sympa-thetic to the football players. Not right off. But leading the procession across the picket line? That is a totally, completely asinine thing for Bradshaw to say."[19]

Bradshaw certainly did not advocate for himself and others to cross a picket line. He advocated for negotiations in good faith. Perhaps that position came from his Southern roots. He added, "I just don't like strikes. Mature people ought to be able to sit down and work things out." When money and power were at issue, it is not uncommon for otherwise reasonable people to find themselves unable to reach an agreement.[20]

An illustration of that reality came when the media obtained a survey of the players receiving the highest salaries in the NFL. New Orleans quarterback Archie Manning ranked as the league's top-salaried player, earning $600,000. Walter Payton, the Chicago Bears' running back,

placed second with a $500,000 salary. Bradshaw's $470,000 annual salary placed him in the third position. Steelers Franco Harris, Joe Greene,
Lynn Swann, and Jack Ham also ranked among the highest-paid players
at their respective positions. As professor of labor history at the University of Pittsburgh, Dr. Mark McColloch noted, "[F]or the small man in
an industry to make gains, you have to have the big men go along."
Thus, Bradshaw and the other well-paid players needed to support the
strike if one occurred so the others could possibly make more money.[21]

The league owners and players began the new football season without a collective bargaining agreement in place. They would either have
to come to an agreement within two weeks or there would be a strike.
No one wanted to focus on that when they could discuss the strengths
and weaknesses of the teams. Coming off an uninspiring 8–8 season,
few experts thought much of the Steelers' chances in 1982. The defense
had experienced drastic changes with Joe Greene's retirement and the
release of both L. C. Greenwood and John Banaszak. The team would
rely on their offense to score a fair amount of points to win. Bradshaw
would be the key. Yet, during the warm-ups before a preseason game,
Bradshaw injured his elbow. "It's torn bad," he revealed. But a team
spokesman said the injury was not serious. The Steelers organization
said the quarterback would play in the next preseason game.

The Steelers completed their exhibition season with their cross-state
rivals, the Philadelphia Eagles. The game started out all Eagles, but
Bradshaw led a big second-half comeback that gave Pittsburgh Pennsylvania's bragging rights for the year. The regular season began with a
battle against the Dallas Cowboys in the *Monday Night Football* contest. The Cowboys grabbed a 14–13 halftime lead; however, the Steelers came out in the third quarter and rambled over their opponent. Two
touchdowns and a field goal gave them a 16-point lead on their way to
victory.

Bradshaw's elbow "killed" him, and the team physicians chose to
inject the area with a cortisone shot. A powerful anti-inflammatory
medication, the medicine offers relief of inflamed muscles, joints, and
tendons. Despite the beginning of the 24-hour sports cycle with the
development of the Entertainment and Sports Programming Network
(ESPN), off-the-field topics in sports received significantly less coverage in the early 1980s. The greater number of news outlets, increased
attention to the game, and the expansion of the Internet and its infor-

mation sources remained years in the future. Instead, sports news about injuries, like the one that Bradshaw encountered, received coverage when they happened. Bradshaw knew this and tried to hide his identity, to no avail. [22]

Teams and the league frequently disregarded player health in violent sports like football. Playing through an injury helped reinforce a version of the rugged, masculine man. It demonstrated that the player had an appropriate toughness in a sport where players wanted to project a high degree of toughness. Playing with pain impressed others and offered prestige and a manly identity within the team setting.

Game two brought the AFC champion Bengals into Three Rivers Stadium. Veteran quarterbacks Ken Anderson and Terry Bradshaw both threw the ball well. The Steelers held a 10-3 halftime lead, and the game grew in intensity. The teams traded touchdowns, and then Anderson led his team to the tying touchdown and a go-ahead field goal. Bradshaw took the offense deep into Bengals territory. With 35 seconds remaining in the game, Anderson kicked the game-tying field goal. The teams went into overtime. Pittsburgh's defense made a key interception, and Bradshaw called the play that resulted in the winning touchdown. [23]

Fans had to make do with the memories of that last play and game. The owners and players failed to craft a new bargaining agreement and the players declared themselves out on strike. Despite being vocal critics of the union, Bradshaw and Jack Lambert said they would walk out. "I'm not going to break a strike, I go with the majority and if the majority goes (on strike), I go," Bradshaw said. In a union town like Pittsburgh, Bradshaw's words would find a lot of support. [24]

Some Steelers "megafans" maintained their routine and even set up their tailgate parties in the parking lot of the stadium. Although many fans expressed unhappiness with the players for the strike, they also cheered wildly when Franco Harris walked past. Other fans said that they still loved their Steelers.

The love faced a test as the strike lasted over a month. The NFL Players Association claimed that the owners had not attended meetings, but when they did little progress occurred. "I thought it was positive at least that owners were at the table," said Detroit Lions' player representative Stan White. The union tried to stage two all-star games with members from the teams in the AFC and NFC divisions facing one another. Many of the players selected to appear in the game turned down the offer. As Bradshaw put it, "I play for the Pittsburgh Steelers. When the Pittsburgh Steelers play again, that's when I play. I don't plan on getting hurt and not be able to play for my team."[25]

The NFL came out with different versions of shortened schedules, some with 14 games, others with 12. The settlement in early November resulted in the creation of a nine-game schedule. Pittsburgh picked up where it left off, with a win. The team's perfect season came to an end with a shutout at the hands of the Seattle Seahawks. Cliff Stoudt took over for an injured Bradshaw and threw three interceptions in the loss. The Steelers then lost two of their next three to fall to a 4–3 record. With the odd season, the league would place the top eight teams from each league into the playoffs. The team with the best record played the one in the eighth slot (with the worst record), the team with the second-best record played the seventh-place team, the third played the sixth, and the fourth battled the fifth. The Steelers' record placed them among the lower-ranked playoff teams, and any additional losses would hurt their chances. Fortunately, they played two of the teams battling them for the remaining playoff spots. Under Bradshaw's guidance, the offense scored 37 points against each of the teams, and Pittsburgh assured itself of the fifth position and a playoff game at home against San Diego.

During the regular season, a few critics had reportedly talked about Bradshaw having an aging arm. Some members of the Steelers organization mentioned anonymously that they had no idea what they would get from Bradshaw on any given day. Some days were great, while on others he performed poorly. Bradshaw admitted that a few years earlier he had the arm strength to zip the ball to any location. "Now I can't throw it like I used to, so I have to be sure my mechanics are better," he stated. While the focus of the organization and fans stayed on Bradshaw, the team had only three games where a running back gained more than 100 yards. Harris had carried out the feat in the last two games, and the team needed that kind of balance to win the playoff game.[26]

Against San Diego, the two teams combined for more than 900 yards of offense and five touchdown passes. San Diego had a rusher who gained more than 100 yards, but the Chargers trailed in the third quarter. Bradshaw and the Steelers tried a ball-control offense, but it failed to move the team. "I just played a more conservative game. That's what you do when you're leading," explained Bradshaw. San Diego completed a comeback with two touchdowns in the fourth quarter to win, 31–28, helped by a Bradshaw interception, a holding penalty on defense, the Steelers' inability to run the ball, and a shanked punt that gave the Chargers great field position.[27]

As he did in the past, Bradshaw remained the stand-up guy. He addressed reporters' questions after the game. He took responsibility for his interception and said nothing negative about the effectiveness of his teammates' performances. Bradshaw appeared as the truly gallant figure, able to accept responsibility when something did not go as he wanted.[28]

Surprisingly, Bradshaw had played the entire year with pain in his throwing arm. When examined, it turned out that he had tears in the muscle surrounding his elbow. Surgery would be necessary. A "Thomas Brady" checked into a Shreveport, Louisiana, hospital with tennis elbow. Dr. Bill Bundrick operated on Terry Bradshaw for football elbow. The doctor said Bradshaw would be able to start throwing a football in June and should have no further problems with his elbow. Bradshaw cleared the operation with the Steelers organization, including Dan Rooney, trainer Ralph Berlin, and Dr. Paul Steele, the team's orthopedic surgeon. The quarterback did not inform Chuck Noll directly and thought the Steelers acted indecisively by not pushing for him to have the operation or setting up an operation for him.

After a few weeks, the pain in the elbow disappeared. He exercised in the weight room and on cardiovascular machines but had not lifted a football. In the minicamp during the spring of 1983, Bradshaw picked up a ball and lobbed a throw, sparking a sharp pain in his elbow. When he got home, the elbow looked like a purple tennis ball from internal bleeding. The doctor ordered complete rest for at least two months. The Steelers opted to place their star on the "physically unable to perform" list. Noll explained when the team met for training camp in July that the listing allowed Bradshaw to run and rehabilitate himself, but he could not practice in pads or join in any contact practices.

Bradshaw noted how angry Noll acted, and the pair returned to their confrontational positions. On another occasion, Noll came to Bradshaw's room at camp and asked, "Why did you get this thing operated on? You threw the ball great last year." Bradshaw replied, "Chuck, I

know I threw it great, but my elbow hurt constantly." Noll's consterna-
tion grew as he was peppered with questions about Bradshaw's injury.
After one reporter's question, Noll responded, "I don't know if he can
throw or not. Maybe he's ready for his life's work." Bradshaw felt the
comment like a stinging head slap. Noll responded in that way after he
felt Bradshaw could no longer contribute as a football player. Bradshaw
had not reached that conclusion; he expected to heal in six to eight
weeks. The quarterback was upset that his coach and general manager
seemed to believe that his playing career had neared the end. The
predictions for the team seemed rosy, with one calling the Steelers
sound and expecting them to win the division.[29]

The Steelers started out the 1983 season by winning two and losing
two. The defense grew stronger and held opponents to an average of 17
points a game, while the team's offense proved strong enough behind
Harris's 1,000-yard season and Stoudt's play at quarterback. The team
stood at 9–2, three games ahead of the second-place Cleveland Browns.
Then the bottom fell out. The defense sprang big leaks, and the offense
forgot how to score. The Steelers lost two games. The sniping in the
media between Noll and Bradshaw increased. Then they lost again. At
9–5, the Steelers had a one-game advantage on Cleveland, and only two
games remained.

The Steelers had sent Bradshaw for physical therapy, but it had not
worked. He went back to Shreveport, and the surgeon introduced him
to a new machine called an Acuscope. This electronic medical instru-
ment used electricity to reduce pain by stimulating the nervous system
of the body. Bradshaw's elbow felt great again. He could not only lift
things with his right arm without dropping to his knees in pain, but also
throw the football again.

He returned to the starting lineup against the New York Jets at Shea
Stadium in New York. As he threw a touchdown pass, Bradshaw felt
something inside his arm snap. His teammates cheered, as did the fans
visiting from Pittsburgh or living in the New York area. Bradshaw ran
off the field holding his elbow to his chest. He told one person on the
way to the bench and then sat down and hoped that the Jets would be
out on offense for a little while.

The Jets fumbled the ball away; the Steelers offense went back on
the field. Bradshaw threw a second touchdown pass and came off the
field. Noll asked, "You okay?" "No sir, I tore my elbow up," he re-

sponded. He had torn a ligament in the elbow. Stoudt finished the game with two more touchdown passes and one interception, and the Steelers won the game. Inside the locker room, the media asked questions about the team clinching the Central Division title. The Steelers would have an extra week off before starting the playoffs, and the hero vowed he'd be back for that big game. Memories of Bradshaw in the Jets game remained strong in the minds of some fans. One Steelers fan noted that he thought Bradshaw appeared so courageous on the field, but he also feared he had seen the last game of Bradshaw's career. Professional sports executives sensed the possibility as well. Terry O'Neil, of CBS Sports, said, "Right away I called Brad's agent and said we would love to hire Terry as a commentator." [30]

The remaining game on the schedule called for a trip to Cleveland. Pittsburgh fell behind, 16–3, and never caught up. Stoudt threw one touchdown and two interceptions, and Harris ran for only 56 yards. The Steelers had one week off while the two wild-card games took place during the Christmas holiday. Then they flew to Los Angeles to take on the Raiders, and Bradshaw stood on the visiting team's sidelines and watched.

The Steelers took a 3–0 lead in the first quarter and began another drive deep in their territory. Stoudt took the snap, backed up, and threw, but Lester Haynes picked off the ball and went in for the touchdown. With Bradshaw, the team found itself in situations like this and expected to go back onto the field and march for a touchdown of their own. But the offense stalled, and in the second quarter, Marcus Allen ran in for one touchdown and the Raiders got a field goal to take a 10-point lead. The third quarter featured three more Raiders touchdowns to one for the visitors. The scoreboard read 38–10, and neither team added any additional points. "To stand there and watch, and not be able to play was sickening. I don't want it to end like this," Bradshaw said. [31]

Oakland owner Al Davis doubted Bradshaw's presence on the field would have changed the result. Davis talked highly of his current Raiders team, but also about how close his old Raiders teams were to the Steelers during the championship years. He claimed that Bradshaw wanted to play for the Raiders when he sat on the Steelers bench in 1974. When Davis still sat on the competition committee, he recalled talking about the best quarterbacks: "Don Shula liked Griese, Tex Schramm liked Roger Staubach, and they thought I would pick Snake,

Kenny Stabler, but I picked Bradshaw. He's the best, the most productive quarterback I've ever seen."[32]

The quarterback faced media questions about his health. "I think I'll be all right, but if I'm not fine, I'll retire," he said. Chuck Noll also faced the questions and responded, "Right now he's not healthy, but if he can throw the ball, we want him." The plan featured rest until April, when he would start weight training to strengthen the arm. A couple weeks later, while at Louisiana Tech's annual football banquet, Bradshaw said the elbow injury would not force him out of football. "I'm going to play," he said.[33]

The 1984 team faced uncertainty at the quarterback position. Cliff Stoudt left for the United States Football League. This latest attempt at a new professional league lasted three full seasons before a few of its on-field innovations and many of its star players and coaches became part of the NFL. Without Stoudt, the Steelers traded with the Miami Dolphins for quarterback David Woodley. Facing reporters' questions, Noll explained the move by saying, "We're not sure about Terry. We expect it will be just like it was last year with respect that he hasn't had any improvement." Bradshaw responded forcefully, "If he wants opinions, he ought to call and ask me, and stop making all these comments. He doesn't talk to me. He doesn't call me, but he makes these statements. . . . My plans are to get myself ready to go to camp in July and be able to perform."[34]

Indeed, when Bradshaw came to the minicamp in May, he underwent the usual physical exam. He achieved the highest score ever on the team's physical stress exam, grading "superior" in all areas. He ran four to five miles daily and worked with weights at his ranch. Despite the ranking, his elbow remained uncooperative.

Every professional athlete is eventually faced with the decision of when to retire. There are instances when no real choice exists; a small number of professionals in football have faced catastrophic injuries that completely end their careers. One of the most famous examples involved New England Patriots wide receiver Darryl Stingley, who broke two vertebrae and had his spinal cord compressed in 1978. Another well-known event occurred in 1985, when Washington Redskins quarterback Joe Theismann broke bones in his lower right leg. Fortunately, that type of situation is rare.

Much more frequently, stars find themselves in a situation where their longtime team no longer wants them. They can be traded, elect to retire, or sign a contract with another team as a free agent after being released. One of the most famous of the trade circumstances was Johnny Unitas, who left the Colts after 17 years. He shared the role of quarterback for the San Diego Chargers with rookie Dan Fouts in 1973. Joe Namath left the Jets for the Los Angeles Rams and started four games on gimpy knees before giving way to Pat Haden. The Steelers soon put Franco Harris on this list, releasing him during training camp in 1984, before the Seattle Seahawks signed him for half the season.

The situation Bradshaw faced occurs less frequently than the star being released or traded away. In this instance, the player remains in great physical shape, and observers think he still has a few more good years left to play. The player believes what others tell him and what he wants to hear. But many players suffer from one debilitating injury that makes playing the game nearly impossible. Greg Cook of Cincinnati suffered a shoulder injury that derailed him after being named American Football League (AFL) Rookie of the Year in 1969. In 1972, Gayle Sayers, running back for the Chicago Bears, stopped playing because of a bad left knee. That same year, Bart Starr, legendary Green Bay Packers quarterback, spent 10 days in consultation with doctors about his shoulder. The pain continued, and he realized he needed to retire. Bradshaw's old friend Bert Jones retired after the 1982 season. He received a helmet to his chin that fractured a cervical vertebra, ending his career. Later in the 1984 season, running back Billy Sims of the Detroit Lions suffered a knee injury that abruptly forced him to end his career.[35]

Two weeks after the minicamp, Bradshaw weighed his options. He could hope for his elbow to heal naturally or undergo an operation. His arm felt "deader than road kill." Surgeons informed him that the elbow would take anywhere from one year to 18 months to recover. Most people believed that taking that path spelled retirement for the quarterback, but Bradshaw did not offer the media a formal announcement. He recalled informing Chuck Noll, saying, "Chuck, that's it. I can't play anymore. It's over." They shook hands; Bradshaw left for his apartment and sobbed.[36]

Both CBS Sports and NBC Sports sought to hire Bradshaw as a color commentator/analyst. After being asked what would happen if

ailing Pittsburgh Steelers QB Terry Bradshaw became available, a CBS
spokesman replied, "We'll be interested. Terry O'Neil would just make
adjustments to the present roster." O'Neil promised Bradshaw that he
would not have to perform an audition, while NBC expected one. Bradshaw selected CBS and elected to arrange for the announcement of his
retirement to occur during the announcement of the hiring at CBS
headquarters in New York City. Photographs featured Pat Summerall,
CBS broadcaster, along with two CBS Sports executives. There were no
photographs of Bradshaw standing with Steelers executives.

Bradshaw chose not to hold his retirement announcement in Pittsburgh despite the advice of the team's public relations director, Joe
Gordon. The quarterback said he didn't want to make a fuss about it.
"That was my style," he quipped. Bradshaw believed that he would have
had an emotional breakdown in Pittsburgh, saying, "I couldn't stand in
front of my friends and the writers I came to like and respect and not
completely fall apart. I just couldn't have done it, although that is the
way most players do it. Right or wrong, that's the way it had to be."[37]

A quick survey of retirements of star players indicated that most
have held press conferences in their team's offices. Johnny Unitas held
a press conference for his, saying, "I hate to quit playing football." Starr
held his inside the Packers' offices. Longtime Kansas City Chiefs quarterback Len Dawson asked the team to hastily arrange a media conference for Saturday. While mentioning his retirement, Dawson also informed everyone that he signed a three year contract to work with NBC
doing football coverage. Bradshaw's teammates confirmed that a press
conference with the team was often the way a player announced their
retirement. Safety Mike Wagner stepped up and "handled his last Steeler press conference the way he always handled himself on the field. In
the midst of an emotional moment, he was composed." Joe Green did
the same one year later, followed by Jack Ham in the winter of 1983.[38]

In westerns, the lawman or hero who helps the town eventually has
to retire or leave town. The movie contains a scene where the hero says
good-bye to the gathered townspeople or a special group of them. The
hero lets them know why he must take his leave; the townspeople express their appreciation for his heroic efforts. For Bradshaw, the news
articles noted that the retirement took place in New York. One fan
observed that it mattered that there was no ceremony with the team,
saying, "I knew that he wasn't getting along with either the front office

or Coach Noll. I figured it was Noll, but I wasn't sure why and who was to blame." Steelers fans did not have the opportunity to say farewell to their longtime, ailing hero and quarterback icon.[39]

The relationship between the expectations of Steelers fans and Bradshaw's comments, opinions, and actions would become more complicated during the next few years. Fans often want their favorite players to continue to look back on their playing career and revel in the good ol' days, like they do. They want former teammates to like one another and participate in reunions—be the perfect team. Bradshaw often went his own way and expressed his thoughts in his new position as a color commentator for CBS Sports.

8

PRESS BOX VIEW

The Colorful, Unfiltered Commentator

"I have not been able to determine whether Bradshaw considers himself (a) a singer, (b) Brent Musburger's court jester, or (c) a commentator in position to provide rare insights."—William Taaffe, columnist[1]

After years of participating in the NFL playoffs, the Steelers finished the 1980 season with a 9–7 record, situating them in third place in the Central Division. Producer Terry O'Neil had recently come over to CBS Sports after working at ABC. He saw Terry Bradshaw as a natural for television and hired him to appear as a guest commentator on the network during the upcoming playoffs. As the quarterback described it, "I wore a cowboy hat and sang 'On the Road Again,' and yukked it up with Brent [Musburger]."[2] He appeared to not take the job very seriously.

A NEW CAREER

Bradshaw returned to CBS to cover the playoffs the next season, talking in the studio during the pregame, halftime, and postgame segments. The network also assigned Bradshaw and Roger Staubach to do postgame interviews, with Bradshaw getting to interview the winning team. But Dallas lost to the San Francisco 49ers in the NFC Championship

Game, known as "The Catch," and no one felt comfortable sending Staubach in to ask his former teammates how they felt after the loss. Bradshaw accepted the switch and the unenviable assignment of interviewing the heartbroken Cowboys. Players were furious, cussing and throwing helmets, and Bradshaw had prepared questions for the winners. Fortunately, Tom Landry created an atmosphere where Bradshaw felt comfortable asking questions that needed to be asked.

After completing the stint with CBS's football coverage by working the wrap-around coverage of Super Bowl XVI in 1982, some network executives liked Bradshaw's work. They realized he enjoyed stock car racing and hired him to work in the network's coverage for both the Daytona 500 and Michigan 400 later that year.

Two years later, during the summer of 1984, Bradshaw and CBS executives scheduled a press conference to take place at the network's headquarters in Manhattan. He simultaneously announced his retirement from the NFL and his joining the CBS Sports television crew. "Terry has excelled in everything he's tried . . . I'm very excited and happy to have him join our staff of NFL announcers," said Peter A. Lund, executive vice president of CBS Sports. As O'Neil phrased it later, Bradshaw would be a good broadcaster because he lacked the filter others had between their heads and their mouths. Bradshaw spoke at the luncheon. "This is a proud moment for me and a sad one," he said. Later he gave an unvarnished opinion of his current situation, saying, "I wouldn't be surprised if my booth career turns out to be not unlike my football career—I'll start slow and be good in time."[3]

O'Neil and others wanted to get Bradshaw some practice. The CBS staff started by having the quarterback practice calling a game in the studio to a videotape machine. At that time, fans demanded more than competency from the announcers and wanted something that would distinguish one announcer or color commentator from another. CBS executives teamed Bradshaw with announcer, Verne Lundquist, who had joined CBS in 1982. The broadcaster lived in Dallas and had broadcast Cowboys games for many years. He also worked on a variety of assignments, ranging from boxing and golf to the North American Soccer League while working for ABC Sports beginning in the mid-1970s.

The pair got along great, but Lundquist observed that they were among the lower-ranked duos at the network. This was because most of the games that they called were for the Atlanta Falcons, Tampa Bay

Buccaneers, and New Orleans Saints. At least the Saints won their first five games, which were called by the Louisiana native. "We reached 10 percent of the market at best," Lundquist observed. Several of these contests were called "point-to-point games." In these instances, the market for the game consisted of two markets, one for the home team and the other for the visitor's broadcast station. One Falcons–Buccaneers game that the pair announced was blacked out in the Tampa Bay area. The veteran announcer knew that the game drew such low interest that only one station in Atlanta received the feed. Despite working for a national network, Lundquist had fun and used the Atlanta broadcasting station's call letters one time before cutting to a commercial break.[4]

Bradshaw thought the network assigned him these games because of his Southern accent. The people from the South could understand the way he talked, whereas those from other parts of the nation could not. At the same time, Lundquist thought the network executives believed the games with fewer viewers would serve as a good practice ground for their new hire. The quarterback quickly discovered that there were many aspects to the job, including knowing the team's style of play and the names of the players, and realizing when to speak. It took one quarter in his first game for Bradshaw to realize that he could not see the field well, let alone the players' numbers. He also found that he lacked the necessary preparation.

However, guidance from Lundquist and O'Neil helped Bradshaw improve his announcing throughout the course of that first season in 1984. Another important adjustment came with connecting Bradshaw and producer David Michaels via an earpiece in Bradshaw's ear during the games. He found the earpiece with the little voice disconcerting but appreciated the insight he received from the broadcasting truck, for example, "Terry, look at the left guard. Watch what happens here."[5]

Bradshaw and Lundquist also adopted a version of the famous telestrator that John Madden used to illustrate plays. They used a real blackboard, calling it "Terry's blackboard," and the color commentator used chalk or markers to illustrate the plays on the field. They also adapted well to another O'Neil innovation: sitting down with the coaches before the game to gain insight into the upcoming game. One of Lundquist's favorite games in their first years together involved the Cincinnati Bengals and the Dallas Cowboys. Coach Sam Wyche had been liberal in sharing a strategy during the pregame, and it helped call out a big running play during the telecast. "A lot of coaches share information, but a lot don't. I was thrilled that he trusted us not to run and tell the Cowboys about that play," Lundquist noted.[6]

The pair established a routine that included Lundquist playing straight man to Bradshaw's funny comments and stories. Their interaction came naturally, as did Bradshaw's responses to questions from Lundquist, like why a certain player was struggling. "Verne that guy really isn't any good," Bradshaw once said. The preparation and some of the other grunt work took more time to become part of the weekly routine.[7]

TAKING OVER THE BOOTHS

Despite Bradshaw's improvement and some other transitions from successful athlete to announcer, a television critic in Washington, DC, observed the trend to include more ex-jocks with dismay. Because former San Francisco 49ers quarterback John Brodie performed as color commentator one time and announcer another, he wondered if former jocks would usurp the play-by-play announcer position as they had the color commentary one. Longtime baseball announcer Red Barber noted that the concern with selling product became paramount with televised sports. Barber claimed this change favored the athlete, who could sell products that a regular sports announcer could not. He predicted that athletes would take over the announcing jobs.[8]

The fear of a takeover by ex-athletes proved somewhat overwrought. The overall number of broadcasting teams at the CBS network dropped from 10 or 11 to a steady 8 beginning in 1981, and lasting into the twenty-first century. Six of the eight play-by-play announcers on the CBS coverage of football in the early 1980s were nonplayers. That number had dropped to five by the mid-1980s, when Bradshaw joined the network. During the final year of Bradshaw's tenure as a color commentator in 1989, the networks filled seven of eight announcer spots with "trained or college-educated" broadcasters. Color commentators would continue to be former players and coaches, and most critics agreed that they brought a required knowledge to the booth.

While former football players and coaches may have the knowledge, several sportswriters and television experts criticized them for their lack of speaking abilities. Famous sports announcer Howard Cosell grumbled in a talk to the Associated Press that the country had fallen under the grip of the sports syndrome. The syndrome featured two major parts: First, it asserted that sports were sacrosanct; second, it implied that sports were mysteries that only former players could understand. Cosell believed neither held true, and he was further irritated by the fact that the former athletes working the games proved themselves to be superbly unqualified to communicate with the masses.[9]

Cosell placed Bradshaw in this second category. George Bell Jr. wrote, "[O]n any given day you may hear Terry Bradshaw . . . struggling to be a communicator." Others harped on Bradshaw for talking too fast or being overly analytical. The quarterback apparently heard it all. "There's been lots of criticism," he told a reporter. He suggested a solution: "Why don't you just cut off my arms? That'll take away my enthusiasm, and that's reflected in the way I talk." The result would be that he would sound like everyone else. He mentioned trying to slow down, but he couldn't.[10]

Regardless of this small amount of criticism, CBS Sports executives continued to believe in Bradshaw's abilities. He had the "big personality" and the ability to say what he thought, both of which made him unique. Those attributes also made him a notable figure who could stand out from the rest and earn strong ratings for the games and publicity for the network and its products. The pairing with Lundquist said a lot about how much the CBS leadership trusted him to guide their new jewel in his first year. The feeling was that the Lundquist–Bradshaw team held the number-two position, although every team would work a game that was broadcast to most of the country. "Verne had the experience of living in the South and was a great mentor," O'Neil thought. Lundquist did a good job of putting Bradshaw's personality on display while adapting it to the needs of the broadcast and the booth. The play-by-play announcer, like producer O'Neil, realized the gem Bradshaw's personality could be.[11]

O'Neil wanted to put Bradshaw's personality on display in other scenarios when football season ended. He also produced the weekend sports program, then known as the *CBS Sports Spectacular*. O'Neil changed the name of the show to *CBS Sports Saturday* and *Sports*

Sunday, and brought in a breaking news focus and a diminished focus on junk sports. The producer used Bradshaw on some episodes. His personal favorite featured Bradshaw covering a 1,000-mile sled dog race. His big personality enabled him to fill the race time. One Japanese man recognized Terry and told him how much he liked him. O'Neil remembered, "When Terry was about to leave he asked the man how you say 'bye' in Japanese, and the man told him, 'sayonara!' Bradshaw said, 'I heard that in a John Wayne movie!'"

O'Neil started the 1985 season with the intention of keeping his announcing teams intact and providing each one with the chance to cover a major game. Each of the teams did receive a prime market slot during the 1985 season. O'Neil and staff did that intentionally to provide opportunities and keep from rotating in a pattern that might indicate who had a position above or below anyone else. Lundquist believed that rankings existed and understood that when starting out you are going to get those games that draw limited attention.[12]

At the halfway point of the season, *Sport* magazine gave fans the opportunity to comment about football broadcasters in a national poll. The magazine subscriber base featured many "mega fans," people into the statistics and highly knowledgeable about the game. The editorial focus of the magazine switched to a "sports in-depth" focus that catered to this readership. These fans named Pat Summerall and Dick Enberg as the best play-by-play announcers. The San Diego-based sportswriter commenting on the poll results generally agreed with these choices. John Madden ran away from the competition among color commentators, gaining 62 percent of the vote, with Merlin Olsen finishing a distant second, with 22 percent. Bradshaw did not appear on the list; however, in the category of broadcaster fans wanted exiled from the booth, Bradshaw finished third, gaining 7 percent of the votes. O. J. Simpson topped the list, with 33 percent, and Joe Namath finished second, with 20 percent. The sportswriter expressed surprise at these results. He thought Simpson knew the game and was surprised Bradshaw appeared on the list at all. He noted, "CBS considers him an up-and-comer."[13]

The Bradshaw–Lundquist team received its big-market game of the year in early December. The Cowboys–Giants game went well, and the duo performed very well. Lundquist related, "[Bradshaw] has not been able to learn his craft in a vacuum. He has had to learn on the job. And he has worked very hard. For us, getting the Cowboys–Giants assignment is a testimony to Bradshaw's growth." The announcer pointed to an earlier game involving the Cincinnati Bengals as their best work, stating, "We watched the tape [of the game after it aired] and thought we handled the thing pretty darn well."[14]

Strong performances from their broadcasters mattered significantly to the NFL and the network executives. The league's television ratings had slipped dramatically in the past few years. The NFL and television leaders tried to figure out the reasons behind this drop in the once-strong ratings. Experts tossed out rationales ranging from the games being too long and having too many commercials to the officiating or the announcing teams. Maybe it was none of the above; maybe the games stunk. Verne Lundquist stated, "There's one reason why ratings are up—good football games. I'm one of those guys who believes the game is everything." While he knew people did not watch a game because of him and Bradshaw, Lundquist knew that people listened. He trusted himself and Bradshaw to know that the pair did not pull punches in their announcing. Their main boss agreed. "I think Lundquist and Bradshaw have had a great year," said O'Neil.[15]

NEW BOSS, REVISED STYLE

Bradshaw and Lundquist may have appreciated the comments from their boss; however, change arrived inside the suites of CBS Sports. A move to consolidate titles led to the departure of the network's executive producer of the NFL, Terry O'Neil, and the promotion of Ted Shaker. Newspapers and other outlets started buzzing with wonder about Bradshaw's future at the network since O'Neil had been one of his biggest supporters. While Bradshaw had improved a lot during the previous season, he had only one more year remaining in his contract. Reportedly, one influential man upstairs at the network thought the former quarterback needed to straighten out his goofiness, and Shaker would likely be listening to broadcasts and the executive's opinions.

New leader Shaker thought the network had a great deal of talent. "I've had the chance to work with some great talent," he said. While he believed in the importance of announcers, Shaker thought the game had the paramount position. He added, "One of the things I always found funny about sports television was the number of people who thought people were tuning in to see them as opposed to watching the game, which is a big mistake because they tune in for the game."[16]

Bradshaw described working with Shaker as being like playing under a new head coach. Shaker pointed out that many fans watched football games because they liked the sport. He wanted Bradshaw to stop being silly, a strong indication that Bradshaw had behaved like few other color commentators that had come before him. Instead, Shaker argued that Bradshaw's job involved offering insightful analysis in an entertaining way. The other important factor for a color commentator could not be taught: the ability to think on one's feet and respond quickly and appropriately to circumstances in the game. An example of Bradshaw and Lundquist's execution of this occurred after Joe Montana fumbled a snap during a 49ers game. The CBS cameramen turned their attention to the men in the television booth after Bradshaw asked Lundquist to bend over into a center's position. Bradshaw stood behind Lundquist's butt and attempted to accept the roll of toilet paper into his hands. He explained to the viewers that a low butt made it tough for a big and tall quarterback like Joe Montana to get in there and take the ball. After requesting for Verne to raise his butt higher, Bradshaw said, "Look at this butt. See how high it is. Now look and see how tall Montana can stand under the sun."[17]

Like a head coach, Shaker also made different use of his personnel and several switches in his pairing of announcers. He put Tim Ryan and Terry Bradshaw together and situated Verne Lundquist with multiple different partners, including John Madden and Pat Haden, among several others. To this day, Lundquist wonders, "Still not sure why they split us up?" The change in announcing partner seemed much like getting new offensive personnel, Bradshaw thought. Tim Ryan came from Canada and spoke fast and frequently. Bradshaw looked for his spots to make comments. He thought Ryan was tough on him, so he cut back on his folksy comments and looked at the game from a gambler's point of view. This viewpoint led to a streamlining of his thinking about the game and helped Bradshaw make sharper, more unvarnished statements.[18]

Some in the media appeared to concentrate on only Bradshaw's odd comments. One southern Virginia newspaper columnist noted, "Bradshaw recently declared that an unexpected play was part of the team's 'imaginary offense.'" Still, he and Ryan enjoyed a few big-market games, like the one where the Minnesota Vikings visited the New York Giants in November. They also covered the Giants again when they went to play the Washington Redskins in December with the division title on the line. The assignment included an interview with Redskins quarterback Jay Schroeder to air on the highly rated pregame show. Bradshaw declared that Schroeder, "reminds me of me." Among the quarterback's positive attributes, Bradshaw said, "He's aggressive. He's got a cannon (of a right arm). He plays fearless. He gives you the impression that everything is under control. And in a business where there are a lot of jerks, he strikes me as a nice person."[19]

The effort that Bradshaw expended during the changes seemed to benefit him professionally. One sportswriter from Seattle listed Bradshaw among his choices for an "all-star" team of broadcasters. He selected only the top announcers and color commentators to work the NFL playoffs and gave Bradshaw a first-round game. He argued, "Bradshaw is still rough-hewn, but his likeable personality and country-boy humor are appealing." He teamed him with Ray Scott, who was a solid announcer who offended CBS management. Others agreed with show business magazine *Variety* when it mentioned that Bradshaw's work was improving.[20]

In the new season, the executives played their latest game of mix and match. CBS Sports executives switched up all the announcer pairings, except the top one of Summerall and Madden. Bradshaw moved to a pairing with Dick Stockton. While one analysis called it a promotion of Bradshaw to the number-two position behind Madden, another take placed the pairing behind Tim Ryan and Joe Theismann. Verne Lundquist received a new partner in the form of former Eagles coach Dick Vermeil. The executives gave Bradshaw a contract extension for two seasons. "I guess I do it well. . . . CBS hired me because I speak my mind," Bradshaw noted. This would hopefully remove the old Li'l Abner stereotype for good. As Bradshaw said, "Some people thought I was a clod, that I couldn't stand up before a crowd and speak an intelligent sentence. That was insulting."[21]

THE REPLACEMENTS

Soon the NFL would be presenting something as insulting as the negative comments being slung at Bradshaw. The threat of a players' strike
loomed after the close of the 1986 season. By early September, player
representatives for the teams realized that the chances of reaching a
collective bargaining agreement and avoiding a strike shrank each day.
The players sought free agency and a larger share of the sport's reve-
nue, and the owners wanted to grant neither. The owners and management of the 28 teams made plans to return to games with nonunion
players on October 4.

As would be expected, few network announcers commented on the
labor strife during the weeks before the walkout. On the day of the first
games with replacement players, some media commentators expected
little commentary regarding the circumstances surrounding the games.
As one said in summarizing the situation, "NFL game announcers, as a
group, have never been known for breaking new ground journalistically,
and viewers rarely seem to mind. Most announcers Sunday covered the
strike games as business as usual." The CBS pairing of Hank Stram and
Tim Brant praised the replacement players, and Merlin Olsen and Dick
Enberg at NBC offered a few comments about plays of "NFL quality."
Brent Musburger called the games "entertaining." He did interview
Pittsburgh Steelers president Dan Rooney and asked, "Isn't management trying to break the union?"[22]

A few made direct comments expressing their dissatisfaction with
the replacement games. Bob Costas closed the NBC pregame show by
saying the games were a "significant blow to the integrity of the game,"
while on *NFL on CBS*, Irv Cross called a replacement game a "black
day for the NFL." Bradshaw's comments were strong about the quality
of play. When his partner Dick Stockton said Bears coach Mike Ditka
told him he was considering keeping quarterback Mike Hohensee when
the strike was over, Bradshaw called the statement ridiculous. The commentator took a lighthearted approach to the game. He reported that
Hohensee was not going to be fazed by the prospect of a small crowd,
telling viewers, "He told me, 'That's great. Now, instead of hand signals,
the coaches can shout the plays to us.'"[23]

Bradshaw and Stockton occasionally put a nice spin on the proceed-
ings. "Dick, I'm really impressed . . . well, not impressed," Bradshaw

said to his partner. Later he observed, "You ask these kids why they came out here, you keep hearing one word: opportunity. That's what it's all about." Bradshaw then took a jab at Indianapolis Colts quarterback Gary Hogeboom, who crossed the picket line and had thrown five touchdown passes at last count. "Hogeboom's gotta be proud today. Five TD's. Gosh, that's great," Bradshaw said, sarcastically.[24]

The NFL's replacement games occurred during a time when unions were losing significant membership. The loss of manufacturing and other large-scale enterprises in the United States cut deep into the membership of industrial unions, including the United Auto Workers (UAW) and United Steelworkers. In 1979, union membership was at a high of 24 percent. It dropped to 17 percent by 1987. Many of the unions, for instance, in the automobile industry, found themselves forced to accept collective bargaining agreements that offered lower salaries and less benefits to new employees. Like the NFL players, some memberships, like the Air Line Pilots Association, rejected lesser agreements and discovered management's plans to use replacement workers.

Here, the critique by Robert Lipsyte and Howard Cosell that the "jockocracy" in the announcing booth lacked journalism training became more significant. Brent Musburger's question to Dan Rooney represented one of the few comments making the connection between the NFL's replacement games and similar activities occurring throughout the United States. The former players often lacked the training or had disinterest in making these types of connections to larger trends. Instead, an athlete brought a name, which helped sell products, and that was what the advertisers paying for television spots wanted; the corporations running the television networks, the NFL, and the companies selling the products during the games preferred for the focus to be on the game and favored a lack of controversy, as controversy might take viewers' attention away from the products. Cosell and others brought journalism to the sports world in the more turbulent and questioning times of the 1960s and 1970s. By the late 1980s, the country held a more conservative attitude and saw that attitude reflected in their sports coverage.

During the second week of the replacement player games, CBS's pregame show featured college football highlights and baseball playoff discussions. Bradshaw offered interesting criticism of the owners and team organizations who delayed before putting their replacement teams together, thus either getting poorer-quality players or not giving them a chance to practice together before the start of the games. "Some of the coaches got caught. They didn't do their homework," he said. That said, Bradshaw followed up the truthful observation, "As long as this goes on, the fans are saying, 'Who cares?'"[25]

By the end of week two, that question had an answer. Whereas week one witnessed small drops in ratings, ratings for the networks fell to all-time lows for NFL games during the second week. Before the start of the third week, the strike had ended, but the replacement games continued for one more week. "Everyone's dreading this week," one network source said. "The announcers don't want to do games without regular players. The producers don't want to. And the business people are dreading the numbers they expect to see."[26]

OBSESSIONS AND LISTS

Once the aftershock of the replacement games disappeared, everyone in the football world could return to their usual activities. One of those activities for the observers and commentators on sports television involved compiling lists that provided readers with some information, if not insight. Like many of the listings complied by observers today, these lists provided expert ranking of who was good and who was bad in the realm of football announcers. One syndicated columnist argued that during most NFL games, much of the talk goes nowhere. "Most analysts are terrible," Norman Chad concluded. After listing Summerall and Madden as the best, he put Al Michaels and Dan Dierdorf second. Lundquist and Vermeil finished third, and Stockton and Bradshaw finished sixth out of 13 teams. Chad believed Bradshaw had improved but added he "still says enough dumb things per telecast to fill all sides of a long-playing double album."[27]

Regardless of the opinions of critics, Bradshaw did get attention from the players. He and Lundquist returned to their partnership, to the pleasure of both. During the 1988 exhibition season, Bradshaw commented on Darrin Nelson sitting out in a contract dispute with the Vikings. Nelson heard Bradshaw and said, "I got a kick out of listening to Terry Bradshaw take a shot at me about sitting out."[28]

Bradshaw continued his regular critical comments. He continued his usual bombardment of Chuck Noll, arguing that things needed to change in Pittsburgh. During his weekly commentary on KDKA-TV, the former quarterback said, "I think Chuck Noll needs to take a serious, hard look at his future." The Steelers had a 1–6 record for the second time in three seasons. The Steelers' public relations director objected to these commentaries. Joe Gordon called Bradshaw and said, "Who do you think you are! You used to be a Steeler, and you owe us!" Bradshaw saw his comments as part of doing his job and received more attempts to "persuade" him to saying nice things about the team.[29]

These comments did not alter the choices made by the team's leadership, but they did have a negative effect on Steelers fans. Many began to resent the continuous attacks, and some questioned Bradshaw's sense of loyalty. They appeared to prefer that the former quarterback stop his attacks because they disliked seeing two of their icons at odds with one another and the resulting internal dissention. Many believed that any criticism needed to be kept within the team.

The Bradshaw comments received attention in a variety of regions throughout the country. With the newsworthiness of the intramural drama and the syndicated nature of the news business, the Bradshaw opinion of the situation in Pittsburgh spread from Kentucky to Minnesota to Los Angeles. The articles noted that some fans perceived Bradshaw as being disloyal, but more fans thought his words demonstrated his independence.

Television critics returned to offer midterm grades to the various NFL announcers at work during the 1988 season, and *Sports Illustrated* hosted the results. It appeared that critic William Taaffe had adopted the bell curve. Among the 11 groupings, he gave "As" to four play-by-play announcers and two "As" to color commentators. Bradshaw scored one of the four "Bs" granted to color men. There were five "Cs" and four "Ds" granted among the color and play-by-play men as well. Taaffe defined Bradshaw's coming into his own as putting away the cowboy hats and down-home humor, and adopting suits and glasses. "His twang can be grating, but he's honest and enthusiastic, and dispenses well-reasoned criticism," reasoned Taaffe.[30]

Despite being merely opinions, these lists at times became news stories in themselves. Columnist John Freeman took Taaffe's list and offered his own ratings. He doled out only four "As," two in each grouping of announcers. Bradshaw earned a B–, one of 11 "Bs" dispended. Freeman provided the following assessment: "Bradshaw sounds like a good ol' boy, which he is, but he's not afraid to speak his mind." He showed this attitude at his own enshrinement into the Pro Football Hall of Fame.[31]

THE PRO FOOTBALL HALL OF FAME

A few years before his first year of eligibility for the Pro Football Hall of Fame, the former Steeler stated, "My relationship with the Steelers is zero. I like the Rooneys, but when I think of the Steelers, I think of Chuck. If I get in the Hall of Fame, you can bet your sweet bleep I won't have him presenting me with the trophy." Bradshaw received a telephone call from the Hall's director, Pete Elliott, that he had made it in his first year, the summer of 1989, and faced a choice about who would introduce him.

Through 1988, the overwhelming majority of inductees to the Hall of Fame in Canton, Ohio, selected a coach, top brass, or former teammate to perform their introductions. A handful picked a former high school or college coach, for example, former Steelers linebacker Jack Ham, who had Joe Paterno from Penn State University introduce him. Two decades earlier, Jim Brown had asked a friend and attorney to perform his introduction, while Mel Blount, who was also part of the class of 1989, asked Steelers president Dan Rooney to present him. Bradshaw selected his friend and colleague Verne Lundquist to give his introduction.[32]

Lundquist focused his presentation on the role of sports in all civilizations. He said sports provided everyone with the opportunity to become the best they can. The athlete served as a mirror to our own humanity as they failed to attain or gained victories on the field. Bradshaw showed fans his humanity and allowed fans to watch him prevail. As Bradshaw stepped up to the podium and started speaking, he roused the partisan Steelers and other fans, saying, "Let's go deep!" and hurling an imaginary football. "I always thought you were supposed to win. If a receiver is open, what do you do with the ball? Throw it!" The hall of famers seated behind him howled with glee. Lundquist observed, "Terry's got an evangelical furor when he speaks, and that is very compelling." Obviously, that came from years of listening to sermons at the various churches he had attended since childhood. He thanked Lynn Swann, John Stallworth, Franco Harris, Rocky Bleier, Mike Webster, and, finally, Art Rooney, saying, "I know you're watching Art. I love you. Thank you," as he pointed to the sky. [33]

Bradshaw also held the crowd accountable. He reminded them, despite their protests, that they booed him during the early years. Those associated with the Steelers expressed their happiness for their former quarterback. Blount said, "What Bradshaw meant to the Steelers was what the captain means to a ship. If I had to pick a guy to go to war with, it would be Terry Bradshaw." Dan Rooney wrote that being elected to the Hall on the first year of eligibility represented one of the best ways to measure the best against the best. His former quarterback passed that measure as a real team leader with no quit in him. A decade later, one fan who had seen Bradshaw's speech when he gave it saw it again posted on a website and commented, "Terry Bradshaw's Hall of Fame speech is the most awesome speech ever. It brought back all the emotion from hearing it for the first time in '89!!!" [34]

The news conference before the ceremonies featured questions regarding Bradshaw's selection for his presenter. He sounded frustrated and a bit annoyed, commenting, "It's the greatest day of my life, and I get nailed down here." He would have chosen Art Rooney, but the Steelers patriarch had passed away. "That's the only person that would have represented me," he revealed. In keeping with his image as a truth-teller, he told the assembled media and others listening, "I'm not going to have some athlete or coach present me who I'm not going to see ever again." Articles mentioned the "stir" Bradshaw supposedly created a week later. [35]

Curiously, one year earlier, no one had seemed focused on the choice of former Minnesota Viking Alan Page for his presenter. Page selected Willarene Beasley, principal of North Community High School in Minneapolis, to give his introduction. Clearly, Beasley had nothing to do with the Minnesota Vikings. Beasley stated in his introduction of Page that education and sports must go together. Several articles highlighted that Page used the induction as an opportunity to discuss the importance of education. While not a controversial subject, Page used the Hall of Fame as a platform and took the event away from football and the NFL. But that did not register a stir. Bradshaw did, however, because in his openness, he declared that he did not feel close to the Steelers organization or former players.

The openness and free flow of opinions continued. When NBC Sports executives hired two new announcers, Bradshaw provided some commentary about the choices, relating, "I think the first thing they had to do was get headlines, so they cleaned house to generate those head-lines and get Bill Walsh and O. J. Simpson." Bradshaw questioned Walsh's immediate placement on the top announcing team, saying, "Walsh is smart, but the question is, Can he condense his remarks in 20 seconds where the average fan can understand it?" Reporters reminded the CBS commentator who was behind hiring the two men. "O'Neil and I are good friends," said Bradshaw. But he could not resist another humorous comment, adding, "He hired me when NBC offered me virtually nothing, although he gave me $100,000 and Walsh $750,000." Bradshaw reiterated that Madden held the number-one color commen-tator spot at CBS and that there was no room for him to become number one. He and Verne Lundquist remained a partnership in the clear number-two slot.[36]

Being number two never sat well with Bradshaw, as he explained in *Looking Deep*. Bradshaw's new book with Buddy Martin came on the market as the new season began. Summed up by one sportswriter as a chronicle of the difficult relationship between the quarterback and his coach, the book created a storm in Pittsburgh. On radio stations throughout the Pittsburgh region, many fans expressed a great deal of unhappiness with Bradshaw concerning the rift between him and the team. The quarterback declined to sit for interviews with members of the Pittsburgh media. "I got tired of the negative," he said, sure in his mind that he would continue to speak his feelings and what he thought was the truth. On such national programs as *The Larry King Show*, Steelers fans called in when Bradshaw appeared to discuss the book, and many told him how much they loved him.[37]

At work as a color commentator, Bradshaw continued that tradition. He received plaudits from critics for his insight during games. A sports-writer in New England gave him, John Madden, and Joe Namath spe-cial awards for having the guts to challenge a referee's call or coach's decision. Bradshaw sometimes called out owners, saying, for instance, that only an "idiot" would fire Phoenix Cardinals coach Gene Stallings. Owner Bill Bidwell did agree with the firing, and the team lost their last five games of the 1989 season, won only five games the next year, and came away with a mere four wins in each of the next two seasons under their new coach.

Near the end of the 1989 NFL season, Bradshaw's reputation as a color commentator soared. He expressed more direct criticism of players' performances on the field than ever before. As an example, Bradshaw observed, "It's important to tell why the receiver got to the post. Just saying he got to the post isn't enough. You can see he did that. But who screwed up to let him get to the post? I've got to point that out." After six years in the announcing booth, Bradshaw had a good sense of his profession. "A lot of athletes who go into the broadcast booth have the tendency to be reserved with their criticisms because of relationships built up from their playing days," he declared. He admitted to being outside that circle now. Indeed, such direct and unfiltered critiques resulted in fewer players being open to talk with him before games. "A lot of players won't talk to me now. In a way, that's the greatest compliment," the former quarterback said matter-of-factly. He had developed his own unique style in the booth.[38]

Still, Bradshaw would be supportive of specific players if he saw something of himself in them. This proved particularly true of quarterbacks. His empathy seemed only natural after his experience. As former teammate Andy Russell, a linebacker, documented, "The NFL can be a very harsh place for a young quarterback. I was just as confused as he was in my rookie year, made just as many mistakes. The difference was that no one knew it. With a quarterback, everyone knows it."[39]

As noted earlier, Bradshaw applauded the play of quarterback Jay Schroeder, ranking him as one of the top 10 quarterbacks in the league in 1986. He bestowed the high praise of "natural leader" on Dallas Cowboys quarterback Kevin Sweeney two years later. The team cut him at the end of the 1988 season. Brett Favre represented the one top-flight quarterback Bradshaw supported. "Brett Favre's a great quarterback, and if I have a best friend playing in the NFL, it's Favre," he said. Yet, Bradshaw decided to root against Favre's Green Bay Packers in Super Bowl. Bradshaw's empathy figured prominently in that decision. He revealed, "But in my heart of hearts, I don't want John [Elway, quarterback of Green Bay's opponent, the Denver Broncos] to join Jim Kelly as the only quarterbacks to lose four Super Bowls."[40]

But another young rookie with a lot of potential caught Bradshaw's attention. He observed, "I watch quarterbacks closely, and Vinny is as much like me emotionally as any quarterback I've ever seen. This is a soft kid, and I think you have to treat him differently. This kid can play. In time, he'll grow up." Like Bradshaw, Vinny Testaverde became the first selection in the NFL Draft. The Tampa Bay Buccaneers had a 2–14 record in 1986. Unlike Bradshaw, Testaverde would first learn the game behind veteran Steve DeBerg; however, Testaverde played six games that year and had a 0–4 record (the other two losses were assigned to a different quarterback). He became the starter and salvaged little on two poor teams. During one season, Testaverde sat down in an interview with Terry Bradshaw and admitted he was colorblind.[41]

Tampa Bay fans launched attacks with placards and billboards throughout the stadium. One bright blue billboard said, "Vinny thinks this is orange." Of course, Vinny could see this difference. Since during games one team wore dark and the other white jerseys, his color confusion had no influence on the game. But fans watched Bradshaw on television and took the information to register their anger at how badly their team played.

SUPER BOWL OPINIONS

Bradshaw would have further opportunities to provide his commentary when CBS broadcast Super Bowl XXIV at the end of the 1989 season. It featured the San Francisco 49ers going up against the Denver Broncos. While Pat Summerall and John Madden would broadcast the game, Bradshaw, along with Mike Ditka, Dan Fouts, and Ken Stabler, formed the pregame crew of analysts. At a press conference during the two-week game hype, a reporter asked the former quarterback to compare 49ers starter Joe Montana with Broncos starter John Elway. He did. "Get serious," Bradshaw retorted. "What's John Elway ever won? . . . I mean, John Elway's very good, but he's not great. He's inconsistent." Bradshaw stayed on his roll, throwing in comments about things that bothered Elway much more than they bothered Montana and such personal comments as his opinion that Elway had been babied his entire life. "The game as I see it is a total mismatch. No contest," he concluded. Bradshaw offered a predicted score of 55–3. That last set of comments presumably did wonders for his position at the network, which wanted a close game so viewers would keep watching.[42]

Predictably, the most significant reaction to Bradshaw's comments came from areas where the Denver Broncos had a large fan base. In Colorado's neighboring state of Kansas, the media repeated many of Bradshaw's comments before providing responses from John Elway and Broncos head coach Dan Reeves. After saying Bradshaw reacted as he had because he felt jealous of Elway's large salary, Elway said, "He [Bradshaw] can stick it in his ear." When Reeves heard that Bradshaw's comments occurred at a beer company's promotional news conference, he snapped, "I think he may have had a few too many." A newspaper in Colorado claimed that Bradshaw had betrayed Elway, who thought they had a friendship. The author concluded that Bradshaw had sold out Elway for ratings.[43]

While the Elway comments drew moderate coverage, a few outlets discussed another set of strong opinions Bradshaw had shared. He examined Bill Walsh again, but this time for his work as 49ers coach the previous season. Bradshaw suggested that Walsh was trying to prove how smart he was when he benched Montana early last season. "Walsh was wanting to bench him and play his other guy, (Steve) Young, because if Young can go in there and do it, then Bill looks like another genius again," Pittsburgh's former quarterback contended. Bradshaw asserted that Montana really deserved the genius tag, and he won out in a sort of power struggle over Walsh. The former coach disagreed, stating, "Terry just doesn't know the circumstances in which Joe was unable to play. He has a tendency to make damaging remarks about people almost in an innocent way." After explaining who played when and why, Walsh commented, "It worked out beautifully. Terry doesn't understand how those kinds of remarks can mislead people."[44]

Bradshaw joined a roundtable with Ken Stabler and Dan Fouts to discuss quarterbacks of the 1980s. *NFL Today on CBS* host Brent Musburger cornered Bradshaw about the remarks he had made about Elway earlier in the week. The former helmsman refused to call Elway a great quarterback. CBS recorded Elway's reaction. He said, "Terry's been on my back since I've been in the league. He's a guy that pops off. I've got no respect for him." Bradshaw responded, "I'm not gonna apologize. It's just unfortunate, I guess, that I didn't think he was a great quarterback." Bradshaw's refusal to back down earned him credit from columnists in newspapers in the South.[45]

After the Super Bowl, one San Diego reporter offered Bradshaw kudos for his strong work during half time, particularly he and Mike Ditka engaging in good natured kidding. But Bradshaw deserved credit for proving to be prescient. The Super Bowl ended 55–10, 49ers on top. Several letters from Broncos' fans pointed out Bradshaw's assessment as accurate and sagacious, while a columnist in Fresno noted how accurate he proved to be.[46]

OPPORTUNITY

Verne Lundquist said he had thought two years earlier that Bradshaw would be more effective in a studio than he could ever be in a booth. His gestures were so big, he needed to be seen in a larger space. He knew how frustrated his partner felt being on the number-two announcing team. With Madden holding down the top position, there was no room for Bradshaw at number one. Earlier in the year, he had told the media as much, saying, "I know there's no place for me to become number one with John Madden around."[47]

The executives at CBS Sports decided during the offseason to make a momentous change in their football coverage. Reportedly, CBS Sports president Neal Pilson and executive producer Ted Shaker had made the decision to recreate their pregame show. After 15 years, the network brass fired Brent Musburger. They immediately replaced him as CBS's top baseball announcer but moved more slowly in finding a replacement for the *NFL Today* program. Some television critics, while acknowledging the show as a ratings winner, also argued that it needed revamping. As Terry O'Neil noted, the CBS pregame show always had a built-in advantage in the ratings because the NFL teams from the larger metropolitan areas aired on the network. Still, CBS's pregame ratings slipped from 7.1 in 1986 to 5.9 in 1987 to 5.7 by 1989. If voting from fans in Miami served as an indication, CBS benefited from the switch. Musburger polled as the least favorite announcer in the all-sports category, as well as among studio hosts. Interestingly, Bradshaw pulled in an almost 9 percent disapproval rating among South Florida residents.

Those residents might have enjoyed the satisfaction of having their least favorite personality removed, but the feeling wouldn't last for long. CBS executives noted that they wanted to give some of the younger people on their staff the opportunity to shine. They made a hire, moving Greg Gumbel into the position of *NFL Today on CBS* studio host. Lundquist recalled the pair flying to Orlando for the NFL meeting. Bradshaw said, "I'm really frustrated. I'm gonna go to the CBS offices and I'm gonna ask them if I can move into the studio with Greg Gumbel." They hired Bradshaw as a cohost. Since the network removed all the staff members when they let Musburger go, they brought in Pat O'Brien and Lesley Visser to round out the new crew.[48]

The new staff would reshape both *NFL Today on CBS* and pregame broadcasts. As Bradshaw moved from the press box to the studio, he took his unfiltered opinions and good ol' boy attitude with him. He soon realized that the new position enabled him to dust off some of the zaniness, a part of his personality the network executives had found less than favorable while he had been working the booth for the last half-decade.

9

STUDIO ANALYSIS AND HIJINKS

Playing "Terry Bradshaw"

"When the Bradshaw good-old-boy twang commences, pay attention. Terry's apt to say [and do] anything."—Phil Jackman, columnist[1]

After a half-decade of perfecting the craft of color commentating for NFL games, Terry Bradshaw transitioned from the press box to the television studio in the fall of 1990. Assuming the position of cohost on the one-time premiere pregame program, both the newly formatted *NFL Today* and Bradshaw faced new scrutiny. One Pittsburgh television columnist noted, "[I]f Bradshaw is outspoken enough, the show will succeed; however, Bradshaw is no sure thing." By the time he assumed the cohost position with *NFL on Fox*, Bradshaw was serving as ring master of the football pregame hour. The show contained information and opinions about professional football and much more, featuring skits, banter, and good old fun that created an atmosphere of a good time for everyone. When it proved necessary, Bradshaw spoke out on issues in a way that reflected the thoughts of many viewers.[2]

A NEW CAREER

The cohosts for the network's NFL pregame show represented an interesting contrast—Greg Gumbel's rock 'n' roll, hip, and slick personality versus Bradshaw's country and western, humorous, and wacky ways. Gumbel had a smooth, relaxed style; "Terry Bradshaw, on the other hand, is an in-your-face kind of guy," said CBS Sports executive producer Ted Shaker. The pair would work in an environment that was quite different from the old show, where Brent Musburger had rattled off scores and set story lines effortlessly. "I'll be spontaneous. I promise you that," Bradshaw said. Musburger's costars earned the attention of critics for bringing little to the program and making news with their controversial statements and fights concerning the division of the 22 minutes of on-air time.[3]

Television critics immediately expressed pleasure with the changes. One critic noted that *NFL Today* was stale in its old format. Gumbel, Bradshaw, Lesley Visser. and Pat O'Brien gave the show a jolt of much-needed enthusiasm. Bradshaw set out on his first project, which was to promote such passing offenses as the run-and-shoot. He frequently brought up how boring and unimaginative offenses like the one he ran with the Steelers were. A month in, four pregame shows received an evaluation from a television critic based in Connecticut. ESPN's hour-long programs received the nod as top products. The critic concluded that Gumbel, Visser, and Bradshaw were very good at their profession. But the critic had some fun at their expense, noting, "Watching Bradshaw diagram a blitz with CBS chalk on the CBS blackboard no doubt looks too much like algebra to the squirming eighth graders in the audience." Another critic wrote, "Though he [Bradshaw] deserves strong marks for candor, a tranquilizer for those times he gets too wound up."[4]

Despite the personnel changes, *NFL Today* remained a half-hour program, so the four members shared the 22 minutes of air time. NBC, which also ran a 30-minute program, ranked next, followed by TNT's *The Stadium Show*. Another critic from a Southern California newspaper observed that Bradshaw, with his off-the-wall remarks and busy hands, took some getting used to. Meanwhile, a group of fans in Colorado ranked Bradshaw second on the list of media people who were jerks they hated, and having those people you dislike was part of what made sports more fun to watch.[5]

PATRIOTS AND DESERT STORM

Despite Bradshaw's obvious popularity and his being the most notable name on *NFL Today*, the personnel blended their talents to give the show a successful new footing. Meanwhile, two significant events demanded their attention. Inside the professional football world, a locker room incident sparked a discussion about the role of women reporters. Outside of the sport, the United States became embroiled in a war in the Middle East.

The locker room situation was centered on sexual harassment. Five New England Patriots players had told crude jokes and two fondled their genitals as *Boston Herald* reporter Lisa Olson was covering their locker room after a *Monday Night Football* game in mid-September 1990. After Olson issued a formal complaint, team owner Victor Kiam had a brief exchange with the reporter in the locker room the following week. He turned to a member of his entourage who was standing by his side and said sotto voce, "She's a classic bitch. No wonder the players don't like her." During the next few weeks, fans showered Olson with obscenities and vile suggestions, yelling such statements as, "If you want to go into the men's locker room, you get what you deserve."[6]

After nearly a decade of being kept out of male locker rooms, *Melissa Ludtke v. Bowie Kuhn*, in 1978, had opened the doors, literally, for female reporters. The ruling determined that keeping the *Sports Illustrated* reporter out of the New York Yankees locker room during the 1977 World Series deprived her of the equal opportunity to pursue her profession. The NFL did not enact an equal access policy until 1985. Female sportswriters faced frequent discrimination, harassment, and fraternity-type pranks like wet towels being whipped against their behinds as they waded through the male athletes to reach the person they wanted to interview.

The Steelers maintained a "no-female-sportswriters-inside" policy during the early 1980s. Some sportswriters recalled waiting for stars like Bradshaw to exit the locker room, after which time the interview would be carried out in a designated area. On one occasion, Lesley Visser chased Bradshaw down in the parking lot to interview him. She started working with the *Boston Globe* in 1976, and took a lot of verbal abuse from players who were seeing a female in the locker room for the first time. "I've had to plant the flag every so often. Women in sports media have to roll with the punches," Visser said.[7]

Other sportswriters and commentators offered their perspective on the situation. A Dayton sportswriter described Patriots fans as Puritans. The abuse they directed toward Olson betrayed their male chauvinism, which basically said, "You are a woman; know your place." Unfortunately, in contrast, NBC's Will McDonough rushed a quick response to the incident and claimed Olson "exaggerated her story."[8]

The CBS pregame show made Visser the lead in the discussions on the issue. Bradshaw described how he thought the public saw the issue, contending, "We can be as lenient and we can be as accepting to the opposite sex all we want to. But there comes an area where a man just absolutely closes his mind up and says no." Mary Carillo, analyst for women's and men's tennis on CBS and ESPN, responded, "I think that's valid, a very valid point. Football always has been perceived as a male domain. Tennis isn't like that—(John) McEnroe and (Ivan) Lendl know I have the same skills, so it isn't a stretch." Cathy Barreto became the first female director for NFL games in the late 1980s. She thought that for a female announcer to be accepted, "it's going to have to be a recurring thing—not just once in a while. . . . Really no different than a man—except people aren't used to it." Bradshaw recalled growing up in Shreveport and witnessing the slow dissolution of racial segregation, another instance where people needed to get used to change. He listened to women analyze golf on television and accepted them because he learned from them. "I'm looking for knowledge. I don't care what the sex is," he said.[9]

As the New England controversy raged, the NFL universe was preparing for the playoffs, followed by the Super Bowl in January 1991. Meanwhile, members of the U.S. military and political sphere were readying to take military action against the Iraqi forces and government that had occupied Kuwait since August 1990. A coalition of military forces from numerous governments joined with the United States in attacking Iraqi forces in Kuwait in late January. Before the invasion began, the NFL's commissioner, Paul Tagliabue, decided the games could go on. Bradshaw wished he did not have to be part of Sunday's NFC Championship Game telecast, stating, "[I]f we declare war, or war is declared on us, I will have a tough time seeing any reason for playing any football." Some wondered how comments regarding football play would fare against the backdrop of war. The prediction was that the announcers would downplay the importance of the game. The Super Bowl did provide the usual amount of hype, but fans who attended witnessed the combined efforts of 18 law enforcement agencies to combat possible terrorism at the stadium resulting from the Persian Gulf War. Among the list of items banned from the facility were televisions, camcorders, still cameras, headset radios, bottles, cans, and other containers.[10]

With the end of the Super Bowl came the end of the first season of the new pregame show. The new staff proved unable to arrest the declining ratings. The ESPN pregame show eroded the ratings of both CBS and NBC during the late 1980s. By the last season in the old format, CBS's show had a 5.6 rating. With the new crew, CBS's pregame show fell to a rating of 5.1, and NBC's program had a 4.6 rating. ESPN remained in third but gained on both. The CBS show ended the season with a loss of 10 percent of its viewership.[11]

YEAR TWO

Despite the ratings, the network chose to retain the same cast for the second year; however, producer Ted Shaker promised the show would have less gossip and rumor. "Last year . . . it became tabloid TV. We'll still provide the stories, but we want to return to the days when the games were the most important thing," Shaker said. Bradshaw agreed, saying he was tired of hearing about such issues as players involved in contract negotiations.

The cast members shared time and divided responsibilities during the pregame show. While O'Brien presented a range of feature stories, Visser often provided interviews with players and coaches, and joined the cohosts for comments. Bradshaw did interviews as well, most of which he enjoyed. But when a player lied to him, especially when saying that money was not a major consideration, he would get mad and lose respect for the player. With the advent of free agency, players' salaries ballooned, making money an even more prominent topic. As a former player, Bradshaw ardently supported an "open market." He dismissed the notion that big-city teams from New York or Los Angeles could successfully buy a bunch of superstars and have a happy team. The former quarterback of a dynasty did not want the league to lose dynasties and have a bunch of middling teams making the playoffs. Having a dynasty gave people someone to root against, Bradshaw contended. [12]

Bradshaw's main job on the program remained contributing insights into specific games; however, just as often he delivered comments about players, the NFL, or something of the moment. He railed about the NFL's rule against end zone celebrations. "We're legislating ourselves to boredom. Next thing, they'll make the fans wear suits," he said. His zany but cagey persona developed "Bradshaw Ball" as a tonic to the smash-mouth football that many teams were playing. He also developed the Bradshaw Fun League, where teams played a pass-happy, man-to-man, bump-and-run style of football. "Will the NFL listen to me or pass off this low-scoring humdrum as just a phase?" he asked viewers. Newspapers throughout the eastern part of the country printed articles spreading the word of these "rules changes."

At halftime between the network games, Gumbel and Bradshaw appeared seated across from one another on the set. The pair talked through the highlights of each game. They interacted easily with one another, sharing commentary on what had happened. Bradshaw provided analysis that detailed to viewers why a play unfolded the way it did. What viewers never got to see seemed even more fun—Gumbel and Bradshaw playing practical jokes on players during interviews or scaring them into thinking they said something unfavorable about their team or coach on live television. [13]

When things got slow in the studio, Bradshaw took time to offer counsel to various current quarterbacks. He called Chicago Bears quarterback Mike Tomczak and offered encouragement. "Sometimes it helps to hear things from guys who've been through this before," Tomczak responded. Bradshaw also telephoned Joe Montana, who had suffered an elbow injury similar the one that had ended Bradshaw's career. He warned Montana not to hurry back, stating, "Don't let the performance of Steve Young do something that may cost you a career." [14]

The critics again enjoyed the CBS pregame show that year. The Pittsburgh reporter who had wondered if Bradshaw would succeed concluded, "CBS has a good show. Terry Bradshaw is entertaining and lively. ESPN does a good show for the hardcore football fan." Another for the *New York Times* observed, "Bradshaw is the dominant star of the CBS and NBC shows, an unpredictable and entertaining personality." He offered this comparison: "NBC's Bob Costas is superior to the adept Gumbel as a host and informational traffic cop, but Bradshaw's approach pushes him onto another plane. Bradshaw's endearing character lets you forgive his imperfect English, his dropped gs and his flailing gesticulations."[15]

The network broadcast the Super Bowl in January 1992. Bradshaw appeared in several features and interviews that composed the three hours of pregame before the kickoff. The show featured football insights from astronauts orbiting the earth, a Lesley Visser interview with former Super Bowl hero Doug Williams, and reports on the two teams from color commentators Dan Fouts and Randy Cross. To survive the telethon, one critic suggested that audience members do different things depending on who was on the air. "When the Bradshaw good-old-boy twang commences, pay attention. Terry's apt to say anything," he said. While true, reporters in Southern newspapers noted Bradshaw's football smarts, referring to him as having "graduate-level football knowledge."[16]

THE GAME'S THE THING

For the 1992 season, the *NFL Today* crew retained its stated focus: "The game is the thing." One of the changes made involved getting up from behind the desks more and demonstrating some football action. "It wasn't particularly exciting, but at least we brought something new to the format," Bradshaw stated. The cohosts remained well-liked by critics, who referred to them as smooth Greg Gumbel and affable Terry Bradshaw. They continued to provide the lighthearted and fun but knowledgeable approach to the pregame. Visser offered the hard journalism as she moved to being a sideline reporter before the bigger games of the week. The group enjoyed one another off the set as well. Visser and the cohosts often went out for dinner at the Manhattan eatery Wilson's, which held an open mic night on Sundays. "I'm trying to get Terry to sing 'I'm So Lonesome I Could Cry,'" said Visser. "He can sing. Greg knows every word to every Rolling Stones song, even 'Brown Sugar.' And I'm the only person who knows the words to the theme song for 'Bonanza.'"[17]

Viewers presumably picked up on the feeling and observed that the banter between the cohosts grew increasingly easy. One pregame featured throughout the league before the start of any game included interviews by color commentators at different stadiums. When commentator Hank Stram said to interviewee tight end Keith Jackson, "The quarterback is always right," Jackson chuckled and replied, "The quarterback is always right." They went back to the studio, and Bradshaw thanked Jackson. Greg Gumbel joked, "That's our problem around here. The quarterback is always right." Bradshaw laughed. They started a detailed discussion about what one team needs to expect from their opponent.[18]

Bradshaw fired off a few unvarnished opinions on players, coaches, and situations. He claimed that Philadelphia Eagles quarterback Randall Cunningham had to stop wavering between Mr. Nice Guy and Mr. Me-Me-Me. Bradshaw opined, "Randall has got to make his mind up after seven years on which Randall he wants to be. Great leaders don't change their spots." Mike Ditka, who returned to head coaching, heard Bradshaw question whether he could withstand the Bears needing to go through a rebuilding season. A reporter argued, "Hearing Terry Bradshaw say Ditka doesn't have the disposition to withstand a rebuilding process no doubt motivates da coach into a state of defiance." On one occasion, rookie NFL analyst Matt Millen appeared on the pregame show. Bradshaw said Joe Montana's potential return to the 49ers sidelines would be a "huge distraction" for a team that has been cruising toward the playoffs with Steve Young, the NFL's highest-rated quarterback. Millen responded, "That's a bunch of baloney. Hey, it's the NFL. You want your best people on the field."[19]

During the halftime show, the cohosts continued their rapport as they showed highlights of the various games. They combined slight teasing of one another with a rundown of the games. After showing the single touchdown in Seattle's 10–6 win against New England, Bradshaw quipped, "I hope I got a tape of this. I want to watch it later." Gumbel laughed as well. The host then provided a clip from an important baseball game and explained how a triple play had occurred. Gumbel looked at Bradshaw and said, "You got all that." Bradshaw said, "Nah," shook his head, and continued, "I don't know anything about baseball."[20]

Indeed, the former quarterback was presumably telling the truth regarding baseball; however, two statements illustrated what he believed were the key elements that he provided to the program. During a taping of a behind-the-scenes look at *NFL Today*, Bradshaw admitted, "I try to mess up once a (halftime) segment to show people I have a human side." He added, "I'm not afraid to let people know that I'm kind of an idiot."[21]

Perhaps Bradshaw's onscreen attitude served as a major reason why critics enjoyed him. One television sports columnist in Orange County, California, placed Bradshaw on his list as the third-best talking quarterback on television. Hometown favorite Pat Haden topped the listing, and Joe Theismann finished second. Another television critic observed that Bradshaw was a big success as an analyst. He was Cosell without the ego, Costas without the cuteness, and Madden without the boom—and don't forget to toss in a wide smile and Southern drawl. *Gentleman's Quarterly* offered a flattering article on the pregame host in its November 1992 issue. A New York newspaper television columnist noted that Bradshaw had reached the star stratosphere. The recognition culminated in colleagues recognizing the show. *NFL on CBS* won the Sports Emmy for Outstanding Studio Show for the year.

Nonetheless, a notable group of critics and fans in the San Francisco Bay area appeared to find Bradshaw quite unenjoyable. One critic offered an unflattering remark, referring to a Bradshaw report as "inane." One San Francisco 49ers fan complained about Bradshaw's regular comments about his favorite team. He claimed to want Bradshaw to shut up and was tired of his comments about Joe Montana and the 49ers. Bradshaw called Montana one of only two great quarterbacks in the league during that time, with Buffalo's Jim Kelly being the other. But fans expressed animosity toward anyone who questioned their hero or anyone who supported the "other" quarterback. Montana did return to the team's sidelines but did not play in the 49ers' loss to the Dallas Cowboys in the NFC Championship Game. Before the 1993 season, the 49ers traded Montana to the Kansas City Chiefs, where he played his final two seasons. [22]

CBS GETS OUTFOXED

As they began their fourth season as the network's pregame show, the crew drew many of the same reactions from television critics and fans as they had the previous season. Some television critics appreciated Gumbel's relaxed and informative personality, and others liked Bradshaw's information but cringed about his screaming and wild hand motions. Others noted that among all the networks' "studio clowns," Bradshaw wore the lampshade.

The majority of the fans tuned in for the CBS program, and many appreciated Bradshaw's straight-shooting commentary. Indeed, Bradshaw's thoughts on the Cowboys repeating as Super Bowl champions surprised some: "A lot of people get very satisfied. One ring and they're all fulfilled. If you can figure out who they are, you cut them. (Jimmy) Johnson will figure it out. Watch who he cuts." When Emmitt Smith sat out for more money, Dallas started out the season 0–2. Bradshaw took aim at the team and challenged the players to improve their own performances. He also attacked the league when he felt they were mistaken. He and Dan Fouts stated that the 40-second clock forced offenses to run plays slipshod. Several radio and newspaper commentators agreed.[23]

Bradshaw also offered praise for teams and players. He stated that the Arizona Cardinals' team building was on the right track, mentioning running back Garrison Hearst as an example. "Hearst is a great runner, and great runners open up the passing game and the whole offense looks good. Hearst can be the next Emmitt Smith," Bradshaw told the audience. Unfortunately, the Cardinals did not get this potential out of Hearst, but he succeeded with the 49ers and Eagles. Bradshaw also received praise for his interview with Eagles quarterback Randall Cunningham. The host expressed the criticisms he had made of Cunningham to the quarterback, who provided responses with poise and diplomacy.[24]

Bradshaw and other commentators and analysts complained about the league's product. Some pointed to fewer important games, while others like Bradshaw noted, "[T]he league as a whole isn't fun to watch." A few television columnists held CBS partially to blame. They celebrated the news that the upstart Fox network, in an effort to expand its reach, had outbid CBS for its NFL package. Fox would begin airing the NFC games the following year for the NFL's 1994 season.

The executives at CBS tried to win the rights to the AFC games but lost to incumbent NBC. CBS Sports president Neil Pilson brought all the divisions' personnel together for a rally. He said the network had plenty of sports, including the Masters and the U.S. Open in tennis. One person in the room said Terry Bradshaw raised his hand and asked, "Does the Masters have a pregame show?" That broke everyone up."[25]

Despite the change, the pregame show kept humming along. They invited two actors who played Mr. and Mrs. BIG FAN to the studio. The pair had been plugging NFL games on CBS. "I was so thrilled. I was going to meet Terry Bradshaw! I was afraid he was going to say, 'Who are these hicks?' But he saw us and said, 'The BIG FANS are here!'" said Viki Boyle, the actress who played Mrs. BIG FAN. Her parents and brothers were huge Steelers' fans. After meeting Bradshaw, Ms. Boyle said, "My dad and brothers are thrilled with this. This legitimizes everything I've ever done, and I'm not doing anything but being myself—a premenopausal cheerleader." On their last broadcast for the regular season, Gumbel and Bradshaw wished viewers and one another a happy new year, joked around, and then introduced the upcoming game.[26]

As the playoffs began, Bradshaw continued sharing his comments about the quality of the NFL games, stating, "We are in danger of becoming the National Field Goal League. The games are putting fans to sleep, and this ought to be a wake-up call for the league." He concocted another list to solve this problem, including narrowing the uprights on the goal posts and making the playing field longer and wider.[27]

CBS covered the 1993 NFC Championship Game for the final time. Executive producer Rick Gentile said, "The mood was somber but focused. Everybody was trying their best to get out the idea that this was it, and they did a great job of it. The pregame show guys were incredible because that was a complicated pregame to do." Terry Bradshaw got a little misty-eyed when he said to *NFL Today* partner Greg Gumbel as the telecast was concluding, "We're dear friends; it's a sad day." Of course, Bradshaw had to say to Gumbel, "[A]nd if you were a little bit better looking I'd give you some sugar." The mere playful nod at one male friend kissing another drew editorial comments from newspaper columnists, for example, "Eeyew—sober up, will ya?" Colleagues again saw the program as being tops in its category. *NFL on CBS* won the Sports Emmy for Outstanding Studio Show for the second year in a row, but the football games transferred over to the relatively new network Fox.[28]

The Fox Broadcasting Network started operations in the fall of 1986, and rolled out programming on Saturday and Sunday. Its executives realized that the fastest way for it to solidify its status as a fourth major network would be to show NFL games. They had tried to purchase the NFL in 1987, but failed. The network had 99 stations throughout the United States, many in the harder to receive ultra high frequency (UHF) range. The network struggled in its first years. The 1989–1990 season represented a big triumph with the airing of *The Simpsons* and the success of the series *Cops* and *America's Most Wanted*. Winning the rights to air the NFL games starting in 1994 solidified Fox's position as a member of the Big Four networks.

Fox issued announcements regarding the staffing for its NFL coverage. They selected Ed Goren from CBS to serve as the pregame show's executive producer. The network bought most of the CBS announcing staff, including paying $32 million for John Madden, $2.5 million annually for Pat Summerall, and $1.5 million for Terry Bradshaw.

Summer arrived, and the Fox network unveiled to television and sports columnists its plan for handling the new sports programming. It touted its broadcasts with the slogan, "Same game, new attitude." Network executives promised more pictures, slow-motion video, stereo sound, and more field noise in its coverage. The studio set featured a "demonstration area," where the hosts could illustrate plays in the games, and a "Fox Box," where they could interview celebrities. The network spent a great deal of money on promotions and advertising to draw new fans to the hour-long program.[29]

Fox's notable irreverence and gimmicks caused some sportswriters concern about the way the network would broadcast the game. John Madden appeared to emphasize that the game was the important thing. Bradshaw joked around with everyone but followed with the statement, "You can have fun . . . as long as you cover the game." One of the pregame show hosts, former Dallas Cowboys coach Jimmy Johnson, did not appear at the grand preview of the pregame show. Bradshaw began ribbing Johnson to reporters. "He should be here. We are here. We've been here a whole . . . week. I mean, his butt should be here, 'cause this is the chemistry we're trying to develop," declared Bradshaw. Johnson issued comments to a columnist from *USA Today*, escalating the play fight: "Terry (Bradshaw) talks before he thinks, but I don't think it would make any difference if he thought first."[30]

THE MOVE TO FOX

As the pregame show, called *NFL on Fox*, began during the preseason, some critics offered their opinions. One stated that he enjoyed Bradshaw but doubted that anyone could be having as much fun as his laughing indicated. A second question among critics in Colorado was whether Bradshaw understood the difference between a game and a carnival. The central question for this television critic became, Did he know when to tone down his hyper-humor?

The regular season for the pregame show began with Bradshaw riding horseback in the Hollywood Hills. He galloped down Rodeo Drive to a Hollywood parking space equipped with a hitching post. "Time to go to work," he said. The hosts previewed the upcoming games, and Bradshaw offered a high-energy tour of the studio. Some of the player interviews had a warmed-over feel, but overall, Fox and its staff impressed viewers. Fox increased CBS's ratings for its first-week games by 15 percent, and the pregame marks increased by almost 20 percent.[31]

A few critics expressed pleasure. "The quick, young Fox jumped all over the lazy, old networks," said one West Coast critic. Longtime sportswriter Frank Deford thought too many of the football games received the same coverage, and the pregame shows took themselves too seriously. He applauded Bradshaw's work in the studio as the best of the pregame shows. His role of ringmaster and clown proved much different than the way other hosts and analysts appeared on television. For example, *NFL Live!* on NBC used the dual cohost format, teaming Greg Gumbel with Ahmad Rashad. On ESPN, host Chris Berman may have been loud and made up funny nicknames, but he did not behave outrageously.[32]

Several sports columnists thought the pregame show overplayed itself in its first week. They looked forward to future weeks, when they would rein in some of the entertainment and focus the show—and Bradshaw—more on football. By mid-October, a columnist in San Francisco was continuing the complaints. The pregame number with Bradshaw and Howie Long playing computer football was not funny when "Big Silly and Bald Silly wrestled around on the couch like a couple of frat boys." A television critic in Salt Lake City, Utah, another 49ers stronghold, thought Bradshaw needed to be reined in.[33]

Regardless of their thoughts, Fox designed the program with Brad-shaw and Long playing their personas off of one another. The two-minute filmed bits continued and usually involved a football joke and a joke about Terry's character. In one instance, he and Long were in a barbershop, and when the barber fussed with Bradshaw's hair, he turned out to be wearing a Jimmy Johnson wig. In another, James Brown tried to give Long and Bradshaw some culture in an art mu-seum. Bradshaw said the piece with two push brooms leaning against a wall "showed a certain whimsy," until the janitor came and carried them away.

When the four-man pregame crew talked football, the conversations were usually focused on pertinent information and gave the games a degree of importance. Bradshaw even outdueled Madden by picking the 49ers to defeat the Cowboys in their midseason clash. Still, some people liked their football coverage to be serious, and one *Washington Post* critic thought Bradshaw and his four-legged companion ought to ride off into the sunset and give viewers football, nothing but football. In a rare occurrence, a Southern newspaper critic said one benefit of a year without sports would be that Bradshaw would go away.[34]

Reporters who appreciated Bradshaw's abilities sometimes sought a little less from him. One Texas reporter wrote, "Bradshaw is a terrific presence as a studio analyst, but somebody should start pouring decaf in his coffee mug." He suggested putting Bradshaw in the penalty box for two minutes due to his overacting.[35]

The NFL gave Fox the credibility to gain new affiliates and cover 98 percent of the country. While the Fox games lost in the ratings to the games aired on NBC for the 1994 season, the pregame show won its battle. *NFL on Fox* outpaced its competition handily. Both the games and the pregame won in the coveted demographic of males 18 to 49, and Fox attracted many more young viewers than either NBC or ESPN with its pregame show. The show followed Fox Sports president David Hill's mantra, "Sports aren't a requiem Mass; sports are fun." The trend of moving away from journalists and focusing on stories gained momen-tum at Fox.[36]

But the pregame show sometimes provided commentary on situa-tions occurring within the football world. During season two, Bradshaw wore an orange armband during a pregame show in early November to show his dislike for owner Art Modell moving the Cleveland Browns to

Baltimore. The display of disapproval continued with an interview with NFL commissioner Paul Tagliabue. New York City television critics applauded it as a strong effort to hold the commissioner's feet to the fire. The comments represented an early example of the praise Bradshaw would earn for his interviewing skills. The next month, Bradshaw summarized the relocation as part of football's "all-for-me" attitude. "Athletes now have a dollar value before their name in every article. . . . One of the biggest problems we have is money seems to mean everything," he told the New York City media. His solution to stop the Browns relocation: "Buy him [Modell] out and let him go to Florida and enjoy his life."[37]

The pregame show retained its focus on having fun. Bradshaw attributed the program's success to the crew behaving naturally and the network "allowing people to be themselves and not put a bit in their mouths." He said they had done their research, but the show was not going to try to appeal to the hardcore fan who wanted 60 minutes of information. Instead, he argued, "I think people like to look at people enjoying what they're doing and laughing along the way." A poll of attitudes of Sacramento fans found that they believed the pregame show guys were entertaining and easy to follow. Only one fan thought negatively of Bradshaw as a studio analyst.[38]

Fox executives were considering what to do when Jimmy Johnson left Fox to coach the Miami Dolphins at the beginning of the 1996 season. Bradshaw offered more opinions regarding the focus on money by athletes and owners. Neil O'Donnell quarterbacked the Steelers to the losing side of the Super Bowl and then left as a free agent. Bradshaw predicted that it would be a long time before O'Donnell saw a Super Bowl again and would not acknowledge that his new team had received an upgrade. Indeed, the New York Jets won one game in O'Donnell's first season and finished with an 8–6 record in his only other season.[39]

LOTT'S STAY

The pregame show's executives decided to bring in another cohost to replace Johnson. Ronnie Lott, former San Francisco 49ers safety, became the new hire, and Bradshaw reportedly disliked the move. Critics wondered if Bradshaw simply did not want a third person or if the discord appeared as a ploy for publicity and ratings for the show. Executive producer Ed Goren said, "I look forward to knowing that Terry and Howie may be hit harder than they ever were on the field. It should be an interesting year."[40]

Big-city and national television sports critics argued that the Lott addition proved successful. One noted that he appeared to blend in well with the panel. Lott brought knowledge and bold commentary, and contributed to the enjoyment in the studio that made the pregame show a success. As national syndicated columnist Norman Chad wrote, "I like Fox because I'm not a helmet head." James Brown and Bradshaw incorporated Lott into the mix quite seamlessly. In one instance, sitting inside their studio watching games on their monitors, Bradshaw turned to Lott and asked him what was wrong in the Redskins–Giants game. Bradshaw saw Redskins linebacker Marcus Patton slap Giants quarterback Dave Brown across the face. Brown's teammates did not rush to defend their leader. Bradshaw stated, "That tells me that they don't support him. If that was (Dan) Marino, we would've seen a free-for-all."[41]

The cohosts offered their insight and opinions as always. Bradshaw offered a scathing critique of Washington Redskins receiver Michael Westbrook for not returning to play after a knee injury in the first half. Bradshaw said Westbrook let his team down by not returning in an important game, which the Redskins lost to Dallas. Washington coach Norv Turner defended Westbrook, claiming that a MRI indicated that the receiver suffered a dislodged cartilage in his knee. No one doubted the injury's existence; Bradshaw's reaction emerged from a difference in the culture of the NFL between the late 1970s and the late 1990s.

As described in earlier chapters, during Bradshaw's era, players reentered games with injuries, frequently taking painkillers so they could play. Bradshaw had done this on many occasions, and his view carried the expectation that this is what a player and teammate should do for the team. If a player failed to return, the media would start asking hundreds of questions, and teammates would wonder if the man had "gone soft." In the late 1990s, Westbrook's teammates Terry Allen and Brian Mitchell offered jokes to encourage the receiver to come back onto the field. Individual players and teams placed long-term health and viability above short-term gains, for example, helping to win a single game, even if it was the national game aired on Thanksgiving Day.[42]

The 1996 NFL season culminated with a Super Bowl in the Louisiana Superdome. This game represented the Fox network's first Super Bowl. The network offered coverage on the Internet during the two weeks before the game. Bradshaw offered daily commentary as one of the site's features. Other elements included a virtual tour of the Superdome, fan pools, and merchandise ordering forms.

Befitting Fox, the pregame show lasted five hours. Bradshaw admitted, "If I'm a fan, I don't want to watch five hours." The Fox pregame crew hosted the final three and a half hours of the program, the length of the actual game on the field. Among the many segments were John Madden's "All-Time All-Madden Super Bowl Team" selections; NFL Films short videos, called "Super Bowl Diary"; the pregame hosts conducting interviews; Bradshaw's analysis of the opposing quarterbacks; and the Fox pregame crew's keys to the game.[43]

Several television critics expressed pleasure with the pregame show. One Milwaukee reviewer saw the pregame as Bradshaw's show and noted he could be a terrific analyst. Another from Ohio observed that Bradshaw predicted the winning team for accurate reasons. A Northern California critic rated the Fox pregame quartet the best in the business and the most entertaining. Even in the area where the losing team resided, television critics said Fox delivered a near-flawless performance. "Bradshaw's rapid-fire, unscripted game summary could not have been better executed by a career broadcaster," the New England critic declared.[44]

The pregame crew still had their critics among the people paid to comment on television programming. Critics in Colorado remained hostile, even after Bradshaw's relationship with Broncos star quarterback John Elway improved. One called Bradshaw the "buffoon of 'Fox NFL Sunday,'" which stung Bradshaw. In an interview with *TV Guide*, Bradshaw explained, "I stutter, I stammer, I scratch, and I do it all on live television. That's why I've never been able to watch myself, 'cause I embarrass myself. . . . I can't help it, it's me. What are you gonna do about it? You can't change who you are." A critic for the *New York Times* argued that Bradshaw served as an antidote to boredom on the show. Bradshaw admitted he liked to take chances for entertainment value and did not intend to play the fool. "I want people to feel good when I'm on the air. Millions of people like what I do. We're not creating the world. It's a game," he said. His statement appeared accurate, as *TV Guide's* readers named Bradshaw, along with John Madden, Bob Costas, and Greg Gumbel, as the finalists in the Favorite Sportscaster category for 1998.[45]

New members would join the group of sportscasters as CBS won the AFC football contract from NBC for the 1998 season. Its sports president, Sean McManus, highlighted the need for changes to the coverage. Fox had "raised the bar" on game broadcasts since acquiring the NFC games five years earlier. McManus sought to bring a fresh look to the CBS broadcasts in the form of a new pregame show and new booth pairings. The new group would need to have the TV savvy and personable figures that had become notable with the pregame show. The Fox pregame show had obviously set the standing, winning the Sports Emmy for Outstanding Studio Show in two of the last three years.

NFL on CBS featured host Jim Nantz and three analysts, former Oakland/Los Angeles Raider Marcus Allen, former San Francisco 49er Brent Jones, and former 49ers coach George Seifert. The trio lasted one season. Before the 1999 season, producers paired Nantz with Randy Cross, Craig James, and the Elvis-loving motorcycle and stock car driver Jerry Glanville, hoping to spice up the show with more personality. A critic from Colorado labeled Glanville the worst television personality, disliking what he called an "irritating show-biz presence." One season later, a television critic from Baltimore also wanted Glanville gone. His observation was that Glanville attempted to play the "Terry Bradshaw 'aw shucks' role but with half the intelligence and none of the charm." A Florida critic tersely called it an "awful show with everybody's sweetheart Jerry Glanville." Glanville revealed the difficulty in successfully playing the "Bradshaw role."[46]

The Fox pregame show's cohosts played a key part in the success of the program. Colleagues had recognized this when they nominated all three analysts for the Sports Emmy in the category of Outstanding Sports Personality/In-Studio Analyst for the past few years. While one critic from Buffalo called the group smart and sassy, another summarized their contributions as providing honest, colorful commentary and having fun without going overboard, adding, "They know when to make a point and when to trade barbs." Another change occurred when Ronnie Lott left the program to return to the broadcast booth.[47]

ADDITIONS TO THE SHOW

The loss of football on NBC left many of the network's analysts without work. Fox hired Cris Collinsworth to join as the newest third analyst on its pregame show. This time the three already on the show thought that having a fourth person would work out fine. Bradshaw introduced Collinsworth to the top executives at the Fox annual affiliates meeting. "We got this new guy on our show this year, but you don't have to worry about him. . . . A lot of people didn't want to work with Cris Collinsworth because they said the boy was two-faced . . . if the boy had another face, don't you think he'd use it?" Collinsworth said it was a real honor to work with someone who is living proof that Hooked on Phonics really works. [48]

The new man became the person who received the majority of the barbs from Bradshaw and Long, and he played along well with the gags. But it took a few weeks for Collinsworth to understand the way the hosts worked—they may rehearse, but the show had little to do with what they had discussed. Collinsworth brought more of the hard-line football commentary to the program, which neither Bradshaw nor Long wanted to do.

NFL on Fox also added two other new features. Comedian Jimmy Kimmel joined to offer predictions for the games. He brought one-liners and comedic skits. He also exchanged barbs that played well off of Bradshaw. The second addition came one year later, when Jillian Barberie joined the cast, providing weather forecasts for each week's game sites.

The new group exchanged opinions about football, including individual games and teams, players, and organizations. Bradshaw used information acquired from networking to offer informed opinions about the status of current teams, for instance, "Listen, most of the offensive coordinators around the league will tell you that the Carolina defense is one of the best around, and Jacksonville is pretty good, too." The following season, when Carolina's defense helped the team reach the NFC Championship Game, Bradshaw expressed happiness with the arrival of a new top team despite the Panthers not being one of the most popular clubs. "Sure, I'm concerned about the ratings," the former quarterback said, "but from a pure football standpoint, I think what has happened is great. My network might have a problem with it, but I don't have a problem with it. You can't have Dallas, the 49ers, the Jets, or the Giants every year."[49]

Current players received some timely critiques. Much of the criticism came when Bradshaw perceived the player was not giving his all or had been letting the team down, as in the aforementioned Michael Westbrook situation. Occasionally, a player combined these flaws with a bad personal decision. The night before Super Bowl, Atlanta Falcons safety Eugene Robinson faced arrest on charges of soliciting sex. The network kept the event in context overall, but the cohosts discussed the issue. Howie Long tried to defend Robinson's character, but Bradshaw disagreed, saying, "How stupid, how stupid."[50]

The cohost would even offer a critique of a former player when the topic arose. On occasion, Bradshaw's opinions revealed that he could have a sharp edge. He dressed down the Washington Redskins leadership for deciding to sign quarterback Jeff George as a free agent. Previously, Bradshaw had voiced his opinion that George was "not a winner." Instead of leveling a critique at the organizational leaders, Bradshaw's sources indicated that a former player had made the recommendation. "Sonny Jurgensen gained [Redskins owner] Dan Snyder's ear and told him how great George was and then Snyder ran out and signed him. Why? I don't know." The analyst took aim at the former Redskins quarterback, saying, "Sonny played 18 years and only made four playoff appearances. Both Jurgensen and George have one thing in common— they've never won anything." George finished his career with Washington, starting the last five games of the season. The team ended up with a 1–4 record in those games. He then had only two starts for the second year, earning a 0–2 record in his final season in the NFL. [51]

Bradshaw reserved criticism for the Washington Redskins organization as well. Some fans wrote comments on various pro-Redskins websites, fulminating about when Bradshaw was finally going to get off the Redskins' backs. The team's sorry state of affairs resulted in that question going unanswered for quite some time. Other dysfunctional organizations received some attacks as well. When analysts realized that Carson Palmer would become the first pick in the NFL Draft in 2003, by the management-challenged Cincinnati Bengals, Bradshaw summarized the situation as follows: "He'll [Palmer] soon hear, 'With the first pick, Cincinnati takes Carson Palmer.' Then he should go and get his master's degree."[52]

Bradshaw continued to show a range in his interviewing abilities. While interviewing executives, players, and even player wives, he showed strength in getting to the heart of the story and the situation. He reminded Green Bay Packers defensive end Reggie White of White annually telling his teammates about their commitment to getting to the Super Bowl the year he achieved that goal. Bradshaw also conducted a strong interview with Dallas Cowboys owner Jerry Jones. As he had done earlier with the NFL commissioner, Bradshaw felt comfortable holding Jones accountable for his decisions as general manager of the team. After asking him point-blank if he could truly evaluate talent, Jones attempted to deflect and Bradshaw held firm. Finally, Jones slipped out of that answer by saying it comes down to who signs the checks. If the interview provided Jones with a little challenge, the one with Packers quarterback Brett Favre and his wife Deena was even more so, as Bradshaw asked the couple to address some deeply personal issues. Deena had talked to an attorney about getting a divorce because Brett had been drinking too much while hanging out with his teammates. Favre said Deena told him, "I love you to death. We have been together since we were little kids. We have been through a lot together." He admitted she basically said, "It's us or the partying."[53]

Even a media critic who admitted to never liking Bradshaw said that the analyst had to have something special. He admitted this after watching Bradshaw complete two interviews—when Bradshaw got Atlanta Falcons kicker Morten Andersen to shout in Danish and the team's coach, Dan Reeves, to do the Dirty Bird.[54]

The show's fans enjoyed Bradshaw's interviews and the way his infectious personality rubbed off on the people being interviewed. They really enjoyed when that enthusiasm spurred Bradshaw to lead the crew over to the field to demonstrate a play. During the San Francisco 49ers–Atlanta Falcons playoff game, Bradshaw got excited about what he thought was a bad call that negated a fumble. He got up from the desk, took off his wristwatch, and demonstrated the play and why it should have been ruled a fumble. Voting colleagues appreciated these elements too, as Bradshaw won the Sports Emmy for Outstanding Sports Personality/Studio Analyst for the first time in 1999.[55]

RESPONSE TO SEPTEMBER 11, 2001

Regardless of winning awards, sometimes circumstances demand that businesses, people, and programs adopt a change in tone. The NFL and Fox chose to make modifications after the United States suffered terrorist attacks on September 11, 2001. The series of four coordinated attacks by the Islamic terrorist group al-Qaeda involved hijacking four passenger airliners and crashing them into the World Trade Center complex in Manhattan, New York City, and the Pentagon in Arlington County, Virginia. The fourth airplane crashed into a field in Shanksville, Pennsylvania, due to the efforts of its passengers. Almost 3,000 people died and more than 6,000 received injuries. Many more suffered during the rescue work after the attacks.

The NFL decided to postpone a week of games the Sunday following the Tuesday attacks. At football stadiums throughout the country, the gates were chained shut, and acres of parking lots were empty. No boos, no cheers. Just quiet. Dead quiet. Sports bars and restaurants, usually filled with crowds standing in front of the many big-screen televisions, appeared partially filled. The few patrons and sportswriters admitted to missing their bad football team and even Terry Bradshaw.

When the sport returned after the weeklong hiatus, the Fox pregame show was more reserved. Host James Brown aired stories related to the tragedy that he, his wife, and production people had collected during a bus trip across the country. Bradshaw and Long bantered less, and Jimmy Kimmel delivered fewer one-liners. Even Bradshaw's severest critics gave him high marks for his presentation.[56]

The next week, during a portion of the show, Bradshaw held his Bible above his head. He cited Old Testament scripture. He quoted from Psalms 10 to help himself, his studio partners, and viewers find some peace during the tumultuous period. Each member had a few moments to talk about how they felt, and Bradshaw devoted his time to addressing any fears people might have so they would not lash out and torture themselves wondering why God had done this. He noted, "I know all prayers are answered, it just may not be the answer you want. I find that when things like this happen, I tend to go to my faith more so than normal. I think that's what the nation is doing." He also sought to remind people that sports are only a game and only so important.

The analyst's response drew support from the program's fans. One man from Marietta, Cobb County, Georgia, wrote that he was impressed and overjoyed with Terry's comments, saying, "Terry cuts right thru and reminds everyone there is the Bible, the Word of God, we can turn to for comfort."[57]

SINGING WITH SIR PAUL

Four months later, Fox broadcast Super Bowl XXXVI and planned a respectful, patriotic presentation. The usual parties and concerts included celebrities from various musical genres, from Sting to Paul McCartney. The pregame contained less than usual about New Orleans and more about the mood of the country with a patriotic flourish. Bradshaw and the other analysts provided their usual pregame analysis and interviews but with a quieter tone. The show also featured performances with a patriotic theme. These included Mary J. Blige and Marc Anthony singing "America the Beautiful"; Barry Manilow, with Patti LaBelle, Wynonna Judd, Yolanda Adams, and James Ingram, performing "Let Freedom Ring"; and Paul McCartney signing a new song entitled "Freedom."

Television critics responded favorably to the majority of the show. The decision to include segments where America's greatest historical documents were read went over well. Most thought the additions proved successful, and the producers resisted any pressure to become maudlin. The show's watercooler-conversation moment came at halftime, when Bradshaw interviewed Paul McCartney. As one viewer described the event, Bradshaw's body language, expressions, and overall excitement seemed to say, "Hey everyone, I'm interviewing Paul McCartney!" When McCartney joined the roundtable of analysts, the country singer asked the former Beatle to sing a duet with him. Bradshaw started, "It's been a hard day's night, and I've been workin' like a dog." McCartney joined in. After they stopped and moved toward the commercial break, McCartney leaned forward and started singing, prompting Bradshaw to join in.[58]

The moment generated a range of reactions from reviewers, which were generally critical. Two critics admired Bradshaw's nerve and his having the experience of singing with a Beatle. The majority of the critics disliked the duet. While one likened Bradshaw's proclamation, "I sang with the Beatles!" to McCartney playing quarterback for the Steelers, another sarcastically called it a "super TV highlight." Others referred to the duet as frightening or disgusting. A Houston-based critic called it the most horrible thing ever on TV, adding, "I thought 'Hee Haw' was canceled 20 years ago." The comment linked Bradshaw to "cornpone" entertainment and revealed that the reviewer held an anti-rural, if not anti-old-country Southern, bias. John Stewart used the clip of the duet to end his show the next day referring to it as a "Moment of Zen."[59]

Fans seemed to mirror this reaction. One thought the duet was awesome, saying, "McCartney was doing his little shuck-n-jive vaudeville bit 'ello 'ello and 'ere we go yadda yadda, and Bradshaw burst into a jocko howl of 'A Hard Day's Night.'" Most Beatles fans ardently disliked the performance. While one man noted, "It made me want to die," a woman described seeing the two men together as "creepy." They idolized McCartney and other members of the group, and his knighthood only confirmed his sense of royalty. A "royal" singing with a "commoner" seemed to be the core problem for many Beatles fans.[60]

Indeed, one Beatles fan tried to understand the duet through rationalization, stating, "The McCartney–Bradshaw thing was just so horrible. He [McCartney] must be really broke." The person tried a second approach, adding, "I thought he [McCartney] was just humoring him [Bradshaw], which was horrible but forgivable." But the structure to his belief crumbled as he revisited the actual event. The fan continued, "[A]s they were going to commercial, it was McCartney who started in again, and Bradshaw followed along." The person had to admit to themselves that the "royal" may have enjoyed his moment with the "commoner," the spontaneous moment pleasing both stars.[61]

The duet stayed in the minds of critics for a long time. Three months later, a review of McCartney's tour included a mention of the moment. When McCartney returned three years later to play at the Super Bowl, the duet returned as a matter of discussion. As one critic fretted, "The bad news is that Fox has the Super Bowl this year, so there's a chance that Terry Bradshaw will try to sing with McCartney once more." In 2014, in an article on the Beatles and sports, the staff of *Sports Illustrated* ranked the duet as one of the top 10 moments where the Beatles and sports intertwined.[62]

Regardless of the critical responses about his singing with a former Beatle, Bradshaw won the Sports Emmy for Outstanding Sports Personality/Studio Analyst for 2001. As Bradshaw wrote at that time, the more important thing was that the family at the pregame show enjoyed working together and the show kept winning in the ratings. The program's audience outpaced the audiences for the CBS and ESPN shows combined.

ANOTHER DEPARTURE AND CHANGES

The *NFL on Fox* crew had little time to revel in its ratings success. Once again the program lost the man in the fourth chair, as Collinsworth returned to the broadcast booth. He would occasionally contribute features and interviews to the pregame show. The producers decided to use a rotating system for the additional analyst position. After the third week, Jimmy Johnson returned to the set and has been with the show ever since.

The pregame show incorporated elements from other popular programs into its structure. One critic likened the debates between Howie Long and Terry Bradshaw to those on CNNs popular news program *Crossfire*. The two analysts argued and demeaned one another, much in the same way the journalists from the conservative and liberal political perspectives did on *Crossfire*. Bradshaw offered up a top 10 list, which one critic viewed as not nearly as funny as talk show host Dave Letterman's lists but worthy of a chuckle or two. "Terry's Top 10 Young Quarterbacks" sparked at least several sportswriters to provide their own lists because of how much they disagreed with the order of Bradshaw's compilation.[63]

Other additions to the program included an award segment and an interview session. Bradshaw devised a prize called the "Terry Award," to reward players who performed more like duds than studs. His first award, in 2003, went to defensive end Bruce Smith. The 11-time Pro Bowler failed to make the squad during his four seasons in Washington. His value on the field declined, and he received fewer opportunities to play. "Hey, Bruce, you had a great career, but whining about playing time so you could break the sack record? I could have broken every record in the book if I had played until I was 50. Hello!" Bradshaw said.

The new interview segment, called "Ten Yards with Terry Bradshaw," pleased some but annoyed most television critics. A sportswriter from Oklahoma said the segment made Bradshaw appear to be a male Barbara Walters. Pittsburgh's former quarterback asked players and coaches such questions as, "If you could come back as a pastry, what would it be?"[64]

The analysts continued to offer their opinions on franchises and ownership as well. Bradshaw pounded away at Washington Redskins owner Dan Snyder, who paid big money for free agents who were past their prime and made poor decisions when it came to coaching and general manager hires. The analyst said, "I'd like to congratulate Mr. [Danny] Snyder for taking a storied franchise like the Washington Redskins and virtually destroying it. And to prove my point, Jimmy, have you heard from Mr. Snyder by any chance?" Dallas' owner and general manager, Jerry Jones, took some fire as well. According to Bradshaw, the team's burgeoning quarterback controversy indicated the cluelessness of Cowboys management: "[T]they brought in Drew Henson and Chad Hutchinson—two baseball guys? This front office wouldn't know a good quarterback if he fell into their lap."[65]

The overall critical view regarding the pregame shows was that *NFL on Fox* was still the best show. James Brown kept the show moving, and Terry Bradshaw and Howie Long remained interesting and entertaining. One longtime television critic noted that *Fox NFL Sunday* remained really, really good, while CBS's *NFL Today* was not as good. He thought Fox's program revolved around Bradshaw playing the role of village idiot.[66]

"SPYGATE" AND INTEGRITY ISSUES

The pregame show continued to remain relevant as news within the football world stoked controversies. Super Bowl XXXVI, where Terry Bradshaw had sung with Paul McCartney, featured the New England Patriots defeating the St. Louis Rams. Six years later, revelations emerged suggesting that Patriots coaches had illegally videotaped Rams practices after videotapes of the Patriots taping other teams became public knowledge. The scandal became known as "Spygate" and also included documents indicating that the Patriots had handwritten diagrams of the defensive signals used by the Pittsburgh Steelers during the 2002 AFC Championship Game, which the Patriots won by a touchdown. While no one knows for certain the role the videotapes and diagrams played in the Patriot victories, the decision to acquire the material raised questions about the integrity of Fox's pregame show hosts and other members of the league.

Among the Fox pregame crew, analyst Jimmy Johnson and former Cowboys coach Barry Switzer admitted to various degrees of cheating during their coaching careers; however, they said it was mostly during their days as college coaches. Bradshaw stated, "A cheater doesn't sound too good. It's embarrassing, not only to yourself, but to your players. . . . You've hurt your team, and you've hurt the fans in your city all because of your arrogance." He thought the revelation placed a cloud of suspicion over New England's Super Bowl victories. Long and Johnson disagreed, labeling Bradshaw "naïve."[67]

On CBS's pregame show, former Steelers coach Bill Cowher seemed to agree with Long and Johnson. He stated, "Trying to steal signals is part of the game. We understand that as a coach. You see walkie-talkies, tape recorders." Cowher did seem to agree with Bradshaw that Patriots coach Bill Belichick had overstepped a line. He added, "[W]hen you take the camera on the field, that's just arrogance." Bradshaw's former Fox colleague Cris Collinsworth and ESPN's pregame show stalwart Tom Jackson agreed with Bradshaw about the severity of the Patriots' actions. They thought NFL commissioner Roger Goodell needed to suspend Belichick, as well as impose a $500,000 fine.[68]

Bradshaw and other analysts expressed indignation at the behavior of New York Jets coach Rex Ryan. While appearing on the HBO program *Hard Knocks*, Ryan looked like a plainspoken, excitable, charismatic schlub who transmitted his love for what he's doing. NBC analyst Tony Dungy disliked Ryan's penchant for cursing. Bradshaw blasted Ryan for putting pressure on his players by talking so much, saying, "He doesn't even play, so it's easy for him to shoot his mouth off. He doesn't make a tackle, he doesn't run a ball, he doesn't make a catch or throw a ball. He just sits over there. Unfortunately, I don't think his players are quite as strong-minded as he is." Bradshaw also spoke out when football intersected with significant social and cultural issues.[69]

SPEAKING OUT ON ISSUES

In early 2011, Bradshaw admitted that he had experienced problems with memory and other things he attributed to brain damage suffered on the football field. He stated, "The memory loss made me jittery at times. It was driving me crazy that I couldn't remember something that I studied the night before. All it did was trigger my anxiety, and all of sudden everything would snowball on me." He advocated for the NFL to do more to improve conditions for today's players.[70]

He continued to discuss concussions during the next few years in media articles and on such television shows as *The Tonight Show with Jay Leno*. Bradshaw told host Jay Leno that if he had a son he would not let him play football. He asserted that he would still play the game if he could do it all over and had the same choices to make. But when he retired in 1983, he felt it was evident that no one cared about his future and that many former players did not expect the league to care. But suddenly the NFL did care because it was politically correct to care. Bradshaw added that lawsuits make you care. While he did not join former NFL players in suing the NFL for concussions and head injuries suffered on the field, Bradshaw wanted the best for the former players.[71]

Bradshaw issued strong warnings to current players about their actions off the field. He warned Steelers quarterback Ben Roethlisberger about riding a motorcycle without a helmet. Roethlisberger suffered serious injuries in a major accident, hurting his performance during the 2006 season. Bradshaw sought more maturity from Roethlisberger, but two more sexual misconduct incidents in 2009 and 2010 raised additional issues.

Most often the criticism came when players' actions distracted them from playing their best football. Bradshaw believed that it was in the best interest of players, teams, and fans for players to concentrate on football and improving their game. The analyst called out New York Giants receiver Victor Cruz for spending more time on commercials than his game. Bradshaw quipped that he saw Cruz catch more passes in commercials filmed during the offseason than against the Cowboys. These "old-school graduates" criticized the "entitlement jock culture," which provided talented athletes with a lifetime of special treatment. As Bradshaw noted, "[T]hese kids are just placed up on a pedestal, and they're phenomenal, talented people, and they just get special treatment, and I think if you're not mature enough you can't handle it."[72]

Sometimes no one was hurt by the choices made by entitled players; however, Bradshaw criticized those players for being clueless about how their actions appeared within the context of the larger world. When a Miami Dolphins defensive lineman lost a $50,000 earring during practice, Bradshaw commented, "I hope they never find it—$50,000. Go tell that to somebody that can't pay for his kid's education or can't get them into a hospital room and get them treated properly. . . . I hope they stomped on it, and I hope he never found it."[73]

The NFL was facing a large number of legal problems related to its current players. With more than 1,600 players and the staff in their organizations, it wasn't surprising that the league was experiencing off-field issues. The vast majority of the attention was focused on the players, and with the advent of cell phone cameras, portable video cameras, and gossip websites and programs like *TMZ* to broadcast the incidents, the attention greatly increased. In the 16 years since 2000, more than 800 NFL players have faced charges for a variety of crimes. More than 224 of the incidents were related to driving under the influence and 103 to drugs. The third highest number of arrests (99) arose from domestic violence and disputes. While less than the number of cases in the law enforcement community and less than the average among American families in general (25 percent), the number of incidents remains high.[74]

The NFL has had many players face domestic violence charges. In 2002, one sportswriter opined that players are singled out for arrests for drunk driving or domestic abuse. Writers have documented how arrests for drunkenness and violence plague teams, as in *The Good, the Bad, and the Ugly: Heart-Pounding, Jaw-Dropping, and Gut-Wrenching Moments in Minnesota Vikings History*, which chronicles the issues experienced by the Minnesota Vikings teams of the 1990s. The root of the problem extends well beyond the inception of the NFL, as domestic violence, rape, and other violence, primarily against women, have been a longstanding concerns on college campuses.

By the late 2000s, attitudes started to change, as people displayed greater awareness of these crimes and less tolerance for sports figures who commit these acts. Several college football coaches lost their positions after news of domestic violence incidents broke, even if it took

months to reach settlements. Some marginal players who had committed crimes related to domestic violence faced quick release from their
NFL teams as well, largely because the NFL had come to realize
through various demographic studies that an increasing number of
women supported teams and were major fans.

There was a "breakthrough" moment when Baltimore Ravens running back Ray Rice was arrested for striking his then-fiancé at an Atlan-
tic City casino. The video from the casino showed Rice dragging his
unconscious fiancé out of an elevator. The sordid affair included incomplete statements, news conferences, and certainly lies on many sides.
Initially, the Ravens and the NFL supported Rice; however, as more
video of the incident surfaced, including footage of Rice punching his
girlfriend, the Ravens organization eventually moved to release him,
and Commissioner Goodell elevated Rice's punishment from a two-
game suspension to an indefinite one. After the case made its way
through court, Rice received reinstatement into the NFL, although to
date no team has given him a tryout. Goodell received intense criticism
for his handling of the case and experienced such embarrassment that
he instituted a new domestic violence policy with a mandated six-game
suspension.

The crew of Fox's pregame show and many of the commentators for
the CBS program spoke out about the incident but added little depth.
ESPN, with its show running three hours, provided more details. *NFL
on Fox* did bring in reporters Pam Oliver and *USA Today*'s Christine
Brennan, who discussed the Rice case in detail and provided some
insight. Months later, when the commissioner was again forced to act as
judge, jury, and executioner during his suspension of Adrian Peterson,
many applauded Bradshaw for his stinging commentary, where he held
Goodell responsible for his latest action. The commentator reminded
everyone that Goodell admitted to bungling the Rice situation and
asked for a second chance. The Peterson misdemeanor reckless assault
charge gave Goodell that opportunity to redeem himself, but there was
no consistency in his handling of the situation, and Bradshaw criticized
him for having a double standard. [75]

One season later, the NFL faced another major domestic violence
case with defensive lineman Greg Hardy. Hardy was found guilty of
assaulting an ex-girlfriend and earned an 18-month probation sentence
and a 10-game suspension from the league. Despite pleas from team-

mates and staff members to give Hardy a second chance, Carolina Panthers owner Jerry Richardson released the troubled player, because, as Richardson stated, "We do the right things." Hardy signed with the Dallas Cowboys, and Goodell reduced the suspension to four games. Bradshaw criticized Hardy's violence and Jerry Jones's hiring of him, stating there should be no place in the league for people like him.[76]

So, what is Terry Bradshaw's legacy in the booth and studio? Years later, sports broadcasting historian David J. Halberstam wrote an article naming the "50 greatest network announcers." His ranking took five factors into account. Aside from the individual's national reach and distinction in an on-air role, he considered their legacy, the measure and length of their visibility, and their trendsetting and pioneering contributions. Howard Cosell, John Madden, and Brent Musburger topped the list, with solid professionals like Al Michaels, Bob Costas, and Jim McKay being among the top 10. Bradshaw was ranked number 31, for his cross of edge and self-deprecation, as well as his reliable energy, praise, and criticism.[77]

10

HOST, GUEST STAR, AND COMMERCIALS

Zany Uncle Terry

"In this day and age, face it, personality is the rule of the day."—
Kathy Bates, actress[1]

In 1990, their first year at the helm of CBS's pregame show, cohosts
Greg Gumbel and Terry Bradshaw reshaped the stodgy *NFL Today*
into a program with a lighter touch and greater humor. Bradshaw successfully demonstrated what both his former broadcast booth partner
Verne Lundquist and former boss Terry O'Neil had thought all along—
that he would do well as a studio host for pregame football. A former
CBS Sports executive, O'Neil also knew Bradshaw could host other
sporting events because he had done so in the mid-1980s.

An executive at another network also saw Bradshaw's potential as
television host. In 1990, the former quarterback appeared in Times
Square, New York, as a correspondent during a New Year's Eve celebration. He joined radio and television personality Mark McEwen that
night and performed well; however, CBS did not use Bradshaw much
outside of the pregame show. His friend Burt Reynolds put him on his
show *Evening Shade* once in 1991, and again in 1992, where he played
himself. Perhaps executives did not see the potential for cross-program-
ming. Bradshaw might have brought football fans to a sitcom or other
program, and the viewers of that show would have been introduced to
him and might have watched *NFL Today*.[2]

Eventually, the Fox network and other creative producers recognized the benefit of bringing Bradshaw on their shows and adding him to their commercials. The many appearances he would make from the mid-1990s through the mid-2000s created a recognizable image. He resembled that zany uncle that many people liked or at least recognized because they had one in the family.

NAME RECOGNITION

The CBS network might have missed a significant opportunity. Memorabilia sales demonstrated that among fans, Bradshaw's name had substantial recognition and value. QVC, the product sales broadcast network, sold mass-produced souvenirs on its sports collectibles show. Since its debut in the summer of 1989, the show had offered such products as autographed bats and baseballs with the names of retired baseball players on them. Fewer products featured the names of then-current figures like Darryl Strawberry. Items autographed by baseball players accounted for 80 percent of sales, and Terry Bradshaw was the only nonbaseball personality whose autographed items appeared on the show.

Other sporting goods companies realized the value of Bradshaw's name among purchasers of football products. Wilson issued collectible footballs autographed by Joe Montana, Joe Namath, Jim Brown, Terry Bradshaw, and Johnny Unitas. The footballs cost $250 and were sold through a special vendor. Topps issued a subset of player cards called "Football Legend." The Stadium Club Series II featured six cards for notable quarterbacks from the past. The front of the cards had a photograph of either George Blanda, Terry Bradshaw, Bart Starr, Roger Staubach, Y. A. Tittle, or Johnny Unitas, and the back listed biographical information, career stats, and a picture from the player's rookie card.

Even a toy company recognized the profitability of the memorabilia market. Kenner Company created a new line called "Timeless Legends" to add to its starting lineup collection. Figures added included boxers Joe Louis and Rocky Marciano, hockey's Gordie Howe and Bobby Hull, basketball players Wilt Chamberlain and Kareem Abdul-Jabbar, and Walter Payton and Terry Bradshaw of NFL fame.[3]

FRIEND OF BILL

Others saw the benefit of building connections with Bradshaw. The 1992 Democratic Party presidential primaries started with nine candidates, including a former governor from Arkansas, William J. Clinton. The first Southerner with a strong chance to win the nomination since Jimmy Carter, Clinton eventually faced off against Edmund G. Brown and accumulated enough delegates to secure the nomination. The "baby boomer" with small-town roots defeated incumbent president George H. W. Bush and independent Ross Perot.

The future president enjoyed appearing on national television shows. He went on a talk show on MTV and sat for an interview with Greg Gumbel that appeared on *NFL Today*. Clinton confessed to being a "frustrated athlete" and said he would rather be a sports star like his friend Terry Bradshaw. Gumbel mused that his cohost would be a good choice for secretary of offense. "I think he'd be pretty good," Clinton responded. Both men embodied the rising success of Southern white men exuding a folksy charm. As Clinton took office in the White House, Bradshaw received new advertising offers.[4]

Dick's Clothing & Sporting Goods moved its headquarters to Pittsburgh and decided to use Bradshaw for its advertising campaign. The billboard slogan "Guess Who's Back in Town?" played on Bradshaw's decade-long absence from the region. "He has huge name recognition," said Kevin Flynn, president of the Flynn Agency, developer of the campaign. Several hardcore Steelers fans expressed displeasure, including Joseph Chiodo, owner of Chiodo's Tavern in Homestead. "I don't believe in biting the hand that feeds you—criticizing Noll, the Steelers, the fans," said the tavern owner. Eddie Stanko of White Oak noted, "Here is a man who made his name as a Steeler great—hall of famer, four-time Super Bowl winner—and then criticized Chuck Noll and local sportswriters continuously after his retirement."[5]

Steelers fans seemed unconcerned about the reasons for or context of Bradshaw's criticism of Noll and the team. Bradshaw thought Noll had lost his coaching and drafting abilities. Despite the number of poor seasons seemingly validating the quarterback's words, many Pittsburgh fans perceived the voicing of those opinions as wrong.

GUEST APPEARANCES

By the time the NFL moved to Fox, Bradshaw was appearing regularly as a guest on national talk shows. Phyllis George featured him on one of her hour-long specials, where he talked about his role as a father and his emotional side. The program appeared on the Nashville Network. Both David Letterman and Jay Leno featured Bradshaw on their late-night programs. Leno's *Tonight Show* routines tended to be more mundane with broader appeal. Set in Los Angeles, the show seemed smooth and friendly for guests. Letterman's edgier program took place in New York City, and some guests found the host slightly combative and unpredictable.

Bradshaw appeared on the *Tonight Show* on a few occasions. Some television critics thought he often talked about nothing, but Leno enjoyed Bradshaw's stories and his ability to say anything. He often made the host laugh. Bradshaw thought he and Letterman didn't hit it off as well, taking longer to get used to one another. "I'd rather stir things up . . . I could cut out all the humor and do all football. But why?" he said. Bradshaw admitted that he liked to take chances for entertainment value.

During his first appearance on *Late Night with David Letterman*, Bradshaw did not know that the host was sensitive about his neck and did not want anyone touching it. After Letterman made an off-the-wall comment, Bradshaw reached over and gently popped him on the face. Letterman got out of his chair and ran around his desk for protection. Bradshaw interpreted this incorrectly as play and chased after him. Letterman backed away. The show went to commercial, and they ushered Bradshaw out of the studio. The Fox studio analyst made a second appearance on the show, and the pair made fun of the incident. From then onward, Bradshaw made regular appearances, one time wearing only a one-piece bathing suit. In another instance, Bradshaw took off on a quintessential verbal ramble. Letterman turned to the audience and said, "It's like talking to Jethro." Bradshaw enjoyed going on and talking with Letterman.[6]

He felt similarly comfortable being on Leno's show. He was often surprised by what he said on the show. Leno usually asked questions about how Bradshaw's family was doing back in the woods. He once said his mother had a problem with her tooth and told about an incident that occurred back at her welding job. When Mrs. Bradshaw attended church, a man walked up to her after the service and said, "I didn't know you weld." She tsk-tsked him and said, "Oh that's just Terry."[7]

Leno's staff often devised something for Bradshaw to do when he appeared on the show. After Bradshaw joined Fox and rode a horse to the studio for the opening day, Leno's crew tried to surprise their boss by pulling the sound stage curtain back and revealing Bradshaw atop a horse. They had many conversations, discussing everything from baseball, which Bradshaw disliked, to alimony payments, one area he admitted to saying too much about on more than one occasion. Fans mentioned seeing Bradshaw's appearances on Leno, expressing their admiration for him as a player and even how he developed his talents in other directions.[8]

The comedic potential displayed by Bradshaw attracted the attention of some television sitcom producers. One Fox sitcom called *The Sinbad Show* used Bradshaw twice in its first season in 1994. One time Bradshaw appeared as himself and another as a character named "Terry Bradshaw" in the episode entitled "The Mr. Science Show." The group behind the show *Blossom* hired Bradshaw to appear as the high school baseball coach of character Joey Russo. Coach Morton, a high-energy fellow, arrived at the Russo home claiming to have big news. He told Joey he had been drafted while excitedly shaking the boy. The two celebrated before engaging in a conversation to convince Joey's father Nick that playing baseball was the best idea. The comic scene ended with Bradshaw on his knees begging Joey to take the opportunity. The show reached its peak popularity in its third season and fourth seasons, drawing more than 12 million viewers on average and finishing 32nd in the ratings. Regarding playing these kinds of roles, Bradshaw observed, "That's the kind of thing I used to do. I have no doubt that I can do more than that."[9]

Bradshaw played against type on a new show that struggled with low ratings. Fox's Western series *The Adventures of Brisco County Jr.* blended cartoonish action with pop-culture satire but ranked near the bottom of the Nielsen ratings. For their two-part finale, they hired Bradshaw to play the villainous Forrest March, a crooked cavalry officer who charged the two protagonists with treason. "I was playing a heavy for the first time. It was fun to be a heel, but I was determined not to make a fool of myself. I still don't know diddly about acting," he revealed. Even with the all-star finale, the network did not renew the show for a second season.[10]

PROGRAM HOST

With the increased acting roles, Bradshaw received more opportunities to host programs. *Sports Illustrated* brought its *Sportsman of the Year* to television for 1995. They hired Bradshaw to serve as host for the one-hour special. A new television arm of the magazine would reveal the winner for the first time on national television. Bradshaw seemed an excellent choice for host, as he had already performed hosting duties and cultivated an image on the screen. As he noted, "Throughout my television career I have said hello to all the people who appreciate hard work." The network knew of his appeal to these Southern and Midwestern people.[11]

Fox also had Bradshaw host or provide commentary during a few bull-riding competitions. At the Tulsa State Fair, he voiced his appreciation for those who could do the difficult task of staying on top of a bull, calling bull riding the greatest sport there was and saying linebackers are nothing compared to bulls.[12]

Bradshaw's success in these ventures convinced executives at Twentieth Century Fox to offer him the opportunity to host a syndicated talk show. Called *The Home Team with Terry Bradshaw*, the show would run during the daytime throughout 85 percent of the country. Veteran producer E. V. Erni Di Massa Jr. signed on as the show's coexecutive producer. Di Massa knew Bradshaw from his days as a producer with *The Mike Douglas Show*. He made Bradshaw a guest on that program on a few occasions after enjoying hearing him tell stories.

Home Team originally put Bradshaw in the position of quarterback with a group of regularly appearing contributors. These included a woman who could do household repairs, "Mrs. Fix It"; a personal trainer; and a style reporter. Among the other segments planned was one where Bradshaw interviewed children, a la Art Linkletter. Backed by Comcast and Planet Hollywood, the show received promises that top-flight Hollywood stars and other major celebrities would regularly appear.

Any new program airing during the daytime needed the "celebrity wattage." In the late 1990s, there was fierce competition for ratings among the dozen returning talk shows, local news programs, and game shows. Oprah Winfrey's program dominated, with double the ratings of the next-closest programs: *The Rosie O'Donnell Show* and *Live with Regis and Kathie Lee*. These three celebrity talk shows ranked on top because they not only booked the most notable celebrities, but also the hosts were widely admired and enjoyed. Single-issue programs, for example, *The Jenny Jones Show* and *The Montel Williams Show*, garnered respectable ratings, and shows centered on people behaving badly, for instance, *The Jerry Springer Show*, had climbed in ratings during the last few years.

However, Bradshaw's program and five other "softer-edged" shows entered the market in the fall of 1997. None garnered ratings higher than 1.6 million national households in mid-September. "The competition for top guests, even with a big-name host, is cutthroat. . . . You got Rosie, Regis, *Access Hollywood*, *Hollywood Squares*, and *Donny and Marie*. There are not enough quality guests to go around," exclaimed Twentieth Century Fox president Rick Jacobson.[13]

Indeed, critics of the program agreed with the lack of stars. "Bradshaw leans heavily on "B"-team celebrities; here," said one television critic in a review of the glut of syndicated talk shows. Rosie and Oprah raised the bar with their programs, and others found it hard to keep up. Bradshaw's program leaned heavily on him, according to another critic, so people who liked him liked the program and those who did not would not. The critic noted that Bradshaw had to be the sweetest, most sincere, and manic person ever to don the mic, which added up to an awfully dull hour. Dressed in crew neck shirt, dark vest, and cowboy boots, Bradshaw acted pumped and fired up but also fawned all over his guests. He discussed film, music, cooking, and relationships, and several critics thought this was akin to rock star Stevie Nicks hosting a football roundtable. Janeen Bjork, vice president of programming for representative firm Seltel, maintained that Bradshaw seemed unlikely to draw female viewers who were at home during the day, saying, "[I]t was still a failed concept in the producers' believing he had something to tell women between the ages of 18 and 49—as if we cared what Terry Bradshaw thought. His forte is in sports. No one is interested in seeing him cook."[14]

Bradshaw thought the show suffered low ratings for a few reasons. Primarily, Planet Hollywood did not deliver the stars. Other factors included the show's varying formula and the fact that the program faced off against Oprah and Rosie in several big cities. Still, Bradshaw recalled that NSYNC did his program first and that he enjoyed interviewing Charlton Heston and Whoopi Goldberg. The program lasted half a year before being pulled for low ratings.

While he may have not lasted as a full-time host, Bradshaw continued to emcee specific events. He continued his connection with rodeos. He and Fox baseball announcer Bob Brenly cohosted the Ranger Millennium M1 bass tournament. Fox invested some of its prime weekend air time and wanted its hosts to help it be a ratings success. Executive producer Ed Goren said, "A number that is hard to ignore is that over 55 million people in the United States consider themselves anglers." The 2.5 rating pleasantly surprised Fox, with viewership high in Detroit, St. Louis, and Milwaukee, and low in Florida.[15]

The Arts & Entertainment (A&E) channel hired Bradshaw as host of an offbeat reality show. The program, called *The Competition*, featured contestants who engaged in strange contests. The show started slowly in ratings and struggled. TNN and its partners for the Country Music Awards hired Bradshaw to cohost the ceremony with singer Lee Ann Womack.

Two years after the end of *Home Team*, a full-time gig emerged in talk radio. A new sports radio station had recently started in Los Angeles, and Bradshaw received a show called *Lunch with Terry*. The program aired for one hour on KXTA at noon. Bradshaw certainly wanted to launch this new venue, and many considered the show an audition of sorts. Pittsburgh's former quarterback related, "Maybe it sounds like I'm winging it, but it takes a lot of preparation." Bradshaw talked about his life and activities, and not sports, most of which he disliked. He brought along characters, including exaggerated versions of his ex-wife and his mother. The executives slotted the program in between sports talk shows, and Bradshaw believed he really did not fit in at the station. The program lasted six months. By early 2000, there was talk of Bradshaw returning to the radio. Fox entered into an agreement with Premiere Radio to create shows for their sports personalities, including Bradshaw, Howie Long, Cris Collinsworth, and Keith Olbermann. Bradshaw never did return as a radio host.[16]

NATIONAL COMMERCIALS

The acting roles, hosting gigs, and high profile at Fox sparked more chances for Bradshaw to appear in national commercials. Credit card company Visa hired ex-football players Bradshaw and Dick Butkus for a commercial in 1996. By then, what had started with Diner's Card and proprietary credit cards issued by stores had become a national business. Visa became the new name for the former BankAmericard in 1976. Credit card usage skyrocketed after 1978, when a Supreme Court ruling allowed nationally chartered banks to charge out-of-state customers the interest rate set in the bank's home state.

Credit cards became easier to obtain, and by the mid-1980s, government deregulation had enabled the companies to charge users higher fees and interest rates. The banks and Visa, MasterCard, Diner's Club, and American Express sought to extend their stakes in the lucrative business. This market neared saturation by the beginning of the 1990s. Companies looked to new customers and found two demographics they had previously avoided. One side included customers who had not been seen as creditworthy, for example, students and others with poor or no credit history. The second featured affluent customers who did not need credit.

Advertising proved an effective method for reaching the two groups. American Express had long depended on exclusivity and celebrity to entice potential members to join its growing family of colorful cards, with the slogan, "Membership has its privileges." Visa sought to get into the affluent market with its sponsorship of its first Olympic Games in 1988. Next, Visa built advertising campaigns that focused on pointing out the growing number of places where its credit cards were accepted, while showing self-indulgence and conspicuous consumption. These commercials indicted the legitimacy of Visa to the affluent, and their display of conspicuous consumption also appealed to the middle and working classes.[17]

The Visa commercials of the 1990s occasionally featured celebrities. One featured the performers from *A Chorus Line*. A second from the same era featured the 1992 U.S. men's Olympic basketball team, known as the "Dream Team." A new campaign featured individual entertainers. Bradshaw and Butkus performed a specially written version of the song "I Remember It Well," from the musical *Gigi*. In the show, an elderly man and woman recall the beginning of their relationship, and he gets every detail wrong. For the commercial, the two hall of famers are dressed in tuxedos and can be seen strolling through the Pro Football Hall of Fame. Bradshaw played the forgetful one of the pair, with each mistake highlighted by video of him sustaining a vicious hit on the playing field. It closed with Bradshaw saying, "See you Nitschke," and Butkus corrected him again. [18]

It required many takes to complete filming of the commercial, and during the night both players felt hot, tired, and aggravated. Late one evening, as they were pausing to let the crew reset the lights, Butkus leaned over to Bradshaw and growled, "You better not screw up your lines!" "Me? Screw up my lines?" Bradshaw replied. Bradshaw thought to himself, "What would he do, hit me?" Given the situation, Bradshaw thought that might be a possibility, so he answered, "I'll do my best, Mr. Butkus." [19]

Bradshaw enjoyed the finished product. The commercial proved a big hit with the public as well. He found himself getting stopped by all sorts of people, who told him how much they enjoyed the advertisement. Butkus felt differently, wishing he could regain some of his privacy. Receiving extra attention from nice "average Jane and Joes" rarely bothered Bradshaw. He took commercials with regionally based companies in his home area, which elevated his profile among his neighbors. The next year, he filmed commercials for a Texas company called the "Associates," which provided home equity loans.

Once called second mortgages, home equity loans used to be the last resort for those hoping to borrow money because of the risk of homeowners losing their homes; however, lenders realized a lucrative market existed if consumers could borrow and pay back high interest and principal. When a consumer failed to make payments, banks also collected high fees. A potentially large market existed, as more than 70 percent of Americans owned homes by the mid-1980s. The industry needed to draw the interest of their possible consumers. They rebranded the loan with the name "home equity loan," which carried connotations of ownership and fairness. They embarked on advertising campaigns to interest users and removed the stigma many in society held about being in debt. [20]

As with Visa and other credit card advertising, bank marketing came into its own in the 1980s and early 1990s. "Banking started using consumer advertising techniques more like a department store than like a bank," said Barbara Lippert, an advertising critic for the magazine *Adweek*. Executives for credit divisions thought everything would work out well because the people taking out loans would not "pledge the house to buy a blouse." With wages remaining stagnant for 40 years and the loss of jobs in certain sectors, practical need led to more Americans accumulating debt. With banks receiving returns of 25 to 50 percent from the high fees, other lenders wanted to get into the business.

Several businesses like the Associates emerged as regional lenders. The Money Store, based in Sacramento, California, marketed in the New York City area. Beneficial Finance set up its headquarters in Delaware. The Dallas-based Associates represented one of the largest in the business, with $18 billion in receivables.

The Money Store ran advertisements in the New York area featuring former New York Yankees shortstop and announcer Phil Rizzuto. He appeared as their television spokesman during the 1980s and early 1990s. By the mid-1990s, the industry was engaged in the "Battle of the Jock Endorsers." The Money Store featured former Baltimore Orioles pitcher Jim Palmer in the mid- to late 1990s, as Beneficial used former heavyweight champion from the 1970s George Foreman as their pitchman. The Associates made Bradshaw their corporate spokesman for two years. Chairman and chief executive officer Keith W. Hughes said, "We are delighted to have Terry Bradshaw as our spokesman in this initiative. He epitomizes hard work, honesty, and integrity, which are the very attributes we hope our customers see in us."[21]

One of the company's goals was centered on locating branches within a 20-minute drive of the majority of Texans. The advertisements sought to create a customer base that would support that infrastructure. In one commercial, Bradshaw and a man trailing behind in a suit knocked on the front door of a house. The woman opened it, and Bradshaw barged in saying, "Mrs. Lear, hello. Got your call about a home equity loan. I'm here for your bills." As he walked toward the dining room table, he called out to her husband, who was seated at a table, "Hey boy, how you doing?" While Bradshaw recited the couple's problem bills, the wife asked her husband who this man was. "Terry Bradshaw, four-time Super Bowl winner," the man responded. The wife smiled wanly.

The announcer intoned the company's pitch and guarantees. In the final scene, Bradshaw and the man in the suit stood in the driveway behind a car. "We have a very simple procedure," the suited man said. Bradshaw put a milk carton full of money in the trunk and turned to his companion, stating, "Just get them the money, Frank."

The commercial used a typical scene from a police drama and added Bradshaw as the humorous element. Bradshaw played the smart, nice policeman out to do whatever it took to help the people. The high-energy, loud, and friendly character exhibited a no-nonsense manner. He swept into the house to quickly clean up the couple's mess. His partner wanted to follow procedures, but Bradshaw's good-cop mentality simply wanted the people to get the help they needed.[22]

Bradshaw fulfilled his contract and moved on. Meanwhile, Citigroup acquired the Associates First Capital for $31 billion in 2000, despite the company having been widely denounced for predatory lending practices. Renamed Associates Home Equity Services, Citigroup stopped doing business with about 20 percent of the loan brokers in its new unit. The roughly 1,000 staffers suffered from "integrity concerns" or lacked proper licensing.[23]

After completing the contract with the Associates, Bradshaw signed on with a national advertising campaign for a discount long-distance telephone company. The deregulation of the telephone industry in the United States during the early 1980s split up the old American Telephone & Telegraph (AT&T) monopoly. AT&T became primarily a long-distance telephone provider, while local calls were handled by seven regional "Baby Bells." The federal government argued that breaking up the monopoly would spur competition and benefit consumers through lower prices.

Some competition did emerge in the long-distance telephone consumer market. GTE created Sprint and joined the fray. Nextel and others emerged in the early 1990s. The development of the Internet and expansion of fiber optics led to new opportunities in the telephone services area. Companies, including Sprint, MCI, and Nextel, emerged as interexchange carriers that enabled consumers to dial around their primary long-distance carrier. The service these companies used offered a significantly reduced rate than AT&T offered at the time. The services charged the same rate regardless of time of day, a rarity for long-distance service during that time period.[24]

The competing services needed to reach the awaiting market. They advertised heavily on radio and television, promising low rates. One of the earliest products came from MCI and sold itself as 1-800-COL-LECT. It advertised with many comic actors, including David Spade, Ed O'Neill, and Wayne Knight of *Seinfeld* fame. Spade used his insult humor, while Knight appeared as a goofy nerd. Mr. T, Arsenio Hall, and others appeared in their own commercials as well. Three years later, the 10-10-321 service emerged. The company used actors John Lithgow, Reginald VelJohnson, and Marla Gibbs to market its product. The scenes featured these actors as everyday people discussing the cost of long-distance calls with family members and friends in sets made up to look like their homes.

The 10-10-220 commercials from MCI featured such notable personalities as comedians George Carlin and Dennis Miller, and professional wrestler Hulk Hogan, playing themselves. Actors like Christopher Lloyd played various characters, all with the direct pitch of getting long-distance calls for less than a dollar.

Terry Bradshaw appeared in several commercials, usually without being identified. In one, former NFL quarterback Doug Flutie and Bradshaw shot baskets in the driveway of a house. They told a small, older man about the service, and he took the basketball and dunked it. In another, Bradshaw teamed with Hogan. The humor began when the two of them started talking ballet and trying to learn the dance. After discussing the 10-10-220 service, Bradshaw pirouetted until falling backward, and Hogan caught him.

Bradshaw did other commercials with the company into the 2000s. He yukked it up with country singer and friend Toby Keith, playing a bartender in a country western bar. As Keith pitched the slogan, Bradshaw repeated the line, "Get outta here," followed by, "Get yourself outta here." One male viewer observed that he enjoyed Bradshaw in the ad because of his glorious sense of humor. He did a few of these commercials with New York Mets star catcher Mike Piazza. In one, they ran out of gas in the middle of nowhere, but Bradshaw still managed to enjoy the open road. They stopped a farmer and convinced him to give them a ride. He told them to sit in the back. As they sat next to the chickens and cows, Piazza said, "Great trip." Bradshaw stroked the back end of a calf and responded, "Oh be quiet." Bradshaw observed that the "nice part about making these commercials is that the client allows us to create our own endings.[25]

RETURN TO RECORDING

The commercials for long-distance telephone service provided Bradshaw and others with some artistic freedom. Bradshaw also received that freedom and camaraderie after his return to recording music in the mid-1990s. As Bradshaw explained when he took the job as cohost for the football pregame shows, he realized that he did not have the time to record music. "I still pick a guitar and sing at home," he revealed.

While Bradshaw did not record, more actors and athletes began to move into the music business starting in the late 1980s. As one might expect in this capitalist country, once an actor became popular, someone instantly thought, "They're hot right now. Let's sign them to a record deal!" *Miami Vice* star Don Johnson had a top 10 single in 1986. After his success on the show *Moonlighting*, actor Bruce Willis played harmonica on a 1987 album. David Hasselhoff released almost 20 albums, many of which proved successful in Europe. While these actors performed double duty in the entertainment world, many athletes thought they could do the same. Shaquille O'Neal recorded several albums between 1993 and 1998, and achieved a few gold and platinum plaques for big sales. Basketball and later baseball players teamed with rappers and hip-hop artists on compilation albums. Most of these efforts were met with lukewarm fanfare despite some players' abilities to sing and perform. [26]

Given the mild success of the hip-hop compilation album featuring NBA players, it made financial sense for other professional leagues to follow suit. Bradshaw joined with some other NFL stars in singing on two albums: *NFL Country* and *NFL Jams* in 1996. Teaming up with NFL Properties and the NFL Players Association, Gridiron Records, a young New York City-based label, got established musical stars in country, rhythm and blues, and rap/hip-hop to perform with both current and former NFL stars. The albums were sold at retail stores like Sears and JCPenney, and also at stadiums.

NFL Jams contained 14 songs and featured such hip-hop and R&B musicians as Method Man, Richie Rich, and Ghostface Killah performing songs alongside NFL stars like Andre Rison, Ricky Watters, and Robert Brooks. It proved successful enough to generate a follow-up title of the same name that came out two years later. *NFL Country* consisted of 10 tracks, and a second version also came out a few years after.

On the country album, duets featured Green Bay Packers quarterback Brett Favre and Nashville singer-songwriter Steve Azar, former Pittsburgh Steelers great Terry Bradshaw with Glen Campbell, and Dallas Cowboys running back Herschel Walker with honky-tonker Doug Supernaw. Walker admitted, "I can't sing at all." Yet, one critic found the duet fun and enjoyable. The reviewer described Azar and Favre's "Born with It" as uneventful. Campbell and Bradshaw did a creditable job with the honky-tonk workout "You Never Know Just How Good You've Got It ('Til You Ain't Got It No More)."[27]

Bradshaw enjoyed contributing to the first country version of the NFL compilation album. But Southern gospel ranked among his favorite kinds of music. Like hip-hop during the 1980s and early 1990s, Southern gospel emerged from and represented a way of life. Gospel was born in community singalongs among poor and working-class whites in the southeastern states after the Civil War. Once James D. Vaughn published sheet books and music, he professionalized the music by sending out groups of four men and a pianist that toured, singing songs of faith in Christian life. Through the 1930s, the old-style Southern gospel often followed the music as it was written and featured a little comedy and some gags to make the audience feel more involved.

After World War II, Southern gospel became more of a performers' art, where groups set their own singing style. The Blackwood Brothers, the Statesmen, and J. D. Sumner and the Stamps began writing their own songs, and stars like Hovie Leister and Jake Hess emerged. The groups moved onto the national stage by appearing on variety programs like *The Jimmy Dean Show* or *Arthur Godfrey's Talent Scouts* during the mid-1950s. Terry Bradshaw proved very familiar with the songs from seeing them on television, hearing them on the radio, and attending sold-out shows at auditoriums throughout the South through the mid-1960s. During the next two decades, Southern gospel declined in popularity, but when the baby boomers began to age they reignited the popularity of the genre with a wave of nostalgia. "In the last five years,

Southern gospel has experienced a bigger burst of growth than any other form of gospel," said Ralph Burhe.

Bill and Gloria Gaither realized this resurgence and developed the Gaither Homecoming tours and videos. The Gaither Homecoming began in 1991, as a reunion of many of the best-known and loved Southern gospel music performers. Among the many stars featured in the videos were Vestal Goodman and Jake Hess, who sang many of their old songs. [28]

A friend of Jake's, Mickey Vaughn, read an article about Terry Bradshaw, which said his favorite music was gospel and that the Statesmen were his favorite group. Bradshaw and Hess spoke via the telephone and arranged with Crutchfield to produce an album. "I had never even heard Terry sing, but I knew I liked him. He's tough as nails but a beautiful person. He had been one of my favorite athletes, and I enjoyed him as a football announcer on the Fox network," Jake said. They recorded the album *Jake and Terry*. Hess observed, "[I] didn't have to teach Terry any of the songs. He knew them already." The duo winged things a lot while making the album and had a really good time. [29]

The pair promoted the album. They appeared in some of the Gaither tours and videos. Hess and Bradshaw made stops at stores and other locations to sign albums, appearing in such location as a Wal-Mart in Robinson, Pennsylvania, where many lined up for the autograph session. They held another successful event in Philadelphia. The duo appeared on television shows that had significant audiences in the Mid-South and Deep South, including on the program "Classic Gospel," which played on public television in Tennessee and a few other states.

Some fans of gospel and/or football, for instance, one Texas commentator, seemed unable to get over Bradshaw's singing with Hess; however, a fan in West Virginia heard the album and thought Bradshaw had a rich singing voice. The album received mention in the major Atlanta newspaper in a column that listed new albums listeners should purchase. Years later, the compilation received strong user reviews on Amazon. Five people gave the album the highest rating of five stars. Four of these reviews described how well Bradshaw sang, including saying, "Bradshaw is great on this CD. He needs to make another Christian CD." One reviewer granted the album the lowest rating of one star. One of the positive reviewers received their wish, as Bradshaw recorded an album entitled *Terry Bradshaw Sings Christmas Songs for the Whole World* in 1996.[30]

The exposure to the Gaither's group enabled Bradshaw to meet many of the other stars from the "old-timey" gospel. He made surprise and scheduled appearances with some of these groups during the next few decades. He sang with the Isaacs at a church in a small town in Texas. One parishioner noted, "[Terry was] very down to earth, and he did a great job blending vocals while singing an old hymn favorite, 'What a Day.'" Later he hosted the Isaacs at his home in Hawaii, and the group performed a concert at his local Baptist church. After the concert, Bradshaw and Pastor David Copeland joined the group on the stage, enjoyed some laughs, and sang songs from a range of Protestant traditions. Thanks, in part, to the Homecoming series, Southern gospel music now has fans throughout the United States and in a number of foreign countries, like Ireland and Australia.[31]

AUTHOR, AUTHOR

While Bradshaw continued singing in nonprofessional situations into the 2000s, he received a contract to write two books from one of Simon & Schuster's labels. Working with author David Fisher, the first came out in the summer of 2001. The book, a memoir entitled *It's Only a Game*, has been interpreted as an effort to exorcise past demons and help Bradshaw reconnect with his Steelers family. He admitted, "I think the Steelers' family has had enough negative from me alone. I'm trying to be the goodwill ambassador for the Steelers. I love them, and I miss them." Bradshaw took a zany approach to explain who he is now and who he was as a player.

The book tour included stops throughout the country. At a store in a suburb of Pittsburgh, more than 400 people waited in line to get the former quarterback's signature on a copy of the work. Others wanted to tell him how much he means to them and that they hope he will return to the Steelers fold. There were lots of "I love yous" and "You made the 1970s great, man" mixed in with people's greetings. Fans in a county seat in western Pennsylvania also greeted Bradshaw, who signed copies of his book in a large grocery store. Bradshaw said, "I really do love the fans. They know the game. They support their team. I love them."[32]

Steelers and Bradshaw fans were expected to purchase and enjoy the book. And so were reporters and reviewers. One in Fort Worth, Texas, initially thought, "[T]he last thing we need is one more self-pitying autobiography." He said *It's Only a Game* turned out to be surprisingly entertaining. The book contained some things the reviewer dreaded reading about, for example, Bradshaw's inability to stay married and problems with self-esteem. But for the most part, the author made fun of himself. The reviewer added that Bradshaw is a grown-up country kid who compensated for his lack of social polish by coming up with earthy one-liners and making a good impression. A Southern California reporter agreed that the book was a good read. He noted that the work chronicled Bradshaw's roller-coaster TV career and the network transformation of his on-air persona. What struck him most was the theme of not taking work and football too seriously. The reporter thought the sentiment very appropriate in light of the 9/11 terrorist attacks.

The book sold well, making an appearance on the *New York Times* Best Sellers List in September 2001. The next book came out to less fanfare in 2002. An Orlando-based reviewer observed that *Keep It Simple* featured the ways we can learn to accomplish the easy-to-do things that can make you a happier person and found the book entertaining. Readers enjoyed both books. A veterinarian technician bought them immediately and found both enjoyable. Another fan explained that she laughed so hard while reading the books at the beach that people stopped to ask her what she was reading. The 15 readers who posted reviews on Amazon in 2001, expressed overwhelming enthusiasm, except for one, who gave it one out of five stars, writing, "I deplore his TV and movie work." A few years later, 13 reviews from readers of *It's Only a Game* averaged 4.6 out of five stars, while four reviews for *Keep It Simple* averaged 4.3 out of five stars. [33]

During the year that the second book emerged, Bradshaw pursued another of his passions, becoming the owner of a car racing team. The old quarterback had long enjoyed NASCAR and had served as grand marshal of the TranSouth 4000 in the late 1990s. "I'm a huge fan, and it's great to be here at something like this," he had commented. "There are not a lot of things left for me to experience. This was something I wanted to do." He wanted to drive around the speedway full out, but officials told him to maintain a speed of 55 miles per hour. Three years later, he waved the green flag to start one of the most tragic and mesmerizing Daytona 500 races in years. The 2001 race cost driver Dale Earnhardt Sr. his life.[34]

Fox Sports had picked up the television contract for NASCAR earlier that year. Bradshaw attended the Daytona 500 as a broadcaster. A year later, he felt shivers thinking about his last moments with friend Dale Earnhardt. "Dale Earnhardt grabbed me behind my ears, forehead to forehead, and he said, 'I'm so glad you're here, you're my good-luck charm, man.'"[35]

A few months later, the eldest Earnhardt son, Kerry, joined a new racing team started by Armando Fitz, former vice president of operations for Team SABCO, and Terry Bradshaw. Earnhardt's car was sponsored by Supercuts, the national hair-cutting chain. "With a legendary racing name like Earnhardt and a celebrity with a household name such as Terry Bradshaw, our team is able to provide our sponsor with marketing options and extensions no other team can provide," Fitz said. Bradshaw noted that he had opportunities for partnerships before but waited until he found a partnership with a friend. Similarly, Fitz related, "I just said, 'Let's just see if you and I can even be friends before we do something like this.'" His biggest concern was bringing on a celebrity sponsor who made promises of doing commercials and off-track stuff and then didn't follow through.[36]

The team needed Bradshaw to organize financial support quickly. The bursting of the "dot.com" bubble had led to more than 50 percent of the Internet technology companies going out of business between 2001 and 2004, plunging stock prices, and a decrease in spending. The sputtering economy forced sponsors to withdraw support and some teams to fold because of financial stress. The Fitz–Bradshaw team had recently acquired a motel chain called Knights Inn as a new sponsor. Their decals would accompany those from Supercuts on their number 12 Chevrolet. The companies purchase the names of the owner and driver for their commercials as well, with Bradshaw and Earnhardt both appearing in one Supercuts commercial. Bradshaw handled the team's finances and also served as the team's cheerleader. Earnhardt said Bradshaw did not try to lend any technical racing expertise to the team. "We don't listen to him if he does," Earnhardt said.[37]

In their first year, Fitz–Bradshaw finished 22nd overall in the racing points. They ranked fourth among rookie drivers. Bradshaw admitted it took time for the team to understand one another. "If I pushed too hard he [Kerry Earnhardt] couldn't handle it. Like me. You've got to love on me a little bit, pat me on the back. I'll kill for you. That's Kerry. I had to figure him out. Now I expect big things," said the quarterback. When those things failed to materialize, Bradshaw tried to remove Earnhardt, but the sponsors had their own opinions and his partner wanted to be politically correct. As one fan observed, "And it's tough to understand what a sponsor sees in some drivers." Bradshaw threatened to quit if the team did not replace their driver. After the change, veteran Tim Fedewa recorded the team's three best finishes of the season—12th, 13th, and 13th. "Hello? Does that tell you something?" said Bradshaw. Fedewa tamped down the expectations a little. "We'd like to run better, but right now we're trying to weed the bad (equipment) out and get the good in for over the winter," the driver noted.[38]

The team continued to look for a winning formula. Going into its third year on the Busch racing circuit, Fitz–Bradshaw Racing announced some changes. The team said that the U.S. Navy would continue to sponsor their car. They switched from Chevrolet to Dodge, hired David Stremme as a new driver, and entered a partnership with the Chip Ganassi/Felix Sabates Nextel Cup team. The move made a great deal of sense. "It's a catch-22. When you get big sponsors you've got to produce. But to produce, you've got to spend money on wind tunnel time and chassis and engines. These were things we couldn't afford, so we needed an association," Bradshaw explained.[39]

The expansion of the team to three cars indicated the success Bradshaw had in negotiating with sponsors. Many former NFL players have gotten involved in NASCAR. Brett Favre, Dan Marino, and baseball's Mark McGwire are former car owners. Former Buffalo Bills quarterback Jim Kelly has a team in the Busch series. Receivers Terance Mathis and Tim Brown have both started teams and soon realized that without help from a sponsor, the best race car never leaves the garage. Ex-Dallas Cowboys quarterbacks Roger Staubach and Troy Aikman worked to put together a team. Former Washington Redskins coach Joe Gibbs has been the most successful, with three NASCAR championships.

By 2006, the time and effort required to acquire and retain sponsorships had proven too demanding for Bradshaw. He said, "[M]y schedule is making it harder and harder to fulfill the necessary race team sponsor commitments for personal appearances. It's time to move on." The

Fitz–Bradshaw group lagged in the middle of the pack among the teams in the Busch series. "I love racing, and I treasure the relationships I've made with so many wonderful people connected with NASCAR," Bradshaw stated.[40]

The realization that he might not be able to meet the demands of the racing team came at a time when Bradshaw had just completed shooting one theatrical movie and started shooting one for television. He had retained his love of acting while pursuing his interests as author and race car owner. Bradshaw appeared as the voice of Preston Rogers in an episode from the fifth season of the animated series *King of the Hill* in 2000. He returned to the familiar role of coach in 2002, playing Coach Clarence in two episodes of *Malcolm in the Middle* in the program's third season.

Bradshaw continued to average an appearance in one television series per season. He received a slightly different role during the next television season, playing the father of a boyfriend of Kerry Hennessy on the show *8 Simple Rules*. A Fort Worth television critic applauded Bradshaw for taking a role that did not involve yelling. He appeared on the annual "ghoultide" Halloween episode of *The Simpsons* with former NBA star Dennis Rodman.[41]

Bradshaw's entertainment peers have acknowledged his activities throughout his career. He received his own star on the Hollywood Walk of Fame, in the television category. As of 2016, 17 athletes have stars on the Walk. Bradshaw remains the only former NFL player so honored. Aside from the four Olympians from Hollywood's "Golden Age"—Buster Crabbe, Sonja Henie, Johnny Weissmuller, and Esther Williams—only four professional athletes have joined the quarterback—heavyweight champion Muhammad Ali, former baseball player Chuck Connors, NBA legend Earvin "Magic" Johnson, and professional golfer Joe Kirkwood Jr. The Walk of Fame remains one of the most popular tourist attractions in the city, drawing millions of visitors to the more than 2,500 stars.[42]

Despite having his career immortalized, Bradshaw added to his resume significantly in the mid-2000s. In late 2004 and early 2005, he picked up three movie roles. He performed the voice of "Broken Arm Bot," in the movie *Robots*, released theatrically in March 2005. *Robots* is centered on the story of a young man who created robots to make the world a better place but falls in love with an executive robot and must face a corporate tyrant. Robin Williams led the group of misfit robots, including Bradshaw, that helped the hero succeed. Major movie critics generally appreciated the visual delight but found the story trite.

The reviews appeared in newspapers throughout the country. Most observers mentioned the actors and actresses who voiced the major characters. Other actors and actresses with smaller roles were listed in a large group or in a group of actors and actresses who performed cameo roles. While Bradshaw oftentimes appeared in this group, one Buffalo critic expressed surprise that he failed to see the names Bradshaw, Jay Leno, James Earl Jones, and Al Roker, among others. A small Pennsylvania suburban newspaper commented that the movie included a nice, small part for Steelers great Terry Bradshaw.

Audiences showed significant appreciation for the movie at the box office. After making more than $128 million in the United States, the movie made more than $132 million in foreign sales. Audience reviewers on Rottentomatoes.com have numbered nearly 1,000 since 2008. A majority of them enjoyed the movie, with Williams receiving plaudits, even from those who disliked it. [43]

In the romantic comedy *Failure to Launch*, starring Matthew McConaughey as Tripp and Sarah Jessica Parker as Paula, Bradshaw played Tripp's father, while Kathy Bates played his mother. The parents hire Parker's character to get their 35-year-old bachelor son to move out of their home in suburban Baltimore. Tripp is an overgrown mama's boy who hasn't found the courage to take flight from the nest. The plot hatched by the parents nearly backfires when Tripp falls for the girl of his dreams. Director Tom Dey stated he felt particularly impressed with the chemistry that developed between costars Terry Bradshaw, a Shreveport native and former NFL star, and Oscar winner Kathy Bates. "You really believed that they could be together since high school," he said. [44]

Despite the perception of the director, movie critics expressed derision at the movie. Only one-third of the reviewers in the major news outlets enjoyed the film. The general critical opinion was that it was a flat romantic comedy with a formulaic plot that barely rose, even during its comedic moments. Some argued that fans of McConaughey could breeze through the movie while everyone else groaned and moaned.

Audiences turned out to see the movie. It ranked number one at the box office in its opening week and stayed in the top 10 grossing movies for six weeks. On a budget of $50 million, the film made approximately $89 million in the United States and almost $130 million worldwide.[45]

As a costar in the movie, Bradshaw received a significant amount of critical attention. One critic from Southern California enjoyed the interaction between the parents, noting, "Perhaps the greatest attraction of this film is the chance to see Kathy Bates and Terry Bradshaw." One of the reviewers who enjoyed the movie thought Bates and Bradshaw were quite funny. Another, who gave it 2.5 out of four stars, thought the supporting characters carried the movie. Among the positive critics, Bradshaw earned praise for his comedic turn. One television reviewer said he was impressed with Bradshaw's performance. "He was funny. He was good," he commented. Most interesting, one critic observed that he and Bates provided more than comedy, referring to them as an appealing double act. Another critic felt the pair gave very poignant performances, portraying a couple who rekindled their relationship after their kids left home.[46]

The majority of reviewers expressed negative criticism of the movie. One discussed the poor script but praised the vibrancy of the supporting actors, whereas the critic for *USA Today* could barely find one thing to like. A second national viewpoint, from a major entertainment magazine, devoted only two lines to the movie. A Chicago critic thought the movie's comedy could be summarized by having Bradshaw appear in the nude. He was one of several professional reviewers who mentioned the former quarterback's nudity.[47]

Reviews from audience members were more positive. About half enjoyed the movie, either for the romance or the comedy, but few enjoyed both. A few said they "loved" or "enjoyed" Terry Bradshaw. A big fan of the movie noted, "This movie was pretty good. My husband even watched it! The end is great, and Terry Bradshaw is a scream. Lol." Most who disliked the movie observed a long list of problems. In finding something positive, they usually mentioned the turn by Zooey Deschanel or the supporting characters, played by Justin Bartha and Bradley Cooper, and, of course, Bates and Bradshaw, who "garner the film's few laughs." On a few occasions they praised Bradshaw, saying, for example, "Kathy Bates and Terry Bradshaw were great as Tripp's parents." One reviewer who disliked the film, commenting that it was a "horrible chick flick," offered a backhanded compliment, noting, "Terry Bradshaw is pretty good at acting like himself."[48]

One of seven audience commentators mentioned Bradshaw appearing nude. A fan of the movie matter-of-factly mentioned in a three-line review that they showed the dad's naked butt a lot. A young woman who gave the movie a high rating wrote, "Terry Bradshaw was also hillarious [sic] in his naked room scene." But most audience members seemed bothered by his nude scene. A man who gave the movie a four-star review wrote, "I saw a little more of Bradshaw than I wanted, but I like goofy movies." Another male reviewer who gave the movie 3.5 stars simply wrote, "Put some pants on Bradshaw!" A female fan of the movie noted, "Very good, even with Terry Bradshaw's icky naked body." One reviewer who ardently disliked the movie thought a natural reaction for a character seeing him naked would be, "Eww! Gross!"[49]

Reporters in sports and entertainment also issued statements of grievance related to the Bradshaw display. "Why would it give us such extended looks at Terry Bradshaw's bare behind?" asked one movie reviewer in Kansas. Another from Arkansas called the scene "shocking." A reviewer from Central Florida simply wrote, "I saw Terry Bradshaw's naked butt. Talk about a big mistake." A married movie-reviewing couple asked why Bradshaw did not have a body double and called his scene "terrifying nudity."[50]

Some sports reporters expressed their disgust even more strongly, if that was possible. A St. Louis sports columnist wrote, "Industry experts predict the film will gross a couple of million, and gross out many more." A local Florida journalist quipped, "It's a wonderful country when our friend Terry Bradshaw at 57 . . . with a nude scene." The San Antonio Express-News sports section simply said, "Terry, we don't give a damn. Just don't ever drop trou again."[51]

Several reporters brought up the "bare-buns" scene in an interview with Bradshaw. He admitted that at first the thought doing the scene felt humiliating. "I kind of liked it and said, 'Well, this is no different than taking a shower with a bunch of football players.' It's just my butt. Had it not been funny, I would have never done it. And it is funny," he declared. Later he explained, "I'm a football player. You can't expect me to go from that to doing 'Gone with the Wind.'" Oscar-winning actress Kathy Bates observed her costar's difference in background, saying, "I come from the theater, and he's from the gridiron." But she credited his personality, adding, "Terry made me feel more comfortable being myself. I'm used to hiding behind the mask of a character and have always been shy, and that's something (being himself on screen) that he does so well."[52]

At about the time of the release of *Failure to Launch*, Bradshaw was working on the television movie *Relative Chaos*. The program aired on the ABC Family network and involved the story of the youngest of three siblings, who attempts to win a family athletic competition called the Gilbert Cup and beat his older siblings for the first time. The movie offered a look at a lovably dysfunctional family whose problems formed an extreme version of those shared by some viewers. Bradshaw played the family patriarch, Will Gilbert, a flawed father with out-of-kilter priorities. Actress Charisma Carpenter played one of the leads and gave Bradshaw high praise, relating, "He's incredibly hard working. . . . And I think he excels at whatever he puts his mind to."[53]

The movie generated few reviews from movie critics. There was also little commentary from audience members. One reviewer gave the movie three out of five stars. She wrote, "Bradshaw particularly shines as a flawed father whose priorities are so shaky that he cursed his kids with rhyming names."[54]

After this run of movies, Bradshaw returned to a few television guest spots. He appeared in a tribute to Hank Williams Jr., which aired on the Country Music TV network in mid-November 2007. Early the next year, he played against character as Pete Skinner, a horse-track gambler who arouses suspicion by always being right. He played this more subdued character successfully. Bradshaw also appeared on a holiday special featuring the redneck, blue-collar character "Larry the Cable Guy." The *Larry the Cable Guy Star-Studded Christmas Extravaganza* also included as guest stars country musicians Toby Keith and Blake Shelton, and Southern comedians Jeff Foxworthy and Bill Engvall. A year later, Bradshaw appeared as himself in one episode of the first season of a new comedy called *The League*.[55]

One of Bradshaw's most involved projects in 2008–2009 was serving as an executive producer of a documentary called *Walking on Dead Fish*. The story focused on East St. John High School, in La Place, Louisiana, which took in more than 450 students from New Orleans after Hurricane Katrina. The football team declared all positions open after inviting 20 new players from New Orleans to try out for the team. Rather than be bitter about possibly losing their positions on the squad, the young men banded together to become a team. Bradshaw narrated this inspirational movie about people caring for one another.

One reviewer relished the film, observing that the viewer comes to understand what the situation must have been like for the students and players as they faced c hallenges beyond losing material possessions. He wrote, " Sit back and ride the emotional roller coaster only a hurricane as powerful as Katrina could produce, in the uplifting and heart-wrenching documentary." The critic for New Orleans' major daily thought the movie was a winning sports documentary. And it was some-thing more in its depiction of what it was like moving forward after Hurricane Katrina: "[N]arrator Bradshaw—who, along with New Or-leans Saints running back Reggie Bush, earned an executive producer credit—tamps down his usual high-energy joviality here, and 'Walking on Dead Fish' is a better film for it."[56]

In the five years since appearing on *The League*, most of Bradshaw's television appearances has been on talk shows and reality programs. After sitting in the audience for *Survivor* in 2010, he appeared on *Cubed*, where three office drones killed time at their cubicles discuss-ing sports and pop culture, and creating skits and videos. He appeared on a wide range of talk shows, including *Fox & Friends*, *The Arsenio Hall Show*, *Jimmy Kimmel Live!*, *Larry King Live*, and *Live with Kelly*. This enabled him to gain exposure with all the different demographic groups. Bradshaw and his distinct persona achieved widespread fame.

Bradshaw has filmed many more television commercials as well. From 2012 to 2014, he made several sets of ads for the Nutrisystem dieting plan. The first focused on the system for men only, and the second he shot with Jillian Barberie and Marie Osmond. The ads claimed Bradshaw lost 32 pounds. He spoke in a relaxed tone and mentioned being able to play with his dogs and chase women. The ad clearly focused on men of the baby boomer generation who had gained excess weight and were not as active as they wanted to be.

In 2014, Bradshaw made several commercials, including one for Pepsi with former NFLers Mike Ditka and Deion Sanders. He made one for Ferguson's plumbing and contracting, and a public service an-nouncement and commercials for Merck about shingles. The latter ad played on Bradshaw's aggressive persona but showed him providing helpful information and building a team with the other characters in the commercial. Again, the ad spoke to the baby boomer generation and was centered on their health.[57]

In 2013, Bradshaw completed the process of developing a theatrical show about his life. He brought *Terry Bradshaw: America's Favorite Dumb Blonde—A Life in Four Quarters* to the Las Vegas Strip with producer and director Anita Mann. She observed, "Terry is a unique talent. . . . He's so quick-witted and ad-lib funny with a mind like mine that goes all over the place at once. I don't think we'll work with a script, just bullet points, and let him fly!"[58]

The show featured stories, singing, and jokes. There were innumerable clips from Bradshaw's television and film career (Burt Reynolds popping him in *Hooper* and Bradshaw spitting out a tooth being one highlight). His team hired four of the best backing singers and dancers in Vegas—Maren Wade, Amanda Avila, Lorena Peril, and Sarah Jessica Rhodes. The quartet received the name the "IQties." Bradshaw had audiences roaring when he sang a song about his chili beans in his stage debut at the Mirage.[59]

When asked about the composition of the audience, Bradshaw had another funny response: "I think this show—if the stadium holds 1,000 and there are 400 people there, I would say probably 80 percent of the 400 are people who know me from football and are either fans or curious, and the other 20 percent have nothing better to do." The audience was dotted with his longtime friends from football and broadcasting. "I laughed. I cried," Howie Long said in a quick assessment of the show. "Terry is a classic, old-time performer. It's just really been a big wish of his to do this."[60]

Bradshaw's connections led to more entertainment activities. He made a Christmas album with producer and friend Jerry Crutchfield, which included the single "Lights of Louisiana." It aired on several local Louisiana radio stations. Listeners offered a wide range of reactions. Some said don't listen to the tune while driving, while others called it a true Christmas song.[61]

Bradshaw has frequently been included in music videos. One of the more recent appearances starred the son of former teammate punter Bobby Walden. Robert Walden is the lead singer for Bad Horse, and Terry Bradshaw joined his friend Bobby Walden and the band for some fun with the hit song "It's All Good."[62]

In the fall of 2016, Bradshaw joined three other iconic figures from the 1970s—George Foreman, William Shatner, and Henry Winkler—in a new television program. The four men had costarring roles in a reality show called *Better Late Than Never*. They were joined by a younger comedian named Jeff Dye. They traveled throughout Asia and relied on one another for encouragement and friendship, representing likeable figures with whom the baby boomer generation can identify. The stars went through their "bucket list" items so viewers could as well. Viewers tuned in, providing "solid" ratings and an uptick in the second week.[63]

Bradshaw's status has been elevated from being well known and discussed only when he appeared on screen or in a music video to his name and character being regular subjects in comedy skits for a variety of different comedians. Rattlebrain Comedy Theater, a skit and improvisational comedy troupe based in Denver, created a musical about a town where Christmas is not celebrated. Instead, they had an annual festival of greed. In the show *B.F.E.: The Town That Christmas Forgot*, the doe-eyed ingénue character had the name "Terry Bradshaw." This broad joke played on the gender switch between the real Bradshaw and the character with the same name. A disappointed theater critic asserted that this "rimshot" joke matched the range of the show's comedy.

The Bradshaw persona has become a standard for impressionists like Frank Caliendo. He has performed the impression on talk shows and radio sports programs. Sometimes nonprofessional comedians get in on the act. Former NBA star Shaquille O'Neal impersonated Bradshaw, yelling, "Yee haw!" As one observer who appreciated the skit noted, "Shaq's impersonation was far from anything close to looking like Bradshaw, but at least he was out there doing his best." While doing little to replicate the voice, O'Neal tried to create the Bradshaw persona with jokes about his family and being poor and zany, and about rural living.[64]

NFL on Fox received coverage in the *Onion*, a farcical newspaper featuring world, national, and community news. For nearly three decades, the publication's humor often depended on presenting mundane, everyday events as newsworthy, surreal, or alarming. The article asserted that Fox's studio executives gave a stern warning to Curt Menefee for his failure to razz analyst Terry Bradshaw on at least six separate occasions. Fox Sports CEO David Hill said, "Our award-winning NFL coverage is founded on three central tenets: covering every angle, breaking every story, and really giving it to Terry about his bald head or dopey accent." The article poked fun at the show's structure and humor. It created humor for its audience by making fun of the particulars of the hosts' personalities and the Bradshaw persona.[65]

A fitting finale to the comedic treatment of Bradshaw came with a Friars' Roast. In early 2015, a group of friends, coworkers, and comedians gave Bradshaw a thorough ribbing. Before sitting as the guest of honor, Pittsburgh's former helmsman hobnobbed backstage with the roasters and a number of fellow retired football players. The roasters attacked Bradshaw's hairline, his high interception totals as a player, and his incessant product shilling, with their target guffawing with every barb. After reading a few lines from the teleprompter, Bradshaw went completely off script, making weight-loss jokes about Lisa Lampanelli, mocking Rob Riggle's irrelevance, and even cracking a few more jokes about his own intelligence.[66]

In the twenty-five years since he joined the pregame show at CBS and later the Fox network, Bradshaw has also pursued opportunities as an actor, author, emcee/host for radio and television programs, and singer. In most of these capacities, he performed his persona character, being a zany good ol' boy with a nutty family who may not be the brightest person. The persona has bordered on a caricature of a Southern man. The frequency of his performing this character has made sense, because talk shows, commercials, and situation comedies wanted to hire "Terry Bradshaw." Bradshaw has bemoaned the fact that people confuse him with his character. But celebrities have always faced this problem.

On some occasions, this overshadowing of the persona has hurt celebrities' abilities to perform and work. Some celebrities with a distinctive persona have found it difficult to get jobs because they are unable to escape the shadow of their persona. Bradshaw experienced some good fortune on this account. In one instance, he played a villainous character in a television drama, while also recording a gospel album and a Christmas album, which enabled him to present an image of a Christian Southern man. As an author and an executive producer of a movie about the effects of Hurricane Katrina on a small Louisiana town, Bradshaw also presented his perspective on what is important in life.

CONCLUSION

Sports Icons and Celebrity Entertainers

Terry Bradshaw enjoyed successful careers in two rough-and-tumble businesses: playing professional football and being a celebrity. He forged an iconic status as one of the top quarterbacks of all-time. Throughout the final decades of the twentieth century and into the first decades of the twenty-first, he engaged in various entertainment mediums, from movies and television commercials to music and cohosting a pregame program. Few athletes, let alone iconic ones, have engaged in such a wide variety of entertainment arenas. Even fewer have matched Bradshaw's success and longevity.

Most sports icons do not follow the latter path of a multifaceted entertainment career. Most sports icons, from boxer Joe Louis to baseball centerfielders Willie Mays and Mickey Mantle, generally choose to not engage in a career in another entertainment field after they retire. Many of these athletes lack the media savvy and experience to build that second career.

OTHER ENTERTAINING ICONS

A few iconic athletes engaged in several entertainment opportunities after retirement. Bradshaw contemporary Kareem Abdul-Jabbar accomplished a significant amount off the basketball court. He made slightly more appearances as an actor and many more appearances as himself on a wider array of program types than Bradshaw has. He filmed several commercials for a range of products, ranging from computers and potato chips to a state tourism board. The former center has written a dozen books and many opinion pieces related to race and religion. Unlike Bradshaw, he did not enter the realms of music, serve as a host for his sport's pregame shows, or delve into sportsmen's activities like horse and car racing.

Two professional football contemporaries, New York Jets quarterback Joe Namath and Buffalo Bills running back O. J. Simpson, also engaged in acting. Namath appeared in three movies and two television situation comedies during his playing days. Immediately after retirement, he appeared in a television series that lasted half a season. He made guest appearances on shows through the early 1980s and regularly appeared as himself on talk shows, among other programs. He appeared in many commercials, including famous ones for Haynes pantyhose and Noxzema shaving cream. Namath neither recorded music nor pursued sportsmen activities, and he did not succeeded to the degree Bradshaw has as a color commentator and studio host.

O. J. Simpson also began acting during his football career. He appeared as a guest star on a number of television shows during the early 1970s, before receiving character actor roles in a few movies during the remainder of the decade. Simpson continued to broaden his appeal and fan base with his role running through airports in commercials for Hertz Rental Car. The running back then anticipated the future that wealthy athletes today can indulge in, as he started his own film production company in the late 1970s, producing mostly made-for-TV fare in the 1980s. His greatest success came in a character role in the *Naked Gun* movies beginning in the late 1980s. Despite these achievements, Simpson made fewer appearances as himself on television talk shows than either Namath or Bradshaw. But like Namath, O. J. did not pursue a variety of entertainment areas and succeed to Bradshaw's degree as a color commentator and studio host.

A few notable sports icons from more recent times have made significant inroads into entertainment mediums. Former Miami Dolphins quarterback Dan Marino made a small number of movie and television appearances as a character and himself. Marino filmed many commercials and appeared as a studio analyst for CBS for nine years. He wrote only one book and did not record music or pursue sportsmen's activities.

Iconic quarterback Payton Manning only recently retired. He has not made movies and television shows or recorded albums but has appeared as himself on many programs and filmed numerous commercials. Former basketball center Shaquille O'Neal stands the closest to being as successful and varied as Bradshaw. He has been in a number of movies and television shows, ranging from starring in *Kazaam* in 1996, to voicing Smooth Smurf in *The Smurfs 2* two decades later. He appeared as himself on a number of shows and in many commercials. O'Neal's albums include *Shaq Diesel*, *Shaq Fu: Da Return*, *You Can't Stop the Reign*, and *Respect*, and he is author of five books. He served as an analyst on a pregame show and marketed his jewelry line through Zales. The question remains, Can he survive in the industry for another two decades?

PERSONAS

When iconic athletes find ways to successfully engage in these other entertainment areas, they become more than iconic players. As they appear in more and more shows, commercials, and other activities, they create a "character" for public consumption. This character often becomes the athlete's celebrity persona.

Managing stars' personas served as the cornerstone of the success of the Hollywood studios during the Golden Age. The studios managed the star's persona to maximize their personal appeal to their legions of fans. By the early 1970s, such sports stars as Namath and Simpson had hired consultants like Pro Sports to negotiate their endorsements and frame their images. Namath appeared as a cool, happy-go-lucky, soft-spoken, sinisterly handsome leading man, and also an outsider. Yet, he had a Manhattan penthouse and a town car. Simpson appeared in commercials that made him the athletic everyman but highlighted his attractive appearance and sensuality. Combined with his big smile, this made him appear as a sexy and desirable man. Among sports figures from the 1970s, the running back proved one of the most successful in developing a persona, second only to Bradshaw. His trial for double murder a few years later caused everything to unravel.

Kareem Abdul-Jabbar seemed to have difficulty with being an entertainment celebrity. He battled hard to retain a distinctly private part of his life. Despite his role in the movie *Airplane!* his images in sports news came across as introverted and serious to the extent that many interpreted it as sullen. Much of Abdul-Jabbar's entertainment works enhanced his persona. When they revealed certain private aspects he deemed important to keep private, it sometimes seemed that the effort to appear in the limelight was too much work and not so much fun.

Almost every star athlete since the end of Terry Bradshaw's football career in the early 1980s has hired image consultants. Bradshaw did not have the same level of professional image management. The Pittsburgh media helped forge images of him as a "dumb" Southerner. But by the middle of his playing career, he had presented images of a happy, gregarious man as well. His work as a football commentator and analyst played off these two facets of his persona, as did several of his television and commercial roles. But many of these roles also showed the excitable and zany Bradshaw as knowledgeable, particularly about football.

Intriguingly, in several of Bradshaw's commercials and stories, he took the brunt of the joke or the slapstick action or pratfall. Shaquille O'Neal also had some similar situations with some of his images. Peyton Manning's successful commercials for DirecTV created images of him as lonely and out of sorts. These three iconic athletes experienced success with these types of images. What did fans and nonfans alike enjoy about them? Certainly, most everyone enjoys a pratfall or slapstick, knowing they are not a real, but comedic situations. The commercials contained silly humor that enabled viewers to laugh with and at these icons as they appeared as the butt of the mild joke. Basketball icon Michael Jordan crafted a persona of a "cool winner" in his one movie, and during his television appearances as his self. As the greatest corporate pitchman of all time, Jordan's commercials forged an improvised stylized persona that remains popular years later because it represented greater access to the American Dream for African Americans and a race-less utopia to all.

FAN REACTIONS

The Bradshaw persona and images have generated some intriguing fan reactions. Steelers fans disliked that Bradshaw did not reach his star potential as quarterback in his first few years in the NFL. They showed their displeasure with boos, and some fans expressed displeasure by cheering when Bradshaw suffered an injury and had to be removed from the game. When the Pittsburgh metropolitan area sports media made fun of Bradshaw as a way of understanding him and explaining his deficiencies on the field, groups of Steelers fans believed this characterization.

After obtaining fan adulation with his personal success, as well as that of the team, in winning multiple championships, Bradshaw attained iconic status among Steelers fans in Pittsburgh and throughout the United States. These fans loved him as a player and used him as a measure of the playing ability of future franchise quarterbacks. They included baby boomer and Gen Xer Steelers fans, as well as Gen Xers from throughout the country old enough to become Steelers and Bradshaw fans. This affection enabled Steelers fans to forgive Bradshaw's absences from team reunions and other events. Fans wanted to see the former players come together at these reunions and charity events, seeking a display of unity and the joy and nostalgia of reliving past success. Missing a key player like Bradshaw undermined those experiences. Most significantly, his absences raised troubling questions that torpedoed the nostalgic enterprise by potentially signaling friction.

Steelers fans, like those of other teams, disliked friction among their team and its icons. Many disliked Bradshaw as a commentator and studio cohost because he used his honesty and football knowledge to take aim at the Steelers and Chuck Noll. Bradshaw expressed his displeasure with the Steelers leadership and their management of the team. Groups of fans perceived Bradshaw as being unsupportive and disloyal regardless of the accuracy of his assessments. Fans of other teams noted that these thoughts demonstrated Bradshaw's honesty and knowledge.

Overall, Bradshaw's image as a studio host has proved successful among NFL fans. They enjoy his character. The show has topped its competition among baby boomers, Gen Xers, and now Gen Yers as well, who find Bradshaw funny. As with the commercials he made during the 1990s and early 2000s, fans like the comedic characters played by Bradshaw, always willing to take the pratfall and the gentle ribbing or exhibit goofy smarts, a good example being his role in *Failure to Launch*.

Bradshaw appeared in several Burt Reynolds movies decades earlier and almost turned a supporting character in *The Cannonball Run* into a costarring role in a television sitcom; however, the number of interested fans proved too small for the program to gain admission into NBC's prime-time schedule. The pilot needed to follow the release of the movie, as the show would have benefited from a carryover fan base that was already familiar with the characters. It would have fit neatly into an era that featured such shows as *The Dukes of Hazzard* and other "Southern" programming.

Bradshaw struggled to find a similar niche in the music world, making it difficult to market him to fan groups. He sang country western songs from an earlier era, when the music had a more regional appeal. He did not fit into the stylings of the "Countrypolitan" sound, in vogue in the Nashville of the era, nor did he sound stylistically like the "Outlaw" music of the Southwest. Both sounds had national appeal to specific fan groups that Bradshaw did not quite reach.

SOUTHERN IMAGES

Both the images the media forged for Bradshaw and his persona provided some interesting commentary about the Southern United States and how the region was perceived in a Northern city like Pittsburgh. The media-created images from Bradshaw's early years as a professional quarterback used a stereotype to describe him. It conflated Southerners into one region and, worse, carried the connotation that Southerners were undereducated and dumb. Other professional football players may not have been as open to reporters. Maybe they did not provide the variety of responses that Bradshaw did. But reporters gave Bradshaw the Li'l Abner label primarily because the view fit a commonly held perception of Southerners in the early 1970s.

The stereotype of "dumb Southern male" happened to be decades out of date. Since World War II, the South had gained numerous technical, managerial, and other white-collar jobs. Funding for secondary education and attendance at universities grew throughout the region. The depictions of the South in movies changed for the better, as evidenced by Burt Reynolds's movies, and Southern music began making significant inroads throughout the nation. A few years later, in 1976, a former governor of Georgia won the presidency, becoming the first person from the region to win the office since the Civil War.

The stereotype played a role in shaping Bradshaw's persona. As he said in a roundtable discussion of player images with his fellow pregame show coworkers, the stereotype that led to him being called a "dumb quarterback" hurt him as much as anything in his life. Howie Long contended that Bradshaw had "cultivated part of that," and Bradshaw quickly responded, "[T]o survive I had to."[1] Bradshaw sometimes played the character on talk shows, his own radio program, and *NFL on Fox*, making jokes about being poor or ill-educated, or perpetuating exaggerations about family.

As cohost of *NFL on Fox* and in commercials and guest spots on many television programs, Bradshaw added to the persona. While volume, humor, and good ol' boy friendliness might be considered part of the stereotype, Bradshaw gave those aspects shadings that made them less problematic. He added moments of knowledge, thoughtfulness, and mania that undercut the stereotypical figure. His roles in the Reynolds movies showed that he and other "good ol' boys" felt kinship with others with the same socioeconomic status. His roles showed that Southern boys could support black men and have them as friends.

Other Bradshaw images offered different depictions of Southern men. His initial singing images represented the regional old-style country guy in an era when country music developed two new styles that were more national and mainstream. His forays into gospel singing provided images of a Southern gentleman practicing his faith with likeminded people. These images illuminated a man with a certain humbleness and a sense of community.

Bradshaw's most distinct images have come from his movies of the mid-2000s. In *Failure to Launch*, he represented an everyman with a few unusual interests that he wanted the freedom to pursue. In *Relative Chaos*, his father figure remained happily married to his wife and offered his children traditions and tough love. Both images involved complicated family men with professional backgrounds who were intelligent and had long since abandoned the activities of the good ol' boys, if they ever pursued that lifestyle at all. Bradshaw put these images on display in his theatrical play *Terry Bradshaw: America's Favorite Dumb Blonde*, telling stories about Southern poverty and being an iconic quarterback, quipping about his commercials, and singing songs.

The many public images of Terry Bradshaw have revealed an individual who is very much a man of his time who stood out in it as well. The cartoon nicknames, with their connotations of Bradshaw being dumb, fit the prejudiced view of many people in urban Northern cities regarding people from the South. This perception remained in the minds of many professional football people and fans, even after the quarterback led his team to four Super Bowl championships.

Bradshaw emerged during a period when various aspects of Southern people and culture were gaining more political and cultural attention throughout the country. One of the top box-office stars of the time, fellow Southerner Burt Reynolds, made movies set in and about the region. Bradshaw's background enabled him to be in some of those films, but his unique personality enabled him to forge the connection with Reynolds. But Bradshaw's success in country music proved more limited, as the genre had moved into newer styles; however, his musical foray into gospel earned him plaudits from the music industry and enabled him to ride the revival wave when old-time Southern gospel crested in the 1990s. With these and other images, Bradshaw brought to the fore the changed and complicated region of the South and its people.

NOTES

1. BORN IN FOOTBALL COUNTRY

1. Jerry Byrd, *Jerry Byrd's Football Country* (Shreveport, LA: Shreveport Publishing, 1981), vii.

2. Byrd, *Jerry Byrd's Football Country*, 55.

3. Byrd, *Jerry Byrd's Football Country*, 55.

4. Terry Bradshaw, with Buddy Martin, *Looking Deep* (New York: Berkley Books, 1989), 4–5.

5. Terry Bradshaw, with David Diles, *Terry Bradshaw: Man of Steel* (Grand Rapids, MI: Zondervan, 1979), 63–64.

6. Eric J. Brock, *Eric Brock's Shreveport* (Gretna, LA: Pelican, 2001), 15, 17, 23, 29, 37, 64, 79, 87.

7. Terry Bradshaw, with David Fisher, *Keep It Simple* (New York: Atria, 2002), 54–61.

8. Terry Bradshaw, with David Fisher, *It's Only a Game* (New York: Simon & Shuster, 2001), 16–18.

9. A. L. Williams, telephone interview by author, March 24, 2016.

10. Robert Madison Griffin, telephone interview by author, March 22, 2016.

11. "Sport: Eat 'Em Up, Get 'Em!" *Time*, September 27, 1976, http://content.time.com/time/magazine/article/0,9171,918374,00.html (accessed April 3, 2016).

12. Bradshaw, *Terry Bradshaw: Man of Steel*, 67–69; Nico Van Thyn, "The Team Named Desire," *Nvanthyn.blogspot.com*, August 30, 2012, http://nvanthyn.blogspot.com/2012/08/the-team-named-desire.html (accessed April 3, 2016).

13. Bradshaw, *Terry Bradshaw: Man of Steel*, 67–69.

14. Jimmy Watson, "Lee Hedges Will Have Plenty to Say about A. L. Williams: Terry Bradshaw Says Coach Was a Patient Teacher," *Shreveport Times*, July 25, 2014, http://www.shreveporttimes.com/-lee-hedges-will-have-plenty-to-say-about-aA-l-williams (accessed July 26, 2016).

15. *Terry Bradshaw: Man of Steel*, 69; Jimmy Watson, "Bradshaw, Ferguson Set Stage for Proflic Passing Attacks," *USA Today High School Sports*, September 3, 2015, http://www.usatodayhss.com/2015/bradshaw-ferguson-set-stage-for-proflic-passing-attacks (accessed March 21, 2016).

16. Nico Van Thyn, "'The Blond Bomber' a Bright Star, Then and Now," *Nvanthyn.blogspot.com*, April 14, 2012, http://nvanthyn.blogspot.com/2012/04/blond-bomber-bright-star-then-and-now.html(accessed March 15, 2016).

17. Byrd, *Jerry Byrd's Football Country*, 116–19, 151.

18. Telephone interview with A. L. Williams, Woodlawn High School coach, March 24, 2016.

19. Eddie Jenkins, *Louisiana High School Football Championships: The Complete Reference Book, 1921–1996* (Shreveport, LA: 14-0 Publications, 1997) ; Eddie Jenkins, "Playoff and Title Game Appearances and Titles Won," *WinnfieldTigerFootball.com*, http://www.winnfieldtigerfootball.com/louisiana_high_school_football_championships.html (accessed April 18, 2016); comment by Lee Reece, in Tim McMillen, "Fan Tribute to Terry Bradshaw," *Mcmillenandwife.com*, http://www.mcmillenandwife.com/bradshaw_fans.html (accessed February 26, 2016).

20. Telephone interview with A. L. Williams, Woodlawn High School coach, March 24, 2016.

21. Nico Van Thyn, "A Brutal Day in Murfreesboro," *Nvanthyn.blogspot.com*, January 31, 2014, http://nvanthyn.blogspot.com/2014/01/a-brutal-day-in-murfreesboro.html (accessed April 3, 2016); Williams, telephone interview by author; "Prep Javelin Thrower Has Record Effort," *Sun*, March 27, 1966, A4.

22. Bradshaw, *Looking Deep*, 60–61; *Horse Feathers*, dir. Norman Z. McLeod, perf. Marx Brothers and Thelma Todd. Paramount Pictures, 1932; Andy Staples, "A History of Recruiting: How Coaches Have Stayed a Step Ahead," *Sports Illustrated*, June 23, 2008, http://www.si.com/more-sports/2008/06/23/recruiting-main (accessed April 21, 2016).

23. Bradshaw, *Looking Deep*, 59–61; Bradshaw, *Terry Bradshaw: Man of Steel*, 49–51.

24. Bradshaw, *Terry Bradshaw: Man of Steel*, 79–81; Nico Van Thyn, telephone interview by author, March 15, 2016; "Tennessee Eagles Put . . . ," *Monroe Morning World*, October 30, 1966, 2-C.

25. "Bradshaw Pacing Bulldogs . . . ," *Ruston Daily Leader*, November 3, 1967, 2; Nico Van Thyn, "Phil and Terry and 4–16?" *Nvanthyn.blogspot.com*, June 26, 2013, http://nvanthyn.blogspot.com/2013/06/phil-and-terry-and-4-16. html (accessed March 15, 2016); Glenn Murphy, interview by author, January 12, 2017.

26. Bert Jones, telephone interview by author, April 19, 2016; Bradshaw, *Looking Deep*, 73–74; Nico Van Thyn, "Football Integration at La. Tech: Making It Work," *Nvanthyn.blogspot.com*, April 10, 2015, http://nvanthyn.blogspot. com/2015/04/football-integration-at-la-tech-making.html (accessed March 21, 2016).

27. Byrd, *Jerry Byrd's Football Country*, 143–45.

28. Van Thyn, telephone interview by author; comment by Shirley Cobb, in McMillen, "Fan Tribute to Terry Bradshaw."

29. Van Thyn, "A Brutal Day in Murfreesboro."

30. "So. Mississippi Surprised by Louisiana Tech," *Washington Post*, November 3, 1968, C5; "Akron Loses to La.Tech in Rice Bowl," *Washington Post*, December 15, 1968, C2.

31. Byrd, *Jerry Byrd's Football Country*, 35–37, 52; Bradshaw, *Keep It Simple*, 204.

32. Murphy, interview by author.

33. Neil Amdur, "Bradshaw: Big Man, Tiny College . . . ," *New York Times*, October 28, 1969, 55.

34. "Bulldog History," *LATechSports*, http://grfx.cstv.com/photos/schools/latc/sports/m-baskbl/auto_pdf/0910-mbk-Sec7.pdf (accessed March 31, 2016).

35. Mickey Herskowitz, "The Year of the Quarterback," *Sun*, September 21, 1969, B8; "E. Tennessee Rips La. Tech in Rice Bowl," *Washington Post*, December 14, 1969, 46.

36. Comment by Mike Guzman, in McMillen, "Fan Tribute to Terry Bradshaw."

37. Byrd, *Jerry Byrd's Football Country*, 53.

38. William M. Wallace, "Football Draft Starts Tuesday . . . ," *New York Times*, January 25, 1970, 167.

39. Arthur Daley, "The Wheelers and Dealers," *New York Times*, January 30, 1970, 36.

40. Wallace, "Football Draft Starts Tuesday."

41. "Record Pact Set as . . . ," *Washington Evening Star*, January 28, 1970, 28; "Colts Offer Several for Bradshaw," *Washington Post*, February 4, 1970, D5.

42. "Football: Rookies on a Rampage," *Time*, October 10, 1969, http://content.time.com/time/magazine/article/0,9171,839063,00.html (accessed April 22, 2016).

43. Gary Ronberg, "'I Wanted to Go with a Loser,'" *Sports Illustrated*, February 9, 1970, http://www.si.com/vault/1970/02/09/552493/terry-bradshaw-drafted-steelers-nfl (accessed March 22, 2016).

44. "Despite Confidence, Bradshaw . . . ," *Washington Evening Star*, February 17, 1970, 32; "Louisiana Tech Players Present Ball to President," *Washington Post*, April 8, 1970, D4.

45. Debra Bell, "U.S. News Questions Football's Future Nearly 45 Years Ago," *U.S. News and World Report*, February 1, 2013, http://www.usnews.com/news/blogs/press-past/2013/02/01/us-news-questioned-pro-footballs-future-nearly-45-years-ago (accessed April 30, 2016); Frank Deford, "Hot Pitchmen in the Selling Game," *Sports Illustrated*, November 17, 1969, http://www.si.com/vault/1969/11/17/613826/hot-pitchmen-in-the-selling-game (accessed May 11, 2016).

46. "Bradshaw Signs with Steelers," *Washington Post*, April 26, 1970, C5; Richard Florida, "Which Parts of the Country Produce the Most NFL Players?" *CityLab*, April 26, 2012, http://www.citylab.com/design/2012/04/which-parts-country-produce-most-nfl-players/1840/ (accessed March 31, 2016).

47. Robert Lipsyte, "Sports of the Times . . . ," *New York Times*, May 25, 1970, 62.

2. THE BRADSHAW IMAGE

1. William Shakespeare, *All's Well That Ends Well*, Act II, i, 145.

2. George Vecsey, "Steelers' Bradshaw Stars in 21–6 Defeat of Giants," *New York Times*, August 29, 1970, E4.

3. "Bradshaw Leads Steelers over Giants," *Washington Post*, August 29, 1970, E4; "Rookie Slinger Bradshaw Impresses Steeler Mates . . . ," *Sun*, August 30, 1970, A8.

4. John Mehno, "History of the Stadium," in Pittsburgh Pirates Official 1995 Commemorative Yearbook (Dallas, TX: Sports Media, 1995); Edward K. Muller, "Downtown Pittsburgh: Renaissance and Renewal," in Kevin J. Patrick and Joseph L. Scarpaci Jr., eds., *A Geographic Perspective of Pittsburgh and the Alleghenies* (Pittsburgh, PA: University of Pittsburgh Press, 2006), 7–20.

5. "Bradshaw Fills Need of Steelers," *Washington Post*, August 16, 1970, C3; Bob Addie, "Oh Shoot!" *Washington Post*, April 23, 1970, K5.

6. Dave Anderson, "Namath, the Actor, Unsure of His Role in Pro Football," *New York Times*, May 27, 1970, 52; "Namath Ponders Quitting Football," *Washington Post*, May 27, 1970, F3; William M. Wallace, "Other Passers Have Troubles . . . ," *New York Times*, August 12, 1970, 47.

7. "Simpson's Pact Includes Bonus," *Baltimore Sun*, September 10, 1969, C1; "Oilers Tough on Defense in 17–3 Win over Buffalo," *Baltimore Sun*, September 22, 1969, C5; Arthur Daley, "Sports of the Times: A Time for Growth," *New York Times*, S2.

8. "Bradshaw Fills Need of Steelers," C3.

9. Mark Osele, interview by author, January 18, 2016; Jim Murray, "He Paid Big Penalty . . . ," *Los Angeles Times*, September 17, 1989, 1.

10. William M. Wallace, "Bradshaw Hopes to Put Steelers . . . ," *New York Times*, September 17, 1970, 64; Rodger Brown, "Dogpatch USA: The Road to Hokum," *Southern Changes: The Journal of the Southern Regional Council* 15, no. 3 (1993): 18–26.

11. M. Thomas Inge, "Li'l Abner, Snuffy, Pogo, and Friends: The South in the American Comic Strip," *Southern Quarterly* 48, no. 2 (2011): 6–74; Michael Schumacher and Denis Kitchen, *Al Capp: A Life to the Contrary* (New York: Bloomsbury, 2013); Roy Blount Jr., *About Three Bricks Shy . . . and the Load Filled Up* (Pittsburgh, PA: University of Pittsburgh Press, 2004), 15–16; Nancy Isenberg, *White Trash: The 440-Year Untold History of Class in America* (New York: Viking, 2016), 219–20, 234–36.

12. Blount Jr., *About Three Bricks Shy*, 148–49.

13. Gary M. Pomerantz, *Their Life's Work: The Brotherhood of the 1970s Pittsburgh Steelers* (New York: Simon & Shuster, 2013), 45–55; Terry Bradshaw, with Buddy Martin, *Looking Deep* (New York: Berkley Books, 1989), 74–75.

14. "Oilers, Johnson Spoil Bradshaw Debut, 19–7," *Washington Post*, September 21, 1970, D6; "Redskins Picked by One over Cards," *Washington Post*, September 26, 1970, E5; "Oilers Lose Johnson, Game to Steelers, 7–3," *Washington Post*, October 19, 1970, C2.

15. Lewis F. Atkinson, "Steelers, Fans Dig Bradshaw," *Washington Evening Star*, October 29, 1970, 33.

16. Milton Richman, "Today's Sports Parade," *Lebanon Daily News*, October 20, 1970, 10; "Bradshaw Hit with Fine for Absence," *Washington Post*, October 22, 1970, F1.

17. "2nd Fiddle Prospect Burns Bradshaw . . . ," *Washington Post*, November 4, 1970, B2; comment by TSgt. Tom, in Tim McMillen, "Fan Tribute to Terry Bradshaw," *Mcmillenandwife.com*, http://www.mcmillenandwife.com/bradshaw_fans.html (accessed February 26, 2016).

18. Murray Chass, "Bradshaw to Be Benched . . . ," *New York Times*, November 6, 1970, 67.

19. William M. Wallace, "Heisman Winners Fluctuate as Pros," *New York Times*, November 25, 1970, 58; "Lowly Falcons Finish Steelers," *Sun*, December 14, 1970, C2; Bradshaw, *Looking Deep*, 56–57.

20. Tex Maule, "Tomorrow's Generals," *Sports Illustrated*, February 15, 1971, http://www.si.com/vault/1971/02/15/554294/tomorrows-generals (accessd March 22, 2016).

21. Lewis F. Atkinson, "Bradshaw Gets Lift . . . ," *Washington Evening Star*, August 24, 1971, 20.

22. Lewis F. Atkinson, "Brown Has Bengals . . . ," *Washington Evening Star*, August 24, 1971, 20; "Bradshaw Is Out of Hospital . . . ," *Chicago Daily Defender*, August 25, 1971, 33; William M. Wallace, "Crowds, Revenues, and Pay Lend NFL Rosy Glow," *New York Times*, August 29, 1971, S1.

23. Gerry Mullins, telephone interview by author, March 22, 2016; Scarlett Walden, telephone interview by author, June 23, 2016.

24. William M. Wallace, "NFL's Young Quarterbacks . . . ," *New York Times*, September 2, 1971, 45; John Bunardzya, "Steelers' loss to Bears . . . ,"*Valley Independent*, September 22, 1971, 10.

25. Walden, telephone interview by author.

26. Ira Berkow, "Good Knight Tries Again," *Bucks County Courier Times*, October 27, 1971, 9; "Display Ad," *Washington Post*, November 14, 1971, 20; "Bradshaw Bails Out Steelers," *Washington Post*, December 13, 1971, D2.

27. Terry Bradshaw, with David Fisher, *Keep It Simple* (New York: Atria, 2002), 84–87; "Bradshaw Engaged," *Washington Post*, January 25, 1972, D4; "Bradshaw Passes Click," *New York Times*, January 25, 1972, 30; "Bradshaw Marries," *New York Times*, February 13, 1972, S4.

28. Ken Collier, "NFL Roundup: Pittsburgh Steelers," *Chicago Daily Defender*, September 13, 1972, 30; "Gilliam Eyes Pitt QB Spot," *Chicago Daily Defender*, February 7, 1972, 27.

29. Dave Brady, "Ewbank Creams NFL Critics," *Washington Post*, September 30, 1972, C1.

30. Lewis F. Atkinson, "Bradshaw Predicts a Title . . . ," *Washington Evening Star*, November 13, 1972, D1; "Franco's Army Gets Volunteers," *Albuquerque Journal*, December 25, 1972, E2; Ron Reid, "Sweet 16 on a Super Trip," *Sports Illustrated*, January 8, 1973, http://www.si.com/vault/1973/01/08/567156/sweet-16-on-a-super-trip (accessed March 31, 2016).

31. William N. Wallace, "Pittsburgh Nears Title after Its 30–0 Victory," *New York Times*, December 4, 1972, 57; Red Smith, "Gorilla Warfare," *New York Times*, December 4, 1972, 57.

32. William N. Wallace, "Steeler Touchdown with Five Seconds Left Is Confirmed by TV," *New York Times*, December 24, 1972, S1; Myron Cope, *Double Yoi!* (Champaign, IL: Sports Publishing, 2002), 173–76; Gary Myers, "Top 10 Greatest Plays in NFL History," *New York Daily News*, September 9, 2015, http://www.nydailynews.com/sports/football/top-10-greatest-plays-nfl-history-article-1.2354371 (accessed February 9, 2017).

33. Lewis F. Atkinson, "Dolphins," *Washington Evening Star*, December 26, 1972, 37.

34. "Bradshaw Hit with Flu Bug," *Washington Post*, December 29, 1972, D2.

35. Mullins, telephone interview by author; "Blackout Is Perfect . . . ," *Bradford Era*, December 30, 1972, B1; Reid, "Sweet 16 on a Super Trip."

36. "Display Ad 442," *New York Times*, January 28, 1973, 311; Pomerantz, *Their Life's Work*, 200; Mullins, telephone interview by author.

37. "Terry Bradshaw Irked by Frequent Criticism," *Sun*, June 22, 1973, B8; D. Byron Yake, "Noll Happy with Bradshaw," *Courier-Express*, July 5, 1973, 28.

38. "Bryant Hero as Vikings Rap Steelers," *Washington Post*, August 12, 1973, D8; Neil Amdur, "Giants Down Steelers, 29–24," *New York Times*, August 27, 1973, 39.

39. Neil Amdur, "Steelers at Stadium . . . ," *New York Times*, August 26, 1973, 187.

40. Jennifer Goodin, "Solidarity Lost: The Deindustrialization of Pittsburgh in the 1980s," honors thesis, Rutgers University, New Brunswick, New Jersey, 2012, http://www.history.rutgers.edu/undergraduate/honors-program/honors-papers-2012/400-solidarity-lost-the-deindustrialization-of-pittsburgh-in-the-1980s/file (accessed February 9, 2017); Sean Dinces, "Premium Stadium Data," copy provided to author, August 17, 2014.

41. Maury Chass, "Late Steeler Surge Repels Lions, 24–10," *New York Times*, September 17, 1973, 45.

42. Sam Goldaper, "Steelers Triumph 33–6 over Browns, Take Lead," *New York Times*, September 24, 1973, 44; Ed Bouchette, *The Pittsburgh Steelers* (New York: St. Martin's, 1994), 82.

43. Terry Bradshaw, with Charles Paul Conn, *No Easy Game* (Grand Rapids, MI: F. H. Revell, 1973); "Bradshaw's Book Burns Up Bengals," *Washington Post*, October 25, 1973, D6.

44. "Brown Raps Steeler Fans," *Washington Post*, October 30, 1973, DC2; David Du Pree, "Hanratty Taped but Topped," *Washington Post*, October 30, 1973, C1; Blount Jr., *About Three Bricks Shy*, 162, 176–79.

45. "Bradshaw's Book Burns up Bengals," *Washington Post*, October 25, 1973, D6; Dave Anderson, "Hanratty Replaces Injured Bradshaw, Sparks Victory," *New York Times*, October 29, 1973, 50.

46. Shirley Povich, "This Morning," *Washington Post*, November 1, 1973, D1; David Du Pree, "Hanratty Taped but Topped," *Washington Post*, October 30, 1973, C1; Blount Jr., *About Three Bricks Shy*, 162, 187–88.

47. "Bradshaw Shrugs off Boos . . . ," *Titusville Herald*, November 16, 1973, 6; "Bradshaw Says Fans Making Him Tough," *Bradford Era*, November 16, 1973, 12.

48. "Bradshaw's Ego 'Calloused,'" *Morning Herald*, November 16, 1973, 14; Blount Jr., *About Three Bricks Shy*, 253–55.

49. William N. Wallace, "Broncos Beat Indifferent Steelers, 23–13," *New York Times*, November 19, 1973, 49.

50. "Steelers Looking for Second Title," *Washington Evening Star*, December 15, 1973, 15; Bob Maisel, "The Morning After," *Washington Post*, December 22, 1973, B1.

51. Leonard Koppett, "Steelers Crushed, 33–14," *New York Times*, December 23, 1973, 117; "Steelers Coach, Players Agree . . . ," *New York Times*, December 23, 1973, 122.

3. TWO GOLDEN RINGS

1. Debra Bell, "45 Years Ago . . . ," *U.S. News and World Report*, February 1, 2013, https://www.usnews.com/news/blogs/press-past/2013/02/01/us-news-questioned-pro-footballs-future-nearly-45-years-ago (accessed April 30, 2016).

2. "Bradshaw Signs, Rejects Offer by Stars of WFL," *New York Times*, June 3, 1974, 45.

3. "Gallery," *Washington Evening Star*, June 3, 1974, 44.

4. "Gallery," 44.

5. *The Superstars*, http://www.thesuperstars.org/ (accessed April 23, 2016); "Hal Jackson, Lane . . . ," *Afro-American*, March 2, 1974, 10; "Raider Guy Tops NFL Olympia," *Washington Post*, March 11, 1974, D2; "Fun and Money in NFL Olympia," *Washington Evening Star*, March 11, 1974, 34.

6. "543 F. 2d 606: *John Mackey et al., Appelles v. National Football League et al., Appellants*," *PublicResource.org*, November 23, 1976, http://law.justia.com/cases/federal/appellate-courts/F2/543/606/338695/ (accessed May 1, 2016); Donald Novick, "The Legality of the Rozelle Rule and Related Practices in the National Football League," *Fordham Urban Law Journal* 4, no. 3 (1975), http://ir.lawnet.fordham.edu/cgi/viewcontent.cgi?article=1048&context=ulj (accessed May 1, 2016).

7. Andrew E. Masich, Dan Rooney, and David F. Halaas, *Dan Rooney: My 75 Years with the Pittsburgh Steelers and the NFL* (New York: Da Capo, 2008), 196–97; "National Football League's Players Association: History," *NFLPA.com*, https://www.nflpa.com/about/history (accessed April 23, 2016).

8. Bob Addie, "TVS Package Is Puffy," *Washington Post*, February 24, 1974, D7; "WFL Commissioner Davidson Resigns under Pressure," *Washing-*

ton Post, October 30, 1974, F6; "Most Football Fans Welcome World Football League," *The Harris Survey*, August 22, 1974.

9. Mike Roberts, "Role in Victory . . . ," *Washington Evening Star*, August 31, 1974, 32.

10. "Steelers Squash Cowboys," *Washington Post*, September 6, 1974, E4.

11. "Olympian, 86, Finally Gets Medal," *New York Times*, September 12, 1974, 52; "Bradshaw Would Rather Leave Than Accept Bench," *Sun*, September 12, 1974, C10.

12. Terry Bradshaw, with Buddy Martin, *Looking Deep* (New York: Berkley Books, 1989), 57; Gary M. Pomerantz, *Their Life's Work: The Brotherhood of the 1970s Pittsburgh Steelers* (New York: Simon & Shuster, 2013), 129.

13. Steve Hershey, "Role in Victory . . . ," *Washington Evening Star*, September 30, 1974, 38.

14. "Noll Pondering a Change at QB," *Washington Evening Star*, October 26, 1974, 74.

15. Bradshaw, *Looking Deep*, 57; Roy Blount Jr., *About Three Bricks Shy . . . and the Load Filled Up* (Pittsburgh, PA: University of Pittsburgh Press, 2004), 185; Pomerantz, *Their Life's Work*, 133–34.

16. William N. Wallace, "Situation Cramped in Steelers Camp . . . ," *New York Times*, November 19, 1974, 46.

17. William N. Wallace, "Steelers Take Division Title . . . ," *New York Times*, December 9, 1974, 46; "Steelers Defeat Bengals, 27–3," *New York Times*, December 15, 1974, 247.

18. Gerald Strine, "'Dumb Bradshaw' at Head of Class . . . ," *Washington Post*, December 21, 1974, E5.

19. "Bradshaw Returns to Bible," *Washington Post*, December 23, 1974, F2.

20. Roy Blount Jr., "You're a Part of All This," *Sports Illustrated*, February 17, 1975, http://www.si.com/vault/1975/02/17/557877/youre-a-part-of-all-this (accessed March 31, 2016); "My Best Game," *Washington Evening Star*, December 23, 1974, 29; Cameron C. Snyder, "Bradshaw Quiets Detractors . . . ," *Sun*, December 23, 1974, C3.

21. "Pittsburgh Football Fans Rampage through Streets," *Indiana Evening Gazette*, December 30, 1974, 14.

22. Steve Guback, "Prediction: Vikings to Bend Steelers," *Washington Evening Star*, December 31, 1974, 29; Murray Olderman, "Tarkenton Will Make the Difference," *Courier-Express*, January 11, 1975, 9.

23. Dave Brady, "Much to Prove for Bradshaw," *Washington Post*, January 8, 1975, D1.

24. "Bradshaw's Brightness Defended by Steeler Coach, Quarterback," *Leader-Times*, January 8, 1975, 8; Steve Guback, "Tale of Two Quarterbacks," *Washington Evening Star*, January 9, 1975, 42.

25. Gary Mihoches, "Rozelle Throws Party . . . ," *Courier-Express*, January 11, 1975, 9.

26. Dan Jenkins, "Pittsburgh Punches It Out," *Sports Illustrated*, January 20, 1975, 12; Pomerantz, *Their Life's Work*, 179.

27. Jenkins, "Pittsburgh Punches It Out," 12; Pomerantz, *Their Life's Work*, 179.

28. Dave Brady, "Bradshaw Now Super Folk Hero," *Washington Post*, January 13, 1975, D1.

29. Norman O. Ungar, "Gilliam: A Troubled Quarterback," *Chicago Defender*, January 14, 1975, 24; "Scorecard," *Washington Evening Star*, April 8, 1975, 36; "Noll's Mind Made Up . . . ," *New Castle News*, July 22, 1975, 15.

30. "Bradshaw to Sign Recording Contract," *Sun*, June 22, 1975, B8.

31. Chico Renfroe, "It Pays to Be White in Sports," *Atlanta Daily World*, August 7, 1975, 8; A. S. Doc Young, "Good Morning Sports!" *Chicago Daily Defender*, August 6, 1975, 25.

32. Estebon On, "The 11 Biggest NFL Quarterback Controversies of All Time," *TotalProSports.com*, December 4, 2012, http://www.totalprosports.com/2012/12/04/11-biggest-nfl-quarterback-controversies-of-all-time/ (accessed May 3, 2016).

33. "Bradshaw to the Rescue," *Washington Evening Star*, November 10, 1975, 36; "Steelers Beat Oilers," *Sun*, November 10, 1975, C9.

34. Steve Guback, "I'm Sad for You . . . ," *Washington Evening Star*, December 29, 1975, B1.

35. Comment by Erasmo Mungula, in Tim McMillen, "Fan Tribute to Terry Bradshaw," *Mcmillenandwife.com*, http://www.mcmillenandwife.com/bradshaw_fans.html (accessed February 26, 2016).

36. Mark Mulvoy, "The Steelers Are on the Loose," *SportsIllustrated.com*, January 12, 1976, http://www.si.com/vault/1976/01/12/557906/the-steelers-are-on-the-loose.

37. "1975 Raiders vs. Steelers (AFC Championship)," *Vimeo.com*, September 15, 2014, https://vimeo.com/106254472 (accessed May 3, 2016); Mark Mulvoy, "The Steelers Are on the Loose," *Sports Illustrated*, January 12, 1976, http://www.si.com/vault/1976/01/12/557906/the-steelers-are-on-the-loose (accessed May 3, 2016).

38. University of Maryland Global Terrorism Database, National Consortium for the Study of Terrorism and Responses to Terrorism, "Incidents over Time, 1970–1979," *Start.umd.edu*, 2009–2015, https://www.start.umd.edu/gtd/search/Results.aspx?start_yearonly=1970&end_yearonly=1979&start_year=&

start_month=&start_day=&end_year=&end_month=&end_day=&country= 217&asmSelect1=&dtp2=all&success=yes&casualties_type=b&casualties_max (accessed May 10, 2016).

39. Dave Brady, "Dumb Talk Still Haunts Bradshaw," *Washington Post*, January 10, 1976, D3.

40. Byron Rosen, "Ex-Coach Would Settle . . . ," *Washington Post*, January 30, 1976, C4; David Tarrant, "Terry Bradshaw . . . ," *Dallas Morning News*, August 27, 1995, 1E.

41. Dan Jenkins, "Dallas Feels the Steeler Crunch," *Sports Illustrated*, January 26, 1976, http://www.si.com/vault/1976/01/26/541835/dallas-feels-the-steeler-crunch (accessed May 3, 2016).

42. Jenkins, "Dallas Feels the Steeler Crunch"; Fred Brewer, "Super Sunday Metamorphosis," *Big Spring Herald*, January 18, 1976, B1; Ted Stinson, "Madhouse . . . ," *Naples Daily News¸* January 20, 1976, C1; "Super Bowl X: Cowboys vs. Steelers," *Youtube* , https://www.youtube.com/watch?v=MBdY_YGGXwk (accessed May 3, 2016).

43. Steve Guback, "Swann Difference," *Washington Evening Star*, January 19, 1976, 41.

44. "100,000 Greet Victorious Steelers," *Sun*, January 20, 1976, C5.

4. TWO MORE GOLDEN RINGS

1. Byron Rosen, "Ex-Coach Would Settle . . . ," *Washington Post*, January 30, 1976, C4.

2. Dave Brady, "Starbuck Finds Bradshaw . . . ," *Washington Post*, January 28, 1976, D3; comment by Tim McMillen, in Tim McMillen, "Fan Tribute to Terry Bradshaw," *Mcmillenandwife.com*, http://www.mcmillenandwife.com/bradshaw_fans.html (accessed February 26, 2016); comment by Larry D., in McMillen, "Fan Tribute to Terry Bradshaw"; comment by Kathie Townsend, in McMillen, "Fan Tribute to Terry Bradshaw."

3. Terry Bradshaw, with David Fisher, *It's Only a Game* (New York: Simon & Shuster, 2001), 99.

4. "Steelers Have Fan Club," *Valley Independent*, October 19, 1976, 8.

5. Michael Katz, "Steelers Trounce Colts 40–14 . . . ," *New York Times*, December 20, 1976, 34

6. "150–200 Welcome Steelers Home," *Washington Evening Star*, December 27, 1976, 54; Bob Maisel, "The Morning After," *Sun*, December 27, 1976, C9.

7. National Football League Operations, "Bent but Not Broken: The History of the Rules," *NFL.com*, http://operations.nfl.com/the-rules/evolution-of-

the-nfl-rules/ (accessed May 12, 2016); "American Conference: Raiders Rugged . . . ," *Sun*, September 26, 1977, C8.

   8. "Steelers Hope Bradshaw Plays," *Washington Post*, October 17, 1977, D7.

   9. Alan Goldstein, "Bradshaw Shoulders Blame . . . ," *Sun*, October 31, 1977, C3.

   10. Leonard Koppett, "Late Spree Topples Steelers . . . ," *New York Times*, December 25, 1977, 115.

   11. Dave Brady, "Bradshaw Loses Game, Wins the Ad," *Washington Post*, November 21, 1977, B1; Dan Jenkins, "Once More, with No Hard Feelings," *Sports Illustrated*, October 3, 1977, http://www.si.com/vault/1977/10/03/626756/once-more-with-no-hard-feelings (accessed May 2, 2016).

   12. "Ballet and 'Summer Evening on Ice,'" *New York Times*, June 6, 1978, C2.

   13. Alan Goldstein, "Despite His QB Feats . . . ," *Sun*, December 7, 1978, B1.

   14. "Sports News Briefs . . . ," *New York Times*, December 22, 1978, A26; "Fusina, Bradshaw Honored," *Valley Independent*, December 22, 1978, 9.

   15. "Sign of the Year . . . ," *Valley Independent*, December 30, 1978, 16; Murray Chass, "Steelers Crush Broncos in Playoffs," *New York Times*, December 31, 1978, S1; "Bradshaw's Finest Hour . . . ," *Sun*, January 1, 1979, C8.

   16. Murray Chass, "Bradshaw Is a Joker . . . ," *New York Times*, January 5, 1979, A15.

   17. "Steelers Show Rare Emotion . . . ," *Washington Post*, January 1, 1979, D5.

   18. "1970s/1978 AFC Championship Game," *YouRememberThat.com*, http://www.yourememberthat.com/media/8950/1978_AFC_Championship_Game/#.VzfSlPkrLIU (accessed May 14, 2016).

   19. David Moffit, "Steelers Won't Be Intimidated . . . ," *Tyrone Daily Herald*, January 17, 1979, 7.

   20. Dave Anderson, "It's Hollywood's Bowl . . . ," *New York Times*, January 18, 1979, B5.

   21. Murray Chass, "Images of Quarterbacks Persists," *New York Times*, January 19, 1979, A17; Vic Ziegel, "Thundering Fatties," *New York Times*, February 5, 1979, 47; Bradshaw, *It's Only a Game*, 52.

   22. "Greatest Games of All Time," *NFL.com*, http://www.nfl.com/videos/greatest-games-of-all-time/0ap3000000477078/Super-Bowl-XIII-Steelers-vs-Cowboys-highlights (accessed May 13, 2016); Ron Fimrite, "Li'l Abner Finally Makes It Big," *Sports Illustrated*, December 18, 1978, http://www.si.com/vault/1978/12/18/823255/lil-abner-finally-makes-it-big-when-pittsburgh-won-two-super-bowls-terry-bradshaw-was-praised-primarily-for-his-strong-arm-

but-this-season-theres-no-denying-his-arrival-as-a-play-caller-and-the-leader-of-the-steelers-now-they-co (accessed April 2, 2016).

23. "Greatest Games of All Time," *NFL.com*, http://www.nfl.com/videos/greatest-games-of-all-time/0ap3000000477078/Super-Bowl-XIII-Steelers-vs-Cowboys-highlights, accessed May 13, 2016.

24. "Steelers Salute Fans . . . ," *Indiana Evening Gazette*, January 22, 1979, 21; "Pittsburgh Wins in Super Bowl, 35–31," *New York Times*, January 22, 1979, A1.

25. "Sports Rarely Any Better," *Globe and Mail*, January 22, 1979, S3.

26. "Terry Sore, Looking Forward to Playing," *Valley Independent*, January 24, 1979, 13.

27. "Marvelous Marino Whips Steelers Again," *Altoona Mirror*, January 7, 1983, D1; Bob Rubin, "Pittsburgh Dan's the Man," *Miami Herald*, April 29, 1983, 1F; Jeffrey Landau, interview by author, May 13, 2016; Dexter Germany, interview by author, May 25, 2016; comment by Allen Harper, in Tim McMillen, "Fan Tribute to Terry Bradshaw," *Mcmillenandwife.com*, http://www.mcmillenandwife.com/bradshaw_fans.html (accessed February 26, 2016); comment by Cy Harris, in McMillen, "Fan Tribute to Terry Bradshaw"; comment by Victoria Grismore, in McMillen, "Fan Tribute to Terry Bradshaw."

28. "Most of the East Is Strong . . . ," *New York Times*, August 26, 1979, 172.

29. William Wallace, "Steelers Defeat Patriots," *New York Times*, September 4, 1979, B5; "Steelers Stop Bills, 28–0, for Sixth Division Title," *Sun*, December 17, 1979, C8; Jim Wexell, *Tales from behind the Steel Curtain* (Champaign, IL: Sports Publishing, 2004), xiii.

30. Gerald Eskenazi, "Steelers' Bradshaw Is Best under Pressure," *New York Times*, January 2, 1980, B13.

31. "Bradshaw: So What If Renfro Scored . . . ," *Washington Post*, January 7, 1980, D1; Peter Stopchinski, "1979 AFC Championship Game," *YouTube*, https://www.youtube.com/watch?v=a71vEjU3buQ (accessed May 16, 2016).

32. Will Grimsley, "Stargell, a Super Steeler Fan . . . ," *Progress*, January 15, 1980, 12; Dave Kindred, "Steeler Crazies . . . ," *Washington Post*, January 16, 1980, A1.

33. "The Rams' Three Wise Men," *New York Times*, January 20, 1980, S4.

34. El Jo Lui II, "Super Bowl XIII: Pittsburgh 35, Dallas 31," *YouTube*, https://www.youtube.com/watch?v=qwhwaK9Pdkk (accessed May 13, 2016).

35. El Jo Lui II, "Super Bowl XIII: Pittsburgh 35, Dallas 31."

36. Michael Katz, "Steelers Beat Rams to Win a Fourth . . . ," *New York Times*, January 21, 1980, A1; William N. Wallace, "Bradshaw Seen as Key to Game . . . ," *New York Times*, January 21, 1980, C9.

37. Louis Brewer, telephone interview by author, March 29, 2016.

5. A LITTLE BIT COUNTRY AND
A LITTLE BIT GOSPEL

1. "Bradshaw," *Washington Post*, February 11, 1979, N9.

2. Terry Bradshaw, with David Fisher, *Keep It Simple* (New York: Atria, 2002), 54; *Tillman S. Franks vs. Terry Bradshaw, et al.*, Civil District Court, Parish of Caddo, State of Louisiana, February 17, 1977," in Box 1, Folder 3, Collection 649, *Louisiana Hayride*, Louisiana State University Shreveport Archives and Special Collections.

3. "Bradshaw to Sign Recording Contract," *Sun*, June 22, 1975, B8.

4. "Super Bowl Quarterbacks," *Lakeland Ledger*, January 14, 1976, 14.

5. Dave Anderson, "The Super Contrast in Quarterbacks," *New York Times*, January 15, 1976, 43; Terry Bradshaw, with David Fisher, *It's Only a Game* (New York: Simon & Shuster, 2001), 246.

6. Gerry House, *Country Music Broke My Brain: A Behind-the-Microphone Peek at Nashville* (Dallas, TX: BenBella Books, 2014), 217.

7. "The Megalist of Actors Who Tried to Sing," *Dyers.org*, March 3, 2006, http://www.dyers.org/blog/archives/2006/03/03/the-megalist-of-actors-who-tried-to-sing/ (accessed May 21, 2016).

8. Jason Ankeny, "Tony Conigliaro Biography," *Allmusic.com*, http://www.allmusic.com/artist/tony-conigliaro-mn0002034222 (accessed May 21, 2016); Nate Patrin, "The Swinging Pitcher . . . ," *Vicesports.com*, April 24, 2015, https://sports.vice.com/en_us/article/the-swinging-pitcher-a-look-at-denny-mclains-easy-listening-career (accessed May 21, 2016).

9. Nate Patrin, "Joe Frazier's Forgotten R&B Career . . . ," *Vicesports.com*, April 10, 2015, https://sports.vice.com/en_us/article/joe-fraziers-forgotten-rb-career (accessed May 21, 2016).

10. House, *Country Music Broke My Brain*, 217.

11. "Feeling More at Ease," *Lincoln Evening Journal*, January 31, 1976, 10; Red O'Donnell, "Banjo Wizard Back in Action," *Laurel Leader Call*, February 7, 1976, 8.

12. "Scorecard," *Washington Evening Star*, February 28, 1976, 4; Byron Rosen, "Hard Running Man Races . . . ," *Washington Post*, February 28, 1976, E5.

13. Gerry Mullins, telephone interview by author, March 22, 2016; Gary M. Pomerantz, *Their Life's Work: The Brotherhood of the 1970s Pittsburgh Steelers* (New York: Simon & Shuster, 2013), 198–99; "Giving Singing a Fling," *Greeley Tribune*, March 1, 1976, 27.

14. *Tillman S. Franks vs. Terry Bradshaw*; Roy Blount Jr., "For Bradshaw, Belting Out Country Music Is Not Just a Passing Fancy," *Sports Illustrated*, April 5, 1976, http://www.si.com/vault/1976/04/05/614778/for-bradshaw-

belting-out-country-music-is-not-just-a-passing-fancy (accessed March 15, 2016); Scarlett Walden, telephone interview by author, June 23, 2016.

15. Blount Jr., "For Bradshaw, Belting Out Country Music . . ."; Bill Hart, "Recordings," *Abilene Reporter*, July 11, 1976, 3B; William Taaffe, "Scorecard," *Washington Evening Star*, July 15, 1976, 26.

16. Gerald S. Burnett, letter to Ike Hawkins Jr., June 3, 1976, *Louisiana Hayride* , Louisiana State University Shreveport Archives and Special Collections, Box 1, Folder 2, Shreveport, LA; "TV Listings," *Washington Evening Star*, April 18, 1976, 111; "TV Personality/Singer Mike Douglas Dies," *Billboard.com*, August 11, 2006, http://www.billboard.com/articles/news/57559/tv-personalitysinger-mike-douglas-dies-at-81 (accessed May 23, 2016).

17. James H. Duncan Jr., "1976 American Radio," spring edition, *Americanradiohistory.com*, http://www.americanradiohistory.com/Archive-Duncan-American-Radio/Duncan-1976-Spring.pdf (accessed March 31, 2016); Bill Gavin, "Disk Soundings," *Variety*, January 23, 1976, 28.

18. Roxanne Hovland, Joyce M. Wolburg, and Eric E. Haley, *Readings in Advertising, Society, and Consumer Culture* (New York: Routledge, 2007), 100; "The Broadcasting Playlist, March 8," *Broadcasting*, March 8, 1976, 63; "*Cash Box* Top 100 Country," *Cash Box*, April 24, 1976, 45.

19. Randy McDaniel, "Terry Bradshaw Isn't Only a Pro Football Hall of Famer, He's a Calssic Country Artist," *Kxrb.com*, January 14, 2014, http://kxrb.com/terry-bradshaw-isnt-only-a-pro-football-hall-of-famer-hes-a-classic-country-artist/ (accessed May 22, 2016); "I'm So Lonesome I Could Cry/Making Plans," *Rateyourmusic.com*, http://rateyourmusic.com/release/single/terry_bradshaw/im_so_lonesome_i_could, _cry___making_plans/ (accessed April 2, 2016); Mr. Moderator, "What's So Funny 'bout Terry Bradshaw Singing Country Music?" *Rocktownhall.com*, September 19, 2011, http://www.rocktownhall.com/blogs/whats-so-funny-bout-terry-bradshaw-singing-country-music/ (accessed April 2, 2016).

20. Douglas K. Welde, "From Slingin' to Singin' ," *Amazon.com*, March 23, 2010, http://www.amazon.com/lonesome-could-cry-LP/dp/B004F1RFBW (accessed April 2, 2016); Andy Thomas, "The Four Worst Football Players Turned Musicians—and Terry Bradshaw," *Westword.com*, January 25, 2016, http://www.westword.com/music/the-four-worst-football-players-turned-musicians-and-terry-bradshaw-7536394 (accessed March 29, 2016).

21. Vito Stellano, "Terry's Singing Career Hits Sour Notes," *Pittsburgh Post-Gazette*, May 24, 1977, 12.

22. Stellano, "Terry's Singing Career Hits Sour Notes," 12.

23. Stellano, "Terry's Singing Career Hits Sour Notes," 12; "Short Shots," *Tennessean*, May 25, 1977, 25; "See 500,000 Admissions to New Florida Fair Site on First Date," *Variety*, February 9, 1977, 128; Brad Olson, "Terry Brad-

shaw's Brief Country Music Career," *Steve Hoffman Music Forums*, September 3, 2011, http://forums.stevehoffman.tv/threads/terry-bradshaws-brief-country-music-career.261717/page-2 (accessed March 22, 2016).

24. "Bob Levey's Potomac Journal," *Washington Post*, February 17, 1977, C1; Olson, "Terry Bradshaw's Brief Country Music Career"; Dimitri Vassilaros, "WDVA, Jack Maloy . . . ," *Pittsburgh Tribune-Review*, July 19, 2003, 1C.

25. "The Country Column," *Cash Box*, February 3, 1979, 38; "Bradshaw," N9.

26. "Bradshaw," N9.

27. "People . . . ," *Ottawa Citizen*, January 22, 1980, 47.

28. Daniel K. Williams, *God's Own Party: The Making of the Christian Right* (New York: Oxford University Press, 2010), 1–5; "The People: The Spirit of the South," *Time*, September 27, 1976, http://content.time.com/time/magazine/article/0,9171,918349,00.html (accessed March 22, 2016); Terry Bradshaw, with Buddy Martin, *Looking Deep* (New York: Berkley Books, 1989), 201–3.

29. Bradshaw, *Looking Deep*, 201–3.

30. "People . . . ," 47.

31. "Bradshaw the Quarterback Returns to Singing," *Bluefield Daily Telegraph*, February 3, 1980, 4C.

32. Jack Burke, "Gospel According to LP," *Janesville Gazette*, August 1, 1980, 20; Tim Walter, "Amarillo Braces for a Country Shootout," *Billboard*, April 4, 1981, 31.

33. "Studio Track," *Billboard*, May 2, 1981, 53; Sam McClure, interview by author, July 11, 2016.

34. "Until You," *Rateyourmusic.com*, http://rateyourmusic.com/release/album/terry_bradshaw/until_you/ (accessed April 2, 2016); Wilbur Scott, "Terry Bradshaw, 'Until You,'" *YouTube*, https://www.youtube.com/watch?v=BW0JBIB-UGs (accessed April 29, 2016); "Here in My Heart," *Rateyourmusic.com*, http://rateyourmusic.com/release/album/terry_bradshaw/here_in_my_heart/ (accessed April 29, 2016).

35. "Album Reviews," *Cash Box*, December 26, 1981, 35.

36. "Until You"; Scott, "Terry Bradshaw, 'Until You'"; "Here in My Heart"; Doug Clark, "A Pioneer in Country Music . . . ," *Sampson Independent*, September 23, 2007, A1.

37. "Dove Award Nominations," *Cash Box*, February 6, 1982, 27.

38. Dave Pego, "Oklahoma Singer Is Going West," *Daily Oklahoman*, October 16, 1983, 1C, 10A; Kimberly Link, "The Witnesses—Hear Them Tomorrow," *Star*, April 3, 1988, D3.

6. FROM ADVERTISING TO ACTING

1. Hollie I. West, "Bernie Casey . . . ," *Washington Post*, May 7, 1977, C5.

2. Terry Bradshaw, with David Fisher, *It's Only a Game* (New York: Simon & Shuster, 2001), 204; Bob Tatrn, *Bob Tatrn's Sports Minutes* (Tarentum, PA: Word Association, 2011), 18; Marj Charlier, "Southern Cafeteria Chains Plot Expansion into North," *Wall Street Journal*, June 17, 1988, 1.

3. "The History of Chewing Tobacco in America," *Smokelessaficiona-do.com*, http://www.smokelessaficionado.com/index.php/otp/chewing-tobacco/56-the-history-of-chewing-tobacco-in-america (accessed May 31, 2016); "History of Cowboy Boots," *Sheplers.com*, http://www.sheplers.com/custserv/custserv.jsp?pageName=HistoryCowboyBoots (accessed May 31, 2016); "History of the Cowboy Boot," *America's Horse Daily*, March 30, 2015, http://americashorsedaily.com/the-history-of-the-cowboy-boot/#.V0yhU_krLIU (accessed May 31, 2016); Bradshaw, *It's Only a Game*, 205; John Mutka, "Bradshaw: Super Bowls Not So Fun," *Post-Tribune*, May 15, 1991, C1.

4. *It's Only a Game*, 206–8

5. Dave Brady, "Bradshaw Loses Game, Wins the Ad," *Washington Post*, November 8, 1977, D3; "Rugs and Plugs," *Time*, June 10, 1970, http://content.time.com/time/magazine/article/0,9171,909329,00.html (accessed May 31, 2016); Lynne Luciano, *Looking Good: Male Body Image in Modern America* (New York: Hill & Wang, 2001), 4–25; Bradshaw, *It's Only a Game*, 206–8.

6. Ken Moran, "At 80, Gowdy Still the American Sportsman," *New York Post*, February 3, 2002; http://nypost.com/2002/02/03/at-80-gowdy-still-the-american-sportsman/, accessed May 31, 2016.

7. Gerry Mullins, telephone interview by author, March 22, 2016; Ken Moran, "At 80, Gowdy Still the American Sportsman," *New York Post*, February 3, 2002, http://nypost.com/2002/02/03/at-80-gowdy-still-the-american-sportsman/ (accessed May 31, 2016).

8. "And Next Sunday on TV," *Washington Evening Star*, January 28, 1973, 110; "Sunday Previews," *Washington Evening Star*, February 3, 1973, 37; "Special Section: The Good Life," *Time*, September 27, 1976, http://content.time.com/time/magazine/article/0,9171,918350,00.html (accessed May 31, 2016).

9. Gary M. Pomerantz, *Their Life's Work: The Brotherhood of the 1970s Pittsburgh Steelers* (New York: Simon & Shuster, 2013), 199; Patricia Simmons, "Warming Up for the 4th," *Washington Evening Star*, July 3, 1975, 35; WKY KTVY KFOR Archives, from the Oklahoma Historical Society, "Stars and Stripes 1975," *YouTube*, June 27, 2014, https://www.youtube.com/watch?v=ywOvmdLNkoo (accessed June 3, 2016).

10. "Television," *New York Times*, January 22, 1979, C21; *Dinah!*, Season 4, Episode 127, *TV.com*, March 22, 1978, http://www.tv.com/shows/dinah/march-22-1978-1340157/ (accessed June 4, 2016); *Dinah!*, Season 5, Episode 102, *TV.com*, February 19, 1979, http://www.tv.com/shows/dinah/february-19-1979-1341574/ (accessed June 4, 2016).

11. Cable Neuhaus, "Terry Bradshaw Is a Hero, but When Wife JoJo Skates Off, He's So Lonesome He Could Cry," *People*, January 22, 1979, 26; Cable Neuhaus, "Even Prayer Couldn't Make the JoJo Starbuck–Terry Bradshaw Union a Marriage Made in Heaven," *People*, August 25, 1980, 90.

12. Gary Minhoches, "Bradshaw No Real Playboy," *Progress*, January 15, 1980, 12; Dave Brady, "Bradshaw Gets across His Message," *Washington Post*, January 16, 1980, E6; Maury Z. Levy and Samantha Stevenson, "Terry Bradshaw: The Playboy Interview," *Playboy*, March 1980, https://mauryzlevy.wordpress.com/2009/09/14/terry-bradshaw-the-playboy-interview/(accessed January 24, 2016).

13. Byron Smialek, "Burt's Monologue, but Terry Gets the Last Laugh," *Observer-Reporter*, January 20, 1976, B4; Terry Bradshaw, with Buddy Martin, *Looking Deep* (New York: Berkley Books, 1989), 193.

14. Pomerantz, *Their Life's Work*, 199, 202; "Crooner," *Pittsburgh Post-Gazette*, February 28, 1976, 6; Army Archerd, "Just for Variety," *Variety*, March 21, 1978, 3.

15. Edward L. Blank, "Terry Bradshaw, Burt Reynolds Have a Brawl," *Pittsburgh Post-Gazette*, July 23, 1978, F1.

16. "Hooper: Scene 10," *YouTube*, https://www.youtube.com/watch?v=SBxUfbSAG2I (accessed November 11, 2015); *Hooper*, dir. Hal Needham, perf. Burt Reynolds, Sally Field, Brian Keith, and Jan-Michael Vincent. Warner Brothers, 1978.

17. "Hooper," *Variety*, December 31, 1977, 50; Janet Maslin, "Burt Reynolds in Action in 'Hooper': Moviemaking Fun," *New York Times*, August 4, 1978, C11; Gary Arnold, "The Fall Guys Take a Bow," *Washington Post*, August 4, 1978, C11.

18. Pomerantz, *Their Life's Work*, 199; Matthew J. Ferrence, *All-American Redneck: Variations on an Icon, from James Fenimore Cooper to the Dixie Chicks* (Knoxville: University of Tennessee Press, 2014), 53–55; Derek Nystrom, *Hard Hats, Rednecks, and Macho Men* (New York: Oxford University Press, 2009), 81–91.

19. "Top-Grossing Films of 1978," *Listal*, September 24, 2012, www.listal.com/list/top-grossing-films-1978 (accessed November 11, 2015); "Film–Radio Link Boosts Hooper," *Billboard*, July 28, 1979, 20; Confabulat, "The Final Stunt Scene from the 1977 Movie *Hooper* . . . ," *Fark.com*, August 2, 2008, http://www.fark.com/comments/3777138/The-final-stunt-scene-from-1977-

movie-Hooper-starring-Burt-Reynolds-Jan-Michael-Vincent-This-movie-is-
better-than-you-remember-it-clip-includes-some-profanity (accessed December 2, 2015).

20. "Alan Milberg," *Imdb.com*, http://www.imdb.com/name/nm7812623/
(accessed June 14, 2016); "Terry Bradshaw and Wife Cast in 'Star Marriage,'"
Variety, March 30, 1979; "Update," *Los Angeles Times*, April 22, 1979, W3;
"The Osbournes," *Imdb.com*, http://www.imdb.com/title/tt0306370/ullcredits?
ref_=tt_ov_st_sm (accessed June 16, 2016); "Newlyweds: Nick & Jessica,"
Imdb.com, http://www.imdb.com/title/tt0380934/?ref_=fn_al_tt_1 (accessed
June 16, 2016); "The Anna Nicole Show," *Imdb.com*, http://www.imdb.com/
title/tt0328732/ (accessed June 16, 2016).

21. "Jim Brown," *Imdb.com*, http://www.imdb.com/name/nm0000987/bio?
ref_=nm_ov_bio_sm (accessed June 14, 2016); "Fred Williamson," *Imdb.com*,
http://www.imdb.com/name/nm0004365/?ref_=nmbio_bio_nm (accessed June
14, 2016); Stephanie Pitera, "Thirteen Football Players Who Became Actors,"
Backstage.com, October 8, 2015, http://www.backstage.com/news/13-football-
players-became-actors/ (accessed May 2, 2016); *O. J. Simpson: Made in America*, dir. Ezra Edelman, perf. Mike Albanese, Muhammad Ali, and Marcus
Allen. ESPN Films, 2016.

22. Byron Rosen, "San Diego Christens NBA Clippers," *Washington Post*,
August 9, 1978, D7; "Oral History 41: Hal Needham," *Academy of Motion
Picture Arts and Sciences*, 214; Woods, Mae, *An oral history with Hal Need-
ham*, transcript of an oral history conducted 2006 by Mae Woods, Oral History
Program, Academy of Motion Picture Arts and Sciences, Beverly Hills, Califor-
nia 2006, 401 p.

23. "Stadium Scene," *Smokey and the Bandit II*, *YouTube*, https://www.
youtube.com/watch?v=01NTLWm5MbU (accessed November 11, 2015);
Smokey and the Bandit II, dir. Hal Needham, perf. Burt Reynolds, Sally Field,
and Jackie Gleason. Universal, 1980.

24. "Pix, People, Pickups," *Variety*, March 26, 1980, 39; "Smokey and the
Bandit II," *Variety*, August 20, 1980, 20; "Smokey and the Bandit II," *Afro-
American*, August 23, 1980, 11; Kevin A. Ranson, "Smokey and the Bandit II,"
Rottontomatoes.com, June 13, 2005, http://www.rottentomatoes.com/m/
smokey_and_the_bandit_ii/?search=smokey%20and%20the%20b (accessed
November 15, 2015).

25. "'Smokey and the Bandit II' Box Office Information," *Boxofficemo-
jo.com*, http://www.boxofficemojo.com/movies/?id=smokeyandthebandit2.htm
(accessed November 11, 2015); Moni K., "Smokey and the Bandit II Reviews,"
Rottentomatoes.com, 2012, http://www.rottentomatoes.com/m/smokey_and_
the_bandit_ii/reviews/?page=5&type=user (accessed December 1, 2015); Ger-
ard-21, jrs-8, Dimarc, and Len, "Reviews and Ratings for Smokey and the

Bandit II," *Imdb.com*, April 2010, http://www.imdb.com/title/tt0081529/reviews?ref_=tt_urv (accessed December 6, 2015).

26. "Thursday: Cable/Subscription TV of Special Interest," *New York Times*, November 16, 1980, D51; Tom Buckley, "TV: 'Kenny Rogers's America' Takes Him to Cities and Farms," *New York Times*, November 20, 1980, C34.

27. *The Cannonball Run*, dir. Hal Needham, perf. Burt Reynolds, Roger Moore, and Farrah Fawcett. Twentieth Century Fox, 1981; "The Cannonball Run," *Imdb.com*, http://www.imdb.com/title/tt0082136/ (accessed December 1, 2015).

28. "Bet on TV for Bradshaw's Future," *Sun*, January 14, 1981, B7; "Sports File," *New Pittsburgh Courier*, February 7, 1981, A12; Maggie Daly, "Mitch, Orchestra to 'Barge in' Here," *Chicago Tribune*, February 9, 1981, C6; "Terry Bradshaw and Mel Tillis May Be All Wet . . . ," *People*, March 16, 1981, http://www.people.com/people/archive/article/0,,20078809,00.html (accessed December 1, 2015).

29. "Television: Top Weekend Films," *New York Times*, April 24, 1981, C31; "Morning Briefing," *Los Angeles Times*, April 26, 1981, D2; Red Smith, "Thespian Quarterback," *New York Times*, April 27, 1981, 42; Dick Heller, "Sports Today," *Washington Star*, April 28, 1981, 22.

30. "The Stockers," *Variety*, April 28, 1981, 11; "The Stockers," *Variety*, April 29, 1981, 60; "Morning Briefing," *Los Angeles Times*, April 30, 1981, B2; Terry Price, "Notable: Back in Harness . . . ," *Hartford Courant*, May 26, 1981, D3A; "Oral History 41: Hal Needham"; Woods, Mae, *An oral history with Hal Needham*, transcript of an oral history conducted 2006 by Mae Woods, Oral History Program, Academy of Motion Picture Arts and Sciences, Beverly Hills, California 2006, 401 p.

31. "'The Cannonball Run' Box Office Information," *Boxofficemojo.com*, http://www.boxofficemojo.com/movies/?id=cannonballrun.htm (accessed November 11, 2015); "1981 Domestic Grosses," *Boxofficemojo.com*, http://www.boxofficemojo.com/yearly/chart/?yr=1981&p=.htm (accessed November 11, 2015).

32. "Reviews and Ratings for the Cannonball Run," *Imdb.com*, http://www.imdb.com/title/tt0082136/reviews?start=20 (accessed December 7, 2015); "The Cannonball Run Reviews," *Rottentomatoes.com*, http://www.rottentomatoes.com/m/cannonball_run/reviews/?type=user (accessed December 7, 2015); Doug Wyatt, "Sunday Is the Big Show," *Savannah Morning News*, January 26, 2001, 4D.

33. Joe Dinneen, "Sports Pulse," *Boston Globe*, August 22, 1981, 26; Vito Sellino, "It's No Act—Bradshaw's the Star of This Show," *Boston Globe*, Sep-

tember 5, 1981, 31; *Bucks County Playhouse v. Bradshaw*, 577 F. Supp. 1203 (1983).

7. LEAVING IT ON THE FIELD

1. Bert Jones, telephone interview by author, April 19, 2016.

2. Byron Rosen, "Bradshaw Aims to Quit After...," *Washington Post*, February 14, 1980, F8.

3. Tony Kornheiser, "Crowd Pleasers . . . ," *Washington Post*, February 9, 1980, C1; Byron Rosen, "Bradshaw Aims to Quit after . . . ," *Washington Post*, February 14, 1980, F8; Nathan Cobb, "City of Steelers . . . ,"*Boston Globe*, April 27, 1980, 1; Jim Pane, "Steeler Fans: They Oughta . . . ," *Evening Gazette*, July 25, 1980, 16; "Bradshaw Faces Divorce Suit," *Washington Post*, August 7, 1980, F6; "Football Fanatics," *Leader-Times*, September 6, 1980, 6.

4. Steve Cady, "Pittsburgh's Awesome Steelers," *New York Times*, September 7, 1980, A46.

5. R. Mitchell Steen, "Steelers Still No. 1," *Valley Independent*, September 17, 1980, 14; Gary M. Pomerantz, *Their Life's Work: The Brotherhood of the 1970s Pittsburgh Steelers* (New York: Simon & Shuster, 2013), 238–39, 263; Thomas Rogers, "Bengals Win Again from Steelers," *New York Times*, October 13, 1980, C3.

6. "Quarterback Hoped for a Quiet Visit to Canton," *Hutchinson News*, October 16, 1980, 3.

7. William N. Wallace, "Steelers' Long Playoff Run Nears an End," *New York Times*, December 6, 1980, 17; "Steelers Rally, Beat Chiefs on Bleier's Run," *Washington Post*, December 15, 1980, D3.

8. Larry Allen, "Bradshaw Still Seeking Super Bowl Ring for His Thumb," *Los Angeles Herald Examiner*, November 27, 1981, B1.

9. "Bradshaw Still Undecided," *Los Angeles Herald Examiner*, May 1, 1981, B1; Terry Price, "Notable: Back in Harness . . . ," *Hartford Courant*, May 26, 1981, D3A; Lewis Freedman, "Profile: Bradshaw Still Has the Knack . . . ," *Philadelphia Inquirer*, November 16, 1981, C4.

10. Gary M. Pomerantz, "Steelers Insist They They're . . . ," *Washington Post*, August 4, 1981, D1; William N. Wallace, "Can the Steelers Revive?" *New York Times*, August 17, 1981, C1.

11. "Pro Football 1981," *New York Times*, August 31, 1981, 38.

12. Bill Livingston, "Ferguson in Command . . . ," *Philadelphia Inquirer*, September 16, 1981, D1.

13. "Steelers Regain Old Form, 38–10," *Washington Post*, September 21, 1981, C3; "Steelers Keep Patriots Winless," *Washington Post*, September 28, 1981, C3.

14. "Believe It: 49ers Remain . . . ," *Anderson Daily Bulletin*, November 2, 1981, 25; "Harris Propels Steelers to 24–0 Silencing of Rams," *Sun*, November 30, 1981, 32.

15. Freedman, "Profile," C4.

16. Ira Berkow, "Steelers Trying to . . . ," *New York Times*, December 7, 1981, C1; "Steelers Lose as Bradshaw Breaks Hand," *Sun*, December 8, 1981, C1; "Bradshaw Hurt as Raiders Triumph," *New York Times*, December 8, 1981, D27.

17. Gordon Forbes, "Eagles Are Lining Up . . . ," *Philadelphia Inquirer*, February 15, 1982, C4.

18. Ira Berkow, "Of Unionism and the NFL," *New York Times*, May 29, 1982, 31.

19. Berkow, "Of Unionism and the NFL," 31.

20. Berkow, "Of Unionism and the NFL," 31; "Manning Had Best Salary," *New York Times*, February 1, 1982, http://www.nytimes.com/1982/02/01/sports/manning-had-best-salary.html (accessed May 21, 2016).

21. "Manning Had Best Salary."

22. Michael Madden, "NFL Players Call Strike," *Boston Globe*, September 26, 1982, D1; Alan Goldstein, "Player Demands Inspire Orvis to Finally Unzip Lip," *Sun*, April 15, 1982, E1.

23. Bill Fleischman, "Noll Lets Bradshaw Do His Thinking," *Philadelphia Daily News*, September 20, 1982, 79; Terry Bradshaw, with David Fisher, *It's Only a Game* (New York: Simon & Shuster, 2001), 55–58.

24. Madden, "NFL Players Call Strike," D1.

25. Rich Hoffman, "Strike Standstill Exists . . . ," *Philadelphia Daily News*, October 6, 1982, 76; Gordon Forbes, "Strike Foes Meet . . . ," *Philadelphia Inquirer*, October 6, 1982, C1.

26. David Remnick, "Most Fans—But Not All . . . ," *New York Times*, November 17, 1982, A31; "AFC: Steelers Fall, 16–0," *Sun*, November 29, 1982, C3; "AFC: Bills Blank Steelers," *Sun*, December 13, 1982, D5; Will McDonough, "Wither Bradshaw's Mental Mettle," *Boston Globe*, December 26, 1982, D1.

27. Murray Chass, "Late Charger Pass Tops Steelers, 31–28," *New York Times*, January 10, 1983, C4.

28. "NFL Strike Seemingly . . . ," *Lexington Herald-Leader*, January 2, 1983, B8; Chass, "Late Charger Pass Tops Steelers," C4; Ken Denlinger, "Bradshaw, Shy a Ring, Admits to Excess Brass," *Washington Post*, January 10, 1983, C1.

29. "Bradshaw to Begin Camp Listed 'Physically Unable,'" *Washington Post*, July 11, 1983, D2; Terry Bradshaw, with Buddy Martin, *Looking Deep* (New York: Berkley Books, 1989), 153, 159–61; "More Time Needed," *New York Times* , September 9, 1983, B8.

30. "Bradshaw Gets New Hope from the Scope . . . ," *Sports Illustrated*, December 19, 1983, http://www.si.com/vault/1983/12/19/619679/bradshaw-gets-new-hope-from-the-scope (accessed February 19, 2016); Terry O'Neil, Interview by author, Telephone. March 11, 2016; Bradshaw, *Looking Deep*, 159–61.

31. "'Sickened' Bradshaw Wants Comeback," *Sun*, January 2, 1984, C5; Bradshaw, *It's Only a Game*, 61–63.

32. Jeffrey Landau, interview by author, May 13, 2016; Dave Anderson, "Al Davis Ranks His Champions," *New York Times*, January 24, 1984, A21.

33. Dave Anderson, "Bradshaw Ponders His Future," *New York Times*, January 2, 1984, 34; "Sports People . . . ," *New York Times*, January 15, 1984, S6.

34. "Sports People . . . ," *Sun*, February 29, 1984, E7; "Bradshaw Weighs Another Operation," *New York Times*, June 6, 1984, B11.

35. Chris Wesseling, "NFL Players with Most Memorable Careers Cut Short," *NFL.com*, July 18, 2013, http://www.nfl.com/news/story/0ap1000000218711/article/nfl-players-with-most-memorable-careers-cut-short (accessed May 19, 2016); Amber Lee, "25 of the Worst Career-Ending Injuries in Sports," *Bleacher Report*, June 25, 2012, http://bleacherreport.com/articles/1235089-25-of-the-worst-career-ending-injuries-in-sports/page/22 (accessed May 19, 2016); FanDuel, "All-Time Greats Who Hung around Too Long," *Fanduel.com*, June 29, 2011, https://www.fanduel.com/insider/2011/06/29/all-time-nfl-greats-who-hung-around-too-long/ (accessed May 19, 2016).

36. Bradshaw, *Looking Deep*, 164–66.

37. Robert McG. Thomas Jr., "Bradshaw Retires, Joins CBS," *New York Times*, July 25, 1984, B9; "Bradshaw Joins CBS Sports . . . ," *Atlanta Daily World*, July 31, 1984, 5; O'Neil, telephone interview by author.

38. "Johnny Unitas Announces Pro Football Retirement," *Times Daily*, July 25, 1974, 13; "Len Dawson Retires . . . ," *Florence Times*, May 2, 1976, 20; Vito Stellino, "Wagner Bows Out," *Pittsburgh Post-Gazette*, January 9, 1981, 9; Landau, interview by author.

39. Landau, interview by author.

8. PRESS BOX VIEW

1. William Taaffe, "CBS's Game Face at Times Maddening . . . ," *Washington Post*, January 25, 1982, C3.

2. Terry Bradshaw, with Buddy Martin, *Looking Deep* (New York: Berkley Books, 1989), 174–75; Terry Bradshaw, with David Fisher, *It's Only a Game* (New York: Simon & Shuster, 2001), 131–33.

3. "TV Listings," *Northwest Arkansas Times*, January 24, 1982, 6C; Robert McG. Thomas Jr., "Bradshaw Retires, Joins CBS," *New York Times*, July 25, 1984, B9; Terry O'Neil, Interview by author, Telephone. March 11, 2016.

4. Verne Lundquist, telephone interview by author, May 2, 2016; Mike Coaklin, "Bradshaw Tackles TV Job . . . ," *Sun*, August 5, 1984, 20D.

5. Bradshaw, *It's Only a Game*, 138–41.

6. Lundquist, telephone interview by author.

7. O'Neil, telephone interview by author; Cathy Harasta, "Lundquist, Bradshaw Hit Stride," *Dallas Morning News*, December 13, 1985, 12B.

8. Taaffe, "CBS's Game Face at Times Maddening . . . ," C3.

9. Bradshaw, *Looking Deep*, 153, 159.

10. "A Look at Super Bits and Pieces," *Daily Breeze*, January 11, 1985, D4; George Bell Jr., "Speaking of Sports . . . ," *Dallas Morning News*, May 7, 1985, 1B; "John Moser as Howard Cosell on the 'Jockocracy,'" *Youtube*, https://www.youtube.com/watch?v=OCzn0HU7sNs (accessed June 14, 2016).

11. O'Neil, telephone interview by author.

12. O'Neil, telephone interview by author.

13. "Personalities," *Variety*, September 4, 1985, 62; Nick Canepa, "Summerall, Madden Are the Fan Favorites," *Evening Tribune*, December 6, 1985, E11.

14. Nick Canepa, "A Modest Lundquist Suggests . . . ," *Evening Tribune*, December 13, 1985, E10.

15. Cathy Harasta, "Lundquist, Bradshaw Hit Stride," *Dallas Morning News*, December 13, 1985, 12B.

16. Cathy Harasta, "Announcing World Cup Not . . . ," *Dallas Morning News*, June 29, 1986, 13B; Tyler Tumminia, "Be Your Own Fan TV," interview with Ted Shaker, https://vimeo.com/9131578 (accessed May 22, 2016).

17. Bradshaw, *It's Only a Game*, 146–50; Terry Bradshaw, with David Fisher, *Keep It Simple* (New York: Atria, 2002), 240–42.

18. Lundquist, telephone interview by author.

19. Jon Roe, "Kurtz, Angel Get Sign-off . . . ," *Richmond Times-Dispatch*, November 14, 1986, 1D; Bill Millsaps, "Sold on Schroeder . . . ," *Richmond Times-Dispatch*, December 4, 1986, 1D.

20. Stan Isaacs, "Here Are Grid Announcers . . . ," *Seattle Times*, December 21, 1986, C10.

21. Mike Kern, "He's Not Too Dumb for TV," *Philadelphia Daily News*, August 13, 1987, 83.

22. "Coverage by Networks Light but Pulls No Punches," *Houston Chronicle*, October 5, 1987, 7; Phil Rosenthal, "Show Goes on as Usual for NFL," *Daily News of Los Angeles*, October 5, 1987, S4.

23. "Coverage by Networks Light," 7; P. J. Bednarski, "TV Cameras Convey Strike Confusion," *Chicago Sun-Times*, October 5, 1987, 5.

24. Bednarski, "TV Cameras Convey Strike Confusion," 5; Dan Vierra, "Giants Replacing 49ers . . . ," *Sacramento Bee*, October 13, 1987, S4.

25. Vierra, "Giants Replacing 49ers . . . ," S4.

26. David Hyde, "NFL Ratings Take a Beating," *Miami Herald*, October 16, 1987, E8.

27. Norman Chad, "Madden Is Great . . . ," *Seattle Times*, November 22, 1987, C5.

28. Dan Barreiro, "Hold On: Vikings Need Holdout," *Star Tribune*, August 17, 1988, 1C.

29. Bradshaw, *Looking Deep*, 178–79.

30. William Taaffe, "The Midterm Grades Are In," *Sports Illustrated*, November 28, 1988, http://www.si.com/vault/1988/11/28/118956/ (accessed June 22, 2016).

31. John Freeman, "It's Time to Voice an Opinion on the NFL Broadcasters," *Evening Tribune*, December 2, 1988, E6.

32. "Bradshaw Defends Choice . . . ," *Lexington Herald-Leader*, August 6, 1989, C2.

33. Cooper Rollow, "Bradshaw's Speech Puts Crowd . . . ," *Buffalo News*, August 6, 1989, C1.

34. Comment by Zrelak188@aol.com, in Tim McMillen, "Fan Tribute to Terry Bradshaw," *Mcmillenandwife.com*, http://www.mcmillenandwife.com/bradshaw_fans.html (accessed February 26, 2016).

35. "Bradshaw Defends Choice . . . ," C2.

36. Prentis Rogers, "For Fans Only . . . ," *Atlanta Journal & Atlanta Constitution*, August 8, 1989, F2.

37. "People in Sports," *Houston Chronicle*, October 5, 1989, 10.

38. Paul J. Pacelli, "The Gift Bag Opens for Naughty and Nice," *New Haven Register*, December 24, 1989, C5; Bill Doyle, "Bradshaw Lets Criticism . . . ," *Worcester Telegram & Gazette*, January 11, 1990, B2.

39. Andy Russell, *Andy Russell: A Steeler Odyssey* (Champaign, IL: Sports Publishing, 2001), 130–32.

40. Mike Freeman, "Bradshaw Throws Support . . . ," *Dallas Morning News*, November 9, 1988, 1D; "Bradshaw Is Cheering for Elway on Sunday," *Milwaukee Journal Sentinel*, January 23, 1998, SS1.

41. Nick Pugliese, "'Tis the Season to Listen to the Grapevine," *Tampa Tribune*, December 2, 1990, 19B; Mike Preston, "Public Image Limited . . . ," *Sun*, July 18, 1996, 1D.

42. "Bradshaw Is Cheering for Elway on Sunday," SS1.

43. "Bradshaw Takes His Shots," *Wichita Eagle*, January 25, 1990, 4B.

44. Eric Noland, "New Orleans Diary," *Daily News of Los Angeles*, January 26, 1990, S4.

45. Doug Nye, "CBS's Bomb Squad . . . ," *State*, January 29, 1990, 4C.

46. "Sports," *Fresno Bee*, February 6, 1990, C2; John Freeman, "CBS's Crew Called It What It Was . . . ," *Evening Tribune*, January 29, 1990, D8; Ralph Routon, "Super Bowl Mail Outshines Game," *Gazette*, February 5, 1990, 1D.

47. Rogers, "For Fans Only . . . ," F2.

48. Lundquist, telephone interview by author; Steve Nidetz, "Musburger Charges Two CBS Execs 'Conspired to Get Me,'" *Chicago Tribune*, April 6, 1990, http://articles.chicagotribune.com/1990-04-06/sports/9001290976_1_executive-producer-ted-shaker-cbs-spokeswoman-susan-kerr-brent-musburger (accessed August 31, 2016).

9. STUDIO ANALYSIS AND HIJINKS

1. Phil Jackman, "CBS Offers All You Want, and Two Hours More," *Sun*, January 24, 1992, C2.

2. Bill Modoono, "Pregame Shows a Lot of Dressing," *Pittsburgh Post-Gazette*, August 23, 1990, D2.

3. "Greg Gumbel, Bradshaw Head New Team . . . ," *St. Louis Post-Dispatch*, September 2, 1990, 11F.

4. "Greg Gumbel, Bradshaw Head New Team . . . ," 11F; "Duo Takes over 'NFL Today' . . . ," *Orlando Sentinel*, September 9, 1990, C3.

5. John Altavilla, "On Game Day, ESPN Prime Choice for NFL Information," *New Haven Register*, September 21, 1990, C1.

6. Michael Madden, "Return to the Scene of the Grime," *Boston Globe*, September 24, 1990, 41; Michael Madden, "Even in His Backhanded Apology," *Boston Globe*, September 30, 1990, 60.

7. *Melissa Ludtke v. Bowie Kuhn*, 461 F. Supp. 86 (S.D.N.Y. 1978), September 25, 1978, http://law.justia.com/cases/federal/district-courts/FSupp/461/86/2266331/ (accessed June 28, 2016); Gary Nuhn, " Chauvinism Rears Its Ugly Head," *Dayton Daily News*, October 3, 1990, 1B; Alan Pergament, "Visser More Than Window . . . ," *Buffalo News*, October 20, 1990, B2.

8. Paola Boivin, "Best Wishes for the New Year," *Daily News of Los Angeles*, December 21, 1990, S4.

9. Len Hochberg, "Women Sportscasters Make Headway . . . ," *Chicago Sun-Times*, December 9, 1990, 7; Glenn Sheeley, "TV/Radio," *Atlanta Journal & Atlanta Constitution*, December 11, 1990, E2.

10. John Freeman, "TV's Priority Must Be with War," *Evening Tribune*, January 18, 1991, E6; Bill Modoono, "Duty Calls . . . ," *Pittsburgh Post-Gazette*, January 20, 1991, D5.

11. Joe Lapointe, "TV Shows Have Gains and Losses," *New York Times*, October 7, 1990, S2; Modoono, "Duty Calls . . . ," D5.

12. Terry Blount, "Bradshaw: NFL Legislating Games to Boredom," *Houston Chronicle*, September 6, 1991, 11.

13. Blount, "Bradshaw: NFL Legislating Games to Boredom," 11; "Halftime Report," *YouTube*, https://www.youtube.com/watch?v=JP1p2Fbi874 (accessed June 30, 2016); Terry Bradshaw, with David Fisher, *It's Only a Game* (New York: Simon & Shuster, 2001), 164–71.

14. Tim Cowlishaw, "Tim Cowlishaw's NFL Report," *Dallas Morning News*, September 8, 1991, 14b; George Hostetter, "Bradshaw Scores Big as Analyst," *Fresno Bee*, September 29, 1992, C1.

15. Richard Sandomir, "Pro Football: In Studio Show . . . ," *New York Times*, October 28, 1991, C8.

16. Jackman, "CBS Offers All You Want," C2; Eyeontv, "CBS Super Bowl Pregame and Open 1992," *YouTube*, https://www.youtube.com/watch?v=LOFfkNwfaYc&index=6&list=PLcFcQzGJXbKDIyEjXcbloX9RLJzKu9Cxv (accessed June 29, 2016).

17. Gail Shister, "Lesley Visser Knows Her Sports Statistics . . . ," *Tampa Tribune*, November 22, 1992, 55.

18. Wreytube, "NFL Today Intro October 1992," *YouTube*, https://www.youtube.com/watch?v=sjRjvyNJ_vw&index=26&list=PL03ePUlNXKFU1Aq06VNKIr5rHcsVUilnz (accessed June 30, 2016).

19. "Hunch: Ditka Will Be Here . . . ," *State Journal-Register*, November 18, 1992, 21; Terry Blount, "ESPN Set to Air Racism Special," *Houston Chronicle*, December 13, 1992, 20.

20. Classicsportsvids, "1992-09-20 NFL Today Halftime Report," *YouTube*, https://www.youtube.com/watch?v=JxW80-KThtU&list=PL03ePUlNXKFU1Aq06VNKIr5rHcsVUilnz&index=116 (accessed June 30, 2016).

21. Tom Hoffarth, "The Media . . . ," *Daily News of Los Angeles*, December 25, 1992, S1.

22. Glenn Dickey, "Montana Is Good . . . ," *San Francisco Chronicle*, December 30, 1992, B1; Jonathan Curiel, "Airwaves . . . ," *San Francisco Chroni-*

cle, January 18, 1993, C8; Bob Raissman, "Lundquist–Kellogg Duo . . . ," *Pittsburgh Post-Gazette*, April 4, 1993, D3.

23. Mark Wangrin, "Cowboys Camp Report," *Austin American-Statesman*, August 6, 1993, D6.

24. Dave Eubank, "TV Plays a Role in Proliferation . . . ," *Arizona Daily Star*, September 17, 1993, 1D; Prentis Rogers, "For Fans Only . . . ," *Atlanta Journal & Atlanta Constitution*, September 27, 1993, D2.

25. Eyeontv, "CBS NFL Today and Game Opens 1993," *YouTube*, https://www.youtube.com/watch?v=G2aoEfPWXDc (accessed June 29, 2016); Steve Wulf, "Out Foxed," *Sports Illustrated*, December 27, 1993, http://www.si.com/vault/1993/12/27/130193/out-foxed-rupert-murdochs-upstart-network-snatched-the-nfl-from-cbs-in-a-coup-that-will-change-the-face-of-televised-sports (accessed June 29, 2016).

26. Ron Weiskind, "Terrible Towel . . . ,"*Pittsburgh Post-Gazette*, December 20, 1993, C1.

27. Dave Eubank, "Beginning of the NFL Playoffs Requires a Checklist," *Arizona Daily Star*, January 7, 1994, 5C.

28. "CBS's Finale to Football," *YouTube*, https://www.youtube.com/watch?v=s3RM0DNA0n0 (accessed June 29, 2016); "CBS's Football Finale . . . ," *Sun-Sentinel*, January 24, 1994, 11C.

29. R. D. Heldenfels, "Boom! Madden Won't Change . . . ," *Akron Beacon Journal*, July 17, 1994, D4; Tim Funk, "FOX Network Promises . . . ," *Charlotte Observer*, July 17, 1994, 3H.

30. Mike Fisher, "Cowboys Report," *Fort Worth Star-Telegram*, August 7, 1994, 11.

31. Dusty Saunders, "A Little Bradshaw . . . ," *Rocky Mountain News*, August 15, 1994, 14B; Bob Keisser, "In Week 1 Ratings . . . ," *Press-Telegram*, September 9, 1994, C2.

32. Jeff Hasen, "Fox Has Glitz . . . ," *Deseret News*, September 9, 1994, D3; "Deford Says Football Pregame Shows Are Too Serious," National Public Radio, Morning Edition, Washington, DC, September 14, 1994.

33. C. W. Nevius, "'NFL on Fox': It's a Mixed Bag," *San Francisco Chronicle*, October 19, 1994, D4.

34. Barry Horn, "Ratings Show NBC Getting More . . . ," *Dallas Morning News*, November 29, 1994, 2B; Scott D. Pierce, "1994 Has Been . . . ," *Deseret News*, December 9, 1994, C3; Tom Sorensen, "A Year without Sports . . . ," *Charlotte Observer*, January 14, 1995, 1B.

35. Bill Fleischman, "The Highs and Lows on the Air," *Austin American-Statesman*, December 24, 1994, C2.

36. Gare Joyce, "NHL Broadcasts Land . . . ," *Rocky Mountain News*, April 2, 1995, 9B.

37. Robert Bianco, "A Couple of Football . . . ," *Pittsburgh Post-Gazette*, December 5, 1995, D7.

38. "Madden, Summerall Are Sold Favorites . . . ," *Sacramento Bee*, September 3, 1995, C3; Bob Raissman, "Joe Leads Uncool Fan Treatment," *New York Daily News*, November 14, 1995, 65.

39. Bob Raissman, "Bradshaw No O'Donnell Fan," *New York Daily News*, March 1, 1996, 74.

40. Barry Jackson, "A Lott to Smile About," *Miami Herald*, September 13, 1996, 10D.

41. Marty Mule, "Fan Demonstration . . . ," *Times-Picayune*, October 6, 1996, C18; Bob Raissman, "Not Slaphappy Standing Tall . . . ," *New York Daily News*, September 17, 1996, 54.

42. "NFL Log," *Pittsburgh Post-Gazette*, November 30, 1996, B8; Dave Sell, "Football's Pain-Taking Process," *Washington Post*, December 8, 1996, D1.

43. Barry Jackson, "World's Longest Pregame . . . ," *Miami Herald*, January 24, 1997, 9D.

44. Bob Wolfley, "Fox's Credibility Arrives by Bus," *Milwaukee Journal Sentinel*, January 25, 1997, SS1; John Martin, "Super Bowl XXXI . . . ," *Providence Journal*, January 27, 1997, D11.

45. "People," *Orange County Register*, December 1, 1997, A2; Richard Sandomir, "Fox Uses Bradshaw as Boredom Antidote," *New York Times*, December 26, 1997, C3.

46. Alan Pergament, "ABC Takes Big Chance . . . ," *Buffalo News*, September 9, 1999, S27; "Are You Ready for Some Foxball," *Seattle Post-Intelligencer*, September 2, 1994, F6; Dusty Saunders, "What Pushed My Buttons . . . ," *Rocky Mountain News*, December 27, 1999, 26C.

47. Mark Fitzhenry, "Some Lauds and Frauds . . . ," *Times Leader*, February 1, 1999, 1B.

48. Bradshaw, *It's Only a Game*, 187–91.

49. Robert Kurson, "Fox Analyst Bradshaw Admits . . . ," *Chicago Sun-Times*, November 5, 1995, 25.

50. "Network Drops the Ball . . . ," *Plain Dealer*, February 1, 1999, 10D.

51. John Rowe, "Wanted: True Spirits . . . ," *Record*, October 1, 2000, S2.

52. Tom Hoffarth, "The Writing on and off the Wall . . . ," *Daily News of Los Angeles*, December 16, 2002, S2.

53. "The NFC," *Kansas City Star*, September 26, 1999, 4.

54. Tom Sorensen, "No Fun . . . ," *Charlotte Observer*, January 20, 1999, 1B.

55. Harold Andersen, "Reports on Number . . . ," *Omaha World-Herald*, January 14, 1999, 25.

56. "Weekend Telecasts Will Take Somber Tone," *Press-Telegram*, September 21, 2001, B5; Jerry Lindquist, "Nascar vs. NFL?" *Richmond Times-Dispatch*, September 27, 2001, E2.

57. Tom Hoffarth, "Bradshaw Finds Peace in Bible," *Daily Breeze*, September 28, 2001, C2; comment by Greg Harry, in Tim McMillen, "Fan Tribute to Terry Bradshaw," *Mcmillenandwife.com*, http://www.mcmillenandwife.com/bradshaw_fans.html (accessed February 26, 2016).

58. "Moment of Zen," *Daily Show with John Stewart*, February 4, 2002, http://www.cc.com/video-clips/75ap56/the-daily-show-with-jon-stewart-moment-of-zen---hard-day-s-night (accessed July 29, 2016).

59. John McGrath, "Gleaming Broadcast Has Red, White, and Blue Sheen," *News Tribune*, February 4, 2002, C1; Brad Rock, "Rock on . . . ," *Deseret News*, February 5, 2002, D1; Ken Hoffman, "Comedy Execs Due Here . . . ," *Houston Chronicle*, February 5, 2002, 1; "Moment of Zen."

60. Kristen, "Musical Songs without Sound," *Geminichildetumblr.com*, http://geminichilde.tumblr.com/post/1299937681/terry-bradshaw-and-paul-mccartney-for-some-reason (accessed July 29, 2016); "Paul McCartney and Terry Bradshaw at the Super Bowl," *Ilxor.com*, http://ilxor.com/ILX/ThreadSelectedControllerServlet?boardid=41&threadid=4481 (accessed July 29, 2016).

61. "Halftime Provides a Super Moment," *Maywood Herald*, February 6, 2002, 7; Argus Hamilton, "Improbable Duet at Super Bowl," *Daily Oklahoman*, February 6, 2002, 7A.

62. "The Beatles and Sports," *Sports Illustrated*, February 10, 2014, http://www.si.com/more-sports/photos/2014/02/10/beatles-and-sports (accessed July 29, 2016).

63. Frank Fitzpatrick, "Will NFL Worship at 'Idol's' Feet?" *Philadelphia Inquirer*, September 6, 2002, D2.

64. Jerry Lindquist, "Tired Announcer . . . ," *Richmond Times-Dispatch*, December 30, 1996, C9; "World Picks: Our '05 List? NFL's Most Painful Things," *Tulsa World*, December 22, 2005, B1; "From the Sidelines," *Daily Messenger*, September 18, 2006, C1.

65. Jerry Greene, "Coaching Duo Disappoint," *Orlando Sentinel*, November 3, 2003, D2.

66. Norman Chad, "Pregame Edge Goes to Fox Crew," *Pittsburgh Post-Gazette*, November 21, 2005, E2.

67. Keith Groller, "Scandal Dominates Pregame Shows," *Morning Call*, September 18, 2007, C2; Bill Doyle, "Several TV Voices Take It to Belichick," *Worcester Telegram & Gazette*, September 20, 2007, C1.

68. Groller, "Scandal Dominates Pregame Shows," C2; Doyle, "Several TV Voices Take It to Belichick," C1.

69. Bob Raissman, "A Touch of Madden-ness," *New York Daily News*, September 10, 2010, 82; Rich Cimini, "Terry Bradshaw Rips Rex Ryan," *ESPN.com*, September 4, 2010, http://espn.go.com/new-york/nfl/news/story?id=5529097 (accessed July 29, 2016).

70. Michael David Smith, "Terry Bradshaw: NFL Must Do More on Concussions," *NBC Sports*, April 12, 2011, http://profootballtalk.nbcsports.com/2011/04/12/terry-bradshaw-nfl-must-do-more-on-concussions/ (accessed July 29, 2016).

71. Mike Florio, "Bradshaw Thinks NFL Doesn't Truly Care about Former Players," *NBC Sports*, June 14, 2012, http://profootballtalk.nbcsports.com/2012/06/14/bradshaw-doesnt-think-nfl-truly-cares-about-former-players/ (accessed July 29, 2016); Bill Carey, "Terry Bradshaw: 'If I Had a Son . . . I Would Not Let Him Play Football,'" *Sports Illustrated*, June 14, 2012, http://www.si.com/si-wire/2012/06/14/terry-bradshaw-former-players-concussions (accessed March 21, 2016).

72. Carl Prine and Scott Brown, "Steelers' Off-Field Woes Attributed to 'Entitlement' Jock Culture," *Pittsburgh Tribune-Review*, April 18, 2010, 1D; Ron Cook, "Jealousy Likely Trigger . . . ," *Pittsburgh Post-Gazette*, September 19, 2010, C1; Art Stapleton, "Cruz: I'll Redeem Myself," *Record*, September 11, 2012, S01.

73. "Quotes of the Week XIV," *Kylestack.com*, September 6, 2010, https://kylestacksports.wordpress.com/2010/09/06/quotes-of-the-week-xiv/ (accessed July 29, 2016).

74. "NFL Arrests Database," *USA Today*, November 7, 2013, http://www.usatoday.com/sports/nfl/arrests/ (accessed July 29, 2016).

75. Matt Yoder, "Terry Bradshaw Destroys Roger Goodell," *Awfulannouncing.com*, November 24, 2014, http://awfulannouncing.com/2014/video-terry-bradshaw-destroys-roger-goodell.html (accessed July 29, 2016).

76. Ricky Doyle, "Terry Bradshaw Rips Greg Hardy, Mocks Jerry Jones in Epic Rant," *Sun*, October 11, 2015, http://nesn.com/2015/10/terry-bradshaw-rips-greg-hardy-mocks-jerry-jones-in-epic-rant-video/ (accessed July 29, 2016); J. D. Durkin, "Bradshaw Blasts NFL Owner Jerry Jones and Player Suspended for Abuse," *Mediaite.com*, October 12, 2015, http://www.mediaite.com/online/bradshaw-blasts-nfl-owner-jerry-jones-and-player-suspended-for-abuse/ (accessed July 29, 2016).

77. Verne Lundquist, telephone interview by author, May 2, 2016; David J. Halberstam, "Top 50 Network TV Announcers," January 30, 2009, *Yahoo Sports*, https://sports.yahoo.com/top/news?slug=ys-top50a013009 (accessed September 29, 2016).

10. HOST, GUEST STAR, AND COMMERCIALS

1. "Page 2," *San Antonio Express-News*, January 29, 2006, 2C. Terry Bradshaw is a "natural" in the comedy *Failure to Launch*, in which he stars opposite Oscar winner Bates.

2. "TV Offers Music and Comedy on New Year's Eve," *Sun*, December 31, 1990, 1C; "Terry Bradshaw," *Imdb.com*, http://www.imdb.com/name/nm0103537/ (accessed May 23, 2016); Verne Lundquist, telephone interview by author, May 2, 2016; Terry O'Neill, telephone interview by author, March 11, 2016.

3. Glen Macnow, "Sports Memorabilia Can Mean Money . . . ," *Houston Chronicle*, November 25, 1990, 20; Michelle Meyer, "For the Real Sports . . . ," *Houston Chronicle*, December 19, 1991, B1.

4. Frank J. Murray, "Clinton Carves and Serves, Then Cuts to Family Dinner," *Washington Times*, November 27, 1992, A3; Marty Mule, "'In this Corner' Packs a Punch," *Times-Picayune*, December 13, 1992, C3.

5. Cristina Rouvalis, "Return of the Prodigal . . . ,"*Pittsburgh Post-Gazette*, March 22, 1994, B6; Robert Bianco, "No Need for News . . . ," *Pittsburgh Post-Gazette*, April 11, 1994, C6.

6. "Sports People . . . ," *Fort Worth Star-Telegram*, August 28, 1994, 2; Hal Boedeker, "Dave vs. Jay . . . ," *Orlando Sentinel*, June 30, 1995, E1.

7. Terry Bradshaw, with David Fisher, *It's Only a Game* (New York: Simon & Shuster, 2001), 225–27.

8. Comment by Lisa Todd, "Fan Tribute to Terry Bradshaw," *Mcmillenadnwife.com*, http://www.mcmillenandwife.com/bradshaw_fans.html (accessed February 26, 2016); comment by Kenneth Besig, "Fan Tribute to Terry Bradshaw."

9. "Graduation," *Blossom*, Season 4, Episode 28, May 23, 1994, *YouTube*, https://www.youtube.com/watch?v=QH0I_X2QKhA (accessed May 23, 2016); Lon Grahnke, "Bradshaw Option Play . . . ," *Chicago Sun-Times*, May 16, 1994, 29.

10. Grahnke, "Bradshaw Option Play . . . ," 29.

11. Robert Williams, "SI Award Set for Television," *Omaha World-Herald*, December 8, 1995, 38.

12. Milton Kent, "SI Uses a New Avenue in Telling Story," *Sun*, December 7, 1995, 2D; Glenn Hibdon, "Salley's Hats Versatile for Rodeo," *Tulsa World*, September 25, 1997, B3.

13. "Now Batting for the Home Team," *Broadcasting*, May 26, 1997, 28; "It's Who You Know," *Broadcasting*, June 9, 1997, 18, 44; Bradshaw, *It's Only a Game*, 229–35.

14. Al Brumley, "With Four New Shows . . . ," *Dallas Morning News*, September 16, 1997, 1C; "Special Report: Talk Shows," *Broadcasting*, December 15, 1997, 30.

15. Brett Friedlander, "Fox Hopes Live Fishing Event Is a Keeper," *Fayetteville Observer*, October 31, 1999, 1D; Charles Elmore, "Area Viewers Not Hooked . . . ," *Palm Beach Post*, November 12, 1999, 2C.

16. "TV Listings," *Times-Tribune*, June 9, 2001, 7; Bradshaw, *It's Only a Game*, 239–43.

17. Sarah Schmalbruch, "The Credit Card Was Invented by a Man Who Forgot His Wallet at Dinner," *Businessinsider.com*, March 2, 2015, http://www.businessinsider.com/history-of-credit-cards-2015-2 (accessed August 12, 2016); Andrew Becker, "The Battle over 'Share of Wallet,'" *Frontline*, http://www.pbs.org/wgbh/pages/frontline/shows/credit/more/battle.html (accessed August 12, 2016).

18. Rtrt67, "VISA: A Chorus Line Commercial 1992," *YouTube*, August 18, 2012, https://www.youtube.com/watch?v=ssK5ffa75Mc (accessed August 12, 2016); Jean-Sebastien Blondel, "1992 – VISA – Dream Team," *YouTube*, June 22, 2008, https://www.youtube.com/watch?v=F3cRbg2RbGk&list=PL79508E101B7F0E9E&index=18 (accessed August 12, 2016).

19. Bradshaw, *It's Only a Game*, 216–17; TelevisionDetroit , "1996 Visa Commercial: Terry Bradshaw and Dick Butkus," *YouTube*, April 8, 2011, https://www.youtube.com/watch?v=9yXs3GssD_Q (accessed August 12, 2016).

20. "The Associates Launches Home Equity Campaign . . . ," *Freelibrary.com*, November 5, 1997, http://www.thefreelibrary.com/The+Associates+Launches+Home+Equity+Campaign+in+Texas+with+Terry...-a019954407 (accessed August 12, 2016); Dave Sorter, "The New Money," *Dallas/Fort Worth* 25, no. 2 (February 1, 1998): 16.

21. Sorter, "The New Money," 16.

22. CRS Family, "3/23/1998 Commercials," *YouTube*, August 27, 2012, https://www.youtube.com/watch?v=aLQU3AjXLoo (accessed August 16, 2016).

23. Bradshaw, *It's Only a Game*, 217–18; Richard A. Oppel Jr., "Citigroup Takes Action . . . ," *New York Times*, April 21, 2001, http://www.nytimes.com/2001/04/25/business/citigroup-takes-action-against-brokers-at-consumer-loan-unit.html (accessed August 15, 2016); Felix Salmon, "A Brief History of Home Equity Loans," *Bizjournals.com*, August 15, 2008, http://upstart.bizjournals.com/views/blogs/market-movers/2008/08/15/a-brief-history-of-home-equity-loans.html?page=all (accessed August 15, 2016).

24. "A Short History of the Telephone Industry and Regulation," *Bpastudio.csudh.edu*, http://bpastudio.csudh.edu/fac/lpress/471/hout/telecomHistory/ (accessed August 15, 2016); Harry McCracken, "A Brief History of the Rise

and Fall of Telephone Competition in the U.S., 1982–2011," *Technologiz-er.com*, March 20, 2011, http://www.technologizer.com/2011/03/20/att-buys-t-mobile/ (accessed August 15, 2016).

25. "Terry Bradshaw, Hulk Hogan, 10-10-220 Long Distance Calling Commercial," *YouTube*, February 9, 2010, https://www.youtube.com/watch?v=6ryT61OfKIM (accessed August 16, 2016); Eric Abraham, "10-10-220 Terry Bradshaw and Mike Piazza 'Out of Gas,'" *YouTube*, April 17, 2009, https://www.youtube.com/watch?v=0C1Tx7YZP48 (accessed August 16, 2016).

26. Deborah Jones, "35 Actors You Probably Didn't Know Released Albums," *Sabotagetimes.com*, November 2, 2015, http://sabotagetimes.com/music/35-male-actors-who-released-albums (accessed May 22, 2016); Ellis Ahmed, "The Complete History of NBA Rappers," *Complex.com*, March 2013, http://www.complex.com/sports/2013/03/the-complete-history-of-nba-rappers/ (accessed May 21, 2016).

27. Keith Lawrence, "Owensboro Native Helps Rush NFL Albums into Stores," *Owensboro Messenger-Inquirer*, November 22, 1996, 5C; Dave Hoekstra, "NFL Stars Tackle Country Tunes on Album . . . ," *Chicago Sun-Times*, January 22, 1997, 42; "Recordings," *Times Union*, June 19, 1997, 27.

28. Bill Jarnigan, "Southern Gospel Bursts in Popularity," *Times Daily*, April 25, 1993, 9F; Lon Grahnke, "Bradshaw Option Play . . . ," *Chicago Sun-Times*, May 16, 1994, 29; Jake Hess, with Richard Hyatt, *Nothing but Fine: The Music and the Gospel According to Jake Hess* (Bolingbroke, GA: Buckland Press, 1995), 235–37.

29. Richard Hyatt, telephone interview by author, June 22, 2016.

30. Gospel Hour, "Old Friends: Bill Gaither and Homecoming Friends," *YouTube*, August 13, 2009, https://www.youtube.com/watch?v=tJAujY2Gtj4 (accessed August 17, 2016); Scutter Mann, "Gaither Homecoming, I Shall Not Be Moved, Feat. the Easters, the Nelons, Jake Hess," *YouTube*, July 17, 2010, https://www.youtube.com/watch?v=4pGUmWWkxlE (accessed August 17, 2016); WKNO, "Classic Gospel," *WKNOTV.com*, February 9, 2013, http://www.wkno.org/tvshows/Classic_Gospel8.html (accessed August 17, 2016).

31. Jean Stanley, "Terry Bradshaw Singing with the Isaacs at Clawson Assembly of God, Pollok, TX," *YouTube*, April 13, 2015, https://www.youtube.com/watch?v=o0yBveFC2R8 (accessed August 17, 2016); Michelle S., "The Isaacs and Terry Bradshaw at Waikoloa Baptist Church," July 30, 2015, https://www.youtube.com/watch?v=01KlNv0wk84 (accessed August 17, 2016).

32. Edward G. Robinson III, "Catching Flak . . . ," *Pittsburgh Post-Gazette*, August 3, 2001, C9; "Terry Bradshaw Returns to Roots for Book Signing," *Observer-Reporter*, August 6, 2001, 1D.

33. Jeff Guinn, "Page Turners . . . ," *Fort Worth Star-Telegram*, September 23, 2001, 6; "Love a Parade?" *Orlando Sentinel*, December 18, 2002, D2;

comment by Joyce Wess, "Fan Tribute to Terry Bradshaw"; comment by Donna Vanvalkenburg, "Fan Tribute to Terry Bradshaw."

34. "TranSouth Lures Football Icons . . . ," *Star-Ledger*, March 23, 1998, 41.

35. Dave Kallmann, "Memories of Earnhardt Sr. . . . ," *Milwaukee Journal Sentinel*, February 17, 2002, 10.

36. Rupen Fofaria, "Bradshaw Makes a Pass at Racing," *News & Observer*, November 30, 2001, C7; Fitz–Bradshaw Racing, "News Release," July 5, 2002; Stock Car Racing Collection, Appalachian State University Library, Boone, North Carolina; John Zenor, "Bradshaw Calls the Signals Again," *Star-Ledger*, May 12, 2005, 46.

37. Scott Rabalais, "Bradshaw Quick to Learn Racing," *American Press*, February 15, 2003, 1E; Lewis Lazare, "Tagline Tangles Supercuts Campaign," *Chicago Sun-Times*, April 10, 2003, 59.

38. Rabalais, "Bradshaw Quick to Learn Racing," 1E; "Dave Moody's Speed Reading Column," *Times Argus*, August 13, 2003, 1d.

39. Zenor, "Bradshaw Calls the Signals Again," 46.

40. John Zenor. "Ex-Grid Stars Run Rising Busch Team," *Daily Herald*, May 13, 2005, 1D; Chris Gasiewski, "Dover Notebook," *Delaware State News*, September 23, 2006, 1D.

41. "Company Picnic: Part 1 and Part 2," *Imdb.com*, February 2, 2002, http://www.imdb.com/title/tt0640308/fullcredits?ref_=tt_ov_st_sm (accessed August 24, 2016); "Son-in-Law," *Imdb.com*, October 15, 2002, http://www.imdb.com/title/tt0503843/ (accessed August 24, 2016); Robert Philpot, "Best Bets," *Fort Worth Star-Telegram*, March 18, 2003, 10.

42. "Tag Athlete," *Los Angeles Times*, http://projects.latimes.com/hollywood/star-walk/tag/athlete/page/1/ (accessed August 27, 2016); Shirah Matsuzawa and Patrick Campbell, "The LA You May Not Know," *NBC Los Angeles*, April 3, 2016, http://www.nbclosangeles.com/news/local/374354201.html (accessed August 27, 2016).

43. Frank Wilkins, "Robots: DVD Review," *Reelreviews.com*, May 5, 2010, http://www.franksreelreviews.com/reviews/2005/robots.htm (accessed August 24, 2016); Jen Kopf, "'Robots' Runs Well Enough but Has a Few Loose Parts," *Lancaster New Era*, September 30, 2005, A7; *Robots*, dir. Chris Wedge and Carlos Saldanha, perf. Ewan McGregor, Halle Berry, and Mel Brooks. Twentieth Century Fox, 2005.

44. Michael H. Kleinschrodt, "'Launch' Director Caught Spirit of New Orleans," *Times-Picayune*, March 10, 2006, 7.

45. *Failure to Launch*, dir. Tom Dey, perf. Matthew McConaughey, Sarah Jessica Parker, and Kathy Bates. Paramount, 2006; "Failure to Launch (2006)," *Imdb.com*, http://www.imdb.com/title/tt0427229/ (accessed August 25, 2016);

"Failure to Launch (2006)," *Boxofficemojo.com*, http://www.boxofficemojo. com/movies/?page=main&id=failuretolaunch.htm (accessed August 25, 2016).

46. Jerry Greene, "Silver Stars Bring Sizzle," *Orlando Sentinel*, March 15, 2006, C2; Steven Winn, "Did Someone Say . . . ," *San Francisco Chronicle*, March 15, 2006, E1; "Movie Reviews," *North County Times*, March 15, 2006, 3c; Charles Britton, "Movies," *Daily Breeze*, January 6, 2006, R4.

47. Buddy Martin, "Only You Can Provide All of These Answers," *North Port Sun*, March 19, 2006, 3C; "Page 2," 2D; "At the Movies," *Lubbock Avalanche-Journal*, June 9, 2006, "Around Town" page; Claudia Puig, "'Failure to Launch' Sums It Up," *USA Today*, March 9, 2006, http://usatoday30.usatoday. com/life/movies/reviews/2006-03-09-failure-to-launch_x.htm (accessed June 23, 2016).

48. "Audience Reviews," *Rottentomatoes.com*, https://www.rottentomatoes. com/m/failure_to_launch/reviews/?type=user (accessed June 23, 2016), see Tyler S. and Anne D., among others; "Russell G.," *Rottentomatoes.com*, https:// www.rottentomatoes.com/m/failure_to_launch/reviews/?page=3&type=user (accessed June 23, 2016).

49. "Audience Reviews."

50. Matt Soergel, "New Flick Fails to Launch," *Newton Kansan*, March 11, 2006, Play! Section; Dan and Nancy, "'Failure to Launch' Fails for Dan . . . ," *Broomfield Enterprise*, March 15, 2006, A13; "Cover Your Eyes," *Times Record*, March 12, 2006, Double Take.

51. Dan O'Neill, "Nicklaus Has Tough Time . . . ," *St. Louis Post-Dispatch*, March 16, 2006, B2; Martin, "Only You Can Provide All of These Answers," 3C; "Page 2," 2D.

52. Larry Stewart, "Revealing Role for Bradshaw in 'Failure,'" *Los Angeles Times*, March 10, 2006, Sports 1; Lou Gaul, "Kathy Bates Aims for a Long and Fruitful Career," *Intelligencer*, March 16, 2006, D1.

53. Angel, "IGN Interview: Charisma Carpenter," *Ign.com*, August 31, 2006, http://www.ign.com/articles/2006/08/31/ign-interview-charisma-carpenter (accessed August 25, 2016).

54. Jon Naito, "No, Terry Bradshaw's Not Really Dumb," *Seattle Post Intelligencer*, September 22, 2006, http://www.seattlepi.com/news/article/No-Terry-Bradshaw-s-not-really-dumb-1215380.php (accessed June 30, 2016); Emily Ashby, "Relative Chaos (2006)," *Imdb.com*, http://www.imdb.com/title/ tt0806167/fullcredits?ref_=tt_ov_st_sm (accessed June 30, 2016); "Relative Chaos," *Commonsensemedia.org*, https://www.commonsensemedia.org/tv-reviews/relative-chaos# (accessed June 30, 2016).

55. "Jackson Will Sing in Tribute to Hank Jr. Nov. 17 on CMT," *Times-Herald*, November 6, 2007, 1D; "What's on TV Tonight," *Southtown Star*, February 8, 2008, D5; Cesart Kara, "Las Vegas 517 Win Place Bingo," https://

www.youtube.com/watch?v=BR45ea4nOX8 , http://www.imdb.com/title/ tt1007425/?ref_=nm_flmg_act_3 (accessed August 27, 2016); Walt Belcher, "'Colbert Christmas' Stranger Than Truthiness," *Tampa Tribune*, November 21, 2008, 2.

56. "Documentary: Walking on Dead Fish," *Urbanmecca.net*, November 4, 2008, http://urbanmecca.net/news/2008/11/04/documentary-walking-on-dead-fish/ (accessed August 27, 2016); Mike Scott, "'Dead Fish' Unreels a Slice of Post-Katrina Life," *NOLA.com*, September 19, 2008, http://blog.nola.com/ mikescott/2008/09/dead_fish_unreels_a_slice_of_p.html (accessed August 27, 2016).

57. "Cubed," *Imdb.com*, http://www.imdb.com/title/tt1792654/?ref_=m_ nmfmd_slf_26 (accessed August 27, 2016); "Nutrisystem for Men TV Commercial Featuring Terry Bradshaw," *YouTube*, April 23, 2015, https://www. youtube.com/watch?v=tDuFUgjHyIs (accessed August 27, 2016); BBDO Worldwide, "Merck TV Spot, 'Surprise Door Knock' Featuring Terry Bradshaw," *Ispot.tv*, https://www.ispot.tv/ad/7UEu/merck-surprise-door-knock-featuring-terry-bradshaw (accessed August 27, 2016).

58. "Q+A: NFL Legend Terry Bradshaw . . . ," *Las Vegas Sun*, April 17, 2013, 3D.

59. "Terry Bradshaw's One-Man Show at the Mirage Is Another Mad Scramble," *Las Vegas Sun*, June 30, 2013, 3D; Robin Leach, "Counter Intelligence . . . ," *Las Vegas Sun*, September 24, 2013, 3D.

60. "Terry Bradshaw's One-Man Show," 3D; Mike Forman, "Terry Bradshaw Brings Comedy Show to Victoria," *Victoria Advocate*, December 12, 2013, 1C.

61. "Lights of Louisiana, Single," *Itunes.apple.com*, November 19, 2012, https://itunes.apple.com/us/album/lights-of-louisiana-single/id580963295 (accessed March 31, 2016).

62. Makeupjillian, "Bad Horse 'It's All Good': Behind the Scenes with Former Steelers Terry Bradshaw and Bobby Walden," *YouTube.com*, November 30, 2011, https://www.youtube.com/watch?v=MAQfl65NAIU (accessed March 31, 2016).

63. Dominic Patten, "'Better Late Than Never' Ratings Debut Solid . . . ," *Deadline.com*, August 24, 2016, http://deadline.com/2016/08/better-late-than-never-ratings-debut-solid-william-shatner-americas-got-talent-the-view-nbc-1201808081/ (accessed September 18, 2016); Dominic Patten, "'Better Late Than Never' Ratings Steady . . . ," *Deadline.com*, August 31, 2016, http:// deadline.com/2016/08/better-late-than-never-ratings-steady-with-premiere-william-shatner-americas-got-talwnt-bachelor-in-paradise-after-paradise-rises-nbc-1201811517/ (accessed September 18, 2016).

64. John Moore, "Rattlebrain's Funny Bone Is Out of Joint with 'B.F.E.,'" *Denver Post*, November 23, 2006, F10; John Moore, "Have an Edgier Holiday," *Denver Post*, November 24, 2006, F04; Brosefolophogus , "LOL: Shaq Does Terry Bradshaw during Frank Caliendo Skit on FOX Super Bowl Pregame Show," *YouTube*, February 7, 2011, http://jerseychaser.com/lol-shaq-does-terry-bradshaw-during-frank-caliendo-skit-on-fox-super-bowl-pregame-show/ (accessed August 27, 2016); "Frank Caliendo Impersonates John Madden, Jeff Fisher, and Terry Bradshaw," *YouTube*, February 3, 2012, https://www.youtube.com/watch?v=giu8kVyUM-0 (accessed August 27, 2016).

65. "'NFL on Fox' Host Blasted for Failing to Razz Terry Bradshaw," *Onion*, November 29, 2010, http://www.theonion.com/article/nfl-on-fox-host-blasted-for-failing-to-razz-terry--18529 (accessed August 27, 2016).

66. Chris Strauss, "Terry Bradshaw was Mercilessly . . . ," *USA Today*, January 30, 2015, http://ftw.usatoday.com/2015/01/terry-bradshaw-super-bowl-friars-roast (accessed August 30, 2016).

CONCLUSION

1. Fox Sports, "Terry, Howie, and Jimmy Get Candid about Their Images as Players," *YouTube* , November 27, 2013, https://www.youtube.com/watch?v=uTtj5cPbuBY (accessed September 11, 2016).

BIBLIOGRAPHY

BOOKS, ARTICLES, AND FILMS

"1970s/1978 AFC Championship Game." *Youremembersthat.com*, http://www.youremembersthat.com/media/8950/1978_AFC_Championship_Game/#.VzfSlPkrLIU (accessed June 2, 2016).

"543 F. 2d 606: *John Mackey et al., Appelles v. National Football League et al., Appellants." PublicResource.org*, November 23, 1976, http://law.justia.com/cases/federal/appellate-courts/F2/543/606/338695/ (accessed May 1, 2016).

Aaron, Henry, and Lonnie Wheeler. *I Had a Hammer: The Henry Aaron Story*. New York: Harper, 2007.

Agyekwena, Bernice. "Uses and Gratification Theory Applied to Television." February 2006, https://www.scribd.com/doc/32903764/The-Uses-and-Gratification-Theory-as-Applied-to-Television (accessed June 2, 2016).

Allen, Frederick L. *Only Yesterday*. New York: Harper Perennial Modern Classics, 2010.

Allitt, Patrick. *Religion in America since 1945: A History*. New York: Columbia University Press, 2003.

Baker, Aaron. *Contesting Identities: Sports in American Film*. Champlain: University of Illinois Press, 35–42, 2006.

Bartley, Numan V. *The New South, 1945–1980: The Story of the South's Modernization*. Baton Rouge: Louisiana State University Press, 1995.

Benson, Michael. *Ballparks of North America*. Jefferson, NC: McFarland, 2009.

Blount, Roy, Jr. *About Three Bricks Shy . . . and the Load Filled Up*. Pittsburgh, PA: University of Pittsburgh Press, 2004.

Bouchette, Ed. *The Pittsburgh Steelers*. New York: St. Martin's, 1994.

Bradshaw, Terry, with Buddy Martin. *Looking Deep*. New York: Berkley Books, 1989.

Bradshaw, Terry, with Charles Paul Conn. *No Easy Game*. Grand Rapids, MI: F. H. Revell, 1973.

Bradshaw, Terry, with David Diles. *Terry Bradshaw: Man of Steel*. Grand Rapids, MI: Zondervan, 1979.

Bradshaw, Terry, with David Fisher. *It's Only a Game*. New York: Simon & Shuster, 2001.

———. *Keep It Simple*. New York: Atria, 2002.

Brock, Eric J. *Eric Brock's Shreveport*. Gretna, LA: Pelican, 2001.

Brown, Rodger. "Dogpatch USA: The Road to Hokum." *Southern Changes: The Journal of the Southern Regional Council* 15, no. 3 (1993): 18–26.

"Bulldog History." *LATechSports*, http://grfx.cstv.com/photos/schools/latc/sports/m-baskbl/auto_pdf/0910-mbk-Sec7.pdf (accessed March 31, 2016).

Byrd, Jerry. *Jerry Byrd's Football Country*. Shreveport, LA: Shreveport Publishing, 1981.

Cawelti, John G. *Apostles of the Self-Made Man*. Chicago: University of Chicago Press, 1965.

Chafe, William H. *The Unfinished Journey: America since World War II*. New York: Oxford University Press, 2010.

Chermak, Steven, and Frankie Bailey. *Crimes and Trials of the Century*. Westport, CT: Greenwood Press, 2007.

Cope, Myron. *Double Yoi!* Champaign, IL: Sports Publishing, 2002.

de Jong, Greta. *A Different Day: African American Struggles for Justice in Rural Louisiana, 1900–1970*. Chapel Hill: University of North Carolina Press, 2002.

Dinan, John. *Sports in the Pulp Magazines*. Jefferson, NC: McFarland, 2009.

"Documentary: Walking on Dead Fish." *Urbanmecca.net*, November 4, 2008, http://urbanmecca.net/news/2008/11/04/documentary-walking-on-dead-fish/ (accessed August 27, 2016).

Duncan, James H., Jr. *American Radio*. Indianapolis, IN: Duncan's American Radio, 1976–1988.

Ferrence, Matthew J. *All-American Redneck: Variations on an Icon, from James Fenimore Cooper to the Dixie Chicks*. Knoxville: University of Tennessee Press, 2014.

Foley, Dennis. "Stonecipher: Shreveport Is as Racially Divided Today as in 1960s." *KEEL*, February 3, 2014, http://710keel.com/stonecipher-shreveport-is-as-racially-divided-today-as-in-1960s/ (accessed August 27, 2016).

Freedman, Lew. *Pittsburgh Steelers: The Complete Illustrated History*. Minneapolis, MN: MVP Books, 2011.

Gatlin, Larry, with Jeff Lenburg. *All the Gold in California and Other People: Places and Things*. Nashville, TN: Thomas Nelson, 1998.

Goff, James R. *Close Harmony: A History of Southern Gospel*. Chapel Hill: University of North Carolina Press, 2002.

Goodin, Jennifer. "Solidarity Lost: The Deindustrialization of Pittsburgh in the 1980s." Honors thesis, Rutgers University, New Brunswick, New Jersey, 2012, http://www.history.rutgers.edu/undergraduate/honors-program/honors-papers-2012/400-solidarity-lost-the-deindustrialization-of-pittsburgh-in-the-1980s/file (accessed February 9, 2017).

Harrison, Douglas. *Then Sings My Soul: The Culture of Southern Gospel Music*. Champaign: University of Illinois Press, 2012.

Herman, Didi. *The Antigay Agenda: Orthodox Vision and the Christian Right*. Chicago: University of Chicago Press, 1997.

Hess, Jake, with Richard Hyatt. *Nothing but Fine: The Music and the Gospel according to Jake Hess*. Boilingbroke, GA: Buckland Press, 1995.

Himmelstein, Jerome L. *To the Right: The Transformation of American Conservatism*. Berkeley: University of California Press, 1992.

"The History of Chewing Tobacco in America." *Smokeless Aficionado*, http://www.smokelessaficionado.com/index.php/otp/chewing-tobacco/56-the-history-of-chewing-tobacco-in-america (accessed February 9, 2017).

House, Gerry. *Country Music Broke My Brain: A Behind-the-Microphone Peek at Nashville*. Dallas, TX: BenBella Books, 2014.

Hovland, Roxanne, Joyce M. Wolburg, and Eric E. Haley. *Readings in Advertising, Society, and Consumer Culture*. New York: Routledge, 2007.

Howard, Greg. "The Big Book of Black Quarterbacks." *Deadspin.com*, February 6, 2014, http://deadspin.com/the-big-book-of-black-quarterbacks-1517763742 (accessed February 9, 2017).

Inge, M. Thomas. "Li'l Abner, Snuffy, Pogo, and Friends: The South in the American Comic Strip." *Southern Quarterly* 48, no. 2 (2011): 6–74.

International Directory of Company Histories, vol. 53. New York: St. James Press, 2003.

Isenberg, Nancy. *White Trash: The 440-Year Untold History of Class in America*. New York: Viking, 2016.

Jackson, Kenneth T. *The Ku Klux Klan in the City, 1915–1930*. New York: Oxford University Press, 1992.

Jenkins, Eddie. *Louisiana High School Football Championships: The Complete Reference Book 1921–1996*. Shreveport, LA: 14-0 Publications, 1997.

———. "Playoff and Title Game Appearances and Titles Won." *WinnfieldTigerFootball.com*, http://www.winnfieldtigerfootball.com/louisiana_high_school_football_championships.html (accessed April 18, 2016).

La Botz, Dan. "What Happened to the American Working Class?" *New Politics* 4, no. 48 (Winter 2010), http://newpol.org/content/what-happened-american-working-class (accessed April 18, 2016).

Lafayette High School Lions Din Yearbook (Lafayette, LA), Class of 1966. E-Yearbook.com, http://www.eyearbook.com/yearbooks/Lafayette_High_School_Lions_Din_Yearbook/1966/Page_136.html (accessed February 21, 2017).

Logan, Hoarce. *Louisiana Hayride Years: Making Musical History in Country's Golden Age*. New York: St. Martins, 1999.

Luciano, Lynne. *Looking Good: Male Body Image in Modern America*. New York: Hill & Wang, 2001.

Lumpkin, Angela, and Linda D. Williams. "An Analysis of *Sports Illustrated* Feature Articles, 1954–1987." *Sociology of Sport Journal* 8 (1991): 16–32.

Masich, Andrew E., Dan Rooney, and David F. Halaas. *Dan Rooney: My 75 Years with the Pittsburgh Steelers and the NFL*. New York: Da Capo, 2008.

McMillen, Tim. "Fan Tribute to Terry Bradshaw." *Mcmillenandwife.com*, http://www.mcmillenandwife.com/bradshaw_fans.html (accessed February 26, 2016).

Mehno, John. "History of the Stadium." In Pittsburgh Pirates Official 1995 Commemorative Yearbook. Dallas, TX: Sports Media, 1995.

Muller, Edward K. "Downtown Pittsburgh: Renaissance and Renewal." In Kevin J. Patrick and Joseph L. Scarpaci Jr., eds., *A Geographic Perspective of Pittsburgh and the Alleghenies*, 7–20. Pittsburgh, PA: University of Pittsburgh Press, 2006.

National Association for the Advancement of Colored People (NAACP). "NAACP Legal History." *NAACP.org*, http://www.naacp.org/legal-department/naacp-legal-history/ (accessed February 21, 2017).

National Football League Players Association. "History." *NFLPA.com*, https://www.nflpa.com/about/history (accessed February 21, 2017).

Novick, Donald. "The Legality of the Rozelle Rule and Related Practices in the National Football League." *Fordham Urban Law Journal* 4, no. 3 (1975), http://ir.lawnet.fordham.edu/cgi/viewcontent.cgi?article=1048&context=ulj (accessed May 1, 2016).

Nystrom, Derek. *Hard Hats, Rednecks, and Macho Men*. New York: Oxford University Press, 2009.

"Oral History 41: Hal Needham." *Academy of Motion Picture Arts and Sciences*.

Patrick, Kevin J., and Joseph L. Scarpaci Jr., eds. A Geographic Perspective of Pittsburgh and the Alleghenies. Pittsburgh, PA: University of Pittsburgh Press, 2006.

Patterson, James T. *Brown v. Board of Education: A Civil Rights Milestone and Its Troubled Legacy*. New York: Oxford University Press, 2001.

Pennington, Richard. "Racial Integration of College Football." *Richardpennington.com*, http://richardpennington.com/index.php/publications/entry/racial-integraton-of-college-football-in-texasracial-integraton-of-college (accessed February 20, 2017).

Pilkey, Orrin H., and Mary Edna Fraser. *A Celebration of the World's Barrier Islands*. New York: Columbia University Press, 2003.

Pomerantz, Gary M. *Their Life's Work: The Brotherhood of the 1970s Pittsburgh Steelers*. New York: Simon & Shuster, 2013.

Room, Taylor T. "History of College Football Recruiting Cheating, Part 1." *SB Nation Barking Carnival*, May 30, 2008, http://www.barkingcarnival.com/2008/05/30/the-history-of-college-football-recruiting-cheating-part-1 (accessed February 20, 2017).

———. "History of College Football Recruiting Cheating, Part 2." *SB Nation Barking Carnival*, June 2, 2008, http://www.barkingcarnival.com/2008/06/02/the-history-of-college-football-recruiting-cheating-part-2 (accessed February 20, 2017).

———. "History of College Football Recruiting Cheating, Part 3." *SB Nation Barking Carnival*, June 30, 2008, http://www.barkingcarnival.com/2008/06/30/the-history-of-college-football-recruiting-cheating-part-3 (accessed February 20, 2017).

———. "History of College Football Recruiting Cheating, Part 4." *SB Nation Barking Carnival*, June 9, 2008, http://www.barkingcarnival.com/2008/06/09/the-history-of-college-football-recruiting-cheating-part-4 (accessed February 20, 2017).

———. "History of College Football Recruiting Cheating, Part 5." *SB Nation Barking Carnival*, June 16, 2008, http://www.barkingcarnival.com/2008/06/16/the-history-of-college-football-recruiting-cheating-part-5 (accessed February 20, 2017).

———. "History of College Football Recruiting Cheating, Part 6." *SB Nation Barking Carnival*, July 2, 2008, http://www.barkingcarnival.com/2008/07/02/the-history-of-college-football-recruiting-cheating-part-6 (accessed February 20, 2017).

———. "History of College Football Recruiting Cheating, Part 7." *SB Nation Barking Carnival*, July 9, 2008, http://www.barkingcarnival.com/2008/07/09/the-history-of-college-football-recruiting-cheating-part-7 (accessed February 20, 2017).

———. "History of College Football Recruiting Cheating, Part 8." *SB Nation Barking Carnival*, July 21, 2008, http://www.barkingcarnival.com/2008/07/21/the-history-of-college-football-recruiting-cheating-part-8 (accessed February 20, 2017).

Ruck, Rob L., Maggie Jones Patterson, and Michael P. Weber. *Rooney: A Sporting Life.* Lincoln: University of Nebraska Press, 2010.

Russell, Andy. *Andy Russell: A Steeler Odyssey.* Champaign, IL: Sports Publishing, 2001.

Sabo, Donald, and David F. Gordon, eds. *Men's Health and Illness: Gender, Power, and the Body.* Thousand Oaks, CA: Sage, 1995.

Scaruffi, Piero. *A History of Popular Music before Rock Music.* London: Omniware, 2007.

Scharnhorst, Gary, and Jack Bales. *The Lost Life of Horatio Alger Jr.* Bloomington: Indiana University Press, 1992.

Schumacher, Michael, and Denis Kitchen. *Al Capp: A Life to the Contrary.* New York: Bloomsbury, 2013.

Scott, Mike. "Dead Fish Unreels a Slice of Post-Katrina Life." *NOLA.com*, September 19, 2008, http://blog.nola.com/mikescott/2008/09/dead_fish_unreels_a_slice_of_p.html (accessed March 15, 2016).

Selective Service System. "The Vietnam Lotteries." *SSS.gov*, https://www.sss.gov/About/History-And-Records/lotter1 (accessed February 21, 2017).

Smidt, Corwin E. *American Evangelicals Today.* Lanham, MD: Rowman & Littlefield, 2013.

Society of Independent Motion Picture Producers. "The Hollywood Antitrust Case." *Cobbles.com*, http://www.cobbles.com/simpp_archive/1film_antitrust.htm (accessed February 21, 2017).

Sorter, Dave. "The New Money." *Dallas/Fort Worth* 25, no. 2 (February 1, 1998): 16.

Speck, Mark. "WFL Transactions." *World Football League*, http://wfl.charlottehornetswfl.com/season_book_1974/wfl_transactions.php (accessed February 21, 2017).

Tatrn, Bob. *Bob Tatrn's Sports Minutes.* Tarentum, PA: Word Association, 2011.

University of Maryland Global Terrorism Database, National Consortium for the Study of Terrorism and Responses to Terrorism. "Incidents over Time, 1970–1979." *Start.umd.edu*, 2009–2015, https://www.start.umd.edu/gtd/search/Results.aspx?start_yearonly=1970&end_yearonly=1979&start_year=&start_month=&start_day=&end_year=&end_month=&end_day=&country=217&asmSelect1=&dtp2=all&success=yes&casualties_type=b&casualties_max (accessed May 10, 2016).

Utah Tobacco Prevention and Control Program. "History of Smokeless Tobacco." *Utah Department of Health*, December 2007, http://www.tobaccofreeutah.org/pdfs/hissmkls.pdf (accessed May 10, 2016).

Van Thyn, Nico. "'The Blond Bomber' a Bright Star, Then and Now." *Nvanthyn.blogspot.com*, April 14, 2012, http://nvanthyn.blogspot.com/2012/04/blond-bomber-bright-star-then-and-now.html (accessed March 15, 2016).

———. "A Brutal Day in Murfreesboro." *Nvanthyn.blogspot.com*, January 31, 2014, http://nvanthyn.blogspot.com/2014/01/a-brutal-day-in-murfreesboro.html (accessed April 3, 2016).

———. "Football Integration at La. Tech: Making It Work." *Nvanthyn.blogspot.com*, April 10, 2015, http://nvanthyn.blogspot.com/2015/04/football-integration-at-la-tech-making.html (accessed March 21, 2016).

———. "Phil and Terry and 4–16?" *Nvanthyn.blogspot.com*, June 26, 2013, http://nvanthyn.blogspot.com/2013/06/phil-and-terry-and-4-16.html (accessed March 15, 2016).

———. "Sunset Acres Was Home." *Nvanthyn.blogspot.com*, September 27, 2012, http://nvanthyn.blogspot.com/2012/09/sunset-acres-was-home.html (accessed March 15, 2016).

———. "The Team Named Desire." *Nvanthyn.blogspot.com*, August 30, 2012, http://nvanthyn.blogspot.com/2012/08/the-team-named-desire.html (accessed April 3, 2016).

Washington Speakers Bureau. "Terry Bradshaw." *Plm.automation.siemens.com*, March 2006, http://www.plm.automation.siemens.com/summit/docs/bradshawBio.pdf (accessed February 21, 2017).

Watson, Jimmy. "Bradshaw, Ferguson Set Stage for Prolific Passing Attacks." *USA Today High School Sports*, September 3, 2015, http://www.usatodayhss.com/2015/bradshaw-ferguson-set-stage-for-proflic-passing-attacks (accessed March 21, 2016).

———. "Lee Hedges Will Have Plenty to Say about A. L. Williams: Terry Bradshaw Says Coach Was a Patient Teacher." *Shreveport Times*, July 25, 2014, http://www.shreveporttimes.com/-lee-hedges-will-have-plenty-to-say-about-aA-l-williams (accessed July 26, 2016).

Wexell, Jim. *Tales from behind the Steel Curtain*. Champaign, IL: Sports Publishing, 2004.

Whitburn, Joel. *Top Pop Albums, 1955–1996*, 4th ed. Milwaukee, WI: Hal Leonard, 1996.

Williams, Daniel K. *God's Own Party: The Making of the Christian Right*. New York: Oxford University Press, 2010.

Zoglin, Richard. *Hope: Entertainer of the Century*. New York: Simon & Schuster, 2014.

NEWSPAPERS AND MAGAZINES

Abilene Reporter, 1976–1990
Afro-American, 1965–1990
Akron Beacon Journal, 1990–2000
Albuquerque Journal, 1972
Altoona Mirror, 1980–1990
American Journalism Review, 2005
American Press, 2003
Anderson Daily Bulletin, 1981
Arizona Daily Star, 1993–1994
Atlanta Daily World, 1970–1990
Atlanta Journal & Atlanta Constitution, 1986–2016
Austin American-Statesman, 1990–2010
Baltimore Sun, 1965–2016
Beaver County Times, 1983–1990
Big Spring Herald, 1974–1990
Billboard, 1975–2000
Bluefield Daily Telegraph, 1977–1990
Boston Globe, 1980–2016
Bradford Era, 1972–1973
Broadcasting, 1976–1999
Broomfield Enterprise, 2006
Bucks County Courier Times, 1971–2016
Buffalo News, 1985–2016
Caledonian-Record, 2000–2007
Cash Box, 1976–1990
Charlotte Observer, 1990–2010

Chicago Daily Defender, 1965–1975
Chicago Sun-Times, 1985–2016
Chicago Tribune, 1970–2016
Columbus Dispatch, 1986–2016
Commercial Appeal, 1990–2010
Congressional Quarterly
Courier-Express, 1973–2000
Daily Breeze, 1985–2001
Daily Herald, 2000–2007
Daily Messenger, 2006
Daily News of Los Angeles, 1985–2002
Daily Oklahoman, 1983–2002
Dallas Morning News, 1985–2000
Dayton Daily News, 1990–2000
Delaware County Daily Times
Delaware State News, 2000–2010
Denver Post, 1990–2010
Deseret News, 1990–2010
Evening Gazette, 1980
Evening Tribune, 1985–1991
Fayetteville Observer, 1999
Florence Times, 1976
Fort Worth Star-Telegram, 1990–2010
Fresno Bee, 1990–2010
Globe and Mail, 1973–1990
Greeley Tribune, 1976–1990
Hammond Daily Star, 1976–1990
Hartford Courant, 1981
Houston Chronicle, 1985–2016
Hutchinson News, 1980
Indiana Evening Gazette, 1974–1979
Intelligencer, 2006
Janesville Gazette, 1978–1990
Kansas City Star, 1999
Lakeland Ledger, 1975–1990
Lancaster New Era, 1980–2005
Las Vegas Sun, 2013
Laurel Leader Call, 1976
Leader-Times, 1975–1990
Lebanon Daily News, 1970–1990
Lexington Herald-Leader, 1983–2016
Lincoln Evening Journal, 1976–1990
Los Angeles Herald Examiner, 1981–1990
Los Angeles Times, 1981–2016
Lubbock Avalanche-Journal, 2006
Maywood Herald, 2002
Miami Herald, 1983–2016
Milwaukee Journal Sentinel, 1990–2010
Monroe Morning World, 1965–1990
Morning Call, 2007
Morning Herald, 1973
Naples Daily News, 1974–1990
New Castle News, 1975–1990
New Haven Register, 1986–2000
New Pittsburgh Courier, 1981
New York Daily News, 1970–2016

New York Times, 1967–2016
New Yorker, 2015
News & Observer, 2001
News Post, 1975–1990
News Tribune, 2002
Newsday, 1990–2005
Newsweek, 1965–2009
Newton Kansan, 2006
North County Times, 2006
North Port Sun, 2006
Northwest Arkansas Times, 1982–2000
Observer-Reporter, 1976–2001
Omaha World-Herald, 1995–2005
Orange County Register, 1990–2010
Orlando Sentinel, 1986–2016
Ottawa Citizen, 1975–1989
Owensboro Messenger-Inquirer, 1996
Packer Plus, 2006
Palm Beach Post, 1995–2005
People, 1979
Philadelphia Daily News, 1982–1987
Philadelphia Inquirer, 1981–2016
Pittsburgh Post-Gazette, 1970–2016
Pittsburgh Tribune-Review, 1975–2010
Plain Dealer, 1995–2015
Playboy, 1980
Post-Standard, 1986–2000
Post-Tribune, 1991
Press Democrat, 1986–2000
Press-Telegram, 1994–2001
Progress, 1980
Providence Journal, 1995–2010
Radio & Records, 1976–1985
Record, 2000–2012
Richmond Times-Dispatch, 1985–2001
Rocky Mountain News, 1989–2010
Ruston Daily Leader, 1965–1985
Sacramento Bee, 1986–2016
Sampson Independent, 2007
San Antonio Express-News, 2000–2016
San Diego Union, 1986–2010
San Francisco Chronicle, 1986–2016
San Jose Mercury News, 1990–2016
Savannah Morning News, 2001
Seattle Post Intelligencer, 2006
Seattle Times, 1986–2000
Southtown Star, 2008
Sport, 1965–2000
Sports Illustrated, 1965–2016
St. Louis Post-Dispatch, 1986–2016
St. Paul Pioneer Press, 1986–2000
Star, 1988
Star Tribune, 1986–2016
Star-Ledger, 1995–2015
State, 1990
State Journal-Register, 1992

Sun, 1966–2015
Sun-Sentinel, 1994
Tampa Tribune, 1990–2005
Tennessean, 1977
Time, 1969–2010
Times Argus, 2000–2007
Times Daily, 1974–1993
Times Leader, 1999
Times Record, 2006
Times Union, 1997
Times-Herald, 2005–2011
Times-Picayune, 1992–2016
Times-Tribune, 2001
Titusville Herald, 1973–1990
Tulsa World, 1995–2005
Tyrone Daily Herald, 1979
U.S. News and World Report, 2013
Valley Independent, 1971–1990
Variety, 1975–2010
VFW Magazine, 1997
Victoria Advocate, 2013
Virginian-Pilot, 1990–2005
Wall Street Journal, 1988
Washington Evening Star, 1965–1981
Washington Post, 1967–2016
Washington Times, 1992–2016
Wenatchee World, 2000–2005
Wichita Eagle, 1990–2010
Worcester Telegram & Gazette, 1986–2007
Xenia Daily Gazette

FILMS, DOCUMENTARIES, TV EPISODES, AND VIDEOS

Black Sunday. Dir. John Frankenheimer. Perf. Robert Shaw and Bruce Dern. Paramount Pictures, 1977.

The Cannonball Run. Dir. Hal Needham. Perf. Burt Reynolds, Roger Moore, and Farrah Fawcett. Twentieth Century Fox, 1981.

Dinah! Season 5, Episode 102, *TV.com*, February 19, 1979, http://www.tv.com/shows/dinah/february-19-1979-1341574/ (accessed June 4, 2016).

Failure to Launch. Dir. Tom Dey. Perf. Matthew McConaughey, Sarah Jessica Parker, and Kathy Bates. Paramount, 2006.

"Graduation," *Blossom*. Season 4, Episode 28, May 23, 1994, *YouTube*, https://www.youtube.com/watch?v=QH0I_X2QKhA (accessed May 23, 2016)

Hooper. Dir. Hal Needham. Perf. Burt Reynolds, Sally Field, Brian Keith and Jan Michael Vincent. Warner Brothers, 1978.

Horse Feathers. Dir. Norman Z. McLeod. Perf. Marx Brothers and Thelma Todd. Paramount Pictures, 1932.

O. J. Simpson: Made in America. Dir. Ezra Edelman. Perf. Mike Albanese, Muhammad Ali, and Marcus Allen. ESPN Films, 2016.

Robots. Dir. Chris Wedge and Carlos Saldanha. Perf. Ewan McGregor, Halle Berry, and Mel Brooks. Twentieth Century Fox, 2005.

"The Secret History of the Credit Card," *Frontline*. Season 22, Episode 17, PBS, November 23, 2004.

Smokey and the Bandit II. Dir. Hal Needham. Perf. Burt Reynolds, Sally Field, and Jackie Gleason. Universal, 1980.
Walking on Dead Fish. Dir. Frank Martin. Narr. Terry Bradshaw.
"Win, Place, Bingo," *Las Vegas*. Season 5, Episode 17, NBC, February 8, 2008.

INTERVIEWS

Baronette, Kristi. Interview by author. Telephone, July 11, 2016.
Brewer, Louis. Interview by author. Telephone, March 29, 2016.
Germany, Dexter. Interview by author. May 25, 2016.
Griffin, Robert Madison. Interview by author. Telephone, March 22, 2016.
Hyatt, Richard. Interview by Author. Telephone, June 22, 2016.
Jones, Bert. Interview by author. Telephone, April 19, 2016.
Landau, Jeffrey. Interview by author. May 13, 2016.
Lundquist, Verne. Interview by author. Telephone, May 2, 2016.
McClure, Sam. Interview by author. July 11, 2016.
Mullins, Gerry. Interview by author. Telephone, March 22, 2016.
Murphy, Glenn. Interview by author. January 12, 2017.
O'Neil, Terry. Telephone interview by author. March 11, 2016.
Osele, Marc. Interview by author. January 18, 2016.
Van Thyn, Nico. Interview by author. Telephone, March 15, 2016.
Walden, Scarlett. Interview by author. Telephone, June 23, 2016.
Williams, A. L. Interview by author. Telephone, March 24, 2016.
Woods, Mae, "An oral history with Hal Needham, transcript of an oral history conducted 2006 by Mae Woods, Oral History Program, Academy of Motion Picture Arts and Sciences, Beverly Hills, California 2006.

ARCHIVES AND COLLECTIONS

Louisiana Hayride Collection, Louisiana State University Shreveport Archives and Special Collections, Shreveport, Louisiana.
Oklahoma Historical Society, WKY KTVY KFOR Archives, Oklahoma City, Oklahoma.
Stock Car Racing Collection, Appalachian State University Library, Boone, North Carolina.

WEBSITES

Bleacher Report http://bleacherreport.com
Box Office Mojo http://www.boxofficemojo.com
Business Insider http://www.businessinsider.com
Common Sense Media https://www.commonsensemedia.org
Database Football http://www.databasefootball.com
Deadline http://deadline.com
Grantland http://grantland.com
NBC Los Angeles http://www.nbclosangeles.com
Pew Research Center http://www.pewresearch.org
Pro Football Reference http://www.pro-football-reference.com
Rate Your Music http://rateyourmusic.com
Rotten Tomatoes https://www.rottentomatoes.com

SB Nation http://www.sbnation.com
USA Today http://www.usatoday.com
VICE Sports https://sports.vice.com
YouTube https://www.youtube.com

INDEX

ABOUT THE AUTHOR

Brett L. Abrams is a historian who works as an electronic records archivist, saving the history of the computer age for those who will want to write about it. He has a passion for professional sports, popular culture, and U.S. politics. His books include *Hollywood Bohemians: Transgressive Sexuality and the Selling of the Movieland Dream*; *Capital Sporting Grounds: A History of Stadium and Ballpark Construction in Washington, DC*; and *The Bullets, the Wizards, and Washington, DC, Basketball*. This book started when the author thought about the three things he knew about Terry Bradshaw at the time: He was a Hall of Fame football quarterback, he made movies with Burt Reynolds, and he was born in Louisiana. The author wondered how these pieces fit together, only to discover that the puzzle proved richer than anything he could have anticipated.